D1591502

Volume 4

DIRECTORY OF WORLD CINEMA RUSSIA

Edited by Birgit Beumers

intellect Bristol, UK / Chicago, USA

First Published in the UK in 2011 by Intellect, The Mill, Parnall Road, Fishponds,
Bristol, BS16 3JG, UK

First published in the USA in 2011 by Intellect, The University of Chicago Press,
1427 E. 60th Street, Chicago, IL 60637, USA

Publisher: May Yao
Publishing Assistant: Melanie Marshall

Cover photo: Vasilii Sigarev, Wolfy (2009). Still from the film.
Courtesy Koktebel Studio and Kinotavr.

Cover Design: Holly Rose
Copy Editor: Heather Owen
Typesetting: Mac Style, Beverley, E. Yorkshire

Directory of World Cinema ISSN 2040-7971
Directory of World Cinema eISSN 2040-798X

Directory of World Cinema: Russia ISBN 978-1-84150-372-1
Directory of World Cinema: Russia eISBN 978-1-84150-343-1

Printed and bound by Gutenberg Press, Malta.

DIRECTORY OF
WORLD CINEMA
RUSSIA

This first edition of the *Directory of World Cinema: Russia* is the result of the commitment of a wide range of contributors and an immensely knowledgeable, helpful and patient advisory board, consisting of Nancy Condee, Seth Graham, David Gillespie, David MacFadyen, Stephen Norris, Elena Prokhorova, Alexander Prokhorov, Rimgaila Salys and Denise Youngblood. I would like to thank them all for their co-operation.

I am also very grateful to the team at Intellect, particularly Masoud Yazdani and May Yao for launching this series, and to Melanie Marshall for supporting this volume through its production stages, making it a truly collaborative process. Intellect's contribution to publications in the field of film studies is outstanding, and this Directory is further evidence of the investment they make into the future of the field.

The *Directory of World Cinema: Russia* could not have been illustrated without the assistance of the photo department of *Iskusstvo kino*, where my thanks go to Liudmila Mishunina, now working from the journal's new premises – with her usual efficiency. As an extremely fussy editor when it comes to cover designs, I owe special thanks to the talented Holly Rose for her work, and to Roman Borisevich of Koktebel Studio, Moscow, for granting permission to use a still of *Wolfy/Volchok* for the cover design.

Transliteration is a perennial problem with Russian: This volume follows Library of Congress transliteration throughout, with the soft sign marked by an apostrophe. The sole exception are the names of the studios Mosfilm and Lenfilm, which have been adapted to common usage in English instead of adhering to the transliteration Mosfil'm, Lenfil'm (and the same goes for Soiuzmultfilm and Soiuzdetfilm; and for the Gorky – rather than Gor'kii – Studio). For names with an accepted English spelling, such as Yeltsin, Eisenstein, Meyerhold, Schnittke), the latter has been used.

Birgit Beumers

INTRODUCTION
BY THE EDITOR

Cinema has always played a crucial role in Russia, be it before the Revolution, when it was closely connected with European traditions; or during the Soviet era, when it was used both to voice socialist ideology or dissent with the system; or after the renaissance of the film industry in the post-Soviet era, when Russia joined the league of the major players in terms of world film distribution.

This volume attempts to look at the diverse manifestations of Russian cinema over the hundred-something years in the context of political and cultural developments through a new lens, and one that was rather alien to the high-brow Soviet film culture: genre. Most of the Soviet films known and distributed in the west were *auteur* films, defying a clear genre definition, which is partly a reflection of their dissent with the commercialization of cinema – be that during the 1920s, when Eisenstein's and Vertov's experiments yielded no significant box office at home, or the dissident filmmakers of the post-war Soviet era, Tarkovskii, German and Muratova. As Dawn Seckler shows in her introductory essay on the meaning of *zhanr* in Soviet and Russian cinema, it is only very recently that genre has acquired a more neutral meaning in critical discourse.

The choice of genres represented in this volume has been determined by specificities and characteristics of Soviet and Russian film history: while genres such as the histori-cal film, the biopic or the war films are as prominent as in other film cultures, the genre of action, for example, has a specifically Soviet variety as the Red Western, combining ideological message with the location in the Central Asian steppe and mountain regions. Or the melodrama, frowned upon as bourgeois during the Stalin era, did not yield much of a film harvest in the middle of the twentieth century. As far as possible (given historical constraints) each genre is represented in chronological order by a range of films from dif-ferent historical periods: pre-Revolutionary (where applicable), Soviet and Russian. It may be surprising to discover a relative shortage of films by the filmmakers best known in the West: they do not fit easily into these genre classifications. As Seckler lucidly argues in her essay, it is precisely in their resistance to genre that their *auteurism* manifests itself most clearly. The output of the Soviet satellite republics has been somewhat neglected in this volume: it is hoped that this balance can be re-dressed in future volumes. Simi-larly, the genres of adventure, science fiction and fantasy thrived only at certain moments in Soviet culture, and their phenomena deserve particular attention; they have also been set aside for the future.

The volume opens with several essays that are intended to provide a geographical, historical and cultural framework for the collection. The Film of the Year, Vasilii Sigarev's *Wolfy* (2009), is maybe a daring choice – a debut not by a professional filmmaker but a playwright – but it was the most outstanding discovery of the year 2009, which also marks the second century of Russian filmmaking (if we take its birthday to be the 15 October 1908). The review of the film is followed by an interview with the filmmaker and scriptwriter. An essay on the development of the Russian-Soviet-Russian film industry is followed by a portrayal of the Open Russian Film Festival Kinotavr, which has showcased Russian cinema since the collapse of the USSR and thus made an enormous contribution to the revival if not of the industry, but of cinema art. An essay on genre concludes the introductory section. The choice of the six directors for the biography has been determined by the names most familiar to western audiences. In the choice of films, we have been guided by an effort to include some films that are easily accessible and others that are limited to Russian-language editions (or archives). While some filmmakers, films and periods have been more exposed to scholarly writing, other areas – for example, documentaries of the post-Soviet era; animation; or the cinema of the stagnation era – have so far been denied in-depth scholarship. And if this volume can help in drawing attention to some forgotten, less-known and maybe deserving films, it has over-fulfilled its plan!

Birgit Beumers

Vasilii Sigarev's *Wolfy* (2009). Photo courtesy of Koktebel Studio, Roman Borisevich.

FILM OF THE YEAR
VASILII SIGAREV'S *WOLFY* (2009)

Wolfy

Volchok

Country of Origin:
Russia

Language:
Russian

Studios:
Koktebel, Central Partnership

Director:
Vasilii Sigarev

Producers:
Roman Borisevich, Ruben
Dishdishian

Screenplay:
Vasilii Sigarev

Cinematographer:
Aleksei Arsent'ev

Art Director:
Liudmila Diupina

Duration:
88 minutes

Genre:
Drama

Cast:
Polina Pluchek, Iana Troianova,
Marina Gapchenko, Galina
Dolganova

Year:
2009

Wolfy is a debut film and such an unusual choice for the 'film of the year'. Yet it has impressed critics in Russia, where it won major national film awards (Kinotavr, White Elephant) in the categories of direction, scriptwriting and acting, and also made an impact abroad (competition in Karlovy Vary, Zurich). It is a film with striking originality, which lies in its cold and detached attitude to the main characters – a little girl and her mother – but also in the theme – violence. The film is a shocking manifestation of the lack of emotions – in character portrayal and action – in the modern world, and makes no pleasant viewing for the audience.

The Ekaterinburg playwright Vasilii Sigarev (b. 1977) became famous when his play *Plasticine* (2000) received the Russian Anti-Booker prize and was almost immediately afterwards staged in Moscow by Kirill Serebrennikov at a small and experimental theatre; the production became the sensation of the theatrical season. In 2002 the play was staged by Dominic Cooke at the Royal Court Theatre Upstairs for the festival of young authors and Sigarev went on to win the *London Evening Standard* award as Most Promising Playwright. Handing the award to Sigarev, Tom Stoppard excitedly compared the young playwright to Dostoevsky: 'If Dostoyevsky were writing in the twenty-first century, no doubt he would have written *Plasticine*'. During the following season the Royal Court staged two further plays by Sigarev, *Black Milk* (1999, published 2001) and *Ladybird* (2002, published 2003).[1]

The screenplay *Wolfy* was written in 2006; Sigarev intended to make a film based on his screenplay, which he had refused to sell to the established film production company CTB. Sigarev's screenplay presents a hard task for Sigarev as director, since it contains more narrative than dramatic action. The screenplay is written in the form of monologue by a teenage girl about her unrequited love for her mother – a dazzling, beautiful, sharp-tongued, decisive, merry, irresponsible, cruel whore and a thief with sadistic tendencies. According to the screenplay the mother is locked up for five years for beating up a hospital nurse immediately after her daughter's birth. The film opens with a chase of two cops after a blood-covered woman across the showy field; when they finally catch her she says that she is about to give a birth. After release from the prison she sees her daughter from time to time, mostly teasing and humiliating the child. With her bright make-up the mother stands out amidst the poor and dilapidated world of a workers' settlement somewhere in the Urals. A line of drunken lovers, open sexual scenes with men and women – all this happens in the presence of the small child. The mother is an extremely corporeal figure, almost impregnable in her vitality and at the same time extremely harsh. Iana Troianova has won the Best Actress award at Kinotavr for a very good reason: her performance is nothing short of sensational. The image that she creates manages to bring together glaring contradictions in an organic way: she is attractive and repulsive, charming and monstrous at the same time.

The mother entirely abandons her daughter after the death of the grandmother, who had looked after the child: she literally leaves the seven year old at a railway station. At first the girl is sent to an orphanage, then she is taken in by her crippled aunt where she stays for the next seven years, without hearing a word from the mother (presumed dead). However, the mother returns again – not as beautiful as she used to be, but battered and humiliated; yet, as if nothing had happened, she continues to offend her daughter, now a fourteen-year-old teenager. Ultimately, the girl is stripped of any illusions about her mother. But when the mother leaves again, the girl runs after her. In this chase she is knocked down by a car and dies on the spot.

This is a psychological drama shaped by (post)-Soviet communality; it is a drama within the communal body shaped by a claustrophobic, everyday existence, the lack of perspective, the despair and atmosphere of violence that serves as the only language for communication. Curiously, except for the cops, there are almost no men around the central female characters. Only once in the film do we see a lover whom the mother picked up on the train returning from prison. At first treated as a potential partner, he is literally pulled away by mother and grandmother after a most impressive scene in the film when, defending the mother from being beaten, the girl – propped up on the wardrobe – knocks the man out with a milk jug. Later she sits on the floor and draws patterns with the droplets of blood in the puddle of milk. Tellingly, Sigarev removes from the film the most brutal scenes (present in the screenplay); if they remain (as, for instance, the scene when the drunken mother mockingly urinates on the floor in front of the child and the girl obediently wipes the floor before being forced to wash the mother's genitals) are shot from a distance so they do not shock the viewer. On the whole, the camera position is quite paradoxical: a few scenes are shot from floor level, rendering the child's point of view as she hides under the table. But at the same time, the camera often adopts a position at 'ceiling level', above the characters' heads. The explanation for this may be found in the film's narrative structure. The finale implies that the daughter's voice tells the story of her life and love, but then it comes from the space of death. Sigarev enhances this paradox by the fact that the voiceover (belonging to the daughter) is spoken by Troianova (who plays the mother). Yet this voice carries no markers of the vulgarity that is intrinsic in the mother's speech: in fact, it hardly reminds us of the mother. This device – when the same actress plays the mother and voices the daughter's narrative – suggests that the two protagonists actually represent two facets of the same character: two sides of Russian femininity – meek and tender vs cynical and destructive vitality; life vs death; body vs soul; carnival vs tragedy; violence vs love; freedom vs dependence. All these binaries are applicable to the film, yet they all remain unresolved. This duality is also emphasized by the film's colour palette: frequently white contrasts with red, or blue is juxtaposed to its contrary colour, orange. The daughter's devout love for her unworthy mother, which is the focus of the plot, emphasizes the connection between these binaries rather than their incompatibility. The mother does not seem to notice this devotion; if she does, she coarsely ignores the piercing love of her daughter. Moreover, she sadistically makes fun of the child, telling her that she found her on a cemetery as a wolf cub; or she tells the girl that the grandmother died because of her visits to the cemetery.

The girl is not presented as a sweet and tearful melodramatic victim. She smiles just once in the film, when mother sells their place and takes her to the South (only to abandon her later). On the whole, she is grim and serious. Her love is demanding and fanatical. Furthermore, the daughter does not know how to express her feelings other than through aggression in relation to others, who in her view take the mother's love away from her. Having grown up in the mother's orbit, she does not know another language of self-expression except the language of violence. Very telling in this respect is the episode when the girl suffocates the little hedgehog the mother gives her before leaving with yet another lover. Having forced a cushion over the hedgehog, the girl throws the corpse under a train, as if to allege that not she killed the hedgehog but the train. Subsequently she throws stones at the passing train, the substitute culprit for her own actions. She methodically fights with her mother's lovers – her rivals for attention – and she desecrates the tomb of a boy upon whom she transferred her love for her mother. Indeed, at the cemetery she finds her only friend: a dead boy, at whose monument she articulates her love for her mother: she shares her dreams, gives him gifts (stolen from neighbouring graves) and sings songs. But when the mother tells the girl that the boy 'took away her grandmother', she soils his tomb, in a similar transferral of guilt as in the episode with the hedgehog. This episode is indicative of the film's general logic by which love (Eros) is not only inseparable from death (Thanatos), but inevitably turns into violence, aggression and death.

Wolfy at first invokes and then subverts the melodramatic expectations according to which 'a bad mother' should return to her daughter, seeking forgiveness from the abused and abandoned child. Nothing of the sort happens in the film. On the contrary, when the daughter is hit by a car, the drunken mother laughs happily: she has stolen her sister's money and clothes, and she escaped from her 'boring' daughter – she is free at last.

Sigarev methodically compromises freedom. Freedom as represented by the mother and acquires the characteristics of the uncanny, enhanced by motifs of the cemetery, the girl's communication with the dead, and especially by the horror sequence illustrating the story about the transformation of an abandoned wolf cub (*volchok*) into a child. The mother fits Freud's concept of the uncanny – something very close and familiar that keeps returning as unfamiliar and monstrous, each time more horrifying and destructive, and eventually bringing death. It is indeed a scary image, but Sigarev's attitude to a newly obtained freedom is indicative of his generation with a bitter taste of freedom, vague recollections of the Soviet era and a painful and traumatic experience of coming-of-age during Russia's stormy 1990s.

Russian cultural tradition strongly emphasizes the identification of the mother with the native land, and this allows a reading of the film as an allegory of the relations between the new, post-Soviet generation and a country which has abandoned its children, having wasted their love and eventually killed them, in spite of their continued love for a repulsive 'mother Russia'. In this context, the semi-animalistic existence of the 'body of the Native land' as manifested by the mother with her initially charming energy, gradually kills the soul of her child, the daughter of destructive freedom.

Adapted from a review published in *KinoKultura* 26 (2009) and Chapter 4 of *Performing Violence* (2009)

Mark Lipovetsky and Birgit Beumers

Note

1. All three plays have been translated into English by Sasha Dugdale and published by Nick Hern Books.

Vasilii Sigarev with his Kinotavr award in June 2009. Photo by Birgit Beumers

INTERVIEW
WITH VASILII SIGAREV AND IANA TROIANOVA

'We are malicious children and egoists, and do not want any responsibility'

– What reaction do you expect to your film?

Vasilii Sigarev: I don't expect anything: I do everything just for myself. Knock me over the head if you like: that's the way I am. I've written this script because I was so impressed with the stories told by Iana Troianova, the actress who plays the mother. These are her associations and impressions of childhood. Writing this text, I have not invented anything, but at some point I just faced with the fact that these are my characters and this is how they speak. My characters are born from language. The girl is solely a product of language: human language is my basic tool. We did a reading of this script at the Theatre of the Young Spectator in Ekaterinburg, when Iana played a role of the girl. When I saw that, I thought that I would never find a performer for the role of the child. Iana played the girl in a way that made the audience cry. During the casting, we looked at over 5,000 girls. It was a year of continuous search. [...] We found the girl by sheer coincidence, two weeks before the shooting started. We were in utter despair, when sud-denly Polina Pluchek from Moscow appeared. Only later did we discovered that she is the great-granddaughter of the theatre director and head of the Satire Theatre, Valentin Pluchek, and thus the grand niece of Peter Brook. There was no need to work with her in any special way, and in any case I would not have been able to do that: I'm no pedagogi-cal genius, even if I studied at the Pedagogical Institute. I can't work with children. Polina worked independently, by herself. I worked on the film and would devise things so she could act only in one way, but not another.

– A huge emotional weight rests on the girl. On screen she suffers, her mother leaves her, she loses her grandmother, and there is even a scene at the cemetery. How did you protect Polina?

Sigarev: I'll give you one example of her work. We shot the grandmother's death: the actress is lying in the coffin and probably struggled to stay calm and sane. And Polina went over to rock her and sing her a lullaby. That says everything. Now Polina wants to become an actress.

– The reading of the text took place at the theatre, so this was after all not a film script, but a play?

Sigarev: It's strange, but whatever text I write – everybody starts screaming that I wrote a play. I had to see and hear this text on stage, although it was written precisely as a script. *Wolfy*, as well as *Plasticine* at its time, were scripts. *Wolfy* happened to be presented during a theatre seminar in Ekaterinburg.

– In the theatre you are well known, but in cinema you start from scratch. What were the difficulties you encountered?

Sigarev: There was a script, and there were many people who were grateful to be able to work on it. I had uploaded the script on my website, where the producer Roman Borisevich read it; he called me and asked to buy the rights.

Troianova: But Vasia insisted that he wanted to shoot himself. Roman Borisevich thought that the script had been written by some nobody, and he was happy to have made a discovery. But then Boris Khlebnikov told him who this Vasilii Sigarev is, and a second life began.

Sigarev: With *Plasticine* there's also an interesting story. The text was in an open-access domain, and one day the French producer Jean-Louis Piel got in touch; he had produced *Urga* for Nikita Mikhalkov, he had worked with Wong Kar Wai and Peter Greenaway, and had produced *Ken Park* (dir. Edward Lachman, Larry Clark, 2002). He suggested I should make a film. We had already started to work on *Plasticine*, found a location, drew up the budget, but then the story with *My Blueberry Nights* (2007) happened, which Kar Wai filmed for a long time, so they even ran out of the money which they had set aside for us, and the project was closed. And right there, a week later, Roman Borisevich called. […]

– There are a lot of debuts in your film. Did you deliberately go down that route?

Sigarev: Iana appears on film for the first time; the cameraman Aleksei Arsent'ev is also a debutant, as practically all the people in the crew. We opted for a small-scale production without attracting skilled cinematographers, because it seemed that we needed the purity of the primeval, so we would not have a narrow view in our heads and hearts. We did not want well-known actors. […] We did not want the viewer to recognize anyone in our story.

– Iana, how come you have such profound knowledge of humankind? It seems strange that you never appeared in cinema before.

Troianova: I didn't have a chance, but then I trust in fate: I know that I have made my debut at the right time. […] I didn't play me, but scooped from my inner self, from my dark sides, and uncovered what we normally hide from others. We all carry masks, but here we tried to lift them. It was frightening, because it's like a confession: you bare yourself in front of the camera. But I'm courageous, though I'm also a coward. I've seen lots of women like my heroine. I'm not ashamed to pronounce a phrase like: 'I want to live, I'm young'. I'm a stage actress and if I come to the theatre or the cinema, I have to be prepared to bare myself. That's the only way to exist in this profession. I nurtured this role for two years. I have a direct connection to this script, albeit not as powerful and active as the playwright. This role was my birthday present from Vasilii. This woman crept inside me: everything was new. There were no rehearsals: right away, the camera was running! And amazing things began to happen: I surprised myself, got carried away. I'd never speak like my heroine. But it was really interesting to do something so completely out of sync with my self. […]

– Is the ending of Wolfy *not a little too pessimistic? Why did you decide that the girl should die rather than her mother, who has no love for the child?*

Sigarev: It took me a long time to write the ending: I struggled for over a year. And then came the breakthrough and I decided that the girl, rather than her mother, should die. It is better to die pure than to lose that purity. I did not want to give the mother a second chance. If she had stayed alive, the girl would have turned out just like her mum. In fact, the mother is not capable of loving her own mother (the grandmother) either. If the girl is a wolf cub (*volchok*), then the mother is the wolf (*volchitsa*).

– So nobody can break out of this vicious circle?

Sigarev: Yes, they can. We are not categorical here.

Troianova: I think that the girl leaves of her own will. She is tired of life and understands that her mother's life is senseless. But she is capable of love. In the first version of the ending, the girl perished and thus gave a chance for improvement to her mother, but during the editing Sigarev said: 'No, I won't give her a chance. The girl leaves and the mother stays the way she is'. The spectator must decide for himself what follows from here.

– There appears to be something missing in the film: some shock, some surge of reality that would support the spectator and offer a release after the pain experienced during the film.

Sigarev: This is a very Russian aspiration. We always want to have a light at the end of the tunnel. But I deliberately avoided that.

– Iana, can you find a justification for your heroine?

Troianova: This woman just wants love and her search is egoistic. We talked a lot about this: we are by nature malicious children, egoists who often do not want to take responsibility. The girl clings to her mother, and the mother just says: 'Get off! What do you want from me?' The girl prevents the mother from living her life the way she wants. That is the only justification for my heroine. I cannot call her a monster. [...] our mother is honest, whatever else she may be. I'm all for open attitudes. I found a justification for my heroine: I love her.

Sigarev: First of all, we are all people. Showing ideal heroes in the theatre or the cinema would be false. *Wolfy* is an act of repentance for me, because I'm not an ideal father, and Iana is no ideal mother. We cannot give absolute love. We are all egoists, and love ourselves above all. If we were to love someone else and make a film about that, out comes a lie. [...]

Interview conducted by Svetlana Khokhriakova and Birgit Beumers, Sochi 12 June 2009
Published in full, in Russian, in *Kul'tura* 23 (18–24 June 2009)

Translated by Birgit Beumers

The statue of the Worker and the Peasant by Vera Mukhina, made for the Soviet Pavilion at the World Exhibition in Paris in 1937, which serves as the logo for Mosfilm Studio. Photo by Birgit Beumers

FILM PRODUCTION IN RUSSIA
AN INDUSTRY?

On 4 May 1896 the cinematograph was first presented in Russia at a fairground in the Aquarium Park in St Petersburg. The first Russian shows featured short films made by Auguste and Louis Lumière, while the French companies Gaumont and Pathé soon gained a monopoly on the Russian film market. By spring 1897 the cinematograph was touring Russian towns, acquainting the people with the new attraction and providing cheap entertainment for the masses. Films were mostly shown in booths on fairs and exhibitions rather than in stationary venues. In 1903 two 'electric theatres' opened in Moscow, and when stationary cinemas became more widespread, the cinema drew a different audience: the urban middle class and bourgeoisie.

The attraction of the cinematograph grew rapidly: cinemas increased in number and size. By 1910 there were 84 cinemas in the capital St Petersburg; at the beginning of the Great War in 1914 there were 1,400 cinemas in Russia, with seating capacities of 300–800 each. In contrast to the exhibition sector, which was concentrated in St Petersburg, the production of films was centred in Moscow, with 15 studios operating in 1913. New, purpose-built or specially fitted cinemas opened: the 'Arts' (*Khudozhestvennyi*) on Moscow's Arbat opened in 1909 and still functions today; it had been designed by the leading architect of the period, Fedor Shekhtel, whose art-nouveau architecture has left numerous traces on the Moscow cityscape.

The breakthrough for Russia's own film production came in 1907, when the photographer Aleksandr Drankov announced that he would make films showing views of Russia. Pathé and Gaumont immediately opened their own production studios in Russia. Drankov possessed great skills as a businessman and had a fine understanding of the entertainment business. He produced some seventeen films in a series entitled 'Picturesque Russia', responding to calls for local images (rather than French scenes) on the silver screen. In 1908 Drankov produced the first Russia feature film: *Stenka Razin*, directed by Vladimir Romashkov, was released on 15 October 1908 – the official birthday of Russian cinema. The film told of the popular folk hero and rebel Stenka Razin, focusing on his infatuation with a Persian princess, who detracts his attention from the struggle against oppression.

In the early 1910s Russian film production soared and new companies emerged. Paul Thiemann set up a studio with the tobacco merchant Friedrich Reinhardt; they first distributed foreign films and produced their own. Grigorii Libken from Yaroslavl began to buy, collect and rent films, setting up one of the first Russian 'film exchanges' where films could be leased for theatrical display by cinemas. Aleksandr Khanzhonkov opened his company in 1908, skilfully recruiting young talents – directors, designers, animators and actors, who contributed hugely to the aesthetic development of cinema. In 1914 Iosif Ermol'ev produced his first film, gathering gradually under his elephant logo the leading directors and actors of the time, including the star actor Ivan Mozzhukhin. But Khanzhonkov also developed his studio into one of the leading ventures in pre-Revolutionary Russia: he hired the directors Petr Chardynin and Evgenii Bauer, and counted some 50 actors and five cameramen on the payroll. His greatest coups were the recruitment of the ballerina Vera Karalli, who came to the cinema after a stage injury; and the silent film star Vera Kholodnaia. Russian cinema was growing both as an art and an industry when the Great War struck.

In July 1914 Austria-Hungary and Germany declared war on Russia and soon thereafter the frontiers were closed for trade. Foreign film distribution offices in Russia closed, and film stock – a German import – was in short supply. The rare foreign film imports were the preferred viewing of the upper classes: almost 80 per cent of films shown prior to 1914 had been foreign. During the war Russian film production increased, as did the proportion of Russian films shown in cinemas.

After the February Revolution of 1917 most film studios were still operating; however, the nationalization of the industry was on the cards as the staff of studios and film exchanges refused to work for private proprietors; those packed up their equipment and moved south: Khanzhonkov and Ermol'ev filmed in Yalta. By 1918 most cinemas had been closed and equipment removed, while film stock had become rare, since trade relations had been interrupted; the shortages would continue until the Treaty of Rapallo was signed in 1922, allowing trade with Germany to resume. As the Bolsheviks took hold of the country and resistance was failing, many producers and filmmakers fled via Constantinople to Paris to set up business there (e.g. Ermolieff, whose studio was later taken over by Albatros). Many artists had remained in Moscow, declared capital in 1918, and expressed their loyalty to the new regime. Agit-trains were dispatched across the country to show newsreels to the (largely illiterate) peasant population and the young Denis Kaufman (later known as Dziga Vertov) was in charge of the developing process in a laboratory in Moscow. On 27 August 1919 the film industry was nationalized. Few foreign films found their way to Moscow during the Civil War (1918–1921) and few new films were made.

The following years were marked by the building of a multi-national state: the Union of Socialist Soviet Republics (USSR) was formed in 1922. Yet Soviet Russia found itself in international isolation, because the new regime had not yet been recognized by western nations. Moreover, famines made practical action necessary: the New Economic Policy (NEP 1921–1928) was introduced to alleviate the dismal economic situation by allowing private trade, and with it foreign trade, on the Soviet market. NEP made it possible for film exchanges to open, for commercial concessions to be granted to foreigners so that the ruined infrastructure could be revived through foreign investment. In this climate, the nationalization of the industry took shape. In 1919 the film school was founded as State Film Technikum. Goskino was established in December 1922 with the remit to distribute films, and replaced in 1924 by Sovkino. The production company Mezhrabpom merged with the Rus Studio in 1923, continuing to receive support from International Workers' Relief. However, the development of film art was hampered by the absence of film stock: Lev Kuleshov rehearsed with an empty camera. Only in the mid-1920s did film stock become available again and the number of Soviet films began to rise.

Sovkino reviewed the profitability of studios, leading to numerous closures by 1926. Only Mezhrabpom-Rus continued to work alongside the national studios, the Moscow and Leningrad branches of Sovkino. Sovkino was guided by Lenin's missive for the 'cinefication' of the countryside so the medium could reach the largely illiterate masses. Given the need for cinema to be self-financing, films had to generate income; Sovkino achieved this through the purchase and distribution of popular foreign films that catered for audience taste and financed Soviet film production through their box-office revenue (foreign films brought in 85 per cent of Sovkino's revenue on only 33 per cent of released titles). Sovkino assumed that gradually new Soviet films would be successful enough to sustain the industry. By 1927 the box-office receipts of Soviet films were almost on a par with foreign films.

By 1928 the box-office receipts for Soviet films had overtaken those of foreign films in distribution. At the All-Union Party Conference on Cinema Affairs in March 1928 Party officials demanded that films should be intelligible to the millions. Since cinema was, according to speeches at the Conference, not fulfilling its role of catering for the masses, but spending instead huge sums of money on production, the industry was exposed to vitriolic attacks. The Party officials ignored that the lack of equipment, the ramshackle cinemas and defective projectors, the cameras that were brought back by cameramen from trips abroad and the reliance on imported film stock betrayed the industry's lack of a reliable infrastructure. However, the blame for the huge budget required for Sovkino was placed at the filmmakers' feet. In January 1929 a decree followed, film studios and cinema associations of those who did not make 'films for the millions' and the formalists, targeted for its rejection of linear narratives. Filmmakers and industry staff were accused of economic crimes and put on trial. Sovkino itself was purged in May 1930 and abolished, to be replaced by Soiuzkino on 13 February 1930. Boris Shumiatskii became chairman of Soiuzkino in October 1930. Gradually, foreign films were removed from circulation, while domestic film production dropped to 35 films per year (compared with an average of 120 in the last half of the 1920s). During the so-called Cultural Revolution of 1928, the film industry – only just rebuilt through foreign imports – was almost entirely destroyed. Soiuzkino took over film production under Shumiatskii, who would coin the 'cinema for the millions' in Stalin's Russia, epitomized in the cult film *Chapaev* (1934) and the musical *Circus* (1934). Another effect of the xenophobia of the 1930s was the liquidation in 1936 of the German-funded Mezhrabpom. The children's film studio Soiuzdetfilm (renamed Gorky Film Studio in 1948) was organized on its base and the cartoon industry was established with the formation of Soiuzmultfilm in the same year.

In 1931 the Moscow film studio, Mosfilm, was founded on the base of the former Ermoliev and Khanzhonkov studios. In September 1932 the Film Institute established directors' courses, which were run by Sergei Eisenstein who had returned from Hollywood; in 1934 the State Film Technikum became the Film Institute (VGIK). In 1934 the USSR participated in the Venice Film Festival and Moscow hosted its first international film festival in spring 1935: Soviet films were validated on the national and international stage. In August 1934 the first Congress of the Writers' Union, founded in 1932, resolved that socialist realism was the only acceptable method for artistic work. The All-Union Creative Conference on Cinema Affairs in 1935 adopted the same principles of socialist realism: in order to show the development of history, art would present the (bright) future as present, creating essentially utopian narratives, or 'fairy tales'. The positive hero had to reveal his growing consciousness of the socialist cause that led him to identify with the collective and thus achieve great feats in the name of socialism. Revolutionary leaders, Party officials and historical figures thus lent themselves to reinterpretation, while contemporary man could prove his commitment to socialism through super-human acts in the name of the Party.

The 1930s were also marked by the arrival of sound. In Moscow Pavel Tager was working on sound systems, while Aleksandr Shorin equipped Leningrad's Sovkino with sound. However, sound was slow to be adopted both by filmmakers and the industry, and additional problems were encountered at the level of distribution. In 1932 there were plans for 85 silent and 40 sound films, but the Soviet Union had only 200 sound projectors (compared to 32,000 silent ones); by 1936 the production of sound films had risen to 100 per cent, although not all the cinemas were equipped.

Shumiatskii had grand plans for a Soviet Hollywood on the Black Sea, which were, however, hampered: in 1935 he had delivered merely 43 of the 120 films planned, followed by a further drop in production, which led *Pravda* to accuse him of squandering money (9 January 1938). In the same year the Committee of Cinema Affairs was split from the Committee for Arts and received ministerial status, signalling the importance of the industry as a separate branch. Its new head, Semen Dukelskii, remained in that post until June 1939, when Ivan Bol'shakov took over.

In the autumn of 1941 Lenfilm and Mosfilm were hurriedly evacuated to Alma-Ata, to form the Central United Film Studios (TsOKS). During 1941–1945 the directors and staff of TsOKS made war-chronicles and worked on feature films. The Ukrainian studio was evacuated to Tashkent, Soiuzdetfilm to Stalinabad (now Dushanbe), and Soiuzmultfilm to Samarkand. Immediately after the war, in March 1946, the Directorate of Cinema acquired ministerial status (Ministry of Cinema), with Bol'shakov at its head. A second important cinematic event was the establishment in 1948 of the State Film Archive Gosfilmofond in Belye Stolby, near Moscow. The immediate post-war years saw a sharp drop in production, which led to a film-famine (*malokartin'e*). If in the 1930s production had been around 50 feature films per year, then after the war production dropped to an all time low of under ten. It was not until after Stalin's death on 5 March 1953 that these figures recovered.

The Khrushchev Thaw (1953–1964) saw a boost in film production. The sixth Five-Year-Plan (1956–1960) foresaw investment in cinema infrastructure studios and cinemas in the context of Khrushchev's emphasis on improving leisure facilities. Above all, the cinema network expanded with new cinemas and improved studio facilities; consequently, ticket sales rose. Ivan Pyr'ev became head of Mosfilm Studio in 1954, using his influence to support young film graduates. Mosfilm, as well as other studios, had an artistic council that vetted all scripts and films, and 'creative units' to decentralise control of and responsibility for production. In 1957 Pyr'ev resigned as head of Mosfilm to devote himself to the establishment of a Union of Filmmakers (FU), which held its constituent congress not until in November 1965 when Lev Kulidzhanov was elected chairman. The Union drew its subsidies partly from membership fees, partly from the glossy bi-monthly *Sovetskii ekran*. Its members received medical and social care, and had access to a veteran's residence, sanatoria, and other recreational and leisure services. In 1959 the Moscow International Film Festival was revived: it would take place bi-annually, alternating with Karlovy Vary as A-class festival.

In 1953 the Main Directorate for Cinema (GUK) became part of the newly established Ministry of Culture, but by 1963 its independent ministerial status was restored as Goskino, presided over by Aleksei Romanov from 1963–1972.[1] In 1972 Filipp Ermash was appointed head of Goskino, a position he held until 1986. Goskino supervised export (Sovexport), co-production (Sovinfilm) and festival organization (Sovinterfest), as well as the analytical journals *Iskusstvo kino* (print run: 50,000) and the bi-monthly glossy magazine *Sovetskii ekran* (print run: 2 million). The Film Institute (VGIK), the technical institute (NIKFI), and the research institute NIIK (founded in 1973), as well as Gosfilmofond, an orchestra, the Theatre of the Film Actor, and the Higher Courses for Scriptwriters and Directors were all overseen by Goskino also. Thus the film industry was a fully fledged branch of the Soviet economic and administrative system.

With Gorbachev's glasnost and perestroika the time had come for change: Aleksandr Kamshalov replaced Ermash at Goskino in 1986, while the V Congress of the FU, held from 13–15 May 1986 in the Kremlin, elected as secretary the filmmaker Elem Klimov, who was nominated by Aleksandr Iakovlev from the Central Committee. Moreover, the entire FU secretariat was replaced and substantially enlarged, following Gorbachev's democratic principles for a larger base. The Congress pushed for decentralization and less bureaucracy in film production. Moreover, a Conflict Commission was established under the critic Andrei Plakhov that was put in charge of reviewing banned, shelved and blocked films. Within a year the commission had 'unshelved' some 100 films and found at Gosfilmofond another 250 films that had never been released. Structural changes at Goskino followed: Sovinfilm was relinquished in 1989 and co-production allowed at studio level. Studios were given the right to take control of film production without Goskino's interference. In 1988 the new Cinema Centre (Kinotsentr) opened, accommodating two screens and the Museum of Cinema.

After the demise of the Soviet Union, the new Russia's film industry experienced major problems. Production units were set up on the basis of the national studios; the state-managed distribution system collapsed entirely before private investors could refurbish cinemas; and the role of the producer had to be redefined after 70 years of a state-controlled demand and supply system. In the early 1990s the number of new films doubled because money was laundered through the short-lived production studios. When these sources dried up in the mid-1990s, film production dropped sharply to an all-time low of 28 films in 1996. It was in this climate that the Open Russian Film Festival Kinotavr, founded by Mark Rudinshtein, gained huge importance. In the bleak 1996, the first refurbished cinema fitted with Dolby-Stereo System opened in Moscow: the Kodak Kinomir

(Kodak Cinema World). However, it would take several more years – and into the Putin era – for the infrastructure to recover and for Russia to become a proper film market.

Toward the late 1990s the situation for film production began to stabilize as new laws on cinema and against video piracy (which had even led to a boycott of the MPAA on American imports) began to grip. The three largest film studios were headed by film-makers: Mosfilm's director Vladimir Dostal' was succeeded in 1998 by filmmaker Karen Shakhnazarov; Aleksandr Golutva left Lenfilm in 1997 for the post of deputy minister at Goskino,[2] and was succeeded by filmmaker Viktor Sergeev, while the Gorky Studio was headed in 1995 by Sergei Livnev, and succeeded by Vladimir Grammatikov. At the Filmmakers' Union Sergei Solov'ev was elected chairman in 1994; he was succeeded by Nikita Mikhalkov in 1997.

Cinema gradually emerged from the shadows: initially into a twilight, but then into the limelight of international attention. As the Russian economy stabilized under Putin, the cinema sector began to grow and soon advanced to become the fifth largest film market in the world. The distribution of domestic films picked up as well: a breakthrough for Russian cinema came internationally when Andrei Zviagintsev's *The Return* won the Venice Golden Lion in 2003, while nationally and commercially the watershed was crossed with the success of *Night Watch* (released 11 July 2004), which had a production cost of $3.5 million and was the first film to gross in excess of $10 million at the box office. The exhibition sector has expanded since 2002, when the first multiplex (nine screens, owned by Formula Kino) opened in central Moscow in the new shopping mall Atrium. Other multiplexes followed suit, and already by 2005 Moscow counted 216 screens, followed by St Petersburg with 59 screens and Ekaterinburg with 21 screens. These developments make the Russian film market a considerable player in world cinema distribution and the national distribution networks expanded to cater for a growing number of exhibitors. Production rose, and with it the share of Russian films at the box office: for 20 per cent of titles released, Russian films grossed approximately 30 per cent at the box office in 2006. Russian film production can now build on a developed and sophisticated infrastructure. Films are produced by independent companies, often with backing from television, although many continue to receive subsidies from Goskino or its successor, the Federal Agency for Culture and Cinematography. The major television channels have developed powerful film production arms. Independent studios, in particular Sergei Sel'ianov's CTB in St Petersburg, Armen and Ruben Dishdishian's Central Partnership and Roman Borisevich's Koktebel in Moscow, have found a sound balance between mainstream cinema and auteur films.

Birgit Beumers

Notes

1. During the 1960s and 1970s its status and affiliation changed several times: from 1963–1965 and 1972–1978 it was the State Committee of the Council of Ministers, from 1965–1972 it was subordinated to the Council. In 1978 it became the State Committee for Cinematography until its liquidation in November 1991.
2. Goskino was called Roskomkino until 1996, when it became a state committee, Goskino; in 2000 it was merged with the Ministry of Culture, as the department for Cinematography. It was re-organized into the Federal Agency for Culture and Cinematography in 2004. I use the name Goskino throughout this chapter to avoid confusion.

The poster of Kinotavr Open Russian Film Festival 2010. Courtesy of Sitora Alieva, Kinotavr

FESTIVAL FOCUS
KINOTAVR

Pre-history

'Kinotavr': no one can give a reliable account of the name's origins. Some amateur historians say the word was thought up in endless kitchen conversations where entrepreneur Mark Rudinshtein and writer Mikhail Mishin appear among the explanation's recurring figures; other amateur historians insist that the word's origins are simply unknown. While the festival's etymology is lost, its provenance is not. About 40 kilometres south of Moscow, down the Warsaw Highway, is the industrial town of Podol'sk with a population in the late 1980s of just over 200,000. Podol'sk was the centre of Rudinshtein's family life, a daughter from his first marriage, and of 'Moscow Outskirts', his base of operations. Moscow Outskirts was a showbusiness company that soon branched out into concert production, rock-festival organization, film distribution and video rental. Among the groups and artists whom the fledgling company handled were the rock group Mashina Vremeni, satirist Mikhail Zhvanetskii and actor Gennadii Khazanov. In September 1987 Rudinshtein co-organized the rock festival Podol'sk-87 (sometimes referred to as the Soviet Woodstock), a time and place when rock concerts were still rare; among the performers were DDT (Leningrad), Nautilus Pompilius (Sverdlovsk) and the local group 42. By 1988, Rudinshtein's Moscow Outskirts had acquired an early copy of Petr Todorovskii's smash drama *Intergirl* (1989), the tale of a hospital nurse who becomes a hard-currency prostitute. Although Rudinstein's distribution venture was limited largely to the circulation of the film for two months in Russia's Novosibirsk region, he was able to make a profit of 36 million roubles, a considerable sum at a time, just as late-Soviet cinema was entering a period of increasing instability.

In the two years that followed (1989 and 1990), Moscow Outskirts organized the 'Festival of Unbought Cinema'. By the second year, the festival was already referred to by its alternate name, Kinotavr, and the 1990 event came to be counted retrospectively as the First Open Russian Film Festival, a title that signalled its acceptance of new films from the Newly Independent States (NIS). This First Open Festival managed to attract some twenty 'unbought' films, including such notable entries as Vitalii Kanevskii's drama *Freeze, Die, Come to Life* (1989), but it was Ermek Shinarbaev's drama *Revenge* (1989) which won the festival's Main Prize. It is now inconceivable that a major film such as *Freeze, Die, Come to Life* could have been 'unbought', all the more so in a business environment that allegedly sustained more than 150 private distribution firms, however unreliable many of them proved to be. But Rudinshtein was able to turn this unreliable state of distribution to his advantage. His effort at collecting together and screening 'unbought' cinema was an inspired project, but at the same time it was not unique: another, slightly later effort to revive interest in the domestic industry was Second Premiere, organized by Leonid Mursa, director of the Film Centre (Kinotsentr). What Rudinshtein had to offer, however, was a much larger dream, which concerned the ways in which the entire cinema economy, step by step, could be brought back to health.

Kinotavr moves to the Russian Riviera

By 1991, Moscow Outskirts had moved its fledgling Kinotavr from Podol'sk to Sochi; its activities had shifted from showbusiness to cinema and film-festival organization, and its company emphasis had shifted from 'Unbought' to 'Kinotavr', with Rudinshtein as general director. The move to Sochi was a shrewd effort to capture some of the resonances associated with the Cannes International Film Festival: the sun, the beach, the red carpet, the celebrity status. Rudinshtein correctly calculated that – at a historical moment when the films themselves were not yet in circulation – the national televisual reportage on the Russian cinema industry could gradually rekindle the ceremony, pomp and ambition of the silver screen, drawing the spectator back to the theatre. Relocated to Sochi, Rudinshtein's Kinotavr promised a great many other potential ventures beyond the festival itself. Unlike the older, northern studios – Mosfilm, Lenfilm, Gorky Studio –

where short daylight hours, unfavourable weather and poor climate reduced the number of profitable shooting days, Sochi's subtropics boasted 200 sunny days a year and a wide range of exotic locations. It potentially provided an ideal site for a full range of future plans: a technologically advanced studio, a sophisticated distribution network, a 'Cannes on the Russian Riviera'. As an annual festival, Kinotavr would provide a more flexible, responsive event than the older, biannual Moscow International Film Festival (MIFF), which itself would eventually move to an annual schedule. Moreover, Kinotavr could occupy a different niche than MIFF and Sochi's location promised enormous room for industry growth and diversification.

In broader terms, Kinotavr could also be seen as one of many entrepreneurial responses to the 1988 Law on Cooperatives. During the three-year period from 1988 to 1991, numerous cooperative studios and independent production companies were registered. At the same time, the legitimacy of these operations varied in the extreme; in this atmosphere of new freedom, cinema was among the industries most vulnerable illegal currency practices. It was therefore no surprise that the normally steady annual production rate of roughly 150 films suddenly spiked – a sign not of health, but of the industry's imminent collapse. If in 1991, the country produced 213 full-length feature films, by 1992 this figure had dropped to 172 films, then 152 (1993), and down to 68 (1994). The downward spiral continued to 46 films (1995) and 28 (1996), placing the country in the second tier of European film production, behind Sweden and Poland.

In the face of these daunting circumstances, the opening day of Kinotavr's Second Open Russian Film Festival at Sochi's Winter Theatre in 1991 bravely unveiled the festival's chief programmes, which were to become the hallmark of the early years. The main competition, 'Cinema for Everyone', judged potential box-office entries, with input from the spectators and a jury. A smaller competition, 'Cinema for the Select?' (note the cautionary question mark), screened art house cinema. The Grand Prix in the main competition was awarded to Leonid Filatov's comedy *Sons of Bitches* while the Main Prize for the 'Cinema of the Select?' Competition was shared between Karen Gevorkian's *Spotted Dog Running at the Edge of the Sea* and Dmitrii Astrakhan's comedy *Get Thee Hence!*

The same parallel structure was maintained for the Third Open Russian Festival in 1992, which saw 28 entries, with juries chaired by Vladimir Men'shov (Cinema for Everyone) and Vadim Abdrashitov (Cinema for the Select?). The Grand Prix for box-office cinema went to Georgian director Teimuraz Babluani's crime drama *Sun of the Sleepless*. Sergei Popov won the auteur competition for his drama *The Smile*. While the festival organization and competition apparatus was by now incontestably in good hands, the larger commercial prospects for domestic cinema remained as bleak as ever. Expecting the arrival of nearly 400 potential distributors, Kinotavr had organized a week-long film-market during the festival, billed as international. Surveying the low turnout, Rudinshtein remarked with characteristic good humour that Kinotavr's market initiative should really be described as the festival's comedy number.

By 1993, Kinotavr had formally registered as the Open Russian Film Festival and was actively soliciting entries from the former Soviet republics. The festival had become a fixed feature in the federal media landscape, with news coverage by eight television companies and 130 journalists intermixed with its 1,185 participants, a programme selected by Irina Rubanova. The prize structure consisted of what was now called the Grand Competition, with twenty entries and a Grand Prix of $10,000; and an Auteur Competition, with ten entries and a Grand Prix of $10,000. The actor Oleg Iankovskii joined forces with Rudinshtein and became the festival's president. Petr Todorovskii won the Grand Competition for his comedy *Encore, Another Encore!*, while Oleg Kovalov won the Auteur Competition's for his art house film *Island of the Dead*.

In the following year Kinotavr registered with FIAPF as an international festival concentrating on debut cinema (first, second and third films), with parallel programmes of international and domestic competitions. Preserving the division between box-office and art house cinema, the festival nevertheless inclined toward recognition of quality rather than a strict adherence to its own competition categories. In awarding its main prize in the main competition, for example, to Turkmen director Usman Saparov for his drama *Little Angel, Make Me Happy*, it was investing in a film that would see very little of the box office, but was nevertheless an outstanding work, filmed under the most difficult conditions.

By the Sixth Open Russian Film Festival (1995), Russia had produced a mere 46 films, Kinotavr nevertheless staunchly forged ahead as if the cinema industry were sustaining itself to a much greater degree than was indeed the case. Nearly 80 per cent of the films produced that year were screened at the festival. Fifteen films by younger directors formed the main competition programme, with the Grand Prix awarded to Aleksandr Rogozhkin's comedy *Peculiarities of the National Hunt*, a decision of a jury chaired by writer Vladimir Voinovich. Eighteen entries were comprised in the parallel competition of more experienced directors, and here Vadim Abdrashitov received an award for his drama *Play for a Passenger*. In an (as-yet) unrecognized, but encouraging sign of things to come, producer Igor' Tolstunov joined the Presidential Council; a few brave producers and directors such as Sergei Solov'ev spoke openly of the end of cinema's crisis, and urged the cinema industry to move forward more aggressively with theatre renovation and distribution networking. In many respects, these audacious souls were whistling past the graveyard: in the mid-1990s, the number of annual cinema visits *per capita* had fallen below one per year, but this concerned not only Russian films. The greatest irony was this: in the absence of an audience, Kinotavr and other rapidly proliferating festivals had de facto become a substitute for cinema attendance. The task of the festival was, in a sense, to overcome itself: to generate enough interest in the fact of cinema that those who followed the celebrity news on television would be drawn back into the movie theatre.

The year 1996, the nadir of Russian cinema, marked the most intense moment of the industry's internal contradictions. The Law on Cinema, first initiated in 1991, was signed by Boris Yeltsin on 22 August 1996. At a time when cinema had virtually ceased to exist, the law finally addressed a range of critical tasks, including tax incentives and a wildly optimistic set of tasks and responsibilities for Goskino. The cinema offerings were marked by a high number of adaptations from nineteenth- and early twentieth-century Russian literature. This trend reflected neither laziness nor lack of imagination. It was a calculated risk that, in the popular imagination, the pre-Revolutionary past was indeed that coveted alloy, both worldly glamour and nostalgic provincialism, that could draw the spectator back to the ticket booth. The grand style that dominated many of these productions promised to confer on the newly wealthy the mantle of legitimacy it keenly sought. Yet the convoluted plots and lagging pace were often incompatible with the world of cellular telephones; these adaptations failed in all but one spectacular instance: Lev Tolstoy's 'Prisoner of the Caucasus' (through the mediation of the writer Vladimir Makanin) in Sergei Bodrov's drama *Prisoner of the Mountains*. The competition jury, chaired by Karen Shakhnazarov, chose Bodrov's drama for the Grand Prix of 1996. Another adaptation, Sergei Ursuliak's *Summer People*, won the panorama competition of work by established directors.

In 1997 Kinotavr presented only one competition including twenty films (most of the year's output) for the judgment of the jury chaired by Vladimir Khotinenko. The festival shifted a lot of attention to the international competition (still for first, second and third films), while other slots were taken by a retrospective of Aleksandr Sokurov and screenings of archival discoveries or Soviet films that never enjoyed a full cinema run at the time of release (or even failed to get one). The competition included films from Ukraine, Georgia and Turkmenistan: Murad Aliev's *Night of the Yellow Bull* had been banned in his native country, while Georgi Khaindrava's *Cemetery of Reveries* – about the conflict over Abkhazia – drew crowds to the streets (rather than the cinema) in protest against the film – after all, Sochi was too close for people not to be affected. Sokurov's *Mother and Son* competed alongside Kira Muratova's *Three Stories*, but it was Aleksei Balabanov's *Brother* that won the Grand Prix: it was truly recognized as marker of a new kind of cinema with a new kind of hero (and the Best Actor award went to Sergei Bodrov Jr).

For the 1998 edition Rudinshtein teamed up with Sergei Lisovskii, head of the advertising agency Premier SV. The festival returned to two competition programmes: a main competition and a debut competition, sending out a strong sign of rebirth and rejuvenation to an industry that the festival desperately wanted to see on the road to recovery. The jury, chaired by Rustam Ibragimbekov, judged nineteen films of established filmmakers, all produced or co-produced in Russia, and awarded Abdrashitov's *Time of the Dancer*. The debut competition showed great promise with eight titles, but it was Larisa Sadilova's docu-style drama about a maternity clinic that took away the main award. An information programme screened more Russian films, signalling a steady rise in film production.

For the tenth edition in 1999 Kinotavr showed fifteen films in the main competition, while the debut competition included seven titles, promising a fresh breath in Russian cinema, even if the debuts were significantly weaker than in the previous year. Sokurov's *Moloch* could not fail to impress, having garnered a screenplay award for Iurii Arabov in Cannes, but it was Rogozhkin's *Checkpoint*, addressing the Chechen war and offering a new turn in the oeuvre of a filmmaker best known for comedies, which took the main prize from a jury headed by Armen Medvedev.

By 2000 the festival programme had become very ambitious and included a competition, special screenings, information screenings, a documentary section and a forum for debuts (shorts and animation), presenting the winners of a Debut-Kinotavr competition held in Moscow in the previous spring. The jury had to judge nineteen films of a variety of genres. Lungin's *Wedding* came directly from its screening in Cannes, equipped with a special mention for the acting ensemble, but it was Aleksei Uchitel''s *His Wife's Diary*, about Ivan Bunin, and *Luna Papa* by Tajik-born director Bakhtior Khudoinazarov which took the main awards (which the festival titled Grand Prix and Main Prize from 2000–2004).

The twelfth edition in 2001 presented once again a main and a debut competition, with additional sections for documentaries and for the winners of Debut-Kinotavr. The jury, chaired by theatre director Mark Zakharov, assessed 22 films and awarded Sergei Solov'ev's *Tender Age*, about effect of war on a young man and made in Solov'ev's characteristic fragmentary narrative style. Eleven debuts were screened, all rather unimpressive – except for the winner, Sergei S. Bodrov's *Sisters*, which led to the discovery of the young actress Oksana Akin'shina.

Kinotavr 2002 saw another war film win in a competition of thirteen films: Balabanov's *War* made controversial viewing, because it undermined the perception of enemy as evil and the Russian soldier as essentially good. Valerii Todorovskii's emotional drama *The Lover* also took an award, but it was the debut competition that brought forth the names of Andrei Proshkin and Aleksei Muradov; the latter's film *The Kite* won the competition and established the Ekaterinburg-based filmmaker in cinema. The 2003 edition included eighteen films in the main competition; there was no debut section. Tellingly a turn to folk themes dominated the year's output in films, reflected in the debut award to Gennadii Sidorov's *Old Grannies*. The jury, chaired by Valerii Todorovskii, awarded the main prize to Khudoinazarov's *Chic*.

The fifteenth edition in 2004 included a competition of features and one of shorts, as well as a section of Films on the Square, screening the latest Russian films for the citizens of Sochi free of charge. Of the seventeen films in competition, Pavel Chukhrai's

Driver for Vera and Valerii Todorovskii's *My Stepbrother Frankenstein* clearly stood out. During the festival Rudinshtein negotiated the sale of the brand Kinotavr to Aleksandr Rodnianskii, then CEO of CTC-Media, and the producer Igor' Tolstunov. The 2005 festival saw a change in programme directors, a department now headed by Sitora Alieva. It also established a newly professionalized format, with a more streamlined programme and the firm establishment of a feature and a shorts competition, complemented by a programme of Cinema on the Square. The competition included both mainstream and art house films, ranging from the blockbuster *Shadowboxing* to the experimental *4* by Il'ia Khrzhanovskii and awarding Lungin's *Roots* with the main prize.

The 2006 edition preserved the format of feature and shorts competition, and Cinema on the Square. The fifteen films in competition were the result of strategic selection, since it was possible once again to focus on art house cinema: the infrastructure had recovered sufficiently – especially after the success of *Night Watch*, the first film to break the $10 million barrier at the box office – for mainstream cinema to find its way to the screens through a solid distribution network, while festival could focus on their real role as eye-openers, places for discovery and for the pitching of new projects – and all these areas would be developed to the full in the coming years by the festival management, which also scheduled screenings of sub-titled copies of the films for foreign guests and festival selectors. The discoveries of the debut competition showed immediate results: Valeria Gai-Germaika, whose film *Girls* won the shorts competition, soon embarked on her first feature film *Everybody Dies but Me* which went on to be presented – and win an award – at Cannes. Similarly, in the 2007 edition of the festival the award for the best short went to Dmitrii Mamuliia and Bakur Bakuradze's *Moscow*; a year later Bakuradze won the main award for his feature *Shultes*; or Igor' Voloshin's short *Goat* won an award in 2007, and a year later he received the mention of 'Best Debut' in the main competition for *Nirvana*. The competition programme consisted more and more of films by young filmmakers, reflecting not only a new aesthetic richness of Russian cinema, but also its rejuvenation as a new generation of filmmakers conquered the stage of the (in the meantime also refurbished) Winter Theatre in Sochi. In 2006 the main awards of the festival had gone to Kirill Serebrennikov for his film *Playing the Victim*, based on a play by the Presnyakov Brothers that he had previously staged at the Moscow Art Theatre. Further prizes for Boris Khlebnikov, Aleksei Popogrebskii and Ivan Vyrypaev in the 2007 and 2008 editions signalled the strong foothold that playwrights and people associated with New Drama were gaining in cinema, a tendency that would culminate with the award in 2009 to the playwrights Vasilii Sigarev for *Wolfy* and Ivan Vyrypaev for *Oxygen*.

If Mark Rudinshtein managed to see Russian cinema through its bleakest years, and the rebuilt infrastructure facilitated a rebirth of commercial cinema, it is Kinotavr that is clearly preparing the ground for a new generation of art house filmmakers to emerge from Russia.

Nancy Condee and Birgit Beumers

WHAT DOES *ZHANR* MEAN IN RUSSIAN?

Genre cinema traditionally has a bad reputation among Russo-Soviet filmmakers. It is perceived to be a low-culture, capitalist mass product generated by a film industry. It is not simply distinct from *auteur* cinema (*avtorskoe kino*) but antithetical to it. Explanations for the condemnation of genre cinema align it with the bourgeois West, specifically Hollywood. Denise Youngblood cites the distrust of genre cinema as a dominant factor for the disproportionately few comedies in early Soviet cinema of the 1920s:

> Young directors [...] tended to oppose entertainment films as 'bourgeois,' promoting their own work by way of contrast as somehow truly 'revolutionary.' The press was controlled by critics who likewise believed that Soviet cinema had to distinguish itself from its commercial counterparts in the West. [...] [M]ost established cinematic genres presented daunting challenges to Soviet filmmakers throughout the first decade of Soviet movie production. Genre films were, after all, profoundly 'bourgeois' products of commercial filmmaking – that is, there was nothing intrinsically Marxist or Soviet about them.[1]

Clearly, the judgement of genre cinema as something quintessentially bourgeois stems directly from ideological Soviet rhetoric. However, this way of thinking is not a historically localized phenomenon; it persists into the post-Soviet period. A similar logic can be sensed in comments made by the contemporary directors Aleksei Balabanov, Sergei Solov'ev and Andrei Zviagintsev. When, following the release of *Brother 2* (2000), Balabanov was congratulated for having made the first gangster film in Russian cinema, the praise did not fall on deaf ears, but on insulted ones. In his typical acerbic tone Balabanov retaliated: 'If I had wanted to make a genre film, I would have shot it in English!'[2] This incriminating use of 'in English' signals Balabanov's negative perception of genre as a Hollywood-specific product. Solov'ev and Zviagintsev articulate similar sentiments. Responding to a question regarding the likelihood of American genres taking root in Russia, Solov'ev rejects genre as mercenary and antithetical to good cinema, while art house director Zviagintsev explains: 'Hollywood is a kind of factory and with regard to Hollywood it is possible to speak about genre. But we do not have a factory, we do not have an industry; so what kind of genres can be spoken of?'[3]

For several reasons it is incomplete to interpret this as a battle between east and west, socialist and capitalist, art and commercial product, Russia and America. First, early Soviet attacks on bourgeois filmmaking were aimed just as much at pre-Revolutionary and NEP-era[4] Russian studios as they were at films imported from the West. As entre-preneurs latched onto the cinema's mass appeal, they developed a lucrative industry, complete with a star system playing in 'a rich array of genres' including costume dramas, literary adaptations, comedies, adventure films and, most popular of all, melodramas.[5] Second, despite the on-going tendency to incriminate genre cinema, it has periodically dominated Soviet screens; paradoxically, it is during moments of severe cultural repres-sion that Soviet genre cinema boomed. And, third, following the *auteur*-dominant years of the late 1980s and 1990s, genre cinema is currently enjoying a resurgence. To more fully understand the negative connotation of Russian genre cinema it is imperative to consider the internal politics of the Soviet film industry. This introduction contends that the hostility of Russian directors and film critics toward genre cinema is as much, if not more, a reaction against the repressive cultural environment of Soviet filmmaking that, in fact, demanded genre films, and thereby effectively silenced the *auteurs*, than it is a way to differentiate Russo-Soviet filmmaking from bourgeois Hollywood.

It would be erroneous to separate Soviet cinema from a developed system of genre filmmaking because the centralized state-controlled film industry operated according to a genre-determined production plan. The distinguished Russian film scholar Maya Turovs-kaya has argued that a heterogeneous cultural landscape existed up until approximately 1930, at which point there was a 'change in paradigm'.[6] The new paradigm of socialist real-ism shifted cultural production away from plurality and diversity toward 'a universal char-acter' that was 'accompanied by a shift towards totalitarian structures[7] used to construct a 'stabilised type of consciousness'.[8] These conditions set the stage for a film industry dominated by programmatic narratives – the basis for socialist realist genre cinema.

Turovskaya located an anonymous report from 1927 in the uncatalogued Sovkino files held at the Central State Archive of the October Revolution that asserts:

> The slogan of Soviet cinema enterprises is: 'Our films must be 100 per cent ideo-logically correct and 100 per cent commercially viable.' Soviet film must be highly profitable. It can only be an instrument of Communist enlightenment if it is accepted by the audience with pleasure. We therefore declare that the 'commercially profitable film' and the 'ideologically correct film' are not mutually exclusive categories but rather complementary to one another. The principle place in the repertoire must be occupied by heroic pictures. The aim of these films is to mobilize the masses. The second place must go to pictures on the problems of everyday life in the transitional epoch. In third place – less significant but more numerous – should be entertainment pictures, the aim of which should be to attract the masses to cinema to fight against the more harmful leisure activities of the population such as drunkenness, hooliganism and so on.[9]

Not only do ideological and educative goals crossover with clearly stated economic (i.e., profitable, mercenary and commercial) goals, but the three thematic categories – heroic pictures, pictures of everyday life and entertainment films – can be read as a framework of particular genres. Turovskaya links heroic pictures to the historical-Revolutionary film and it does not take much effort to draw a connection between entertainment pictures and the Stalinist musical.

If in 1927 an industry based on genre cinema was suggested, but lacked a formal spokesman, then by 1934 Boris Shumiatskii, who from 1930–1937 headed Soiuzkino (formerly Sovkino), the centralized Soviet film organization, was poised to articulate such a plan clearly. Shumiatskii called for 'genres that are infused with optimism, mobilizing emotions, cheerfulness, joie-de-vivre, and laughter' and stressed the need for drama, comedy and fairy tales.[10]

It might seem that the flourishing of genre cinema under Stalin contradicts the initial premise of this argument – namely, that genre cinema has since the 1920s been rejected as bourgeois. It is this paradox that complicates attempts to sum up the connotative meaning of genre cinema in the Russian context. The official rhetoric of Stalinism high-lights this inconsistency: even as the production of genre cinema was officially advocated in the thematic plans of the 1930s, specific genres labels were villainized as antithetical to Soviet ideological goals. Richard Taylor grants that '[a]lthough the term *musical* was not used at the time, because it was deemed to be redolent of "bourgeois" Hollywood, […] the terms *comedy* or *musical comedy* prevailed'.[11] Nina Dymshits similarly references genre renaming; she notes that in the 1930s the word 'melodrama' does not appear on posters or in the titles of films. Furthermore, she explains that the category of melo-drama 'gradually disappears from film reference books even in reference to those films of the 1920s, which were consciously constructed in this genre and were openly called melodramas by their authors'.[12] As with street, city and even peoples' names at this time, the melodrama was masked with a more Soviet, or, at least, a less obviously bourgeois designation: '[b]eginning in the 1930s through the mid-1970s melodrama lives under other names: the musical comedy, the film story, the film drama, and sometimes even tragedy'.[13]

This paradox – the rise of genre under Stalinism and the persistent negative connota-tion of genre cinema – is, perhaps, not a paradox at all. The politicized use and rejection of genre categories underscores film genre theorist Rick Altman's assertion that genres 'are not inert categories shared by all […], but discursive claims made by real speakers for particular purposes in specific situations'.[14] With only brief mention of two discrete genres from the Stalinist period (i.e., the historical-Revolutionary film and the musical comedy), this remains a partial picture of genre cinema of the time. The goal here is not to characterize Stalinist genre cinema fully, but to underscore the conscious development of genres within a highly politicized cultural landscape.

That Stalinist culture limited artistic expression is no surprise. The conventional narra-tives articulated via a socialist realist framework functioned as a type of censorship: tell the story one way or don't tell it at all. The difficulty of making films that conformed to the goals laid out in the thematic plans curtailed artistic freedom and is one factor that resulted in fledging film output through the mid-1930s. While the thematic plans of 1935 dictated that 130 films be made and the 1936 plan aimed for 165 films, those years saw only 45 and 46 films, respectively.[15] Thinking about genre cinema within this historical context helps to understand that the narrative limitations intrinsic to Soviet genre cinema during the 1930s and 1940s functioned as a mechanism of political suppression.

Genre cinema did not disappear under Stalin's successor, Nikita Khrushchev, nor did thematic and production plans, which were used to revitalize the industry after hitting its nadir following World War II.[16] However, the Thaw era did provide, if only temporarily, relative artistic freedoms. Josephine Woll, in her characterization of post-Stalinist cinema, asserts that

[a]fter years of imposed aesthetic homogeneity, film-makers were able to explore a spectrum of artistic approaches. Instead of one way to depict objects and individuals on screen, they could choose a variety of ways; instead of a single, predictable and judgmental authorial stance, they could offer multiple perspectives.[17]

The new creative space occupied by this 'creative intelligentsia' propelled *auteur*-driven Soviet cinema onto the international scene in 1958, when Mikhail Kalatozov's *The Cranes are Flying* (1957) captivated audiences and critics from the Soviet Union to Cannes, where it won the Golden Palm. Also during this period, from the late 1950s through the mid-1960s, Soviet *auteurs* debuted (including Kira Muratova and Aleksandr Askol'dov), as well as the *auteur extraordinaire*, Andrei Tarkovskii. However, the rise of the 'cre-ative intelligentsia' was far from permanent. The pendulum quickly swung in the other

direction and the production of *auteur* cinema was curtailed as certain of these directors' films were put 'on the shelf' – the euphemism for censoring a film by taking it out
of circulation. As Soviet culture entered into Brezhnev's Stagnation era, the increasingly
repressive atmosphere forced *auteurs* back into relative silence. Again filmmakers were
forced to privilege the state's political goals over their individual artistic or aesthetic aspirations; again directors returned to cinematic conventions associated with genre-driven
cinema. Thus, another peak in the active production of genre cinema occurs during the
repressive cultural freeze that takes place during Stagnation (1964–1985). The cinema
industry under Brezhnev reinstated rigorous, authoritarian policies while simultaneously
encouraging commercially successful popular culture.

In October 1976 a group of film scholars gathered at the conference 'The Problems of
Genres at the Contemporary Moment of Soviet Cinema Development' organized by the
Research Institute of Cinema Studies and History (NIIK) and the Screenwriting Editorial Board of Goskino. The papers presented at this conference were published in 1979
under the title *Genres of Cinema* (*Zhanry kino*), the only Soviet books dedicated entirely
to film genre. In his introduction to the collection, Boris Pavlenok, the deputy director at
Goskino, writes: 'Of course, it is simple to label any popular film with the almost abusive
epithet "commercial" film'.[18] He goes on, though, to suggest that success must be measured not by box-office figures, but by the ability of films to teach audiences. Thus genre
cinema is characterized as politically correct because it is not economics that matter, but
the teachings of Marxist-Leninism.

The challenge of this ideological imperative comes through in Valentin Chernykh's
contribution to the conference's papers. Chernykh, a screenplay writer, wrote about the
'production film' as a new genre of the era. In the middle of his contribution, buried quietly
among expected political catch-phrases of the day, is a comment that hints at the danger
associated with producing for the state. Chernykh defines Soviet cinema as *auteur* even
within his article on the production film genre. He writes: '[…] our cinema is, on the whole,
a directorial cinema [… a] director makes one film in three years in the best of situations.
Our directors are therefore very afraid of making mistakes. To make a mistake is certainly
for them really terrible: every failure is a trauma that lasts for several years'.[19]

Although couched in the language of the artist's responsibility to his own craft, this
admission of fear hints at the repressive nature of filmmaking under Brezhnev. To understand that Soviet cinema is directorial is to understand that the blame for ideological
impurity is targeted at the director; deviation from acceptable narratives (wittingly or
not) can be a politically dangerous act. The resulting fear, we might conjecture, results in
directors rushing back to genre filmmaking: 'Genres became, one might say, a no man's
land, towards which cinematographers willingly rushed and where they found great
creative freedom'.[20] Genre filmmaking offered safe, predictable territory, where directors
were required to guess less and risk less.

Prominent Soviet film scholar Neya Zorkaya describes the division among Stagnation-
era directors: 'The cinema became a particular social environment thanks to its dual
nature: there was the sphere of government planning, on the one hand, and individual
creative work, on the other'.[21] To the intelligentsia, among whom Zorkaya ranked highly,
directors who succumbed to state pressure and made the genre films required of them
relinquished their status as artists. Describing the three directors she values most highly
in this period – Vasilii Shukshin, Andrei Tarkovskii and Otar Ioseliani – Zorkaya commends
them for having 'spiritually departed from Soviet ideological service' and creating cinema
based on 'dictates of the heart, and not social order'.[22] Whereas Chernykh admits fear,
Zorkaya admires the fearless.

Although tempting to read Zorkaya's division between government hacks and true artists
as parallel to genre and *auteur* cinema, it would be incorrect. Cinema with mass appeal
flourished during Stagnation. While the number of films made annually (approximately

150 per year from 1965–1985) assured a sufficient supply of average-at-best films, there were also an incredible number of popular blockbusters. Certain of the most popular, genre-driven blockbusters bore a distinct authorial stamp. The comedies of Leonid Gaidai and El'dar Riazanov, the master of the sad comedy, regularly broke box-office highs. The prominent and immensely popular Stagnation author and director Shukshin further complicates attempts to divide popular, genre-driven cinema from *auteur* cinema.

At the cusp of the Stagnation and Glasnost eras in the mid-1980s, film directors – like much of the rest of Soviet society – sought to break free from the ideological freeze and cultural strictures that characterized Leonid Brezhnev's rule in late Soviet history. The frustration with a repressive, fear-inducing cinema industry that forced directors to adhere to genre conventions – even if some of these genres films were made by *auteurs* – came to a head at the Fifth Congress of the Russian Filmmakers' Union (May 1986), held three months after Mikhail Gorbachev proclaimed glasnost and perestroika at the 27th Party Congress in February 1986. This Congress of the Filmmakers' Union turned the tables on state control. Among the first orders of business was the establishment of a Conflict Commission, which went on to release hundreds of films that had been censored – or put on the shelf – and curbed the censorship that had prohibited artistically experimental or critical films during Stagnation. This delayed release of confiscated films helped to resurrect *auteur* directors whose careers were initiated, but cut short, during the mid-1960s. For approximately a decade following this 1985 revolt, *auteur* cinema flourished and slowly overtook genre film. As in the Thaw, the cultural liberation experienced during Glasnost prompted the movement away from genre and back to *auteur*. This late Soviet cultural thaw renewed Russian cinema's presence on the foreign festival circuit.

Since 2004, there has been an upsurge in film production. In an effort to revitalize, the post-Soviet Russian cinema industry – which includes the new profession of film producers alongside directors, actors, screenwriters and critics – has begun to think about genre again. The revitalization of the post-Soviet film industry depends on genre cinema. Domestic production of genre cinema not only helps Russian cinema compete against the flood of American movies into its theatres but, moreover, it has catalyzed annual film production. However, despite these benefits, genre cinema continues to be ignored by the vanguard of the intelligentsia within the industry: that is to say, film critics continue to scorn genre cinema as insignificant and undeserving of their attention.

At the 2001 roundtable, 'Director versus Producer', dedicated to an investigation of this relatively new industry relationship, film scholar Elena Stishova made the following scathing remarks of her colleagues:

> The critics endlessly moan about how we need genre cinema capable of competing with and battling against the dominance of American cinema on our screens, etc. Voila! Finally, genre cinema, about which we've dreamt for so long, has appeared. [...] However, last summer at the Open Russian Festival in Sochi, the studio NTV-Profit showed seven new films. For the first time in the last decade it became clear: in our native land they have come up with, devised, made, and offered the audience good or bad, but a totally professional genre cinema. And what kind of the reaction came from the critics? By and large a negative one![23]

This attitude held by Russian film scholars has kept serious study of genre cinema to a minimum. Although the pages of scholarly journals dedicated to cinema are punctuated with genre labels – thus acknowledging that films conform to certain genre conventions – there are virtually no sustained studies of individual genres written by Russian scholars of post-Soviet cinema.

Perhaps the greatest obstacle blocking the Russian intelligentsia's path to genre scholarship is their insistence on separating genre from *auteur*. The Russian university textbook on the history of Russian cinema wisely states on its final pages that 'it has become clear that no uncrossable divide exists between *auteur* and entertainment projects; to the contrary, their interaction often leads to the appearance of great cinema, in which every viewer can find his interest'.[24]

Dawn Seckler

Notes

1. Denise Youngblood, '"We don't know what to laugh at": Comedy and satire in Soviet cinema', in Andrew Horton (ed.), *Inside Soviet Film Satire*, Cambridge: Cambridge UP (1993), pp. 36–47 (37).
2. In Dmitrii Komm, 'Dolzhniki i kreditory', *Iskusstvo kino* 2 (2002), pp. 93–103 (95).
3. Various Contributors, 'Siuzhety i geroi: zapadnye zhanry v rossiiskom kino', *Seans* 19–20 (2004). http://seance.ru/category/n/19-20/sujets_and_heroes/sujets_and_heroes-ganry/. Accessed 27 February 2010.
4. NEP, the New Economic Policy (1921–1928), was a period of compromise during which private enterprise was allowed in small industry with the goal to jump-start the economy following the Civil War.
5. Richard Stites, *Russian Popular Culture: Entertainment and Society since 1900*, Cambridge: Cambridge UP (1992), pp. 30–32.
6. Maya Turovskaya, 'The 1930s and 1940s: Cinema in context', in Richard Taylor and Derek Spring (eds), *Stalinism and Soviet Cinema*, London: Routledge (1993), pp. 34–53 (37).
7. Ibid.
8. Ibid., p. 42.
9. Ibid., p, 43.
10. Boris Shumiatskii, 'Zadachi templana 1934 goda', *Sovetskoe kino* 11 (1933), pp. 1–4.
11. Richard Taylor, 'Singing on the Steppes for Stalin: Ivan Pyr'ev and the Kolkhoz Musical in Soviet Cinema', *Slavic Review* 58.1 (1999), pp. 143–159 (146).
12. Nina Dymshits, *Sovetskaia kinomelodrama vchera i segodnia*, Moscow: Znanie (1987), p. 21.
13. Ibid.
14. Rick Altman, *Film/Genre*. London: British Film Institute (1999), p. 101.
15. Richard Taylor, 'Ideology as mass entertainment: Boris Shumyatsky and Soviet cinema in the 1930s', in Richard Taylor and Ian Christie (eds), *Inside the Film Factory*, London: Routledge (1991), pp. 193–216 (215).
16. From 1945–1950 approximately nineteen films were made annually. In 1951 production hit an all time low; only nine films were completed.
17. Josephine Woll, *Real Images: Soviet Cinema and the Thaw*, London: I.B. Tauris (2000), p. 12.
18. In Valerii Fomin (ed.), *Zhanry kino*, Moscow: Iskusstvo (1979), p. 9.
19. Ibid., p. 271.
20. L. Budiak (ed.), *Istoriia otechestvennogo kino*, Moscow: Progress-Traditsiia (2005), p. 447.
21. Neya Zorkaya, *The Illustrated History of Soviet Cinema*, New York: Hippocrene Books (1989), p. 396.
22. Ibid., p. 395.
23. 'Direktor protiv prodiusera', *Iskusstvo kino* 4 (2001), pp. 166–174 (174).
24. Budiak, p. 510.

Evgenii Bauer

DIRECTORS
EVGENII BAUER

Name:
Evgenii Bauer

Date of Birth:
1865

Place of Birth:
Moscow, Russia

Place of Residence:
Moscow, Russia

Nationality:
Russian

Evgenii Bauer was born to an artistic family: his father was a Russified Czech, Franz Bauer, and a famous zither player; his mother was an opera singer. In 1887 Evgenii Bauer graduated from the Moscow School of Painting, Sculpture and Architecture and started his career in the arts. Before turning to cinematography, Bauer worked as a caricaturist, photographer, theatre producer, impresario and set designer. He joined the film industry at the age of forty-seven. He started at the Drankov studio, where he designed the set for the costume drama *Tercentenary of the Rule of the Romanov Dynasty* (1913). Bauer also shortly worked for Pathé as set designer and later director. However, it was after joining the most powerful studio at the time, the Khanzhonkov studio, in late 1913 that he became one of the most popular and highest paid directors in pre-Revolutionary Russia.

In the 1890s Bauer had married the dancer and actress Lina Ancharova, who proved to be a genuine and talented comedienne and starred in such comedies as *Cold Showers* (1914) and *The 1002nd Ruse* (1915). Generally speaking, Bauer's work can be divided into two parts: theatrical comedies and farces, and psychological dramas. Bauer started with the latter, also known as 'drawing room dramas'; his first film *Twilight of a Woman's Soul* (1913) belongs to this genre. The film tells about a young aristocratic woman who is raped by a commoner and then rejected by her husband after admitting the truth. In typical melodramatic fashion, she rejects her husband when he returns to her years later, and he kills himself. Significantly, Bauer's films were known not only for their dramatic plots but also for experimentation in filmmaking. Already in 1913, in *Twilight of a Woman's*

Soul, he employed close-up photography and experimented with light and shadow to create psychological effects. In addition, the film included a dream sequence shot through a veil, which was a quite innovative for the time.

Another popular film was *Child of the Big City* (1914), a story about a young girl who falls victim to the glamorous life in the city. Among other things, the film was noted for its beautiful decorations used to emphasize the temptations for the young heroine. In the same year Bauer made *Silent Witnesses*, which depicted a tragic love affair between a servant and her master. The film has a minimum of inter-titles, and the storyline builds on concise editing. *Silent Witnesses* is also famous as a new 'encyclopedia' of Russian life, especially fashion and style. With Bauer's experience as stage director and designer, his films were often criticized for being too stylized, too concerned with the set rather than the acting.

Despite his attention to detailed décor and mise-en-scène, Bauer had a profound interest in actors and acting. Actor and director Ivan Perestiani made his debut in Bauer's *Driver, Don't Flog the Horses* (1916) and performed in many other films. Bauer also opened the path for such stars of silent cinema as Vera Kholodnaia, Ivan Moz-zhukhin, Vitol'd Polonskii and the ballerina Vera Karalli. Lev Kuleshov, a prominent Soviet film theorist and director, started working in the film industry as designer for Bauer's films. In 1915 Bauer made *Children of the Age* starring Vera Kholodnaia, a film famous for its décor. In the same year he made two films on the topic of death and love, or life after death: the provocative *Daydreams* and *After Death* (starring Vera Karalli), based on Ivan Turgenev's story 'Klara Milich'. In *After Death* Bauer used one of his favourite techniques: a three-minute 'track out' to emphasize the main character's uneasiness while meeting the guests. In general, Bauer liked to utilize tracking shots for a dramatic effect, as in *The Dying Swan* (1916, with Polonskii and Kar-alli), based on the famous novella by Zoia Barantsevich. In 1916 Bauer made another expensive and fashionable production, *A Life for a Life*, based on the French novel by Georges Ohnet, starring Kholodnaia, Polonskii and Perestiani.

In addition to melodramas and comedies, Bauer created several historical films, making a total of over 80 films between 1913 and 1917. In 1914 Bauer makes a series of patriotic war pictures, includ-ing *Glory to Us* and *Death to the Enemy* with actor Ivan Mozzhukhin. The film is remarkable for an episode of an air-battle in which Bauer fuses documentary footage with acting. During the Great War, when anti-German sentiments were strong, Bauer worked under his wife's maiden name, Ancharov. In 1917 Bauer filmed a historical-Revolu-tionary picture, *The Revolutionary,* which Ivan Perestiani co-wrote and starred in. After the Revolution Bauer and the Khanzhonkov company moved to Yalta. During the making of *For Happiness* Bauer broke his leg but continued to work on his next film, *The King of Paris*. How-ever, the injury was affected by complications and Bauer died in Yalta on 22 June 1917; the actress Olga Rakhmanova completed the film after his death.

Mariya Boston

Sergei Eisenstein, 1931, Kobal

DIRECTORS
SERGEI EISENSTEIN

Name:

Sergei Eisenstein

Date of Birth:

22 January 1898

Place of Birth:

Riga, Russian Empire

Place of Residence:

Moscow

Nationality:

Russian/Soviet

Awards:

Golden Medal at the International Exhibition for Decorative Art, Paris (1925, 1926), Best Film, American Film Academy (*Battleship Potemkin*, 1926), Stalin Prize (1941, 1946)

Sergei Eisenstein is one of the great pioneers of cinema, both as film-maker and film theorist. He had a roller-coaster career in the Soviet Union, alternately benefitting from state commissions and suffering from official rebuke. All of his films use unlikely combinations of formal and narrative elements to challenge viewers into engaging actively in the process of making meaning from visual experience.

Eisenstein was born in Riga, the son of a well-known architect; his parents divorced when he was eleven and he remained with his domineering father, while his mother moved to St Petersburg. Eisenstein was headed for a career in engineering when the Revolution intervened. In the Civil War he fought on the Bolshevik side (though he would never join the Communist Party) and afterwards worked for the revolutionary theatre troupe, Proletkult, but soon left the theatre for film. Between 1924 and 1929 he made four feature films, all on themes of revolution and building socialism: *Strike* (1924), *Battleship 'Potemkin'* (1925), *October* (1928) and *The General Line* (renamed *The Old and the New*, 1929). *Potemkin* made Eisenstein famous around the world for its extensive use of radical montage, or juxtaposition of shots for dramatic and political effect.

In 1929 Eisenstein travelled to Europe and the United States, ostensibly to study new sound technology, but also to explore the possibilities of making films in the West and raising money for the strapped Soviet film industry. Eisenstein's stay in Hollywood produced three treatments and zero films. He was about to return home when the socialist writer Upton Sinclair offered to fund a film about Mexico. Eisenstein spent more than a year shooting *Que Viva Mexico!*, a film about the presence of traditional and indigenous cultures in modern, urban Mexico. Eisenstein loved Mexico; he made many friends there, had his first sexual relationships with men and with women; and reignited his love of drawing, but wild cost-overruns and the discovery of a cache of 'pornographic' drawings led Sinclair to halt the project. At the same time Stalin wanted Eisenstein back in Russia. Sinclair promised to send the footage on to Moscow, but kept it and allowed other filmmakers to edit parts of it, which Eisenstein experienced as a traumatic betrayal.

In his absence, the Soviet Union had gone through a major upheaval with the consolidation of Stalin's power. Exhilarating ideas of the 1920s about art serving society had become rigid guidelines of artistic institutions controlled by the Communist Party. Movies were to be made 'for the masses' and they had to be strictly conventional in terms of narrative and style. Eisenstein struggled to conform to these new requirements, unable to shed his rebellious imagination. Each of his proposals for new projects was denied. In the meantime, he became a popular teacher at the All-Union State Film Institute, he embarked on serious film theory, and he made drawings. He was subject to harsh criticism during this period for the 'formalism' of his theory and his lack of productivity.

Political attacks culminated in 1937, when Eisenstein was nearing completion of a film based on a story by Ivan Turgenev, *Bezhin Meadow*, but organized around a sensationalized incident in which a young boy, Pavlik Morozov, was murdered after denouncing his father as a counter-Revolutionary. Eisenstein turned the film into an Abraham and Isaac parable. The head of the film industry, Boris Shumiatskii, stopped production and denounced Eisenstein to the Central Committee, which decided to allow Eisenstein to continue working as a director and, in a horrifying turn of events, had Shumiatskii arrested and subsequently shot.

In 1938 Eisenstein produced his most conventional film, a hagiographical depiction of medieval ruler Alexander Nevsky. It became his most popular film, though he considered it an embarrassment. If *Bezhin Meadow* threatened his life, *Alexander Nevsky* saved it and then brought him to the heights of fame and success: in 1939 he won the Order of Lenin; in 1941 *Nevsky* won the Stalin Prize. He was given cash, a new apartment and a car. He was made artistic director of Mosfilm.

In January 1941, Eisenstein was commissioned to make a film about Ivan the Terrible as part of a campaign to recruit tsarist rulers as historical precedents for Russian state nationalism and authoritarian rule. Eisenstein wrote a screenplay that emphasized two achievements: the establishment of a centralized state against the will of the aristocratic elite, the boyars; and the successful defeat of non-Russian neighbours in the east and in the west. A draft of the screenplay was finished in spring 1941, but shortly after that Germany invaded the Soviet Union. In October, the film studios were evacuated to Alma-Ata, where Eisenstein would develop ideas for a complex psychological treatment of Ivan's evolution from visionary revolutionary to murderous tyrant. Filming took place between 1943 and 1945. Part I was approved in late 1944, released in early 1945 and received the Stalin Prize in late 1945. Part II was finished in early 1946, but was banned by the Central Committee in March. Eisenstein was in hospital when the film was screened for Stalin, having suffered a heart attack the night he finished Part II. Part II would only be released in 1958 and Part III was never finished. A life of intense work in difficult circumstances took its toll on Eisenstein. He died of a second heart attack in 1948, at age fifty, hard at work at his desk.

From the very beginning of his career, Eisenstein was as interested in thinking about the way we perceive films as in making them: theory and practice were always intertwined. Eisenstein believed that cinema was the highest of the arts, because it was capable of incorporating the history of all the arts into a new form that utilized movement, making its images correspond more closely to the cognitive and emotional responses of our brains. His work in the 1920s was focused on the cognitive and emotional effects of images following one another in cinematic time. 'Montage' or editing, compelled the viewer to supply significance to streams of incongruous images. His work in Mexico brought him in contact with ethnography and cultural evolution, enriching ideas about montage. He came to believe that an art work achieved greatness when it was constructed in ways that corresponded to universal structures of human cognitive perception. Unlike earlier montage, which focused narrowly on visual constructions, his concept in the 1930s and 1940s incorporated sound, colour, movement and complex dialectical structures. The viewer was still to be provoked but now the challenges were organized around multiple layers of dialectical visual cues, including everything from set details, to patterns of actors' movements, to synchronization of musical score with visual images, to rhythms of continuity and disruption, to narrative flow and misdirection and so on.

Joan Neuberger

Dziga Vertov, 1920, Kobal.

DIRECTORS
DZIGA VERTOV

Name:

Dziga Vertov

Date of Birth:

2 January 1896

Place of Birth:

Białystok, Poland

Place of Residence:

Moscow

Nationality:

Russian/Soviet

Awards:

Silver Medal at the International Exhibition for Decorative Art, Paris (1925),Special Jury Prize at the Venice Film Festival (1934)

Dziga Vertov was born David Abelevich (later changed to Denis Arkad'evich) Kaufman on 2 January 1896 in Białystok, Poland (then part of the Russian Empire). After taking on this dynamic, Futurist pseudonym, joining the Moscow Cinema Committee in Spring 1918, Vertov made his reputation with the *Kino-Pravda* Soviet newsreel series, so-called by analogy with the Bolshevik newspaper *Pravda*. This series revolutionized the power of the newsreel form to persuade and analyse, rather than simply inform or describe. While these are all short films, his *History of the Civil War* (1921) and *Kino-Eye* (1924) are among the first attempts at a feature-length documentary, and mark him as a pioneer of the form which was taking shape internationally in this decade. Crucially, this period saw Vertov team up with his brother, Mikhail Kaufman, who was the cameraman for all of his silent films, and his wife, Elizaveta Svilova, who edited all the films, and played an increasingly important role as assistant and co-director after the split with Kaufman in 1929.

In the years 1921–1926, Vertov was the major figure in Soviet newsreel and documentary, and a seminal influence on the montage film style made famous by Sergei Eisenstein, despite the fierce polemics between the two. His theoretical writings in this period range from the early poetic manifesto 'We' to increasingly pragmatic attempts to define documentary according to a minimally staged 'Kino-Eye' method of filming, intended to serve as a template for emulation. In 1926, Vertov was able to make two further technically groundbreaking films in Moscow: *Foward Soviet!*, a celebration of Moscow's progress since the end of the Russian Civil War in 1921, and *A Sixth Part of the Earth*, an apology for the emergent 'Socialism in One Country' policy in fact commissioned to promote Soviet exports. However, Vertov's radical conception of documentary, ambitions for a grassroots movement of film journalists and aspiration that documentary dominate repertoires combined to marginalize him, and he was forced to leave Moscow and to join the semi-autonomous Ukrainian film organization VUFKU in 1926. Here he made three of his most enduring works: *Eleventh Year* (1928), *Man with a Movie Camera* (1929) and one of the first Soviet sound films: *Enthusiasm: Symphony of the Donbass* (1931). While *Man with a Movie Camera* is rightly considered his masterpiece, each of these films was formally innovative, although they did not enjoy critical or commercial success.

After *Enthusiasm*'s hostile domestic reception, especially because of its innovative approach to sound, Vertov left Ukraine and, overcoming numerous administrative and technical obstacles, made his next film, *Three Songs of Lenin* (1934), on location in the Far East for Moscow's Mezhrabpomfilm. This marked a new stage in his evolution, as he adapted to the more rigid political climate, and narrower limitations on the use of sound. Central to this new approach was the emphasis upon the recording of folk music performances as a way of retaining sound with an aura of authenticity and avoiding the stultifying effects of the voice-over. *Three Songs of Lenin* was officially praised, but with noticeable reluctance, due to the marginal role Stalin and Russia (rather than the Far East) occupy in it, and so as not to encourage Vertov unduly. Similarly, when Vertov completed *Lullaby* in 1938, which resembles *Three Songs of Lenin*, but emphasizes Stalin more, it was barely mentioned in part because Vertov's potential influence on documentary filmmakers was still feared, and he had to be tightly controlled. In the last pre-war years, most of Vertov's projects were rejected, and those that were accepted and completed were undistinguished.

During the war (1941) Vertov was evacuated to Kazakhstan, where he was able to make several more films, the most significant of which by far was *For You at the Front* (1942). This continued the folkloric approach of *Three Songs of Lenin* and *Lullaby*, and is effectively the last work in which one can discern Vertov's distinct artistic sensibility. Once again the film was effectively suppressed, and in the anti-Semitic climate that began to intensify in the USSR from 1943 until Stalin's death in 1953, Vertov, ethnically Jewish, was further marginalized, denounced and relegated to editing standardized newsreels.

Since his death, in 1958, Vertov's influence has grown steadily after republication of his writings in the 1960s enabled first the Soviet and then an international public to acquaint themselves first with his rich theoretical legacy, and subsequently with his films. The last decade has seen more works published about Vertov than any other, as his appeal and influence grow on the twenty-first century.

Jeremy Hicks

Andrei Tarkovsky, Kobal.

DIRECTORS
ANDREI TARKOVSKII

Name:

Andrei Tarkovskii

Date of Birth:

4 April 1932

Place of Birth:

Iurevets

Places of Residence:

Moscow and Paris

Nationality:

Soviet

Awards:

Golden Lion, Venice Film Festival (1962); FIPRESCI at Cannes Film Festival (1969, 1972, 1986); Grand Jury Prize at Cannes Film Festival (1972, 1986); Ecumenical Jury Prize at Cannes Film Festival (1979, 1983, 1986); Director Prize at Cannes Film Festival (1983); People's Artist of the RSFSR (1980)

Andrei Tarkovskii was born into a prominent family of intellectuals. His father, Arsenii Tarkovskii, was a respected but somewhat marginal poet who left his family soon after Andrei's birth, and the director grew up in a household consisting of his mother Mariia Vishniakova and sister Marina. He began his university studies at an institute for oriental languages, but soon left and, after a term spent on a geological expedition, enrolled in 1955 at the All-Union State Institute for Cinematography (VGIK) in Moscow, with the intention of becoming a director. Tarkovskii's education at VGIK formed him as a distinctly Soviet filmmaker in the academic tradition established by Sergei Eisenstein. After assisting Marlen Khutsiev on the film *The Two Fedors* in 1956, which starred Tarkovskii's classmate Vasilii Shukshin, Tarkovskii and his future brother-in-law Aleksandr Gordon co-directed the short film *The Killers* in 1956, based on Ernest Hemingway's short story and also featuring Shukshin. More accomplished is Tarkovskii's made-for-television movie *There Will Be No Leave Today* (1958), which became a staple of TV celebrations of World War II.

By contrast with his early noir, Tarkovskii's first feature film *Steamroller and Violin* (1960) appears a quaint and harmless cinematic poem, provocative only in its unabashed innocence. It tells of the friendship between the young musician Sasha and a steamroller driver Sergei, who saves the little boy and his fragile violin from the bullies who hang around Sasha's building in post-war Moscow. A revelry of friendship is curtailed by the intervention of Sasha's mother, and Sasha is left to dream of a symphonic harmony between brightly coloured steamrollers and people in the pristine city-scape. Following *Steamroller and Violin*, Tarkovskii was offered a full position as a director in Mosfilm's First Creative Unit. His first assignment was *Ivan's Childhood* (1962), based on a story by Vladimir Bogomolov about a young child scout during World War II. *Ivan's Childhood* attracted broad praise and instigated extensive comment.

Tarkovskii ran into trouble with *Andrei Rublev* (1966), a historical biopic of medieval Russia's most famous icon-painter. Already during the shoot there emerged reports of Tarkovskii's mistreatment of animals and of historical landmarks. Tarkovskii's first two cuts (the first entitled *The Passion according to Andrei*) were rejected by Goskino. The stalemate persisted until 1969, when the new version of the film was approved under the title *Andrei Rublev* with a duration of 187 minutes. It was sold to a European distributor and was entered at the Cannes Film Festival, out of official competition but to great acclaim. The Soviet authorities allowed its domestic release only in 1971, after Tarkovskii faced down calls for further cuts. Thereafter Tarkovskii and the Goskino resigned themselves to an uneasy accommodation which persisted right up to 1982.

Once the controversies over *Andrei Rublev* died down, Tarkovskii began work in earnest on *Solaris* (1973), based on the sci-fi novel by Stanislaw Lem concerning a team of scientists studying a distant planet which is able to project their thoughts as material forms. Though he toned down the scientific language and underscored the ethical dilemmas of the situation, Tarkovskii basically hewed close to the novel. The main exception is a long prologue on earth that riled with Lem and almost threatened to scuttle the project. His first feature film in colour, *Solaris* showed Tarkovskii eager to develop his aesthetic in new directions. The success of *Solaris* at Cannes and at the box office confirmed Tarkovskii as a major Soviet director and as a thorn in the side of the authorities. *The Mirror* (1975), an autobiographical film originally entitled *Confession*, was tolerated by the authorities more or less as a vanity project. Despite some friction over its complex narrative structure *Mirror* was approved, its harmfulness having been curtailed by limited distribution, despite the studio's often voiced concern to maximize box-office receipts from the film. *Stalker* (1979), based on a screenplay by Arkadii and Boris Strugatskii, showed Tarkovskii continuing to re-think the sci-fi genre as the basis for serious inquiry. The title character leads two others ('writer' and 'professor') through an area contaminated by aliens towards a room where desires are fulfilled. The quest turns out to be a test of their desires, with the result that, upon reaching the room, they hesitate before entering. Tarkovskii's main interest is studying the visual and aural conditions of desire and knowledge; *Stalker* is his most aesthetically rich film.

With a commission from the Italian TV network RAI, Tarkovskii travelled to Italy in 1980 and 1982 to shoot *Tempo di Viaggio* and *Nostalghia* as joint Italian-Soviet productions. *Tempo di Viaggio* documents the search for locations in Italy by Tarkovskii and his co-screenwriter Tonino Guerra. The film itself presents Andrei Gorchakov, a Russian poet in Italy, who is subject to the various stresses of dislocation. He finds resolution in the ideas of a madman Domenico, with whom he seems to merge. Unhappy with the attitude of the Soviet film authorities, in part over *Nostalghia*, in July 1984 Tarkovskii announced he would never return to the USSR.

In the fallow periods between films, Tarkovskii contributed to numerous film projects by other directors and pursued projects outside of film. In 1965, Tarkovskii produced William Faulkner's 'Turnabout' for Soviet radio, and in 1974–1975 he staged *Hamlet* in Moscow. Tarkovskii staged Mussorgsky's *Boris Godunov* at Covent

Garden in 1984, before shooting *The Sacrifice* in Sweden. A Berg-manesque film, which Tarkovskii described as his most dramatic effort, *Sacrifice* presents the crisis of Aleksandr, an aging professor of aesthetics, who makes a series of wagers with God in order to avert nuclear war. The film ends with him burning down his cherished house, in a famous long-take, one of Tarkovskii's longest and most elaborate.

By the time Tarkovskii completed the shoot of *Sacrifice* he had been diagnosed with lung cancer. He died in a Paris clinic on 29 December 1986.

Robert Bird

Nikita Mikhalkov.

DIRECTORS
NIKITA MIKHALKOV

Name:

Nikita Mikhalkov

Date of Birth:

21 October 1945

Place of Birth:

Moscow

Place of Residence:

Moscow

Nationality:

Soviet/Russian

Awards:

Golden Lion at the Venice Film Festival (1991); Grand Prix at the Cannes Film Festival (1994); Oscar for Best Foreign Language Film (1995); Special Prize at the Venice International Film Festival (2007).

Nikita Mikhalkov was born in Moscow into a family belonging to the Soviet intelligentsia. His father Sergei was a poet and playwright; he wrote (with Garold El-Registan) the text of the Soviet national anthem (1943, second version 1977), which he revised when the tune was brought back as the national anthem of the Russian Federation in 2000. Sergei Mikhalkov was one of the most popular authors of children's literature. Mikhalkov's mother, the writer and poet Natalia Konchalovskaia, was the daughter of the painter Petr Konchalovskii. Under the Soviet system, the family changed the stress on the name from Mikhálkov to Mikhalkóv to hide their aristocratic background. Since the collapse of the Soviet Union Mikhalkov has shown excessive pride in the genealogy of his family, altering the stress back to Mikhálkov and producing a family tree that goes back over 200 years and connects the family to the painter Surikov, to the writers Pushkin, Tolstoy, Odoevsky and Gogol, and to Catherine the Great.

Mikhalkov's elder brother, Andrei (family pet-name Andron) (Mikhalkov)-Konchalovskii (b. 1937), is also a filmmaker who made many successful literary adaptations before his emigration in 1980. In some of these early films Nikita appears as an actor (*Nest of Gentlefolk*, 1969 and *Siberiade*, 1978). Andrei Konchalovskii left the Soviet Union to work in Hollywood, where he successfully continued filmmaking. In the early 1990s he returned to Russia where he has made several films and also worked in the theatre.

Mikhalkov is a child of the Victory Year 1945: born in the immediate aftermath of World War II, he grew up during the last decade of Stalin's rule and spent his adolescence in a cultural climate that reflected relaxation after Stalin's purges and the hardship of the war. Mikhalkov went to the school of the Moscow Conservatory, specializing in the piano, until he transferred to an ordinary school for the last three years, during which he took part in an acting group in the studio of the Stanislavsky Theatre. By this time the Khrushchev Thaw (1956–1964) was well underway: Khrushchev had delivered his Secret Speech, denouncing Stalin's crimes, and a period of liberalization had begun in the arts, and in theatre in particular. From 1963 onwards Nikita Mikhalkov trained as an actor at the Shchukin School, a theatre school attached to the Vakhtangov Theatre in Moscow. Having been expelled in 1967 from the Shchukin School for absenting himself from classes in order to film, and, armed with a recommendation from the filmmaker Georgii Daneliia, who had directed young Nikita in *I Walk around Moscow* (1963), Mikhalkov transferred to the All-Union State Institute for Cinematography (VGIK) to study directing under Mikhail Romm. He graduated from the Film Institute in 1971 with his diploma film *A Quiet Day at the End of the War* (1970). Mikhalkov had begun his career as an actor in the 1960s and continued to appear in films after graduating as a film director. During the late 1960s and early 1970s he made a number of short films for the *Fitil'* ('Fuse') series, short satirical clips used as trailers in cinemas. He also began script-writing, and after completing the script for *At Home among Strangers*, he was drafted into the army and served in the Pacific fleet and on the Kamchatka peninsula.

After his army service he made his first feature, *At Home among Strangers, a Stranger at Home* (1974), followed by *A Slave of Love* (1975), both set in the years immediately following the Revolution. *Unfinished Piece for a Mechanical Piano* (1977) bore testimony to Mikhalkov's talent for literary adaptation by presenting a version of an early Anton Chekhov play, frequently referred to under the title *Fatherlessness* (ca. 1878). Adaptations of Aleksandr Volodin's *Five Evenings* (1978) and Ivan Goncharov's *Oblomov* (1979) followed. *Kinfolk* (1981) and *A Private Conversation* (1983) dealt with life in contemporary Russia. Mikhalkov thus moved in his films from the Revolution through the classical heritage and the post-war period towards the portrayal of the present. His growing reputation, nationally and internationally, led to the Italian production of *Dark Eyes* (1987), another adaptation of Chekhov, followed by *Hitchhike* (1990). At a time when Tarkovskii chose to remain in Italy, Mikhalkov was representing Soviet cinema in an international project.

In 1991 he directed the French-Soviet co-production *Urga*, which won the Golden Lion at the Venice Film Festival in the same year and was nominated for the Academy Award in 1993. *Burnt by the Sun* (1994), a melodrama set in 1936 that unfolds against the backdrop of the Purges, won the Grand Prix at the Cannes Film Festival in 1994 and the Oscar for Best Foreign Language Film in 1995. Finally, *The Barber of Siberia* (1999), the most expensive Russian film with a $45 million budget, opened the Cannes Film Festival in 1999, an honour rarely accorded to a Russian director. Although the film was not entered in competition in any major festival, it was popular with Russian audiences, but it did not fare well commercially in international distribution. After an almost ten-year gap, Mikhalkov released *Twelve* (2007), a remake of Sidney Lumet's *12 Angry Men*, for the Venice International Film Festival, where it was awarded a special prize.

Birgit Beumers

Aleksandr Sokurov.

DIRECTORS
ALEKSANDR SOKUROV

Name:

Aleksandr Sokurov

Date of Birth:

14 June 1951

Place of Birth:

Podorvikha, Irkutsk Region

Place of Residence:

Leningrad/St Petersburg

Nationality:

Soviet/Russian

Awards:

Merited Artist of the Russian Federation (1997); State Prize of Russia (1997, 2001); Best Screenplay at Cannes IFF for *Moloch* (1999); FIPRESCI Award at Cannes IFF for *Father and Son* (2003); People's Artist of the Russian Federation (2004)

Sokurov worked at the television studios in Gorky (now Nizhnii Novgorod) while studying history at Gorky University from 1968 to 1974. In 1975 Sokurov enrolled at the All-Union State Institute for Cinematography (VGIK), where he studied in the popular-scientific section of the Department of Film Direction under the direction of filmmaker Aleksandr Zguridi. Originally entitled 'The Return of Platonov', Sokurov's diploma project was supposed to weave scenes from Andrei Platonov's story 'The River Potudan' into the Soviet writer's biography. When the completed film *Solitary Voice of a Man* turned out to be an experimental adaptation of the story, it was rejected by VGIK and the administration ordered the destruction of all copies. Sokurov was able to receive his degree for a documentary he had made for television in Gorky, entitled *The Summer of Mariia Voinova* (1978, later folded into *Mariia*, 1988). Sokurov also preserved *Solitary Voice of a Man*, showed it at Lenfilm, where he was hired as a director, and eventually released a re-edited version of it in 1987 (with a dedication to Andrei Tarkovskii, who had supported Sokurov in his travails).

Over the next ten years Sokurov made numerous films for Lenfilm and for the Leningrad Studio of Documentary Film (LSDF) without any of them reaching the screen. By the time perestroika began Sokurov started to show his sizeable back-catalogue and, together with new films made in the spirit of the time, quickly established himself as one of the leading directors in alternative Soviet cinema (alongside fellow Leningrader Aleksei German). The feature films *Days of Eclipse* (1988) and *Second Circle* (1990) brought him to the attention of the international festival audience. His international status was reinforced by *Mother and Son* (1996) and *Moloch* (1999), and he reached unprecedentedly large audiences with *Russian Ark* (2002). In recent years Sokurov has also worked in the theatre, staging Aleksandr Pushkin's *Mozart and Salieri* and Modest Musorgsky's opera *Boris Godunov* in 2007.

Though his films often defy neat classification as fiction or documentary, Sokurov's uncanny productivity (at the time of writing his filmography numbers 46 items, including 29 documentaries) and his fondness for compiling cycles of films (sometimes where a single effort would suffice) makes it useful to divide his oeuvre into three major groupings: feature films, documentaries and homages (which he calls 'elegies'). Most of Sokurov's elegies commemorate individuals who figure broader histories, from Chaliapin to Yeltsin; here Sokurov seems intent on capturing and preserving (or prolonging) their physical presence in the world. Like his documentaries, these elegies frequently feature voice-overs by the director and utilize video technologies in original ways.

Many of his documentaries chronicle marginal modes of attending to the world, such as farm work (*Mariia*), naval service (*Confession*, 1998), or the labour of an aging writer (*Conversations with Solzhenitsyn*, 1998); long in duration and low on story, they are almost utopian in their melancholy absorption. They frequently build complex landscapes that seem inspired by painterly models. Sokurov has also made several quite stunning documentaries on current events, most notably *Evening Sacrifice* (1987), which shows the firing of a holiday salute over the Neva river and then documents the dispersal of the holiday crowd down Nevsky Prospect; it is an eloquent testimony to the death of Soviet rituals and the birth of new forms of community in the late Soviet Union. His latest documentary is *We Read the Book of the Blockade* (2009), in which residents of Petersburg read fragments from Ales' Adamovich and Daniil Granin's book of testimonies about the siege of Leningrad in 1942–1944.

Sokurov's feature films fall into three sub-categories: literary adaptations, intimate dramas and historical dramas. By contrast with the elegies and the documentaries, which have often been shot on video, Sokurov's feature films often seem designed specifically to pose and test purely formal problems of optics and narrative, some of which Sokurov traces to the Orthodox icon and modernist painting. *Solitary Voice of a Man* extended the experimentation of Tarkovskii's *Mirror* into a study of visual textures. *Days of Eclipse* (1988, based on a science-fiction tale by Arkadii and Boris Strugatskii) and *Second Circle* (1990) are studies in optical alienation, as the camera views the action as if from under a piece of furniture or from the next room, while the focus is unsteady and the colour is washed out. The most conspicuous element of *Mother and Son* is the use of anamorphic lenses, which distort the lines of a vividly coloured garden of wonder. The principles Sokurov established in *Mother and Son* for exploring intimate spaces through various strategies of visual displacement and distortion have been explored further in *Father and Son* (2005) and *Alexandra* (2007), the dreamscapes of which share many features with those of his documentaries.

With *Moloch* Sokurov struck out on a new path by using fictional forms to explore a controversial political subject, namely the home life of Adolf Hitler and Eva Braun. Here Sokurov historicizes the visual strategies of his intimate dramas, exploring the psychological effects of such visual media as the newsreel and technologies of surveillance. The principles Sokurov established here have been extended in *Taurus* (2000, on Lenin) and *Sun* (2004, on Emperor Hirohito). The concluding film in Sokurov's planned tetralogy about power will be devoted to Faust.

Sokurov's numerous literary adaptations mostly combine the formal experimentation of his feature films with elements of the homage (with the exception of *Days of Eclipse*, he has only adapted classical texts). Sokurov is equally interested in the specific atmosphere of the narrative for the reader and its roots in the specific milieu and experience of the author. His adaptations of George Bernard Shaw's *Heartbreak Hotel* (*Mournful Indifference*, 1987) and Gustave Flaubert's *Madame Bovary* (*Save and Preserve*, 1989) are oblique glimpses of motifs derived from the sources with little attempt to reproduce the narratives. *Whispering Pages* (1993) combines an elegiac homage to Dostoevsky with a rigorously experimental study of visual distortion to create a hallucinatory improvisation on 'the motifs of nineteenth-century Russian literature' (primarily *Crime and Punishment*). In accordance with its title, *Whispering Pages* thematizes the mood of the literary medium itself as a material interface of experience, i.e., as a medium. These films confirm Sokurov's reputation as an unrivalled creator of visual textures, though the lack of narrative coherence severely limits their accessibility.

Sokurov has developed a distinctive aesthetic and a dedicated group of collaborators, including screenwriter Iurii Arabov, editor Leda Semenova and actor Leonid Mozgovoi. Though Sokurov's seeming ubiquity on Russian television and art-cinema screens somewhat dilutes his effect, the director's distinctive combination of traditionalist sentiment and optical experiment makes him a leading figure in contemporary Russian culture.

Robert Bird

HISTORICAL FILM

Russia cinematic history began with a historical film. Vladimir Romashkov's *Stenka Razin*, which premiered on 15 October 1908, is about the legendary Cossack rebel and his followers. The ten-minute film features Razin and his men revelling, capturing a Persian Princess and eventually throwing her into the Volga River. Romashkov's turn to this subject fits the time: songs singing the praises of Razin's seventeenth-century rebellion circulated throughout the empire, and just two years before the film, the painter Vasilii Surikov finished his monumental canvas, *Stenka Razin Sailing in the Caspian Sea*. Romashkov's film tapped both into this popularity for the tsarist-era rebel and into the late tsarist interest in the past. At the time of the film's appearance, the tsarist state had established the first History Museum, Vasilii Kliuchevskii dominated the academic study of history and artists of all kinds explored the terrain of Russia's pasts. Four years after *Stenka Razin*, Vasilii Goncharov directed the first Russian feature, *The Defence of Sevastopol*. This 'hit' recreated the heroic defence of the Russian fortress during the Crimean War. From the beginning, therefore, Russian filmmaking saw the re-creation of the past as a vital part of Russian cinema.

After 1917, the relationship between history and cinema acquired a political component. Vladimir Lenin's famous declaration that 'cinema is the most important of the arts' speaks to the significance cinema had for the socialist state. It also captures the way that Bolshevik ideology influenced film in general and the historical film in particular. Sergei Eisenstein's films from the 1920s best express the marriage of the past to contemporary ideology that was at the heart of the initial Bolshevik cultural project. This conflation of past and present for political purposes can best be seen in the films made for the tenth anniversary of the Bolshevik Revolution. Eisenstein's *October* (1927) dramatized the seizure of the Winter Palace and helped to turn that chaotic event into the defining moment of 1917. Vsevolod Pudovkin's *The End of St Petersburg* (1927) recast the Great War as the impetus for Bolshevism, while Esfir' Shub's *The Fall of the Romanov Dynasty* (1927) used documentary footage to create a dynamic history of

1917. All three recreate the past as Marxist-Leninist parables where the evil bourgeoisie exploits the heroic masses. In all three, the chaos, violence and confusion of the actual past did not matter. In 1927, the Revolution film did not recreate 1917; it created a dominant narrative of 1917.

Joseph Stalin's consolidation of power brought with it a new cultural revolution and a new form for the historical film. Stalinist cinematic uses of the past focused on the individual over the collective, turning Great Men of the past into models for the present. The Vasil'ev brothers provided the script for this new cinematic history in their 1934 blockbuster *Chapaev*, Stalin's favourite film. Based on the Dmitrii Furmanov novel, *Chapaev* paints the Civil War as a patriotic defence of the Russo-Soviet motherland. The titular character's rough and gruff style, combined with his natural support for the Bolshevik cause, provided audiences with an ideal screen hero from the past.

Peter the Great, Alexander Nevsky and even Ivan the Terrible also became Soviet patriots in films from the 1930s and 1940s. Soviet films remade Lenin into a Stalinist hero in offerings such as Dziga Vertov's *Three Songs About Lenin* (1934) and Mikhail Romm's *Lenin in October* (1937). When the Nazi armies invaded the USSR in 1941, a host of historical biopics followed that reminded Soviet audiences of the patriotic heroism displayed by their forefathers. Biographies became Stalinist history lessons that stressed how Russians have always defended their motherland and that Russians made the most significant contributions to world culture. Perhaps the greatest example of the biography-as-history in Stalinist cinema was Mikhail Chiaureli's *The Fall of Berlin*, a seventieth birthday present for the Soviet dictator that turned the Victory over the Nazis into Stalin's personal triumph.

After Stalin's death in 1953, filmmakers began to focus on 'unvarnished realism' and 'authenticity' in their films. The heroic history and patriotic biography that had dominated the Stalinist historical film gave way to films that mostly focused on the present. Still, Thaw-era filmmakers did not abandon the past, particularly the recent past. A host of films re-examined the Great Patriotic War and challenged the narrative that Stalin had alone orchestrated the Victory. Pudovkin's 1953 *The Return of Vasilii Bortnikov* began this process. His film explores the difficulties one veteran encounters when he tries to reintegrate into Soviet society after the war, a theme that Sergei Bondarchuk later tackled in his 1959 film *Fate of a Man* and that Grigorii Chukhrai explored in his 1961 *Clear Skies*. Most Thaw-era history films were made by a younger generation of directors, many of whom fought in the war and began their careers after Stalin's death. Mikhail Kalatozov's 1957 *The Cranes are Flying*, Chukhrai's 1959 *Ballad of a Soldier* and Andrei Tarkovskii's 1962 *Ivan's Childhood* all fit onto this generational category. All explored the individual costs of war and overturned the Stalinist historical narrative of the war.

Nikita Khrushchev's call to return to Leninist norms and his denunciation of Stalin's cult of personality helped to reinvigorate the Civil War film. Alov and Naumov's *Pavel Korchagin* (1956) and Chukhrai's *The Forty-First* (1956) both presented an updated, usable Civil War for Soviet viewers. Korchagin was not a Chapaev-like hero while *The Forty-First* had Reds and Whites fall in love. Aleksandr Askol'dov's *The Commissar* (1967) broke more taboos by challenging the myths of the Revolution itself. It was banned, along with a series of other films from the 1960s and 1970s that explored problematic pasts. Andrei Tarkovskii's use of an historical icon-painter in *Andrei Rublev* (1965) also had to go through several revisions before it could be screened because it made too many parallels between the fate of artists in medieval Russia and the fate of artists in Soviet Russia.

Sergei Bondarchuk's *War and Peace* (1965–1967) in many ways signalled a change in the Soviet historical film to fit Brezhnev-era monumentalism. Begun in 1961, the film debuted after films such as *Andrei Rublev* had run into trouble. Bondarchuk's use of Leo Tolstoy's 1812 became a revision of the past that focused more on staggering battle sequences and literary costume drama as history than on unvarnished realism. Iurii

Ozerov's 500-minute *Liberation* (1969–1972) contained staggering battle scenes and returned the narrative of the Great Patriotic War to a neo-Stalinist plotline. Bondarchuk's 1975 *They Fought for Their Motherland* presented the war as a collection of patriotic efforts by Soviet soldiers. Other epics, such as Andrei Mikhalkov-Konchalovskii's *Siberiade* (1979–1980) revisited the myth of Siberia and its role in Russian history over the course of generations while historical melodramas such as Nikita Mikhalkov's *Slave of Love* (1975) romanticized the old Russia that died during the Civil War.

Brezhnev-era films that challenged historical taboos were doomed to censorship: Elem Klimov's *Rasputin* (1974, rel. 1981), which depicted Nicholas II sympathetically and blamed Rasputin for his downfall, sat on the shelf for seven years. Aleksei Iu. German's *Trial on the Road* (1971) spent sixteen years on the shelf because it explored the issues of collaboration and occupation in World War II. By the time it appeared, the landscape for historical films had changed dramatically.

Mikhail Gorbachev's decision to allow openness in Soviet culture created new possibilities for filmmakers to travel back to the past. Filmmakers took part in the efforts to fill in the blank spots of history that Gorbachev called for: Instead of presenting a Thaw-like picture of Leninist norms, they made films that questioned the very foundations of the Soviet experiment. Banned films by Aleksei Iu. German and others became sensations, revealing uncomfortable truths about the Soviet past. Aleksandr Proshkin's *The Cold Summer of 53* (1987), to take one example, became a box-office sensation because it explored the Gulag and the effects of imprisonment among a generation of Soviet citizens. This return of history on the big screen had the effect of presenting the entire Soviet experience as one unending catalogue of horrors. Historical films played their part in the erosion of belief in Soviet socialism.

After 1991, Russian filmmakers continued to mine the past as a means of commenting on the state of the present. Stanislav Govorukhin's documentary *The Russia We Have Lost* (1992) lent its name to cinematic and other artistic recreations of a romantic, pre-Revolutionary past. Other directors continued the Gorbachev-era explorations of history, particularly the Stalin period. Mikhalkov's Oscar-winning film *Burnt by the Sun* (1994) absolves citizens of responsibility for Soviet violence by placing blame on Stalin. Aleksei Iu. German's *Khrustalev, My Car!* (1998), by contrast, depicts a nightmarish society that envelopes and involves everyone.

By the end of the 1990s, with the Russian economy in shambles, many Russian filmmakers wanted cinema to become the source of patriotic pride. They found the past to be ideal territory for revamping contemporary patriotism. Mikhalkov led the way with his epic *The Barber of Siberia* (1999). Set in the 1880s, *The Barber* looks nostalgically at the tsarist-era officer corps while also presenting a *Chapaev*-like hero for the post-Soviet public. His *Burnt by the Sun 2*, released in 2010, resurrects his heroes from the first film and has them defend their Russo-Soviet motherland during World War II. While Mikhalkov's style of patriotic blockbuster history has done well at the Russian box office, other directors have confronted his brand of nostalgic pasts. Aleksei Balabanov's *Cargo 200* depicted 1984 as brutally as Aleksei German had depicted 1953 in *Khrustalev, My Car!* Art house directors such as Pavel Grigor'evich Chukhrai and Aleksei Alekseevich German filmed historical narratives that reframed the pre-Revolutionary, wartime and Brezhnev-era pasts in nuanced ways. Russian filmmakers, it is evident, have not grown tired of using the past to reinvent history for the present. The historical film remains one of the most significant genres in Russian cinema.

Stephen M. Norris

Stenka Razin

Sten'ka Razin

Country of Origin:
Russia

Language:
Russian (intertitles)

Studio:
Aleksandr Drankov

Director:
Vladimir Romashkov

Screenplay:
Vasilii Goncharov

Cinematographers:
Aleksandr Drankov, Nikolai
Kozlovskii

Duration:
6 minutes

Genre:
Historical Melodrama

Cast:
Evgenii Petrov-Kraevskii

Year:
1908

Synopsis

Stenka Razin and his gang engage in 'wild revels' on the Volga River. Their boats mill about as the brigands wave their swords and hoist their tankards. Eventually, all the men crowd onto a single ship. They move to a forest clearing, where their revels are wilder yet. They drink and carouse. A 'Muslim princess', Razin's captive, dances at his command. The men fight. They are jealous that Razin's attention has been drawn away from the brotherhood and plot to destroy the princess. They scheme to get Razin drunk and show him forged letters allegedly between the princess and 'Prince Hassan'. Duped, the jealous Razin drags the princess onto his ship. Although she begs for her life, he lifts her up and throws her into the Volga.

Poster for *Stenka Razin* (1908).

Critique

The story of a seventeenth-century Cossack rebel, *Stenka Razin*
has the honour of being the first fiction film produced by a Russian
studio, that of Aleksandr Drankov, a former court photographer in
St Petersburg. The film reveals some of the defining characteristics
of Russian cinema at its very beginnings: emphasis on a historical
figure (or literary text), a penchant for shooting on location, static
camera, liberal use of the extreme long shot, and long-takes. In the
opening scene, the boats bob aimlessly; one can almost hear the
director shouting at them to get closer to the mother ship. The forest
revels are shot at such a distance that the viewer can hardly tell what
is going on; one cannot distinguish faces, not even Stenka Razin's.
Indeed, Razin himself is scarcely distinguishable from his men unless
he is embracing or dragging the princess. The intertitles are long and
literary, especially the two letters.

The choice of Razin as the 'hero' of Russia's first native production is
an interesting one. A Don Cossack, Razin had achieved folkloric status
among peasants for his thieving escapades in the Caspian region
and quickly attracted a large peasant following when his aims turned
political. After Razin's forces had succeeded in 'liberating' the lands
around the Volga from the nobility, the rebels decided to head for
Moscow in 1670. He was stopped by the Russian army near Simbirsk
and was eventually betrayed by his own Don Cossacks and executed
in 1671. Given that the film was made shortly after the Revolution of
1905–1907, the Razin story obviously had some topical resonance.

Razin's adventures lived on in story and song. Indeed, the film's
script was based on one of these songs, 'From the Island to the Deep
Stream', which proclaims: 'So that there will be no dissension or dis-
cord between the free people, Volga, Volga, my native mother, here
accept this beauty! With a mighty swing, he picks her up, the beautiful
princess, and overboard he throws her into an approaching wave.'

Denise J. Youngblood

Battleship Potemkin

Bronenosets Potemkin

Country of Origin:
Soviet Union

Language:
Silent

Studio:
Goskino

Synopsis

In 1906, the tsarist battleship *Potemkin* lies off the port city of
Odessa in the Black Sea after its return from Russia's disastrous
defeat at the hands of Japan. The sailors, inflamed by intolerable and
squalid conditions on board and led by the sailors Vakulinchuk and
Matiushenko, rise up in mutiny against their callous officers. Once
they dock to bury the murdered Vakulinchuk, the sailors' outrage
spreads to Odessa's citizens, who, themselves chafing under tsarist oppression and moved by the self-sacrifice of this sailor, join the
mutineers in protest against their oppressors. The enraged citizens
march through Odessa, and await the call to arms from the mutineers
aboard the battleship. Odessa becomes a Revolutionary commune,
citizens and sailors standing shoulder-to-shoulder. Without warning,
tsarist troops attack the citizens on the steps of Odessa harbour,

Director:

Sergei Eisenstein

Screenplay:

Nina Agadzhanova-Shutko
Nikolai Aseev
Sergei Eisenstein
Sergei Tretiakov

Cinematographer:

Eduard Tissé

Art Director:

Vasilii Rakhal's

Composers:

Edmund Meisel
Dmitrii Shostakovich

Editors:

Eduard Tissé
Vladimir Popov

Duration:

69 minutes

Genre:

Historical Drama

Cast:

Grigorii Aleksandrov
Aleksandr Antonov
Vladimir Barskii
Ivan Bobrov
Mikhail Gomorov

Year:

1925

bloodily massacring men, women and children. The sailors briefly shell the city, but they decide to return to sea on the *Potemkin* to face the squadron of ships sent to suppress their mutiny. On receiving signals from the sailors aboard the *Potemkin*, however, the crews of these ships show their solidarity by allowing the battleship to pass through the squadron unimpeded.

Critique

This film was an integral part of a broad process of Revolutionary mythologization underway in Soviet Russia during the 1920s, having been commissioned for the twentieth anniversary of the 1905 revolution. Unlike Eisenstein's later *October*, which portrayed the successful dénouement of Russia's revolutions in 1917, *Battleship Potemkin* was a paean to revolution defeated in 1905. Significantly, though, the film ends with the promise of revolution fulfilled, the sailors escaping a blockade of tsarist ships, thanks to the 'revolutionary' acquiescence of their fellow sailors. The narrative is not driven by the 'impersonal forces' of history, but rather by identifiable characters, each clearly responsible and conscious of their own actions (some identified by name by intertitles): the sailor Vakulinchuk, who stirs up the men's anger over the maggot-infested meat; the ship's doctor, Smirnov, who examines it and declares it fit for consumption; Giliarovskii, the officer, who enforces the declaration, eventually by the threat of a firing squad; the Orthodox priest, who calls on the condemned men to see reason, all the while brandishing his crucifix like a weapon.

Eisenstein's story is about the inevitability of revolution by increments. The ship is a microcosm of the world order, its hierarchies mirrored. Sailors are engaged in the petty and meaningless indignities of life: cleaning the guns, polishing the ship's fittings, washing the dishes. Officers seek merely to reinforce those indignities. Power begets violence: an officer's rough awakening of a sleeping sailor becomes a senior officer's physical manhandling of recalcitrant sailors and the captain's threat of lethal violence before a firing squad. Violence begets resistance: Vakulinchuk and Matiushenko voice the sailors' outrage; sailors refuse to eat the borscht; the members of the firing squad refuse to shoot on their comrades. Resistance begets yet more violence, best exemplified in the film's two climactic scenes. The mutineers' righteous vengeance visited upon the officers on board the *Potemkin* and the tsarist soldiers' perfunctory – and far more bloody – slaughter of the citizens on the Odessa steps foreshadow the violence to come in the inevitable Revolution. The victory of the sailors over their masters and the defeat of the citizens by the soldiers are temporary respites in history's grand narrative. Revolution, Eisenstein says in this film, is immanent if not yet imminent.

Like many of Eisenstein's films, key images linger, at least in the modern viewer's memory: the tarpaulin covering the sailors who await execution by firing squad; the wide-eyed, wild-haired priest; phantom bodies hanging from the yardarms; and on the Odessa steps, the anguished mother bearing her dying child towards the advancing soldiers; a child's wrist under a soldier's boot; the bloodied eye of a

Sergei Eisenstein, *Battleship Potemkin* (1925).

screaming woman; the drawn-out descent of the baby-carriage and its baby. Whether these images struck the contemporary viewer in Russia at the time in a similar manner is debatable. Still, the film's narrative is well paced and self-evident, it does not contain the ubiquitous and heavily aestheticized symbolism of Eisenstein's later *October*, and it surely contains some of the most graphic violence ever exhibited on screen at that time.

Frederick C. Corney

New Babylon

Novyi Vavilon

Country of Origin:
Soviet Union

Language:
Russian

Studio:
Sovkino Leningrad

Directors:
Grigorii Kozintsev
Leonid Trauberg

Screenplay:
Grigorii Kozintsev
Leonid Trauberg

Cinematographer:
Andrei Moskvin

Art Director:
Evgenii Enei

Composer:
Dmitrii Shostakovich

Duration:
100 minutes

Genre:
Historical

Cast:
Elena Kuz'mina
Petr Sobolevskii
Sergei Gerasimov

Year:
1929

Synopsis

As troops are dispatched to fight in the Franco-Prussian War (1870–1871), the Parisian bourgeoisie celebrates the opening of a new department store. The emporium's boss invites Louise, a shop-girl, to join him at the party. The French army is crushed, but the workers decide to form a National Guard to defend the city and elect a committee to lead them in a Commune. The Communards attempt to enlist the support of the returning soldiers – among them, the peasant Jean (exhausted, shell-shocked, poorly shod and starving). The Provisional Government, having surrendered to Prussia to protect its own interests, flees to Versailles. The troops side with the Provisional Government. For a short while, the Commune withstands the siege, sustained by idealism and enthusiasm. Then the barricades are breached. The bourgeoisie returns to its frenzied partying in a cabaret called 'Empire' while, outside, the Communards are herded together, summarily court-martialled and shot. Louise refuses an opportunity to save her life, choosing instead to die for the Commune. Jean is thrown a spade and ordered to dig her grave. A wooden Madonna mutely observes proceedings. 'We shall meet again', Louise tells Jean, at the end. 'We shall be back', says another Communard; 'Long live the Commune!'

Critique

SVD (Kozintsev and Trauberg, 1927), also starring Petr Sobolevskii, depicted the 1825 Decembrist Revolt as an historic precedent in Russia's tsarist past for the October Revolution. Likewise, *The New Babylon* turned to the 1871 Paris Commune to legitimize the Soviet Regime: even in failure, Marx foresaw the eventual triumph of the proletariat.

More specifically, Kozintsev and Trauberg drew inspiration from Emile Zola's 1883 novel *Au Bonheur des Dames*, in which a small family business is bankrupted by the Babylon (a surrogate for the Paris store, Bon Marché) and the daughter of the family takes a job in the store. Whereas Zola's heroine marries into wealth, Louise (Kuz'mina) remains loyal to her class. Jean (Sobolevskii), turning like a cur as he storms the barricade, is applauded by the bourgeoisie for his betrayal. There are other literary references: the gargoyles featured as guardians of the city seem to be drawn from Victor Hugo's *Notre Dame de Paris*.

Stylized settings are used to locate the story: wet cobbled streets at night; swirling lace parasols, fans and can-can dancers. The gaudy store mannequin, which Louise burns on a pyre at the barricade, is an effigy of the old France, which the Communards seek to destroy. A rapidly tilted shot of Napoleon I, atop Gondoin's Vendôme Column, marks the temporary fall of Paris to the Commune. Sequences are repeated to present the Communards' dedication to the new order: seamstresses, old cobblers and laundresses collapse with fatigue over their labour for the bosses; for themselves they work joyously, happy in their freedom, 'We shall work no more at night' and 'They shan't evict us.' 'We have all eternity before us', says the journalist

Kozintsev and Trauberg, *New Babylon* (1929).

(Gerasimov) heading the elected committee, swearing allegiance with the workers. Many titles are used ironically: 'Going Cheap' announces not only the bargains offered by the store, but also the low esteem in which the soldiers' lives are held. Jean is obviously not 'the mighty and brave soldier of France' proclaimed by the government minister: he simply wants to return to his village.

Similarly, Kozintsev and Trauberg pursue a style of caricature in costume and gesture previously developed as 'eccentrism'. Through satire they explicitly condemn characters here intended for audience disapproval. Some devices employed are familiar throughout contemporary Soviet propaganda: the bourgeois woman's lorgnette or opera glass; the pompous, inflated capitalist in shiny top hat and stiff collar. Additionally, Kozintsev and Trauberg looked to the drawings of Honoré Daumier for period details. In a notable series of vignettes of ill-matched couples wining and dining, Kozintsev and Trauberg efficiently convey the desperate decadence of France under Napoleon III: a lone dancer capers tipsily across the floor into the morning. The tragic history of the French Revolution and its aftermath is repeated and enacted as farce.

New Babylon now commands attention as much for its orchestral accompaniment as for its direction and fine performances. The former cinema pianist, Dmitrii Shostakovich, worked simultaneously on the score, taking the general theme of an episode rather than slavishly illustrating particular motifs and completed scenes. Strains from Offenbach and a mockingly distorted version of the Marseillaise match the tone. 'We had the same idea', commented Kozintsev, 'not to illustrate shots but to give them new quality and scope; the music had to be composed against external events so as to show the inner sense of the action'.

Amy Sargeant

Zvenigora

Zvenygora

Country of Origin:
Soviet Union

Language:
Silent

Studio:
VUFKU (All-Union Agency for Photography and Cinema)

Director:
Aleksandr Dovzhenko

Synopsis

Dovzhenko's first full-length feature is set in the timeless landscape of Ukrainian legend. It conceals, we are told, a treasure, symbolized by the beauty Oksana. A Ukrainian elder, 'overgrown with moss', is enlisted by the Polish overlords to find the treasure, but at the last moment it disappears into smoke. Centuries pass, and the same old man is now the grandfather of Pavlo and Tymish. The eternal rhythms of agricultural life are disrupted by the horrors of World War I and the ensuing Civil War. The idle and cowardly Pavlo sides with the oppressors, both home-grown and foreign, while Tymish joins the Revolution and begins studying assiduously. Pavlo ends up in Prague where he falls in with bourgeois counter-revolutionaries and kills his beloved Roksana, before returning to Soviet Ukraine to wreak havoc. The film ends with the grandfather disrupting Pavlo's sabotage of a train driven by Tymish.

Screenplay:
Mikhail Iogansen
Iurko Iurtyk

Cinematographer:
Boris Zavel'ev

Art Director:
Vasilii Krichevskii

Duration:
66 minutes

Genres:
Historical Drama
Fairy tale

Cast:
Mykola Nademsky
Semyon Savashenko
Les' Podorozhny
Polina Skliar-Otava

Year:
1928

Critique

Zvenigora was Dovzhenko's breakthrough work, in which he first manifested the unique synthesis of aesthetic traditions that characterized all of his subsequent films. Politically the film makes a clear linkage between Ukrainian tradition and the claims of the new Soviet culture; just as Tymish is the true son of Ukraine, so also the grandfather eventually recognizes Soviet construction as an extension of ancient Ukrainian dreams of independence. The ideological point is often obscured by Dovzhenko's exuberant celebration of folk tradition, expressionist gesture and cinematic trickery. Like most of Dovzhenko's subsequent efforts, the film commanded widespread admiration for its aesthetics and deep suspicion for its politics.

Dovzhenko's *Zvenigora* was one of the first exemplars of what one might call magical realism in cinema. A major influence on Dovzhenko was the prose of Nikolai Gogol (1809–1852), especially his early experiments in adapting Ukrainian folklore to the new Russian literary tradition. Many of the characters, especially that of the beautiful temptress Oksana/Roksana, can be traced to Gogol's precedent, as can the elements of the supernatural and Dovzhenko's fascination with the slow rhythms of the Ukrainian countryside. This mythic quality is particularly evident when, following a clash with a foreign invader, a dissolve-shot suggests that Roksana's body literally becomes the ravine that holds the treasure. No less important than these archaic features, however, was the influence of the films of the German expressionists and of such Russian 'eccentrics' as Grigorii Kozintsev and Leonid Trauberg. Dovzhenko adapted their exaggerated gestures, stylized poses and dramatic framings. Dovzhenko's distinctive contribution was to bring all of these aesthetic strategies to bear on a recovery of the eternally fragile beauty of nature.

In these ways Dovzhenko revealed a potential for intimacy both within the new structures of Soviet life and within the technological medium of the cinema. Dovzhenko continued this effort in his following films, especially *Arsenal* (1929) and *Earth* (1930). The latter featured some of the same characters (most notably, Tymish) and received similarly mixed reviews in the Soviet press. Dovzhenko's mythic landscapes and narratives proved a major influence on later experiments in so-called poetic cinema, both in the Soviet Union and abroad.

Robert Bird

Alexander Nevsky

Aleksandr Nevskii

Country of Origin:
Soviet Union

Language:
Russian

Studio:
Mosfilm

Director:
Sergei Eisenstein

Screenplay:
Sergei Eisenstein
Petr Pavlenko

Cinematographer:
Eduard Tissé

Art Directors:
Isaak Shpinel
Nikolai Solov'ev

Composer:
Sergei Prokof'ev

Editors:
Sergei Eisenstein
Esfir' Tobak

Duration:
108 minutes

Genre:
Historical

Cast:
Nikolai Cherkasov
Nikolai Okhlopov
Aleksandr Abrikosov
Dmitrii Orlov
Vasilii Novikov
Nikolai Arskii
Varvara Massalitinova
Vera Ivasheva
Anna Danilova
Vladimir Ershov
Sergei Blinnikov
Ivan Lagutin
Lev Fenin
Naum Rogozhin

Year:
1938

Synopsis

In 1242, the Teutonic knights attack the Russian city of Pskov and commit horrific atrocities. Over the objections of merchants and officials, the ordinary citizens of Novgorod call on Prince Alexander Nevsky, victor against the Swedes, to lead them into battle against the Teutons. Two brave Novgorodian men, Vasilii Buslai and Gavrilo Oleksich, vie for the hand of the beautiful maiden, Ol'ga Danilovna, who declares that the bravest in battle shall be her husband. Also among the Russian warriors is Vasilisa, a maiden of Pskov avenging the death of her father. Inspired by folk wisdom, Nevsky concocts a plan to trap and defeat the Teutonic knights. An epic battle ensues on the frozen Lake Chud. After a hard-fought battle, Nevsky's strategy succeeds. As the Teutons flee across the frozen lake, the ice cracks and many drown. The Russians return home solemnly to mourn their dead. The crowd enacts popular justice by killing Russian traitors, but Nevsky ransoms the Teutonic knights and allows the ordinary soldiers to return home. Since both Vasilii and Gavrilo have performed bravely, Ol'ga cannot decide whom to marry. Vasilii declares that the maiden Vasilisa was the bravest of all, and Gavrilo second best. Ol'ga becomes betrothed to Gavrilo and Vasilii to Vasilisa. The population celebrates the great victory.

Critique

Released in November 1938 shortly after the Munich agreement, Sergei Eisenstein's *Alexander Nevsky* exemplifies the Soviet turn to Russian patriotism as the Nazi military threat intensified. Soviet artists and writers were encouraged to invoke earlier historical examples of defeating 'German invaders' to reassure audiences that the contemporary army had precedents for vanquishing the Germans in spite of the failures of the Russian army in World War I. Lest anyone miss the contemporary implications of the film, various Teutonic symbols in the film looked quite a bit like swastikas. Nevsky's final pronouncement in the film that 'whosoever comes to us with the sword shall perish by the sword' was equally unambiguous. While this patriotic theme struck a new chord in Soviet culture, the film contained many familiar Soviet plot elements, including vilifying the Teutonic knights as a religious order, emphasizing the class differences between those who heroically wanted to fight and those who sought to capitulate to the Germans, and highlighting the actions of Russian traitors in causing misfortune for the Russians. The film underscored the common people's love of their native land, and one of the heroic characters – Ignat the armourer – prefigured industrialization. Likewise, the shining heroic figure of Prince Alexander Nevsky corresponded to the Soviet leader cult's representation of the leader as simultaneously wise and pure, modest and commanding.

The film remains a classic because of its formal composition: the striking visual images of the enemy Teutons, 'mongrel knights' dehumanized by headgear that allowed only tiny cross-shaped slits for the eyes; the mechanical repetition of Teutonic knights throwing Russian male children into the fire; the remarkably intricate and choreographed battle on the ice; and the powerful score and choral music by Sergei Prokof'ev with lyrics by Vladimir Lugovskoi that sculpted the emotional appeal of the film. The iconic two-dimensional and epic nature of good and evil characters who battle to the death gives the film a stylized and exaggerated 'over the top' feeling that is well suited to the film's mobilizing message.

Like many war and adventure films, *Alexander Nevsky* also has a romantic sub-plot signalling women's symbolic inclusion in the Russian citizenry as wives and mothers, but strikingly also as soldiers. The maiden Vasilisa of Pskov fights and kills alongside the Novgorodian men in order to avenge her father. Because of her bravery, she wins the affection of the male warrior-hero Vasilii. The film thus suggests that both fighting and nurturing women will be the mothers of the future Russian nation.

Alexander Nevsky received popular and critical acclaim in the first ten months after it was released, and its popularity resumed when it returned to movie screens after the German invasion in the summer of 1941, after having being banned during the Soviet-German non-aggression pact.

Karen Petrone

Andrei Rublev

Country of Origin:
Soviet Union

Languages:
Russian
Italian
Kazakh

Studio:
Mosfilm

Director:
Andrei Tarkovskii

Producer:
Tamara Ogorodnikova

Screenplay:
Andrei Konchalovskii
Andrei Tarkovskii

Cinematographer:
Vadim Iusov

Art Directors:
Evgenii Cherniaev
Ippolit Novoderzhkin

Synopsis

The prologue sets the film in medieval Russia, where a bold individual escapes a pursuing crowd to mount a rough balloon and launch into flight across the waterlogged landscape. There follow seven episodes from the (largely imagined) life of Andrei Rublev (ca. 1370–ca. 1420), medieval Russia's best-known icon-painter. First we see him alongside his colleagues Kirill and Daniil as they witness the cruel repression of a folk performer. We then see Andrei's departure from the monastery (causing a rift between him and both of his colleagues), his apprenticeship with Theophanes the Greek, his sexual awakening during a pagan celebration, his frustrated attempts to create a fresco of the Last Judgment in Vladimir, his saving of a retarded woman during a Mongol attack and his life with her at the monastery during a vow of silence. The narrative culminates in Rublev witnessing the young boy Boriska founding a bell, which redeems Rublev's faith in artistic creation. The film closes with a display in colour of Rublev's icons and a shot of three horses grazing on a spit of land in a body of water.

Critique

Tarkovskii's sparse landscapes, silent protagonists and discontinuous narrative, punctuated by mysterious vignettes and transformations, make for an uncompromisingly difficult film which seems at first to repel any attempt at viewer 'identification'. In this multi-dimensional world each life has its own truth. The characters in *Andrei Rublev* represent various types of spirituality, from the stern but spineless intellectualism of Kirill (brilliantly played by Ivan Lapikov) to the pagan

Composer:

Viacheslav Ovchinnikov

Editors:

Liudmila Feiginova
Ol'ga Shevkunenko
Tat'iana Egorycheva

Duration:

185 minutes

Genres:

Historical
Biography

Cast:

Anatolii Solonitsyn
Ivan Lapikov
Nikolai Grin'ko
Nikolai Sergeev
Irma Rausch (Raush)
Nikolai Burliaev
Iurii Nazarov
Rolan Bykov
Nikolai Grabbe
Mikhail Kononov
Stepan Krylov
Bolot Beishenaliev
Iurii Nikulin

Year:

1966

revellers' exuberant carnality, to Rublev's humanist questioning. Andrei's point of view is privileged only insofar as he remains a spectator alongside the viewer, immune to the allure of action. We are never quite sure what he sees and how he sees it, and so we can neither be sure that we are seeing properly either. Nonetheless we feel an almost ethical imperative to keep watching and to elevate our vision. It reminds us of the original meaning of the word 'martyr'; Tarkovskii's films bear witness to his world and posit the spectator also as *witness*.

Quite apart from its inherent difficulties, appreciation of *Andrei Rublev* has been handicapped by the form in which it has reached viewers, especially outside Russia. Tarkovskii completed the film at 205 minutes in duration in mid-1966 as *The Passion According to Andrei*. The State Committee on Cinema then drew up a list of changes to be made before the film could be officially accepted. By the end of August 1966 Tarkovskii had made many of these changes, mostly by re-taping dialogue and cutting scenes and shots, amounting to a loss of about fifteen minutes of film. In the meantime, however, the controversy had been stoked by discussion of Tarkovskii's cruel treatment of animals, and the Committee returned to the matter and demanded more changes. After initially refusing Tarkovskii did make some further changes, removing a further five minutes from the film's duration, but *Andrei Rublev* remained shelved until 1969, when a second premiere was held, a print was sent to the Cannes Film Festival and foreign distribution rights were sold to a company linked to Columbia Pictures. At Cannes *Andrei Rublev* won the FIPRESCI International Critics' Prize for the screenplay and embarked on a successful run in French theatres. Tarkovskii finally saw the film released in the USSR at the very end of 1971. The best available version of the film is the first, namely *The Passion According to Andrei* (available on DVD, though an intermediate version is scheduled to be shown in 2010).

The shock of its aesthetic difficulty has inclined viewers from across the ideological spectrum to reduce *Andrei Rublev* to a tidy 'message', invariably ignoring the multivalent texture of the film. This was not surprising in the Soviet Union, which ideologized all discourse,

Andrei Tarkovskii, *Andrei Rublev* (1966).

whether artistic, religious or personal. Moreover, Tarkovskii never shirked from explaining what his film 'meant', but his pronouncements were often tailored to the needs of the moment. For official Soviet outlets Tarkovskii stressed the epic qualities of the film, which presents a panorama of the nation at a crucial historical moment. Elsewhere Tarkovskii stressed the film's retrieval of traditional Russian art, society and religion. However *Andrei Rublev* has proven disconcerting to those who would seek in it a salve for wounded national pride. Aleksandr Solzhenitsyn found that Tarkovskii contaminated Holy Russia with Sovietisms (such as Boriska, the Stakhanovite bell-founder) and 'besmirched' Rublev's faith by having him wander around spouting 'humanistic platitudes'. Such criticism highlights *Andrei Rublev*'s controversial image of Russia and Russian spirituality, though the film itself is sometimes viewed as a sacred object that has miraculously survived the conflagration of history and has been preserved, like Rublev's icons, in the embers of time.

Robert Bird

Sibiriade

Sibiriada

Country of Origin:
Soviet Union

Language:
Russian

Studio:
Mosfilm

Director:
Andrei Konchalovskii

Screenplay:
Valentin Ezhov
Andrei Konchalovskii

Cinematography:
Levan Paatashvili

Art Directors:
Aleksandr Adabashian
Nikolai Dvigubskii

Composer:
Eduard Artem'ev

Editor:
Valentina Kulagina

Duration:
275 minutes

Synopsis

At the time of the Revolution, the young Kolia Ustiuzhanin from the Siberian village of Elan' falls in love with Nastia Solomina, who is engaged to Filipp Solomin, and runs away with her to join the Revolution. A decade later, Kolia returns to Elan' with his son, Alesha, to construct a road to the marshlands in the hope of discovering oil there. Nastia has died 'defending the Revolution', which sparks enmity between Kolia and his brother-in-law Spiridon, who murders Kolia. Alesha escapes, vowing to avenge his father's death. When he returns a decade later, he learns from Taia Solomina that Spiridon has been sentenced and Alesha falls in love with Taia, when news of the German attack reach the village. After the war, as a decorated war hero, Alesha receives a technical education and becomes Master Oil Driller. He returns to Elan' with a drilling team, working for several months without luck. Meanwhile Filipp Solomin, now a Party functionary, attempts to block a plan for a hydroelectric power plant near the village. Just as leaders in Moscow are making their final decision, oil bursts forth from the well in Elan'. As the well ignites, Alesha dies in the flames. Filipp rushes from Moscow to Elan' and Taia reveals that she is pregnant with Alesha's child, the last of the Ustiuzhanins.

Critique

Sibiriade was the final film that Andrei Konchalovskii made in the Soviet Union, before emigrating to France and eventually Hollywood. This four and a half hour epic was a fantastically expensive film, made during a year when attendance for Soviet films was at a fifteen-year low. The fact that *Sibiriade* was made in the first place indicates Konchalovskii's cultural cache in the Soviet film industry, despite the continued trouble that had plagued his career, from the controversy in Kirghizstan over his depiction of Kirghiz peasants in *The First Teacher*

Genre:

Historical Drama

Cast:

Vladimir Samoilov
Vitalii Solomin
Sergei Shakurov
Natal'ia Andreichenko
Evgenii Perov
Elena Koreneva
Nikolai Skorobogatov
Pavel Kadochnikov
Nikita Mikhalkov
Liudmila Gurchenko

Year:

1978

(1964) to the banning of his next film, *The Story of Asia Kliachina, Who Loved But Never Married* (1967, rel. 1987). Nonetheless, authorities in the Soviet film industry recognized him as a talented director, and like many *auteurs*, gave him unprecedented access to resources and money to make the film that he wanted to make.

A project that began as a Stagnation-era production film about the lives of Siberian oil workers, Konchalovskii transformed *Sibiriade* into an ambivalent meditation on modernity and tradition. From an imperial backwater at the turn of the century to the centre of the Soviet Union's oil production region at the end of the 1960s, the village of Elan' comes to signify both Soviet progress and the destruction to peasant communities wrought by industrialization. Moreover, in its ethical complexity, *Sibiriade* contains both clear socialist realist conventions, along with moments of sympathy for class enemies and a critical attitude toward social heroes. For example, when Filipp discovers that Aleksei has been killed in the oil well conflagration, he asks officials sitting in the Kremlin Palace to rise in memory of a 'common worker'. Yet such socialist realist myths exist alongside the conventions of Thaw cinema, with its focus on the individual and private life. In *Sibiriade*, for example, the Revolution becomes a means for local communities to understand and articulate their differences and personal conflicts. At the same time, Konchalovskii refrains from presenting a simple dichotomy of interior and exterior forces on Elan'. Modernization is not a force imposed from the outside, but emerges from within the community, from individuals whose identities are torn between the village and the city.

Stylistically, *Sibiriade* combines elements of classical narrative cinema with several eclectic touches: Fast-paced newsreels of the Revolution, Civil War, the First Five-Year Plan and the Great Patriotic War – history proper – are intercut with the slow-moving drama of Elan'. In its mix of rapid and slow pacing, *Sibiriade* takes influence from the early work of Aleksandr Dovzhenko, and his *Zvenigora* (1927) in particular. In addition, Konchalovskii is able to mobilize both tonal and aural shifts, which adds to the stylistic eclecticism of the film. For example, the image frequently shifts between colour and a sepia-toned black and white, focusing our mental engagement with the material in different ways. The realm of memory and dreams is typically rendered without colour in *Sibiriade*, although this does not encapsulate the full extent to which Konchalovskii employs tonal shifts in any given section in the film. Instead, Elan' appears to exist simultaneously within the dreamlike space of memory and nostalgia, on the one hand, and the socially defined space of class conflict and rural backwardness, on the other. *Sibiriade*'s soundtrack also defines the village as liminal space, with its mix of orchestral music, contemporary Soviet popular songs and 1970s electronic music. While successful as a work of European art cinema, Konchalovskii's film failed to draw audiences at home.

Joshua First

Farewell

Proshchanie s Materoi

Country of Origin:
Soviet Union

Year:
1982

Language:
Russian

Studio:
Mosfilm

Director:
Elem Klimov

Screenplay:
Larisa Shepit'ko
German Klimov
Rudol'f Tiurin

Cinematographers:
Aleksei Rodionov, Iurii
Skhirtladze

Art Director:
Viktor Petrov

Composers:
Alfred Schnittke
Viacheslav Artemov

Editor:
Valeriia Belova

Duration:
130 minutes

Genres:
Literary Adaptation, Historical

Cast:
Stefaniia Staniuta
Lev Durov
Aleksei Petrenko
Iurii Katin-Iartsev
Maia Bulgakova
Vadim Iakovenko

Synopsis

The film is set over the last weeks of summer and the onset of autumn during the Brezhnev era. The inhabitants of a small island community in Siberia prepare to leave their homes in preparation for the flooding of the entire area as part of a huge hydroelectric dam project further up river. The film focuses on the reactions of three members of the Pinigin family covering three generations: the younger Andrei (Vadim Iakovenko), who is committed to the process of modernization; his father Pavel (Lev Durov), aware that progress is inevitable though painful; and his grandmother Dar'ia (Stefaniia Staniuta), who represents the values of the past, fears their passing and the destruction of her community.

Critique

The film is based on the 1976 novella (*povest'*) 'Farewell to Matera' by Valentin Rasputin, generally considered to be the last great work of 'village prose' of the 1960s–1970s, and one which thematically and stylistically brought that movement to a close. The film was to be directed by Larisa Shepit'ko, but she, along with cameraman Vladimir Chukhnov and art director Iurii Fomenko, was killed in a car accident in 1979. Her husband, Elem Klimov, then took on and completed the project in 1982, though the film was released only in 1984. Rasputin's work is suffused with a mysticism that is meant to symbolize the link of past and present in this rural community. The island community represents the transience of human life in the never-ending waters of time, and the island itself is protected by the spirit of the past.

The very name 'Matera' evokes notions of Mother Russia and Mother Earth. Klimov's film plays down the us-and-them antagonisms between the planners and the villagers, showing not the relentless workings of ideology, but rather emphasizing that even those in charge of the implementation of plans drawn up in distant Moscow are victims of impersonal social processes. Shots of the chaotic urban settlement where the villagers are to be resettled reinforce the impression that those making key decisions affecting people's everyday lives bear no accountability for the grim consequences of their actions. Some of Rasputin's symbolism remains, such as that of destruction by fire and water, suggesting the end of the world, and old and young, with the implication that official teleology is rejected. Shniitke's evocative music further suggests the link between the villagers and their ancestral past. Both Rasputin and Klimov stress the link of these villagers with the land that for centuries was the home of their forebears, and the film features a scene of communal bathing in the river that is reminiscent of the scene of the pagans' 'festival' in Andrei Tarkovskii's *Andrei Rublev* (1966). Rasputin's original novel is linguistically complex, containing many words and phrases peculiar to the Lake Baikal region of Siberia, making the work difficult even for other Russians not native to Siberia, but also aligning the author with the victims of progress. Klimov wisely uses standard Russian throughout the film, but keeps Rasputin's vague, possibly tragic ending. A few villagers remain on the island as the floodgates are about to open and the island will disappear in the ensuing deluge, and a boat sets off to rescue them. The boat gets lost in the fog, the villagers remain on the island and both novel and film end at this point. Time remains suspended, history does not move forward and the future remains uncertain.

David Gillespie

My Friend Ivan Lapshin

Moi drug Ivan Lapshin

Country of Origin:
Soviet Union

Language:
Russian

Studio:
Lenfilm

Director:
Aleksei Iu. German

Screenplay:
Iurii German (novel)
Eduard Volodarskii

Cinematographer:
Valerii Fedosov

Art Director:
Iurii Pugach

Composer:
Arkadii Gagulashvili

Editor:
Leda Semenova

Runtime:
100 minutes

Genre:
Historical

Cast:
Andrei Boltnev
Nina Ruslanova

Synopsis

The film is set in the years 1935–1936, at the onset of Stalinist terror. A young boy, Aleksandr, lives together with his father, Zanadvorov, in the provincial town of Unchansk. They live in a communal apartment with Ivan Lapshin and Vasili Okoshkin, both policemen, and Patrikeevna, a housekeeper. Lapshin and his team are trying to track down a criminal, Solov'ev. Meanwhile, Lapshin's best friend, the writer Khanin, arrives in Unchansk. He is grieving from his wife's sudden death from diphtheria. A company of actors arrives in Unchansk to perform an agitprop theatre piece. One of them, the actress Natasha Adashova, enlists Lapshin's help to find a real prostitute so that she can give a better performance in her role as a prostitute. Lapshin falls in love with Adashova, but she falls in love with Khanin. Because Khanin has recently lost his wife, he rebuffs Adashova. Some months later, Lapshin finds Solov'ev. He kills him even though the criminal asked for and is promised mercy. Khanin leaves town and Adashova and Lapshin go their separate ways.

Critique

My Friend Ivan Lapshin can be considered as one of the most important films of late Soviet cinema. German subverted the official interpretation of history by showing the harsh life of Soviet citizens at the onset of Stalinist terror. Moreover, German sets aside conventional structure, making it difficult for the viewer to determine the sequence of events and situations depicted. *My Friend Ivan Lapshin*, therefore, was challenging both in content and style. After the first screening, the film was immediately attacked from within Lenfilm. Goskino, the State Committee for Cinematography, told German to reshoot half of the film, which German refused to do. After a two-year skirmish with Goskino, the film was released in 1985, at the very beginning of Gorbachev's glasnost.

The film is based on a novel written by Aleksei German's father, Iurii German (1910–1967). The film's frame is set in 1983 and consists of a prologue and epilogue. This frame determines the narration's point of view of Aleksandr, who tries to remember the events set in his childhood. German evokes the atmosphere of provincial life on both the figurative level by using a documentary style and on the narrative level through a focus on ordinary life. He created Aleksandr's memo-

Aleksei Iu. German, *My Friend Ivan Lapshin* (1984).

Andrei Mironov
Aleksei Zharkov
Zinaida Adamovich
Aleksandr Filippenko
Iurii Kuznetsov
Valerii Filonov
Anatolii Slivnikov
Andrei Dudarenko

Year:
1984

ries by ignoring conventional techniques. The long travelling shots and the subjective camera are somewhat disorientating to the viewer, especially given the lack of establishing shots and shot-reverse shots. The dialogue is frequently drowned out by chatter and screaming. At first sight, there is no explicit mention of the Stalinist terror in *My Friend Ivan Lapshin*. The year 1935, after Kirov was assassinated, was the last moment before the outbreak of the Great Terror. By means of omens, the director helps the viewer to imagine the dark future of the story's characters after the ending of the film. There are clear premonitions of a dark future when a mirror is shattered and Zanadvorov says: 'This is a bad omen. And by the way, for all of us'. Near the end of the film Lapshin is about to leave town for a 'refresher course'. He seems to have no idea of the dark fate that awaits him. The detective story and love triangle overshadow these omens, which in turn inform the viewer that many of the film's characters will soon become victims of the Great Terror. Communist idealism is ultimately represented as a lost dream.

The film reached Soviet audiences only in 1986, when it was shown on television, and became the subject of heated debate. At once exciting and disturbing, it offered a glimpse of a sensitive period in Soviet history. Yet it proved to be quite disturbing simply because it was too soon for the general public to take in what it was seeing. German's film marked the beginning of the cinematic investigation into one of the blank spots of Soviet history, the Stalinist terror. *My Friend Ivan Lapshin* therefore contributed to the debunking of Stalinist myth.

Jasmijn Van Gorp

Cold Summer of '53

Kholodnoe let 53-ego

Country of Origin:
Soviet Union

Language:
Russian

Studio:
Mosfilm

Director:
Aleksandr Proshkin

Screenplay:
Edgar Dubrovskii

Cinematographer:
Boris Brozhovskii

Art Director:
Valerii Filippov

Composer:
Vladimir Martynov

Editor:
Elena Mikhailova

Runtime:
96 minutes

Genres:
Action
Historical

Cast:
Valerii Priemykhov
Anatolii Papanov
Zoia Buriak
Viktor Stepanov
Iurii Kuznetsov
Vladimir Kashpur
Nina Usatova

Year:
1987

Synopsis

Just three weeks after the death of Stalin an amnesty was decreed, leading to the release of over a million prisoners from the Gulag. This film depicts the impact of the amnesty on a small fishing hamlet in northern Russia. The village is already home to two political exiles: Luzga, a taciturn, distant man and former captain in the intelligence service, and Kopalych, once a chief engineer in Moscow. Despite their marginal status in the village, they turn out to be its saviours. The amnesty of March 1953 released not only deserving prisoners but also groups of dangerous bandits and a gang lays siege to the village. While the local authorities cave in quickly to the criminals' demands, only Luzga is ready to fight the criminals, aided by the elderly Kopalych. A dangerous shoot-out ensues. Eventually the bandits are defeated and peace brought to the hamlet, but not before a young girl and Kopalych are killed. The ending of the film shows Luzga returning to Moscow two years later, rehabilitated. He remains essentially alone, however, and the final shot shows him walking by himself with his battered suitcase along the capital's busy streets.

Critique

In many ways, the film has all the elements of a traditional Western: a village is under siege from a group of criminals, the authorities are powerless and only the heroism of a lone, somewhat marginalized, individual can save the day. Yet the film evades easy classification for it is much more than an action movie.

After Mikhail Gorbachev came to power in 1985, filmmakers were quick to embark on a reconsideration of the Soviet past in a more critical manner, with Tengiz Abuladze's *Repentance*, released in 1986, leading the way. Making *Cold Summer of '53* just a year later, Aleksandr Proshkin also took advantage of the new cultural environment. His film deals with the legacies of Stalinism, though there is little direct portrayal of the pre-1953 era: he does not use flashbacks or dreams to reveal his characters' experiences under Stalin; and the protagonists, Luzga and Kopalych, speak sparingly of their ordeals. One of the key figures in the village, the mother of the girl killed, is a mute, and her character can be seen to symbolize the silencing effect of Stalinism. Perhaps because the crimes of the Stalinist era remain unarticulated in this film, their continued hold over the present appears even greater, and Proshkin effectively shows how very difficult the effects of the terror were to overcome.

Proshkin's film suggests that in the summer after Stalin's death the first moves to dismantle the enormous prison-camp system he had created already proved highly destabilizing. From the very start the viewer is aware of the suspicion in which former prisoners are held and, even after Luzga and Kopalych's acts of heroism, the villagers' reservations do not disappear and they are reluctant to offer Kopalych, as an exile, a proper burial. In the final scenes of the film, Luzga, having returned to Moscow, visits Kopalych's wife and son to give them news of his death, but the encounter is an awkward one. The scene suggests that the returning prisoners made some people uncomfortable, triggering feelings of shame they preferred to suppress. Such issues became the staple of many of the literary and cinematic treatments of Stalinist terror under Gorbachev. A more unusual aspect of Proshkin's film is his readiness to recognize that political prisoners represented only one type of Gulag returnee. At the time of Stalin's death the majority of prisoners were serving time for non-political crimes and, while few were the violent bandits depicted here, the amnesty does seem to have resulted in a spike in criminal activity in the summer of 1953. The violent impact of the amnesty, at least in some areas of the Soviet Union, perhaps helped to reinforce people's anxieties regarding Gulag releases. In Proshkin's vision of 1950s society, people found it hard to distinguish between different groups of returnees, regarding all with suspicion and caution.

Proshkin's film implicitly raised questions about whether the Gorbachev generation would deal with the Stalinist past more easily than the Khrushchev generation. The film's huge popularity, both in the box office and among critics, certainly suggests that there was an audience eager to engage with these difficult topics. Its popularity was also, though, the result of both the filmmaking and the acting. Although *Cold Summer* is a film full of action, it is beautifully shot, the characters nuanced and its messages subtly conveyed.

Miriam Dobson

Burnt by the Sun

Utomlennye solntsem
(Soleil trompeur)

Country of Origin:
Russia

Language:
Russian

Studios:
TriTe
Camera One
Roskomkino

Director:
Nikita Mikhalkov

Producers:
Michel Seydoux
Nikita Mikhalkov

Synopsis

On a Sunday in June 1936 the secret service (NKVD) officer Mitia accepts and carries out a special assignment: the arrest of the Red Army Commander Kotov at his family's dacha near Moscow. Meanwhile, Kotov enjoys domestic happiness with his wife Marusia and daughter Nadia. Mitia, a friend of the family and Marusia's first love, arrives and spends the day with the family, taking Kotov back to Moscow with him in the evening. Upon his return to Moscow Mitia succeeds in his second suicide attempt (having tried to shoot himself the day before): he cuts his wrists in the bath.

Critique

Set in June 1936, the film's action unfolds before Stalin's Great Purges and the show trials, but already anticipates the Great Terror that would soon become obvious: the impending threat is tangible, audible and visible. The film captures a moment when the belief in Revolutionary ideals and a pre-Revolutionary lifestyle was still possible. *Burnt by the Sun* contrasts that pre-Revolutionary lifestyle as represented by Marusia's family with that of the Soviet reality of Revolutionary leaders (Kotov), juxtaposes the ideals of the Whites against those of the Reds and ultimately insists on the destructive power of political ideas as opposed to personal happiness.

Nikita Mikhalkov, *Burnt by the Sun* (1994).

Screenplay:
Nikita Mikhalkov
Rustam Ibragimbekov

Cinematographer:
Vilen Kaliuta

Art Directors:
Vladimir Aronin
Aleksandr Samulekin

Composer:
Eduard Artem'ev

Editor:
Enzo Meniconi

Runtime:
151 minutes

The film explores the marriage between the old Russian intelligentsia and the Revolutionary system through Marusia and Kotov. Their marriage is based on lies; it is held together by Marusia's attempt to forget the past; and it survives largely because of Kotov's energy and (sexual) power, but only in a protected and enclosed space, on the island of the past in the midst of the Soviet reality of the 1930s: Marusia's family dacha.

Kotov confidently executes Stalin's political will and builds his own image as leader. Yet while Kotov believes in his own power and relies on Stalin's support, Mitia is aware of being a mere arm of power. Indeed, Mitia is an actor in other ways too: he first appears as an old, blind man emerging from the Young Pioneers marching past the dacha; for Nadia, he poses as Father Frost and as a magician; for the household, he claims to be a doctor. He recites the tunes he taught Marusia, repeats the steps he learnt in Paris, quotes Hamlet and plays an invalid at the beach to be helped up by a fat lady. Moreover, when Mitia tells of the past, he chooses the form of a fairy tale: in a story

Genres:

Historical

Drama

Cast:

Oleg Men'shikov

Nikita Mikhalkov

Ingeborga Dapkunaite

Nadia Mikhalkova

Viacheslav Tikhonov

Svetlana Kriuchkova

Vladimir Il'in

Alla Kazanskaia

Nina Arkhipova

Avangard Leont'ev

André Umansky

Inna Ulianova

Liubov' Rudneva

Vladimir Riabov

Vladimir Belousov

Aleksei Pokatilov

Evgenii Mironov

Year:

1994

with inverted names, Mitia tells of his lost love – how Yatim fought in the war, left Russia and returned to find Yasum married to the man who sent him abroad in the first place. The paradigm of Soviet culture of the 1930s does not work here: not the fairy tale is turned into reality, but reality is turned into a horror story where an ogre, Kotov, destroys the love between Yatim and Yasum.

The impact of destruction is underlined by a special effect, the fireball: when Mitia tells his tale, the fireball whizzes over the forest, collides with a falcon and crashes into a single tree; the second fireball effect accompanies Mitia's physical destruction, his suicide. Mitia is politically successful, but his personal life has failed. Kotov has personal happiness and political power, and he loses both. Mitia realizes the potential permanence of personal happiness as opposed to the transience of political success. The absence of a personalized past – parents – is important: Mitia's parents died during the Civil War; when Stalin appears as an all-powerful pagan god, rising on the banner attached to the balloon as the sun is setting, it becomes clear that he is a father-surrogate to Mitia. Kotov may enjoy protection from Stalin but, when he realizes that Stalin is now a father for Mitia, he cries like a child deprived of paternal love.

Stalin's totalitarian regime is interpreted as a part of history that neither Kotov nor Mitia are directly responsible for. The film relieves the individual of responsibility for history, and glorifies the Russia of the past, including its Bolshevik heroes. Mikhalkov here creates an apologia for the intelligentsia's inertia and sways between a neo-Leninist and Russophile position.

Birgit Beumers

Khrustalev, My Car!

Khrustalev, mashinu!

Country of Origin:

Russia

France

Language:

Russian

Studio:

Lenfilm

Director:

Aleksei Iu. German

Producers:

Aleksandr Golutva

Armen Medvedev

Synopsis

The film is set in the last days of Stalin's rule, in February 1953. Red Army General Iurii Klenskii works as a military brain surgeon in a Moscow hospital. After he notices that he is being shadowed by Stalin's secret police, he flees to the countryside. One day later he is arrested as a prime suspect in the 'Doctor's plot'. Stalin's secret police incriminate him with the conspiracy against prominent Soviet politicians and generals. After being tortured and raped, he is sent to Siberia. Upon arrival, he is called back by Beria to tend the dying leader. When Klenskii arrives at the leader's dacha, he massages the comatose man's stomach and witnesses how Beria closes the leader's eyes after he has breathed his last. Beria kisses Klenskii, opens the door and shouts 'Khrustalev, my car!'

Critique

Khrustalev, My Car! is the late apotheosis of the anti-Soviet films of Aleksei German. German pushes content and style much further than in his other masterpieces, making *Khrustalev, My Car!* at once the most artistic and most disturbing one of his oeuvre. While his previous

Screenplay:
Aleksei Iu. German
Svetlana Karmalita

Cinematographer:
Vladimir Il'in

Art Directors:
Mikhail Gerasimov
Georgii Kropachev
Vladimir Svetozarov

Composer:
Andrei Petrov

Editor:
Irina Gorokhovskaia

Runtime:
150 minutes

Genre:
Historical

Cast:
Iurii Tsurilo
Misha Dement'ev
Nina Ruslanova
Aleksandr Bashirov
Dmitrii Prigov

Year:
1998

Aleksei Iu. German, *Khrustalev, My Car!* (1998).

films were made during the Soviet era and its oppressive artistic climate, *Khrustalev, My Car!* was made and released in the 1990s, when filmmakers enjoyed artistic freedom. However, together with the vast majority of Russian filmmakers, German was for the first time in his life confronted with financial restraints because of the transition from a state-led to a market-based film industry and the economic crisis of the 1990s. It took German seven years to finish the film.

Khrustalev, My Car! depicts the paranoia in Moscow during the last days of Stalin's life. The film is told retrospectively by the son of the main character, Iurii Klenskii. The film is shot in black and white, emphasizing the gloom and despair of the period, and with a hand-held camera, stumbling into Klenskii's life without establishing shots. The film's focus is on the harsh lives of Klenskii and his Jewish relatives during Stalin's last anti-Semitic campaign. Jewish families are evicted from their apartments; a Jewish boy is molested on a play ground; and the Jewish nieces of Klenskii's wife live in the wardrobe of their communal apartment. The film's cast consists of carnivalesque characters, contributing to German's hellish vision on history. Characters spit, swear and vomit. Everyone screams and lives in a permanent state of insanity. In one of the most disturbing sex scenes in film history, Klenskii is raped and sodomized by a gang of criminal thugs. In its realistic depiction of human cruelty, the film can easily stand next to such films as Michael Haneke's *Funny Games* (1997, US version 2007) and Aleksei Balabanov's *Cargo 200* (2007). The film's anti-Sovietism and anti-Stalinism is best revealed in the scene of the dying leader. Stalin's death is not more than a banal fact. Just one press on the stomach and a command to make him break wind make up the attempts to tend to the leader, who lies on the ground.

In 1998 the film premiered at the Cannes film festival as the opening film. The premiere turned out to be a disaster: half of the audience left the theatre during the screening. *Khrustalev, My Car!* proved to be hard to watch because of its nervous stylistics, explicit violence and grotesque characters. After the fiasco in Cannes, a crushed German withdrew the film a year from circulation. After a year, it got a limited release in Russia. It was highly praised by Russian critics and received five Nika awards in 2000. Meanwhile, the film achieved cult status in European art house circuits.

Jasmijn Van Gorp

The Barber of Siberia

Sibirskii tsiriul'nik

Country of Origin:
Russia

Languages:
Russian
English

Studios:
TriTe
Camera One
Barandov
France 2
Medusa

Director:
Nikita Mikhalkov

Producers:
Michel Seydoux
Nikita Mikhalkov

Screenplay:
Rustam Ibragimbekov
Nikita Mikhalkov

Cinematographer:
Pavel Lebeshev

Art Director:
Vladimir Aronin

Editor:
Enzo Meniconi

Duration:
179 minutes

Genre:
Historical epic

Cast:
Julia Ormond
Richard Harris
Oleg Men'shikov
Aleksei Petrenko
Marina Neelova
Vladimir Il'in
Daniel Olbrychski

Synopsis

In 1885 Jane Callaghan travels to Russia because she has been hired by the inventor Douglas McCracken, who is under pressure from his creditors, to help him secure funding for his tree-cutting machine. Jane pretends to be McCracken's daughter and charms General Radlov, spending the day with him at a Shrovetide fair, so he exercises his influence on the Grand Duke. When the cadet Andrei Tolstoy falls in love with her, Jane is unwilling to abandon her scheme for love's sake. Tolstoy sees Jane flirt with the general in the theatre and attacks his rival with a violin bow during a performance of *The Marriage of Figaro* which is attended by the Grand Duke. Radlov subsequently accuses Tolstoy of an attempt upon the Grand Duke's life, securing his own promotion, while Tolstoy is sent to a prison camp in Siberia.

In 1895 Jane is married to McCracken and has a child – Tolstoy's son. When McCracken launches his invention, Jane travels with him to Siberia and finds the house where Tolstoy now lives with his family, but she fails to meet Tolstoy. In 1905 Jane writes a letter to her son Andrew, now a recruit at an American military base. He has inherited his father's stubborn nature, as Jane explains to his commander during a visit.

Critique

The film is set in the Russia of Tsar Aleksandr III (1881–1894), a reactionary and nationalist ruler, who is here portrayed as a benevolent tsar: he loves children, as can be seen when he takes his son Mikhail on horseback to a parade. During the same scene, the camera captures a sparrow at the cadets' feet as they stand to attention and closes up on the bird; the shot conveys how the Tsar never neglects the small at the expense of the grand. The tsar (played by Mikhalkov) is presented as an ideal father, for his child as well as for the nation.

Mikhalkov conflates time as he sketches an image of Russia that is derived more from artistic representations than historical fact. Although the action unfolds in 1885, Mikhalkov's Russia resembles that of the mid-nineteenth century under Aleksandr II or even Nicholas I. Indeed, the terrorist activities of the Popular Will (Narodnaia volia) had come to an end by 1883; there were no fireworks, silver samovars or silk garments during the Shrovetide festivities; French and German, but not English, were spoken at the time; and so continues a list of historical infelicities. Mikhalkov glorifies instead a range of features of nineteenth-century life.

The theme of broken families is important in the film: in the absence of an intact family life, the military community replaces the family, while the tsar substitutes the father-figure. Thus, in Mikhalkov's vision the whole of Russian society is transformed into one large family with father-tsar at its head.

The moral values of the young Russian cadet Tolstoy are held up as a model designed to help contemporary audiences value and love their fatherland. The film gives a biased view of traditions: Russian rituals and traditions are shown in great detail, such as Forgiveness Sunday and the Shrovetide celebrations, offering a view on Russia through the eyes

Anna Mikhalkova
Marat Basharov
Nikita Tatarenkov
Artem Mikhalkov
Egor Dronov
Avangard Leont'ev
Robert Hardy
Elizabeth Spriggs

Year:

1998

of a foreign visitor. These values are typical of the nineteenth century, which Mikhalkov connects to the beauty and the deep sense of Russian folk traditions. Likewise, the heroism displayed by Tolstoy is possible only in a setting of the last century. *The Barber of Siberia* instils in the spectator nostalgia for tsarist, pre-Revolutionary Russia, related to the present through the historical event that dominated the year of the film's release: the laying to rest of the remains of the last tsar and his family, the Romanovs, in St Petersburg in July 1998.

The *Barber of Siberia* makes a moral statement by asserting the need to have principles; it presents a positive hero with the potential to instil hope in contemporary Russian audiences. Mikhalkov wanted to boost the image of Russia as a nation with high ideals, unwilling to compromise and with a strong leadership. The film is past and future, objective and subjective, national and international at once, attempting to create a myth for audiences at home and abroad. *The Barber of Siberia* aims at the creation of an idealized view of Russia for foreign audiences through the eyes of a foreigner. However, in international distribution it failed to make an impact.

As a political manifesto the film contains a strangely nationalistic statement for the future of Russia, envisaging the resurrection of order and discipline which would reinstate a value system and thus benefit the Russian population.

Birgit Beumers

Cargo 200

Gruz 200

Country:
Russia

Language:
Russian

Studio:
CTB

Director:
Aleksei Balabanov

Producer:
Sergei Sel'ianov

Screenplay:
Aleksei Balabanov

Cinematographer:
Aleksandr Simonov

Art Director:
Pavel Parkhomenko

Synopsis

Set in 1984, *Cargo 200* is a dark, brutal attack on late Soviet life. It opens as Artem, a professor of scientific atheism, is visiting his army colonel brother. On his way back home, Artem's car breaks down in front of a former Gulag prisoner's home. As they drink moonshine, Artem and the *zek* argue about God's existence. Just as Artem departs, a young man named Valera arrives with Angelika, the daughter of the local Communist Party secretary. Valera leaves Angelika behind as he and the *zek* get drunk. She is kidnapped by a sadistic militia captain, Zhurov, who chains her to his bed. Angelika claims that her fiancé serving in Afghanistan will come back and kill her captor. Zhurov learns that the paratrooper has been killed in action, manages to claim the lead-lined coffin of the fiancé (the name for these Afghan coffins is 'Cargo 200'), opens it up, and deposits the corpse on Angelika's bed. He then momentarily frees a criminal to rape Angelika in the same bed while he watches. After he has killed the prisoner, he reads Angelika's letters from the dead fiancé whose body rots alongside her. Eventually the captain is killed, but the horror onscreen has painted a vivid picture of late Soviet history.

Critique

Cargo 200 caused controversy from the moment it debuted at the 2007 Kinotavr Festival in Sochi. Before it aired, pregnant women were warned to leave the cinema. Some audience members and critics walked out; others hailed it as a masterpiece. Although it was an art

Aleksei Balabanov, *Cargo 200* (2006).

Editor:

Tat'iana Kuzmicheva

Duration:

89 minutes

Genre:

Historical

Cast:

Aleksei Serebriakov
Leonid Gromov
Iurii Stepanov
Agniia Kuznetsova
Aleksei Poluian

Year:

2007

house movie, *Cargo 200* generated a great deal of press coverage and debate. History – or historical accuracy – fuelled the arguments about Balabanov's film.

The director himself has stated that the 'clearly expressed hero is a negative'. *Cargo 200* is in part the story of how Artem has sold his soul to the communist devil. Aleksei, the former *zek*, tells Artem that 'all the evil comes from you, the communists. You want to replace God with your Party and your Lenin. […] There's no God, so everything goes. You can kill millions'. What has happened, in Aleksei Balabanov's view, is that communism deprived its citizens of souls and therefore created a real-life horror film.

The actions of all of Balabanov's characters reveal a depraved, indifferent, violent, sadistic and impotent citizenry, attributes that the director believed emerged out of the Soviet experiment and that found full expression in late socialism. The historical setting of the film is crucial to this point – this is not the Stalinist era, but 1984. Balabanov's USSR is not the nostalgic Brezhnev era that many contemporary audience members yearned for. Nor is it the dystopian world created by George Orwell. Instead, *Cargo 200*'s 1984 is a horror show, a nightmarish world far more frightening that anything conjured up by Orwell because it has a basis in reality. Tellingly, Balabanov's 1984 is also more frightening than what was to come under Gorbachev and Yeltsin.

The unflinching violence and sadism that Zhurov employs has two roots. First, as a representative of the state, Zhurov embodies the moral decay of communism. He does what he does, Balabanov suggests, simply because he can and because he can get away with it. Second, the roots of Zhurov's evil stems from the time, when the Afghan war had gone on for five years and the numbers of Cargo 200 had increased dramatically. It is an era, as Artem tells his brother at the beginning of the film, when 'everyone has begun to fidget'. The long history of state violence employed by the Bolsheviks and their successors, Balabanov suggests, has reached its logical if horrific apex in the form of Zhurov.

Audiences and participants in various discussions about *Cargo 200* tended to divide into generational camps. For those who remembered 1984 well, the film was a shock and a source of anger; for the younger generation the film was a revelation, representing an entirely different story than the one told to them by their parents and at school. *Cargo 200*, in other words, served as a cinematic history lesson for the internet generation. In the end, *Cargo 200* is not just about 1984 but also 2007. Much like Danila in Balabanov's *Brother* films provided a flawed hero for the 1990s, *Cargo 200* provided an antidote to the Putin patriotic nostalgia for the USSR under Brezhnev, a cinematic shock therapy against forgetfulness.

Stephen M. Norris

Paper Soldier

Bumazhnyi soldat

Country of Origin:
Russia

Language:
Russian

Studio:
Lenfilm

Director:
Aleksei A. German

Producers:
Artem Vasil'ev
Sergei Shumakov

Screenplay:
Vladimir Arkusha
Aleksei A. German
Iuliia Glezarova

Cinematographers:
Maksim Drozdov
Alisher Khamidkhodzhaev

Art Directors:
El'dar Karkhalev
Sergei Kokovkin
Sergei Rakutov

Synopsis

This historical drama takes place in 1961 in the months leading up to Iurii Gagarin's historic flight into space on 12 April 1961. The action takes place in Moscow and in Baikonur, the Soviet launch site in present-day Kazakhstan. The story revolves around Daniil Pokrovskii, the physician for the first group of cosmonauts. Pokrovskii attempts to be both a friend and a doctor to the first cosmonaut candidates. He is also part of a love triangle involving his wife Nina (who works as his assistant in Moscow during cosmonaut training) and his lover Vera in Baikonur. Pokrovskii is torn between the responsibility for the cosmonauts and the demands of his job, as well as his private life. After Pokrovskii's death, which occurs just before Gagarin's successful launch, his wife and his lover remain devoted to Pokrovskii and Vera moves into the Moscow family apartment.

Critique

Aleksei A. German's period piece uses the events leading to Gagarin's historic flight as a backdrop for a love story. It is a romance, however, that operates on multiple levels: the conventional story of private love and an equally passionate romance with building a new and more just society. The public and private romances intersect constantly in the film, setting the characters' private interests against their public duties.

At the level of a more conventional love story, the film is a love triangle between the physician to the first group of cosmonaut candidates, Daniil Pokrovskii, his wife Nina and lover Vera. One would expect the story to revolve around tensions between the two women as they compete for the doctor's love. Both women, however, are really in competition with something far more compelling: Pokrovskii's obsession with launching the first man into the cosmos. Pokrovskii is a tortured soul – the 'Paper Soldier' of Bulat Okudzhava's 1959 song, which inspired the title of the movie. Pokrovskii's Paper Soldier, like

Composer:

Fedor Sofronov

Editor:

Sergei Ivanov

Runtime:

118 minutes

Genre:

Historical

Cast:

Merab Ninidze
Anastasiia Sheveleva
Chulpan Khamatova
Denis Reishakhrit
Ruslan Ibragimov
Aleksandr Glebov
Fedor Lavrov
Valentin Kuznetsov

Year:

2008

Okudzhava's, is determined to eliminate injustice and remake the world – and dies in the process. Looming large over all the relationships in the film is the omnipresent threat of death and sacrifice for the state. The cosmonauts, as well as their trainers and physicians, are well aware that their mission is merely to survive – and that they will probably die a dog's death, just like Laika, the first creature in space. The anticipation of death intensifies the personal dramas and friendships.

German's film is part of a trend among Russian filmmakers to use iconic episodes and figures from the glorious chapters of Soviet space history. Those include Aleksei Uchitel''s *Dreaming of Space* (2005) and Andrei Panin's *Gagarin's Grandson* (2007). As with those films, German's film exploits nostalgia for the Soviet era. But it is also a creative attempt to re-spin the Soviet myth of space conquest for the twenty-first century.

Despite its fictional flights of fancy, German's film in many ways hews closer to the truth of the Soviet space programme than the earlier mythologies. German's retelling weaves a tale in which sacrifice for private love and for the state intertwine and mix in complex ways. The film, of course, is not a documentary, but its focus on the tangled nexus of public service and private life expresses a quality of life among those, like Gagarin, who were ready to make the ultimate sacrifice for the Soviet state. German conveys the bleak, empty and impoverished landscape of Baikonur. Trucks, bicycles, cars, carts and people are constantly getting stuck in mounds of mud – a nearly permanent state of being 'en'-mired that contrasts with the rocket that finally succeeds in pulling away from earth's gravity. Set against a backdrop of unrelenting bleakness, *Paper Soldier* puts the romance of Soviet space flight into proper historical context: a country exhausted by war and poverty yet determined to shock the world with its grand vision.

Ultimately, the movie suggests that the Soviet dream of launching humans into space was as much an escape from the challenges of everyday life as a formula for overcoming them. The doctor's tragedy is that he believes that the method of escape – the flight – is actually a means for overcoming the problems on earth that torment him. As he notes at the beginning of the film, the doctor awoke in a cold sweat every night, overwhelmed by an intense feeling of 'impending doom'.

Andrew Jenks

Aleksei A. German, *Paper Soldier* (2008).

WAR FILM

The war film has been an exceptionally important genre in Russian cinema, not just in terms of numbers, but also for the quality of the films made. Indeed, the first full-length film in Russian cinema history, Vasilii Goncharov's *The Defence of Sevastopol* (1912), was a movie about the Crimean War. As with any genre, it is often difficult to decide whether a picture should be considered a 'war film', rather than, say, a 'historical film'. Since the bulk of Russian war films have concerned Russia's twentieth-century wars, this essay shall focus on movies of World Wars I and II, the Russian Civil War, and the Afghan and Chechen conflicts.

World War I inspired great filmmaking in Europe and even in America; not so in Russia, where revolutionary events quickly eclipsed the 'imperialist' war. Even during the war itself, the war film was not a popular genre, save in the year 1915. By 1916, disaffection with the war was so great that audiences strongly preferred escapist melo-drama to patriotic fare. In the first years of Soviet power, the 1920s, the 'historical-Revolutionary' film dominated, with the Great War relegated to a footnote in films like Vsevolod Pudovkin's Revolution-ary masterpiece *The End of St Petersburg* (1927). The only significant movie about World War I is, therefore, Boris Barnet's sound film *Borderlands* (1931), which concerns two brothers who go to war and the fate of their father and sister left behind in a small provincial town. *Borderlands* exemplifies the ambivalent attitudes toward the war; Barnet chose to stress internationalism and the brotherhood of work-ers, rather than jingoistic hatred of the foreign enemy, although that is also shown.

The **Russian Civil War** (1918–1921) was among the most terrible civil wars in modern times, with more than 1 million combatants killed and several million civilians dead due to starvation and disease as well as enemy atrocities. The war was a complicated conflict between the Red defenders of the Revolution and the White counter-Revolutionar-ies, with 'Green' anarchists and nationalists and foreign intervention-ists thrown in for good measure. There were three key Civil War films in the 1920s: Iakov Protazanov's *The Forty-First* (1927), about a Red sharpshooter who kills her White lover; Vsevolod Pudovkin's *The Heir of Genghis Khan* (aka *Storm over Asia*, 1928), about the British intervention in Central Asia; and Aleksandr Dovzhenko's *Arsenal* (1929), a drama about the Civil War and Ukrainian nationalism. *Arsenal* stood out for the complexity of its message and beauty of its images.

The most famous of all Civil War films appeared in 1934: *Chapaev*, the Vasil'ev Brothers' rollicking picture about the legendary Civil War hero, which was based on Dmitrii Furmanov's eponymous novel. One of Stalin's all-time favourite movies, *Chapaev* spawned a veritable industry of songs, games, jokes and postcards.

The Civil War faded with the advent of the Great Patriotic War (as World War II is called in Soviet history) but returned to the screen in 1952, with Mikheil Chiaureli's *The Unforgettable Year 1919*, a Stalin cult film that (falsely) places Stalin at the centre of the Civil War. Audiences were saved from more such fare by Stalin's death the following year. Khrushchev's cultural Thaw saw a different take on the Civil War for the 40th anniversary of the revolution, revising the stalwart Civil War hero and giving an achingly human face to those terrible years.

The last gasp for the Civil War films was in the late 1960s, for the 50th anniversary of the Revolution. By this late date, the Civil War had turned into the stuff of mass-market adventure. The final important Soviet film on the Civil War was Aleksandr Askol'dov's *The Commissar* (1968), about a tough female political officer bivouacked with a poor Jewish family for her pregnancy. The film was banned, primarily for its Jewish content, and not released until 1987.

The **Great Patriotic War** quickly replaced the Russian Civil War as the dominant stabilizing myth of Soviet society. Unparalleled disaster – 27 million dead – became victory against all odds, due to the supposedly unwavering courage and sacrifice of the Soviet people to save their motherland (*rodina*) from the German-fascist aggressors. Film directors did not need encouragement to make patriotic films. What sets Soviet World War II film production apart from that of the other combatant nations is the centrality of pictures celebrating the role of women as fighters. The three canonical films of this type are Fridrikh Ermler's *She Defends the Motherland* (1943), Mark Donskoi's *The Rainbow* (1944), Leo Arnshtam's *Zoya* (1944). With the exception of Comrade Pasha in *She Defends the Motherland*, the partisan heroines are executed; in the case of Olena Kostiukh in *The Rainbow*, after she has witnessed the murder of her newborn son at the hands of the Germans.

As the war drew to an end, agency was withdrawn from both male and female heroes, in favour of a return to the socialist realist mask. Late Stalinist war films are peculiar, with dead or maimed heroes predominating, like the unfortunate youth in Sergei Gerasimov's *The Young Guard* (1948) or the legless pilot in Aleksandr Stolper's *The Story of a Real Man* (1948). Given Stalin's obvious preference for film heroes who could not pose challenges to his role as war-hero-in-chief, it is not surprising that the most vainglorious film in the Stalin cult should be Chiaureli's *The Fall of Berlin* (1949). The film features stylized combat and a kitschy finale in which Stalin descends from the heavens (in an airplane) to greet his smiling multi-ethnic troops in Berlin.

Stalin's death and Khrushchev's Thaw saved the genre from further degeneration, and in fact led to a flowering. It is arguable that the late 1950s and early 1960s were the Golden Age of the Russian war film as directors sought to reclaim the war for the people. They were so successful that the greatest of the war films are also the most important films to emerge from the Thaw: Mikhail Kalatozov's *The Cranes Are Flying* (1957), Grigorii Chukhrai's *The Ballad of a Soldier* (1959), Sergei Bondarchuk's *The Fate of a Man* (1959) and Andrei Tarkovskii's *Ivan's Childhood* (1962). All these films put a human face on the war and complicate the picture of Soviet heroism and sacrifice with views of infidelity, uncertainty and exploitation.

After Khrushchev's ouster in 1964, Leonid Brezhnev set about building a World War II cult with great ambition and earnestness. War movies were an important aspect of the cult and became ever more grandiose; the centrepiece being Iurii Ozerov's eight-hour five-part combat epic *Liberation* (1970–1972), which attracted huge audiences for its first two parts, although attendance dropped precipitously for the final two instalments. There continued, however, to be humanized resistance to such grandiosity, even in commercial films, most notably in Stanislav Rostotskii's *And the Dawns Are Quiet Here* (1972) and Tatiana Lioznova's phenomenally popular television mini-series *Seventeen Moments of Spring* (1973), which became a cult classic.

Art films continued to stretch the limits of the possible: Aleksei Iu. German's *Trial on the Road* (1971) and *Twenty Days without War* (1976) and Larisa Shepit'ko's *The Ascent* (1976). *Twenty Days without War* is an existential journey behind the lines; both *The Trial on the Road* and *The Ascent* deal with the forbidden theme of native collaboration brilliantly, but with differing results. *Trial on the Road* was banned until 1987, while *The Ascent* was shown to great acclaim in international film festivals although its distribution at home was curtailed.

Efforts to break the Brezhnevian mould for the war film became increasingly rare, and by the time of Brezhnev's death in 1982, war film fatigue had set in. The films for the 40th anniversary of Victory Day in 1985 were a forgettable lot, with one startling exception, Elem Klimov's *Come and See* (1985). *Come and See*, which is set in Belorussia in 1943, seeks to bridge the divide between the grand and intimate heritages of the Russian war film and succeeds brilliantly with its story of a teenaged boy's journey through hell. After *Come and See*, the World War II film slipped out of mind as the Soviet film industry collapsed along with the fall of the Soviet Union. There were no '50th anniversary' films in 1995.

The 60th anniversary of the war was another story, as a number of sensational World War II films hit the screen, including the television screen, starting in 2002. The main goal was to revision received truths about the war and to focus on the war's dark side, as we see in Nikolai Dostal's eleven-part RTR series, *Penal Battalion* (2004). A number of interesting art films appeared, including Aleksandr Rogozhkin's acclaimed *The Cuckoo* (2002), but the best of these was arguably Dmitrii Meskhiev's *Our Own* (2004), a compelling and complex story about wartime collaboration that shows how difficult it can be to determine who 'belongs'. Interest in retelling the history of the Great Patriotic War continues, but at a slowing pace.

Russia's contemporary wars – the **Afghan and Chechen wars** – have, not surprisingly, excited the attention of filmmakers and filmgoers alike. The first years of the Russian Federation saw a violent combat film, Timur Bekmambetov's *The Peshawar Waltz* (1994), about Russian POWs, and the much more interesting *The Muslim* (1995) by Vladimir Khotinenko, about a returned Russian POW who has 'gone native'. The biggest box-office hit of the lot of Afghan war films was Fedor Bondarchuk's *Company 9* (2005), which demonizes the Afghans in racist fashion, but also shows how the war has dehumanized good Russian boys.

The films about the Chechen wars are also a mixed lot, some relatively quiet and thoughtful: Sergei Bodrov's *The Prisoner of the Mountains* (1996), Rogozhkin's *Checkpoint* (1998) and Andrei Konchalovskii's *The House of Fools* (2003). Others were loud and violent: Aleksandr Nezvorov's *Purgatory* (1998) and Aleksei Balabanov's *War* (2002). With the exception of *Purgatory*, all these films offer a jaundiced view of Russian involvement in Chechnya, especially *Checkpoint* and *War*, and show how the war has degraded everyone involved.

Generally speaking, Russian film directors have taken their wars very seriously, and films about World War II must be counted one of the most outstanding achievements of Russian cinema.

Denise Youngblood

Arsenal

Country of Origin:
Soviet Union

Language:
Russian intertitles

Studio:
VUFKU

Director:
Aleksandr Dovzhenko

Screenplay:
Aleksandr Dovzhenko

Cinematographer:
Daniil Demutskii

Art Directors:
Iosif Shpinel'
V. Miuller

Composer:
Igor' Belza (restoration:
Viacheslav Ovchinnikov)

Duration:
73 minutes

Genre:
War Film
Revolutionary Film

Cast:
Semen Svashenko
Ambrosii Buchma
Dmitrii Erdman
Sergei Petrov

Year:
1928

Synopsis

Arsenal opens during the late stages of World War I with scenes of hardship in war-torn Ukraine. At the front, Ukrainian troops of the Russian Empire retreat before an advancing German army and many desert. One of the Ukrainian deserters, Timosh, returns to Kiev and joins with Ukrainian Bolsheviks in opposition to the nationalist regime, the Rada. A group of pro-Bolshevik workers declare a strike against the Rada and barricade themselves in Kiev's Arsenal munitions factory. Timosh leads a Red Army detachment which joins the strikers in defending the factory. The Rada army launches counter-assaults, disrupting life in Kiev. After a fierce battle, Rada forces overrun the Arsenal and begin executing its defenders. Timosh makes a last stand against the attackers and proves invincible.

Critique

Arsenal was inspired by historical events, which events in turn figured in Soviet Ukraine's revolutionary lore by the time of the film's production: in January 1918 Ukrainian communists used Kiev's 'Arsenal' factory as the staging area for an armed mutiny against the Central Rada, a newly established nationalist government. The building's battle-damaged exterior wall was preserved in later years as a monument to the Soviet Revolution. In 1928 Dovzhenko was commissioned by the Ukrainian studio VUFKU to make a film on the Kiev uprising so as to mark the tenth anniversary of the event. It was to be a generously budgeted and highly prestigious official project, Ukraine's equivalent of such Russian anniversary films as Eisenstein's *October* (1928) and Pudovkin's *The End of St Petersburg* (1927). 'The assignment to make the film was entirely political', Dovzhenko once noted of *Arsenal's* production, 'set by the [Communist] Party'. *Arsenal* was commissioned as a way to celebrate the revolutionary heroism of the Kiev mutineers, whose armed struggle (according to Soviet histories) helped bring about the eventual Bolshevik victory in Ukraine.

That celebratory dimension remains muted, however, in Dovzhenko's cinematic version of the Soviet Revolution, and this sets *Arsenal* off from most films of the Soviet Revolutionary genre. In fact, the film betrays something of a pacifist strain, as Dovzhenko seems to cast doubt on whether armed revolution is worth the human cost. The film is divided into two unequal parts. The first part concerns the effects of combat during World War I, and predictably – given the Soviet view that the World War was an utterly unredeemed 'imperialist' conflict – the early scenes stress wanton destruction and human suffering. The episode at the front shows soldiers who seem to be helpless against the destructive power of their own weaponry (including poison gas), and scenes in civilian settings show a population rendered catatonic as a side effect of the war experience. The extended second part concerns the revolutionary events in and around Kiev, with armed struggle and its aftermath given considerable dramatic attention. Rather than finding ways to celebrate military heroism in the second part, or even to suggest that the Kiev uprising would lead to ultimate

Bolshevik victory, Dovzhenko dwells on the damage done to the city, to its inhabitants, and to the combatants themselves. Various visual motifs from the World War carry over to the combat scenes in Kiev: e.g., the close-up of a 'laughing gas' victim early in the film finds its visual equivalent at the end in the close-up of a Rada soldier who seems literally to laugh at death. This visual pattern suggests that a cycle of violence from the World War was simply repeated during the Revolution, and the film provides little sense of triumph at the end to justify the conflict.

The conclusion does have one redemptive passage, however, when Timosh proves invincible to the bullets of his counter-revolutionary foes in the film's final moments. Dovzhenko borrows the scene from indigenous folk literature that his original audience would have recognized. In this case, he cites the eighteenth-century legend of a serf rebellion in which the uprising's peasant leader repelled the bullets of his aristocratic enemies. Dovzhenko adapts the motif so as to suggest that a revolutionary spirit can live on, even across the centuries. It is interesting to note, however, that he must appeal to an ancient folk motif so as to justify an episode of modern warfare.

Vance Kepley, Jr

Borderlands (Outskirts)

Okraina

Country of Origin:
Soviet Union

Language:
Russian

Studio:
Mezhrabpomfilm

Director:
Boris Barnet

Screenplay:
Boris Barnet
Konstantin Finn

Cinematographers:
Mikhail Kirillov
Andrei Spiridonov

Art Director:
Sergei Kozlovskii

Synopsis

From 1914 through 1917, families and friendships are torn apart as a town on the outskirts of Tsarist Russia bears the tumult of World War I. Petr Kadkin and his two sons Nikolai and Sen'ka, all cobblers at the local shoe factory, initially stop work in support of fellow strikers at other factories in town. With the arrival of war, Nikolai and Sen'ka eagerly heed the call to defend Russia and are sent to the front, where they experience the horrors of the trenches. Nationalist pride pits Aleksandr Greshin, who runs his own small shoe workshop, against his German boarder and regular partner at checkers, Robert Karlovich. During a bombing raid on the battlefield, Nikolai seeks refuge alongside Müller, a German soldier who is brought back to town as a prisoner of war. Kadkin takes Müller under his care, and romance develops between Müller and Greshin's daughter Man'ka despite Müller's abuse by the angry and resentful townspeople. The Provisional Government takes control and urges a continuance of war, allowing the shoe factory to generate enormous profits manufacturing boots for the Russian troops. Nikolai faces the ultimate punishment for fraternization but is comforted to learn that the Revolution is well underway.

Critique

In Boris Barnet's first sound film, he ambitiously works to reveal the interconnectedness of war to capitalist enterprise and nationalist sentiment, and the film navigates rather complicated ideological terrain to reveal how everyday people are victims of social and economic forces

Composer:

Sergei Vasilenko

Duration:

97 minutes

Genre:

War Film

Cast:

Elena Kuz'mina
Mikhail Zharov
Nikolai Bogoliubov
Nikolai Kriuchkov
Mikhail Ianshin
Khans (Hans) Klering
Aleksandr Chistiakov
Sergei Komarov

Year:

1933

far greater than themselves. There is notably no strong Bolshevik presence throughout the film; therefore, we lack the explicit declaration of correct ideology routinely found in later films, usually manifest in one or more exemplary characters followed across a story arc. Interestingly, the student Aleksandr Kraevich, the principal agitator and presumed mastermind for the strike at the beginning of the film, is quickly exposed as bad, a representative of the Provisional Government. While he is in favour of overthrowing the tsar, he vigorously argues to continue the war on the grounds of patriotism. The film undermines this position both visually and narratively: he is repeatedly framed alongside a bishop and the capitalist factory owner to suggest the ideological alignment between all three, and the plot itself systematically reveals the deadly consequences of such blind devotion to country. Nationalism is shown to be the cause of unnecessary divisiveness; moreover, it is the very means by which the masses are manipulated and sacrificed for the benefit of rich capitalists.

Barnet may not be a typical montage filmmaker in the vein of Eisenstein or Dovzhenko, but in *Borderlands* he skilfully employs montage techniques at key moments in the film in order to underscore the

Boris Barnet, *Borderlands* (1933).

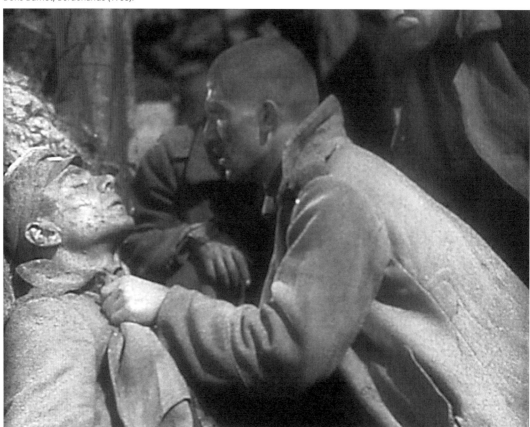

ideological implications of story events. In one particularly bravura example, the film indicts the military-industrial complex of capitalism. After a fellow soldier is killed during a bombing raid, Nikolai tosses the man's now unneeded boot up out of the trench and onto the battlefield. Just before the boot is about to land, there is a cut to two boots landing on a wooden floor. We have been relocated back to the shoe factory, which is now manufacturing these very boots for the military. The factory owner tosses the boots onto an ever-growing pile, and as he moves to toss another pair onto the pile, we get a shot of a bomb exploding. We have returned to another bombardment at the trenches. The editing here indicates both simultaneity and causality, as the labourers and soldiers – one in the same – are being exploited and killed for the economic gain of the factory owner. The boot of the fallen soldier is useless as he is now dead, so it gets tossed away. This single boot is replaced by two brand-new boots, indicating the need to replace this dead soldier as well: the greater the number of soldiers recruited or replaced, the greater the number of boots needing to be manufactured. The steady slaughter of soldiers guarantees the factory owner's continued profits. This message is further emphasized through the use of discordant sound. War profits allow the factory owner to upgrade his manufacturing technology, and in the later half of the film, we see his workers operating large machinery in place of the awls and hammers from before. The sound of this new machinery is exactly the sound of a machine gun, and crosscutting between the new machinery and scenes of battle reinforce the connection. This machinery has replaced the workers in making the boots that these workers now wear as soldiers to be killed on the battlefield; further-more, the machinery has accelerated the rate of replacement for boots and soldiers alike. Similarly, non-diegetic military marches are played ironically throughout the film to both heighten the patriotism of a scene while demonstrating the futility of such a sentiment.

Vincent Bohlinger

Chapaev

Chapaev

Country of Origin:
Soviet Union

Language:
Russian

Studio:
Lenfilm

Directors:
Vasil'ev Brothers (Georgii Vasil'ev, Sergei Vasil'ev)

Synopsis

In 1919 the Russian Civil War hero Vasilii Chapaev leads his Red Army division against the Whites in what is now the province of West Kazakhstan. Commissar Dmitrii Furmanov is sent by the Party to accompany Chapaev on his campaigns. At first, the two argue over matters of leadership, but soon a deep and mutual respect and friendship develops between the two as Chapaev learns much from Furmanov. Young love blossoms as Chapaev's orderly Pet'ka teaches Anna, a new Army recruit, how to operate and maintain a machine gun. In an attempt to prove his worth to Anna and his superiors, Pet'ka sets off to capture a prisoner, only to return after having trapped and released Potapov, a Cossack suffering a cruel test of alle-giance to his White commander, Colonel Borozdin. The Whites launch a 'psychological attack', but are beaten back by Chapaev's forces, with Anna demonstrating great bravery and skill with her machine

Co-director:

Iurii Muzykant

Screenplay:

Vasil'ev Brothers
Anna Furmanova
Dmitrii Furmanov

Cinematographers:

Aleksandr Sigaev
Aleksandr Ksenofontov

Art Director:

Isaak Makhlis

Composer:

Gavriil Popov

Duration:

92 minutes

Genre:

War Film

Cast:

Boris Babochkin
Boris Blinov
Varvara Miasnikova
Leonid Kmit
Illarion Pevtsov
Stepan Shkurat
Viacheslav Volkov
Nikolai Simonov
Boris Chirkov

Year:

1934

gun. Furmanov receives reassignment orders from Mikhail Frunze and takes heartfelt leave of Chapaev. As the Reds encamp in the town Lbishchensk, Borozdin plans a night time sneak attack that leads to a climactic end at the Ural River.

Critique

Based on Anna Furmanova's adaptation of her husband's 1923 novel, *Chapaev* is a pivotal film in the development of socialist realism. The film was released in Moscow on 7 November 1934 in commemoration of the seventeenth anniversary of the Revolution. It proved enormously popular, breaking all attendance records in Moscow. At just one theatre in Leningrad, it was reported that over 80,000 people saw the film within the first three weeks. Indeed, Stalin himself was ultimately reported to have seen the film dozens of times. The commercial and critical success of *Chapaev* was timely, as the film would stand out as the culmination of all the work and progress achieved by the film industry at the fifteenth anniversary of Soviet cinema that January. It was at this January conference that socialist realism was formally adopted by the film industry, and *Chapaev* served as a key example for the appropriate content and style of socialist realist filmmaking.

The narrative trajectory of the film follows Chapaev's growing ideological awareness. At the film's beginning, he has a number of laudable positive traits, and he instinctively knows what is generally right and fair. Throughout the film, however, Furmanov, as the official representative of the Party, systematically explains and instills proper Bolshevik ideology in him – and, by default, in the audience as well. We see Chapaev then impart this new wisdom on his subordinates. Furmanov does not fundamentally change Chapaev; rather, his inherent goodness is refined via his exposure to and adoption of Bolshevik ideology. Similar ideological development takes place across the film within Pet'ka and Potapov.

Scenes in the film often play out a specific ideological lesson embedded within the very action of that scene. For example, after Furmanov places one of Chapaev's officers, Zhikharev, under arrest for permitting his men to pillage from local residents, Chapaev barges in and demands to know who is in charge. Chapaev does not wait to learn Zhikharev's offense; at stake for him is the honour and respect of his troops. As Furmanov and Chapaev argue, a peasant enters and thanks Chapaev for forcing his men to return the stolen goods. It was in fact Furmanov who issued the order, but he allows Chapaev to take the credit. The peasant announces his support for the Red Army because it abstains from the abuses of the Whites. Chapaev is reminded of whom he is fighting for, and he also realizes that he has allegiances and duties to more than just his own men. He then angrily glares at Zhikharev in acknowledgement of the justness of Furmanov's actions. The manner in which this scene is shot and edited helps to underscore the dramatic transition within Chapaev. As Chapaev energetically moves throughout the room while arguing, he and Furmanov are shown in relatively distant shot-reverse shots. At the very moment that Chapaev's loyalties switch from Zhikharev to Furmanov, Chapaev is shown in a dramatic close-up. Moreover, by virtue of the fact that

Vasil'ev Brothers, *Chapaev* (1934).

Chapaev is looking back over his shoulder at Zhikharev, the close-up of Chapaev is a striking diagonal composition. The unusual aesthetic qualities of the shot grab the viewer's attention and expressively reinforce the very moment that Chapaev recognizes the greater Bolshevik cause. With socialist realism, like Soviet montage, ideological transformation is just as important as any plot event.

Over the decades, the film has remained beloved, and it was by far the greatest success of the Vasil'ev Brothers. They are buried together (despite having not been brothers), and an image from *Chapaev* is carved onto their gravestone. Jokes based on the film – of varying degrees of ribaldry – are legion.

Vincent Bohlinger

The Rainbow

Raduga

Country of Origin:
Soviet Union

Language:
Russian

Studio:
Kiev Film Studio

Director:
Mark Donskoi

Screenplay:
Wanda Wasilewska

Cinematographer:
Boris Monastyrskii

Art Director:
Valentina Khmeleva

Composer:
Lev Shvarts

Editor:
N. Gorbenko

Duration:
93 minutes

Genre:
War Film

Cast:
Nataliia Uzhvii
Nina Alisova
Hans Klering
Elena Tiapkina
Anna Lisianskaia
Vera Ivashova

Year:
1944

Synopsis

In a Ukrainian village during World War II, the local population, mostly women, children and old men, unites to resist the German occupiers through death, torture, hunger and extreme cold. The traitors are the mayor, Gaplik, and Pusia, the German commandant Kurt's flighty mistress. Kurt interrogates Olena, a very pregnant, stoic partisan. A boy is shot when he tries to bring her food, and then secretly buried in the family's modest hut. Olena, refusing to give any information, is tortured and shot, but only after Kurt himself mercilessly shoots her baby. Kurt imprisons and threatens to kill villagers who won't say where the grain or the boy are buried. Pusia's attempts to bribe her sister, the stalwart schoolteacher Olga, are unsuccessful. When Germans march prisoners through the village, women and children bring them food despite the danger. Finally the village is liberated, the Germans gunned down, the cowering Pusia shot by her own husband. Fedosia, a strong mother figure, gives a powerful speech trying to keep the village women from killing the Germans with their pitchforks: the Germans should be punished by living to see their armies crushed! A rainbow signals good fortune in the end.

Critique

The Rainbow was filmed in 1943 (released in January 1944), in the middle of fiercest fighting of World War II in the Soviet Union and is perhaps the best of the war films: a realistic, eerily matter-of-fact portrayal of the daily suffering and struggle against the cruel German enemy. The director, Mark Donskoi spent time in recently liberated villages, interviewing the inhabitants, even including the words of a peasant woman in a speech at the film's end. The film had an authenticity and a naked emotional power that amazed audiences, especially abroad, where it was hailed by Italian neo-realist filmmakers and screened at the White House to President Roosevelt's high praise.

Based on a story by a Polish writer, Wanda Wasiliewska, also the film's scriptwriter, *The Rainbow* highlights, like the films *She Defends the Motherland* and *Zoya*, the wartime sacrifice of women. What viewer could forget the agonized face and scream of the partisan Olena, filmed in close-up, as she literally falls towards the viewer while her newborn baby is shot offscreen! Donskoi uses close-ups or shows actual violence sparingly, relegating it offscreen or just demonstrating its results – the many bodies hanging off cruciform-shaped telephone poles. But the mostly spare, realistic cinematography does not offer an emotionally distanced, or nuanced perspective. The film's stark lighting – the Germans' faces shadowed, the heroine's brightly lit or in halo effect, and the powerful orchestral music accompanying the baby's birth and Olena's death, support the renowned critic Neia Zorkaia's statement that 'wartime cinema knew no halftones. We and they, heroism and cowardice, loyalty and betrayal, were the alternatives that dominated every plot, from a short item in newsreels to a full-length feature'. In fact, compared to the unflinching Soviet wartime newsreels with close-ups of dead, mutilated bodies, this emotionally charged film was visually rather restrained.

The film's themes are universal: the village, and the country as family with shared support and sacrifice. When her baby son is killed, Olena speaks of the many 'sons' she has in the forest. A liberator calls a villager 'mother' and she addresses him as 'son'. When Olena is marched barefoot in the snow, the villagers watch, a mother telling her children: 'the German soldier teaches us to value the Soviet way of life'. The word Soviet, however, is soft-pedalled in the film, as are any signs of Soviet power. The Soviet Union here is a Ukrainian/Russian family: while everyone speaks Russian in the film, with an occasional Ukrainianism, the old grandfather actually sings a Ukrainian folk song. Is this Russia or Ukraine? The difference between Ukrainians and Russians is elided as the heroine is played by an acclaimed Ukrainian actress, other villagers are played by Russians and the collaborator, in a daring casting against type, is played by a popular Russian film star.

Whether Ukrainian or Russian, the 'good' villagers share round Slavic features and a hardy Slavic constitution: the weak, sharp-featured, shivering German soldiers are wrapped in many layers against the cold, while Olena survives her forced barefoot march in a light shift. This symbolism of winter destroying the enemy (as it did Napoleon!) was so important that massive artificial snow was created in the summer heat in Ashkhabad (Turkmenistan) where the Kiev Studio had evacuated. Layered with the ever-present Christian symbolism (Olena gives birth in a manger), the film's powerful wartime message was that God, nature and shared Slavic beliefs and traditions would defeat the German enemy.

Vida T. Johnson

The Fall of Berlin

Padenie Berlina

Country of origin:
Soviet Union

Language:
Russian

Studio:
Mosfilm

Director:
Mikhail Chiaureli

Screenplay:
Petr Pavlenko
Mikhail Chiaureli

Synopsis

On the eve of the German invasion, exemplary steelworker Aleksei Ivanov is summoned to Moscow for a meeting with Joseph Stalin. On his return from the capital, an elated Aleksei recounts the impact of this event to his girlfriend Natasha Rumiantseva, but their conversation – which evolves into a mutual declaration of love – is interrupted by a Luftwaffe raid. Wounded by the bombing which also kills his mother, Aleksei loses consciousness. He recovers three months later, only to learn that the Germans have approached Moscow and that Natasha has been captured by the occupiers and driven away to Germany. Vowing vengeance, Aleksei joins the Red Army, soon finding himself in the heat of the Battle of Stalingrad. Aleksei's participation in the Soviet troops' battles is shown against events unfolding in the war's strategic centres: in Stalin's Kremlin and in Adolf Hitler's inner circle, as well as at the Allied conference in Yalta. Finally, Aleksei and his comrades-in-arms take part in the storming of the Nazi capital of Berlin, where he reunites with Natasha and witnesses Stalin's triumphal visit.

Cinematographer:
Leonid Kosmatov

Art Directors:
Vladimir Kaplunovskii
Aleksei Parkhomenko

Composer:
Dmitrii Shostakovich

Editor:
Tat'iana Likhacheva

Duration:
151 minutes

Genre:
War Film
Historical Epic

Cast:
Mikhail Gelovani
Boris Andreev

Year:
1949

Critique

The Fall of Berlin remains one of the most vivid examples of the Soviet genre of 'documentary fiction', a canonic example of the late Stalinist 'Grand Style', a cinematic monument to Stalin's personality cult, and a contribution to the process of the Soviet Union's self-identification as super-power and to the politics of the early, 'acute' Cold War. At the moment of its production and release, it was to represent the late Stalin regime's view of the historical origins of post-WWII global order in a direct, simplified, monologic propagandist mode, and to construe a concise history of the recent war's Soviet episode as a triumph of Stalinist – or rather Stalin's – policy and as a warning to the former allies.

The conscious archaism of *The Fall*'s style is centred on the figure of Stalin, putting his supremacy in the framework of strictly hierarchical religious worship. The extreme artificiality of the film's aesthetic – stylized colour photography, grandiose décor, a glorifying musical score – are summoned to separate Stalin from other, non-divine personages: folkloric characters of common Soviet people, grotesque enemies and the quasi-realistic figures of lesser luminaries, such as FDR or the Soviet marshals and generals. And scenes of combat, the most emblematic and accessible images of war, are assigned in *The Fall* the role of illustrative vignettes within the central narrative of Stalin's wise and effortless decision-making.

In spite of obvious ideological differences, Chiaureli's 'documentary' epic bears a striking resemblance to the Biblical epics produced by the entertainment industry of the Soviet Union's geopolitical adversary not only with the aim of demonstrating the production capabilities of Hollywood but also as the affirmation of traditional religious values in the face of advancing communism. Stalinist culture responded to this challenge on a similar level: with a film no more secular, no less lavish and certainly more ambitious and grandiose than, say, Cecil B. De Mille's *Samson and Delilah* (1949) or Mervin LeRoy's *Quo Vadis?* (1951). However, the cinematic inventiveness of *The Fall of Berlin* is, eventually, an isolated phenomenon, a 'thing-in-itself'; while mass-appeal Hollywood epics contained striking instances of that stylistic and narrative synthesis which irresistibly attracted Soviet filmmakers of the late Stalin era and which could be borrowed by them only to get lost among ideological and narrative immobility.

Sergei Kapterev

The Cranes Are Flying

Letiat zhuravli

Country of Origin:
Soviet Union

Language:
Russian

Studio:
Mosfilm

Director:
Mikhail Kalatozov

Screenplay:
Viktor Rozov

Cinematographer:
Sergei Urusevskii

Art Director:
Evgenii Svidetelev

Composer:
Moisei Vainberg

Editor:
Mariia Timofeeva

Duration:
97 minutes

Genre:
War Melodrama

Cast:
Tat'iana Samoilova
Aleksei Batalov
Vasilii Merkur'ev
Aleksandr Shvorin
Svetlana Kharitonova

Year:
1957

Synopsis

Veronika and Boris Borozdin are in love. When the Nazis attack the USSR, Boris volunteers for service. On the day of his departure Veronika is late and Boris leaves without seeing her. Soon Veronika's family perishes in a bombing raid and the Borozdins take Veronika to their home. Not knowing that his nephew Mark is in love with Veronika too, Boris's father, Fedor, asks him to look after her. Exploiting her emotional vulnerability, Mark rapes Veronika. Boris is killed around the time when Mark rapes Boris's fiancée. Soon Mark announces that Veronika and he have decided to get married. Not knowing about what happened between them, everyone accepts their marriage with visible uneasiness. Veronika doesn't love Mark and cannot forgive herself for betraying Boris. Eventually she leaves Mark. When the Borozdins learn that Boris got killed, Veronika refuses to believe in his death. The war ends and Veronika comes to the train station to meet Boris's friend Stepan who finally confirms Boris's death. In the final scene Veronika gives flowers to people at the station affirming life in the face of her terrible loss.

Critique

Many Russian filmmakers and critics noted that the de-Stalinization of Soviet cinema started with *Cranes*. Kalatozov's home front melodrama redefined the Great Patriotic War as the key event in Soviet culture. If in the decade after the end of the war, war films told primarily the story of Stalin as the architect of victory, for which the entire Soviet nation had to sacrifice itself, Kalatozov chose to depict the war experience as the female protagonist's story of suffering, fall and redemption. In Stalinist films, the representation of the female heroine followed the dictum of Nikolai Simonov's wartime poem 'Wait for Me'. Those who didn't wait for their men were judged as traitors. Kalatozov made such a woman, a woman who failed this ultimate test of the patriarchal order during the war, the sympathetic protagonist of his picture.

Following the storyline of Viktor Rozov's play, on which the film is based, Kalatozov doesn't judge his protagonist and makes the episode of her redemption an ideological alternative to the expected turn of the Stalinist narrative – a state-backed judgment of the traitor. When Veronika works in the hospital, she witnesses a soldier's psychological breakdown when he receives a 'Dear John' letter from his ex-wife. Boris's father pronounces a harsh speech about women who forget about their duty to wait. While he means to support the soldier, he inadvertently hurts Veronika. She is overwhelmed with guilt and tries to commit suicide under the wheels of a train, but in a melodramatic turn of events the place of her attempted suicide turns into a site of last minute rescue and redemption. On her way to the station Veronika saves an orphan boy who is about to be run over by a car. His name turns out to be Boris and she decides to adopt him. The social centre of the melodramatic narrative, the nuclear family, gets miraculously reintegrated and regenerated despite her fiancé's death.

Mikhail Kalatozov, *The Cranes are Flying* (1957).

The potential improvised trial of all the women who failed to wait turns into a melodramatic scene redeeming the perpetrator.

Among the film's numerous awards are the Golden Palm and the first prize for cinematography to the film's cinematographer Sergei Urusevskii (Cannes 1958). Urusevskii, a student of a constructivist artist Alexander Rodchenko, articulated in *Cranes* an innovative visual style that combined the expressive montage evocative of Soviet avant-garde cinema of the 1920s with deep focus and long-takes cinematography characteristic of European art cinema. Most importantly, as opposed to Soviet montage cinema that rejected the individual hero, Urusevskii used conceptual editing inspired by the work of the Soviet filmmakers of the 1920s to represent the individual's inner condition at the moment of crisis. Veronika's attempted suicide and redemption scene is based on such a suspension of continuity editing for the sake of representing Veronika's inner turmoil via montage of attractions: rapid editing, the swirling technique and triple exposures.

To represent an individual in the midst of social upheaval Urusevskii uses long-takes and pans in combination with short focus optics that allowed an unusual depth and layering of space. The long-takes define the style of the farewell scene, in which Veronika runs through Moscow streets in a vain attempt to catch a last glimpse of Boris before he leaves for the frontline. The scene allows Urusevskii to use his mobile camera to a full extent and conclude it with a crane shot of Veronika alone against the tank column. She steps outside the peaceful life into the dehumanized world of war.

Alexander Prokhorov

Ballad of a Soldier

Ballada o soldate

Country of Origin:
Soviet Union

Language:
Russian

Studio:
Mosfilm

Director:
Grigorii Chukhrai

Screenplay:
Valentin Ezhov
Grigorii Chukhrai

Cinematographers:
Vladimir Nikolaev
Era Savel'eva

Composer:
Mikhail Ziv

Editor:
Mariia Timofeeva

Duration:
88 minutes

Genre:
War Film

Cast:
Vladimir Ivashov
Zhanna Prokhorenko
Antonina Maksimova
Nikolai Kriuchkov
Evgenii Urbanskii

Year:
1959

Synopsis

Alesha Skvortsov, a young Russian soldier, shakes off his frontline fears and takes out two Nazi tanks. He is granted a leave to visit his mother to fix her roof, a task he was unable to complete before the war. Alesha claims he only needs one day; his commanding officer grants him six. The young soldier then embarks on a harrowing journey behind the lines of the USSR at war. He encounters a young girl, Shura, who has lost her family; a soldier who has lost his leg and who is afraid to return to his wife; families dislocated by the war; cowardly and brave soldiers; and a woman who has left her soldier husband for another man. Alesha's journey takes him all six days. In the end, he only has time to hug his mother and return to the front. He does not return.

Critique

Ballad of a Soldier is a quintessential Thaw film and one of the most significant Soviet cinematic explorations of World War II. Thaw cinema stressed 'unvarnished reality' over the socialist realism of the Stalin era. Along with other Thaw-era films such as *The Cranes are Flying*, *Fate of a Man* and *Ivan's Childhood*, *Ballad* challenged the prevailing myths of the Great Patriotic War. In particular, Chukhrai subverted the myth that all Soviet citizens responded with heroic patriotism to the Nazi invasion and that all Soviet citizens took part in the Victory. *Ballad* offers nuance where previous Soviet remembrances of the war painted a black and white picture.

Chukhrai's film used a wartime setting to advocate a form of humanist individualism. Alesha is afraid, unsure and naïve. He is motivated more by a desire to help his mother than love for his Soviet motherland or for Stalin (whose absence in the film is particularly important). His fellow Soviet citizens are equally human. Shura is on the run and afraid. The invalid soldier, played by Evgenii Urbanskii, is afraid that his wife will reject him. The families Alesha encounters on his journey are equally unsure about the state of the war and afraid that they will continue to experience more disruptions and more violence. A Soviet soldier who bullies Alesha and Shura and threatens to turn them in for desertion is anything but the heroic defender of the socialist motherland promoted in countless wartime posters and post-war statues. A wife who is unfaithful to her frontline husband also acts out of personal interest and not any commitment to the Soviet cause. In short, what Alesha discovers – and with him, the viewer – is an honest assessment of a society at war. Soviet people, like anyone experiencing the hardships of an invasion, are human beings who are all trying to cope. We see not a monolithic Stalinist citizenry; instead *Ballad* reveals a people struggling during war. At the time, Alesha's consistent acts of kindness offer a believable moral centre to other actions seen on screen. Most importantly, Chukhrai, a decorated veteran, focuses on the individual cost of war. A voice over at the beginning and end of the film explains that Alesha dies at the front. The viewer therefore knows that Alesha's journey home and his brief visit with his

Grigorii Chukhrai, *Ballad of Soldier* (1959).

mother will be his last. *Ballad of a Soldier*, more than any other Soviet film about the war, reveals the sacrifice individuals and individual families made at the front. The Cannes jury awarded it a special prize in 1960 for its 'high humanism and outstanding quality'. Soviet audiences responded to the film for the same reasons – over 30 million people saw it in the cinemas.

Stephen Norris

Ivan's Childhood (My Name is Ivan)

Ivanovo detstvo

Country of Origin:
Soviet Union

Languages:
Russian
German

Studio:
Mosfilm

Director:
Andrei Tarkovskii

Screenplay:
Vladimir Bogomolov
Mikhail Papava

Cinematographer:
Vadim Iusov

Art Director:
Evgenii Cherniaev

Composer:
Viacheslav Ovchinnikov

Editor:
Liudmila Feiginova

Duration:
95 minutes

Genre:
War Film

Cast:
Nikolai Burliaev
Valentin Zubkov
Valentina Maliavina
Evgenii Zharikov
Nikolai Grin'ko
Irina Tarkovskaia

Year:
1962

Synopsis

If one were simply to retell the plot of *Ivan's Childhood*, it could be done in one, albeit long, sentence: a young World War II military scout, a twelve-year-old man-child orphaned during the war, determined and vengeful, wades across a swampy river from behind enemy lines with crucial information on the enemy's whereabouts, and despite his attempt to run away when his superiors try to get him out of the front lines, he goes back on another mission and is killed by the Germans before Russians capture Berlin. But the dark, dirty, sinister and dangerous wartime reality of the story is contrasted with Ivan's vivid dreams – interspersed through the film – of a bright, clean and happy pre-war existence with his mother and sister. Which 'childhood' is the film about then? Although Ivan clearly is killed, as the young lieutenant Galtsev, the only one of Ivan's superiors and caretakers to survive the war, finds his file in a German prison, the film ends with an ambiguous, and unexplained final 'dream' (whose?) of a laughing Ivan running with his sister along the beach, but ominously running towards a dead, black tree which fills the screen in the film's final frame.

Critique

Based on Vladimir Bogomolov's story *Ivan*, a sparse, realistic prose account of the heroic missions and tragic fate of one of the many wartime scouts, Tarkovskii's poetic, and highly subjective, cinematic retelling is no typical war film. There is almost no action, the enemy is mostly unseen, with occasional gun shots and disembodied voices, and two dead scouts eerily sitting on a riverbank with nooses around their necks. Narrative information is spare and imprecise: where is all this taking place? Who is this angry boy who orders about his higher-ups? Why does headquarters know him? What happened to his family? Why does he go back behind enemy lines when his officer friends want him to go to military school to be out of harm's way? In his first feature film, Tarkovskii is already challenging viewers to become what he later described as co-creators of the story. To this end he begins to use what would become some of his favourite devices: elliptical narration, and retroactive explanation of characters' actions. In bits and pieces it is revealed that Ivan is so full of hate for the Germans, and so determined to go on his next reconnaissance mission because his whole family has been killed.

The poetic dream sequences, both lifelike and surreal, revealing Ivan's past, but more importantly his inner feelings, the interweaving of dream and reality, the highly subjective expressionistic camerawork and sound (especially in Ivan's hallucinatory 'game' where, left alone in the bunker, he stalks and kills Germans), the daring use of graphic documentary footage (of the dead bodies in the murder/suicide of Goebbels's family including small children), were a shocking, stylistic and thematic tour-de-force, which challenged and expanded the boundaries of socialist realism. And even among the Thaw-era films which eschewed the large-than-life, patriotic heroes of the late

Stalinist period in favour of real, at times flawed individuals, Ivan was certainly an unconventional 'hero', a warped, damaged man-child. Although it had taken some dozen artistic council meetings and much criticism of the film at the studio, in the liberal Thaw climate, the film was approved for release and almost immediately recognized at home and abroad as a major, though controversial, contribution to Soviet, and world, cinema. Tarkovskii was to become (along with Parajanov) internationally the most highly acclaimed filmmaker from the Soviet Union from the 1960s to his death in the mid-1980s and beyond.

Although Tarkovskii had taken over the filming of *Ivan* from another director, and was not formally credited with any script work, *Ivan's Childhood*, the film he called his 'qualifying examination', already had a distinctive 'Tarkovskian' stamp. In terms of film style he was yet to develop his signature lengthy takes and slow tracking shots (found in his next film, the magisterial *Andrei Rublev*), and soon gave up the self-aware virtuoso camerawork, with odd angles, rapid swish pans and energetic editing (of the dreams and hallucinatory sequences). But his addition of Ivan's dreams introduced a major theme: the inner as well as outward journey of the hero, and a natural world that is both hallucinatory and palpably real, beautiful or ugly, living or dead (the rain and apples in Ivan's dream and the scorched earth of his

Andrei Tarkovskii, *Ivan's Childhood* (1962).

waking reality), but always lovingly shot from extreme close-up to long shot. (Tarkovskii closely oversaw his directors of photography to create his own visual style.) Tarkovskii's favourite motifs – water, fire, horses, trees, bird sounds, much beloved from his own childhood, added in this film, as in many to follow, the personal, autobiographical element that made Tarkovskii's films haunting, mysterious and yet universal.

Vida T. Johnson

The Commissar

Komissar

Country of Origin:
Soviet Union

Languages:
Russian
Yiddish

Studio:
Gorky Studio

Director:
Aleksandr Askol'dov

Screenplay:
Aleksandr Askol'dov

Cinematographer:
Valerii Ginzburg

Art Director:
Sergei Serebrennikov

Composer:
Alfred Schnittke

Editors:
Natal'ia Loginova
Svetlana Liashinskaia
Nina Vasil'eva

Duration:
104 minutes

Genre:
War Drama

Cast:
Nonna Mordiukova
Rolan Bykov
Raisa Nedashkovskaia
Liudmila Volynskaia
Vasilii Shukshin

Year:
1967 (released 1988)

Synopsis

Klavdiia Vavilova, a Red Army commissar during the Russian Civil War, becomes pregnant while away at the front. By the time she returns to base it is too late to have the abortion she wants. She is billeted on the Jewish Magazannik family. At first a very unwilling mother, she grows into the role, especially thanks to her developing friendship with Maria, the devoted mother of many young children; Vavilova becomes the proud mother of Kirill, named for her lover. When the Whites threaten the town in which she is stationed, she realizes the importance of the Revolutionary cause, in part because of a 'pre-vision' of the Holocaust, and what will happen to people like the Magazanniks. She returns to the front, leaving her baby with the Magazanniks. In an open ending the viewer is left wondering what will become of her and her baby.

Critique

Aleksandr Askol'dov's film *The Commissar* needs to be located in three quite separate decades. The movie is set during the post-Revolutionary struggles of the early 1920s; it was made in 1966–1967, just as the Khrushchev inspired 'Thaw' was rapidly drawing to a close. However, sadly for the filmmaker, whose only film this turned out to be, the film saw the light of day only during the glasnost era of the 1980s, when it was released to great acclaim in 1988. In fact, Askol'dov could hardly have chosen a more unpropitious time (in terms of Soviet cultural politics) to try to make this film. Although Askol'dov did not know this at the time, the manuscript of *Life and Fate* by Vasilii Grossman, on whose story 'In the Town of Berdichev' *The Commissar* would be based, had been seized four years earlier. A 'witch hunt' was beginning, signalled by the arrests of Siniavskii and Daniel among others. Later the outbreak in June 1967 of the Six Days War, involving Israel, would be the final blow for the film, with its 'Jewish theme'.

From the period of the film's making onwards, the essence of the controversy surrounding the film has centred around, first, the persona of the female commissar, Klavdiia Vavilova, and second, and more particularly, around her decision towards the end of the film to relinquish her baby son Kirill to the care of the Magazanniks, the Jewish family with whom she has been billeted. On the one hand, Askol'dov himself informed the Goskomitet in 1967 that 'motifs clearly convey

Aleksandr Askol'dov, *The Commissar* (1966).

that, in leaving her baby, the heroine goes on to defend the Revolution and consequently the life and future of her son as well as millions of children around the world'. However, his claims have not persuaded some recent critics as to the meaning of his film and its conclusion. A common view is that, though Vavilova clearly believes in her cause, her zeal leads to inhumanity, in that she abandons her young baby, only (probably) to die shortly afterwards herself. According to this reading, the ending of the film shows how the individual was all too easily sacrificed to the so-called 'common good' – as Askol'dov himself was ironically and tragically to discover.

Indeed, the qualities of *Commissar* show how much might have been achieved in a full directorial career. The film is very simply constructed, with the birth scene at the very centre of the narrative structure. This sequence is also the most striking visually, with a whole series of almost surreal metaphors conveying both the pain of childbirth, but also its symbolic significance for the character and the politics of the film. Mordiukova handles supremely well the transition from burly, brusque, great-coated disciplinarian to smiling new mother in frock and headscarf. The Jewish family is deftly characterized, emphasizing the traditional roles of man and woman, but with both ultimately supporting Vavilova in her dealing with the ethical and political dilemmas she faces. Shot in crisp black and white, with sparing but very effective use of music, the movie captures evocatively the buffer region that is the town of Berdichev. Though ultimately the director's claims for his only film stand up, it was clearly too ambivalent in its opinions – and especially its ending – for the neo-Stalinism of the prevailing political climate of the late 1960s, on the eve, of course, of the crushing of the 'Prague Spring' and other forms of 'socialism with a human face'.

Joe Andrew

The Ascent

Voskhozhdenie

Country of Origin:
Soviet Union

Languages:
Russian
German

Studio:
Mosfilm

Director:
Larisa Shepit'ko

Screenplay:
Iurii Klepikov
Larisa Shepit'ko

Cinematographers:
Pavel Lebeshev
Vladimir Chukhnov

Art Director:
Iurii Raksha

Composer:
Alfred Schnittke

Editor:
Valeriia Belova

Synopsis

The Soviet partisans are fighting an uphill battle against the German invaders in Belarus. After a skirmish, a partisan detachment is stranded in a forest without supplies or ammunition. Two men are dispatched to procure food – a battle-hardened veteran, Rybak, and a schoolteacher turned soldier, Sotnikov. Plowing through a snowy desert, they eventually stock up on provisions, but on the way back run into a German patrol and seek refuge in the house of a local woman. She is unhappy about the visitors, but hides them when the Germans arrive. They are captured and imprisoned along with their hostess. Later they are joined in their cell by the local headman (who is in fact a partisan helper) and a Jewish girl. Sotnikov and Rybak are interrogated by the collaborator Portnov. Sotnikov is put to torture but refuses to divulge any information about his comrades or himself. A more pragmatic Rybak seeks compromise with his captors, hoping to survive, but the next morning all five are led to execution. Rybak finally breaks down and begs for mercy, agreeing to change sides. After Sotnikov and the others are executed, he attempts suicide but fails and is left alone screaming into the wilderness.

Critique

The Ascent, based on the Vasil' Bykov novella Sotnikov, is that rarity, a Soviet war film that has won equal acclaim in the West and at home. It also turned out to be Larisa Shepit'ko's last completed film before her untimely death in a car accident in 1979. The liberal Soviet intelligentsia was thrilled to see a film that overimposed Christian allegory onto a familiar Soviet genre, with Sotnikov standing in for Christ, Rybak as Judas and Portnov as Pilate. The image of telegraph poles that begins and ends the film resembles nothing so much as a row of crucifixes. Some western viewers are still baffled why the Soviet censors let it

Larisa Shepit'ko, *The Ascent* (1976).

Duration:

109 minutes

Genre:

War Drama

Cast:

Boris Plotnikov
Vladimir Gostiukhin
Sergei Iakovlev
Liudmila Poliakova
Victoria Gol'dentul
Anatolii Solonitsyn
Nikolai Sektimenko
Maria Vinogradova

Year:

1976

pass. Hadn't they noticed the religious parallels? They certainly had. Communism had always viewed itself as a quasi-religion, and in the 1970s its waning appeal as an ideology made its custodians seek new ways of legitimization. One was Russian nationalism, another Christian faith. This is not to say that Shepit'ko and her companions were propagating communist dogma, but it does explain the tacit approval from the authorities. However, it is also the reason why some post-communist Russian critics (e.g. Aleksandr Shpagin) are dissatisfied, pointing out that Sotnikov is not a Christ, for he does not carry the Word, only sacrifices himself, like Olena Kostiuk from *The Rainbow* (1943, Mark Donskoi) or *Zoya* (1944, Lev Arnshtam) before him. The Soviet myth cannot be a receptacle for religious consciousness because they teach very different moral lessons and are, in the end, irreconcilable.

Time has certainly made many viewers look at the film's central parable through critical eyes. Ironically, it is the Christ-like Sotnikov that now seems, at least to this reviewer, the weakest and least believable character. He remains a cipher: we never learn what gives him the strength to endure his martyrdom. The frightened Rybak asks him in prison, 'Now what? Into the pit? To feed worms?' Sotnikov's response is: 'That is not the worst. Now I know. The main thing is to have a clear conscience'. It is hard to argue with Rybak's contemptuous retort: 'You are a fool, Sotnikov. And you've been to graduate school'. Earthy, astute and level-headed, Rybak is neither a coward nor a natural-born traitor. He is much easier to identify with than the impossibly angelic Sotnikov. Even the devilish Portnov (Tarkovskii's stalwart Anatolii Solonitsyn) evokes a certain morbid curiosity about man's capacity for evil. A choirmaster before the war, who taught children Revolutionary hymns and nineteenth-century Russian songs, he has turned into a monster playing cat-and-mouse games with his helpless victims. When the Soviet filmmakers wanted to impart a degree of humanness to Nazi collaborators, they usually hinted that they had been victims of dekulakization or other Stalinist terrors. No such explanation is offered here, but the character is not one-dimensional. He seems to be genuinely intrigued and bothered with the Sotnikov case, a case he is bound to lose morally.

Whatever its flaws, *The Ascent* belongs, together with Elem Klimov's *Come and See*, among the best of war films, putting to shame such overpraised but simplistic Hollywood fare as *Saving Private Ryan*. The starkly beautiful black-and-white cinematography captures people's faces and wintry landscapes in crystalline detail. The sketches for the film by production designer Iurii Raksha are works of art in themselves, as is the music by Alfred Schnittke. *The Ascent* is a rich and rewarding viewing experience and the British Film Institute placed it on its 360 best films list in 1993.

Sergey Dobrynin

Come and See

Idi i smotri

Country of Origin:
Soviet Union

Languages:
Russian
Belarusian
German

Studios:
Belarusfilm
Mosfilm

Director:
Elem Klimov

Screenplay:
Ales Adamovich
Elem Klimo

Cinematographer:
Aleksei Rodionov

Art Director:
Viktor Petrov

Composer:
Oleg Ianchenko

Editor:
Valeriia Belova

Duration:
142 minutes

Genre:
War Drama

Cast:
Aleksei Kravchenko
Olga Mironova
Liubomiras Lauciavicius
Vladas Bagdonas
Jüri Lumiste
Viktor Lorents
Kazimir Rabetskii
Evgenii Tilichev

Year:
1985

Synopsis

Nazi-occupied Belarus, 1943. Fifteen-year-old Flera leaves his protest-ing mother and his sisters to join the partisans in the nearby woods. He embraces the life of a resistance fighter until excluded from an important mission. Disgruntled, he wanders away and meets the bewitching partisan girl, Glasha. Together they escape a German air raid which destroys the camp and leaves Flera half-deaf. Upon return to village, Flera learns that his family and others have been mas-sacred, and blames himself. He rejoins the detachment and goes on an ill-fated mission, only to witness the death of his comrades and to seek refuge in another village on the day it is slated for destruction by the SS. The Germans and their collaborators herd the villagers into a barn and set it on fire. Flera is left for dead in the burned-down village. The partisans ambush and execute the Germans. Flera, whose ordeal has turned him into a wizened old man, shoots at the discarded portrait of Hitler. The shooting alternates with documentary footage of Hitler's life run in reverse until he appears as a baby. Flera stops shooting. The final caption says 628 Belarusian villages were destroyed by the Nazis in World War II.

Critique

A perfect companion piece to *The Ascent*, directed by Klimov's wife Larisa Shepit'ko, *Come and See* complements the visual and narrative austerity of the former with baroque imagery and unrestrained emo-tion. Both are based on canonical works of Belarusian 'partisan prose' (Vasil' Bykov's *Sotnikov* and Ales' Adamovich's *The Khatyn Story*, respectively) and both have abandoned the dry, lapidary book titles for ones with biblical allusions (*Come and See* references the Book of Revelation 6:1). The two films capture and bookend a cultural moment when the Great Patriotic War has ceased to be a recent memory and begun to demand a more metaphysical treatment, yet before any historical re-evaluation has become possible.

These films are markedly different from the early, Thaw-era attempts at 'God-seeking' in Soviet war cinema, but they also stand in contrast to each other. While *The Ascent* presents Sotnikov as a Christ figure who wins a spiritual victory over his tormentors, there are no such consolations in *Come and See*, no heroism or hope of redemption, except on the symbolical level. Its would-be hero is unaware of his true role: that of a helpless victim and the viewer's guide on a tour into the heart of darkness. Some of the film's most excruciating moments occur when the character's tender age and idealism are pitted against un-childlike reality. The film's most horrific scene may not be the final fiery death of a village, but Flera's return to his home where everything speaks of tragedy: his little sisters' dolls scattered across the floor, the soup on the stove, untouched and still warm. Flera wilfully misinterprets the ominous signs, blab-bering excitedly that his mother and sisters 'have left'. Is he naïve or in deep denial? A more mature Glasha chokes on the soup offered her and takes the boy away, glancing back only once to see a mound of corpses behind the house. After that, the horrors keep coming without a minute's pause. This relentless insistence on the narrative of victimhood and suffering sets *Come and See* apart from other coming-of-age-in-a-war films, such as Evgenii Evtushenko's contemporaneous, poeticized *Kindergarten* (1983) or Andrei Tarkovskii's *Ivan's Childhood* (1962), which was released by a US video distributor as *The Youngest Spy*. Somebody apparently saw fit to re-package it as a conventional war story. *Come and See* will never be known as *The Youngest Partisan*.

A film like this could appear only at a particular, pivotal moment in Soviet history, coming out as it was on the very eve of glasnost and actually helping usher it in. It could not have been made a few years before – as witnessed by Elem Klimov's seven-year struggle to lift the project, initially called *Kill Hitler*, off the ground. And were it to be made later, its partisan characters would probably be less saintly and its Nazis less single-mindedly evil. However, these vestiges of Soviet propaganda do not distract from the powerful panorama of man's inhumanity to man. The point-of-view Steadicam camerawork of Aleksei Rodionov is masterly without being showy, and the colour palette is suitably sombre, conveying an almost physical sensation of a foggy rural morning or a rainy day in the forest. The dialogue by Klimov and Adamovich (a mix of Russian and Belarusian) was startlingly realistic for its day and still retains its freshness.

Sergey Dobrynin

Checkpoint

Blokpost

Country of Origin:
Russia

Language:
Russian

Director:
Aleksandr Rogozhkin

Screenplay:
Aleksandr Rogozhkin

Producers:
Sergei Sel'ianov
Konstantin Ernst

Cinematographer:
Andrei Zhegalov

Art Director:
Vladimir Kartashov

Editors:
Aleksandr Rogozhkin
Sergei Gusinskii
Iuliia Rumiantseva

Synopsis

During the 1990s Chechen War a Russian military unit enters a house in a local village looking for rebels. A mine explodes killing a boy, and the soldiers are attacked by village women who blame them for the boy's death. A local policeman and a woman are killed. The soldiers are transferred to a remote checkpoint, with an invisible sniper. With little to do the young soldiers settle into a routine. They have sex with a deaf-and-mute woman, who is brought to the outpost by her sister Minimat; they travel to a nearby village to buy dope; they play cards and tricks on one another. One of the soldiers even has a budding romance with Minimat. One day a military convoy arrives from the village where the bloodshed took place. The unit's commander realizes that the Russian general betrayed him and his people to pacify the local population. One soldier is taken away, and a few days later his mutilated body is left on the road by the checkpoint. The soldier who finds the body sits down in despair, and this is when the sniper, who is revealed to be Minimat, takes her shot. The soldier she kills is her lover. Minimat's sister trips over a wire, Minimat cries out in horror.

Critique

Russia's war with Chechnya, which began in 1994, shortly after the collapse of communism, and has continued on and off into the new millennium, became a subject of heated public debate and the setting

Duration:

85 minutes

Genre:

War Drama

Cast:

Roman Romantsov
Kirill Ul'ianov
Denis Kirillov
Andrei Krasko
Zoia Buriak
Aleksei Buldakov
Denis Moiseev
Iurii Grigor'ev

Year:

1998

for many films of the 1990s. Like a score of other war films before and after it, *Checkpoint* portrays Chechens as aliens, unpredictable and incomprehensible. Their speech is never translated. In this respect, the deaf-and-dumb girl – whose fiancé left her after she had been raped by Russian troops – *is* Chechnya. As viewers we might be sympathetic to her but the point-of-view of the film is unmistakable and honestly Russian. In fact, one of the soldiers in the group provides a voice-over narration, and his comment, 'Nobody knows what we are doing here', gives the film an absurdist touch but does not change the fact that these young and nice Russian boys *are* there with guns.

At the same time, *Checkpoint* strikes the viewer by its unconventional minimalism in dealing with such a theme. The narrator introduces each of his buddies by a nickname, explaining the origins of those: Ratso has a pet rat, Scag is a dope fiend, Bones – the narrator himself – shed all his fat in the army. This personal treatment intensifies viewer identification with the young soldiers at the remote checkpoint. They have nothing to do there except for the guard duty, and in that, as the narrator informs us, they are protecting the road to the local cemetery. The camera keeps soldiers in tight close-ups and medium shots, bringing them closer to the viewer and separating them from the surrounding landscape, just as language separates them from the locals. We only get a look at the mountains when soldiers look at them through their rifle sights as they try to locate the sniper.

But this minimalism is well calculated. The film is framed by two instances of violence: the explosion and shoot-out in the village at

Aleksandr Rogozhkin, *Checkpoint* (1998).

the beginning and the rapid series of deaths at the end. These two sequences explode into the narrative abruptly, reminding the viewer that the war – as invisible and absurd as it might seem – is for real. All but one of these deaths seem unpremeditated or accidental. The boy explodes the mine when he plays with it. The two people in the village die during the ensuing commotion. The sniper shoots the soldier she likes because he exchanged his helmet with his buddy. The only premeditated murder is the death of the soldier deemed responsible for the tragedy in the village.

This is a war with no mission or heroism but with real death. The anti-war message is annunciated in the matter-of-fact narration and the mundane activities, including various bodily functions. Rogozhkin, a master of absurd comedy with a 'Russian national' flavour, remains true to himself in *Checkpoint*. At the centre of the narrative space is a perfect symbol of the incongruity: the outhouse. This is a place of privacy and peace, a daily chore of cleaning and a reminder of normalcy. It is also a target for the sniper, a fourteen-year-old Chechen girl who shoots Russians with the very same bullets they pay her with for sex with her dumb sister.

Elena Prokhorova

War

Voina

Country of Origin:
Russia

Language:
Russian

Studio:
CTB

Director:
Aleksei Balabanov

Producer:
Sergei Sel'ianov

Screenplay:
Aleksei Balabanov

Cinematographer:
Sergei Astakhov

Art Director:
Pavel Parkhomenko

Editor:
Marina Lipartiia

Synopsis

Hostages are held for ransom by a band of Chechen terrorists led by Aslan Gugaev: Ivan Ermakov, a young Russian soldier; Captain Medvedev, an inspirational leader; and John and Margaret, two English actors. Aslan sets John and Ivan free to collect ransom for Margaret. When the British and Russian governments refuse to negotiate with the terrorists, John devises a plan to free Margaret and to film the hostage rescue for a British television station. John travels to Tobolsk to enlist Ivan in his scheme. Ivan has tried unsuccessfully to adjust to civilian life, so he accepts John's offer to help rescue the hostages. Back on Chechen territory, Ivan kills some Chechens, steals their jeep, takes a shepherd hostage, and they make their way to Aslan's camp. Ivan and John manage to free the hostages and capture Aslan. When John learns that Margaret had been brutally gang-raped by the Chechens, he kills Aslan in a fit of rage. They flee with Aslan's band in hot pursuit. After a harrowing attempt to escape downriver, they are rescued by Russian helicopter gunships. In the epilogue, we learn that Ivan has been arrested for the murder of Chechens.

Critique

Like his earlier blockbusters *Brother* and *Brother 2*, Aleksei Balabanov's *War* presents a politically charged and controversial look at the aftermath of imperial collapse in the former Soviet Union. While the *Brother* films depicted the mean streets of Petersburg, Moscow and Chicago in the 1990s as an urban free-fire zone in which

Music:

Viacheslav Butuzov

Duration:

120 minutes

Genre:

War Film

Cast:

Aleksei Chadov
Giorgii Gurgulia
Ian Kelly
Ingeborga Dapkunaite
Evklid Kurdzidis
Sergei Bodrov Jr
Vladimir Gostiukhin

Year:

2002

the recently demobilized Danila Bagrov outsmarts and defeats the brutal mobsters who have filled the post-Soviet power vacuum, *War* plays out a similar vigilante narrative in a real free-fire zone during the Second Chechen War (1999–2002). Like Danila Bagrov, Ivan Ermakov is an army veteran and Russian everyman hero who reluctantly takes up arms against a violent band of Chechen terrorists and, against all odds, carries the day. But Ivan's victory is transformed into defeat by a society that, because it neither recognizes its heroes, nor understands what it means to be at war, is doomed to failure.

The central question posed by *War* concerns what lengths a civilized state can legitimately go to defend itself against fanatical enemies who reject the rules of war. Although Balabanov's main interest is with Russia's conduct of the Chechen war, this question is, of course, directly relevant to the Global War on Terror that the West has been fighting since September 11, 2001. Although Ivan's actions in Chechnya are brutal and technically illegal, the film portrays him as a hero for his recognition that in war the only rules are to help your friends and kill the enemy. In this sense, all talk about human rights and rules of engagement is either naïve and wishful thinking or, simply, hypocrisy. By transforming the film's representative liberal, the English actor John, into a cold-blooded killer by the film's end, Balabanov suggests how easily idealistic western principles can disintegrate in the crucible of war. When Ivan is arrested for killing Chechen citizens of the Russian Federation, Balabanov is protesting the absurdity of extending civil protection to people who are openly at war with Russia.

Many critics and viewers have been repulsed by what they see as a crudely nationalistic call to arms to Russians fed up with national weakness, political correctness and western critics of Russia. But while challenging conventional notions of military restraint in anti-terrorist operations and satirizing western liberals, Balabanov's film cannot be reduced to simple propaganda for the harsh anti-terrorist policies put into effect by Putin's government. In fact, the director's depiction of the Russian government, police and armed forces as corrupt, incompetent and apathetic to the needs of ordinary people is no less devastating than his portrait of the Chechen enemy.

For challenging what he sees as the dominant culture of political correctness, Balabanov and his films have often been called racist. The director has, it is true, made such criticism more convincing by provocative and outrageous comments at press conferences and on his movies' official websites. But while Balabanov's characters do use racial epithets and positive Chechen characters are completely absent from *War*, it is difficult to see how this differs from many classic Hollywood war movies, especially those made during on-going military conflicts. Certainly Aslan Gugaev, the leader of the terrorists, is a classic one-dimensional villain, a violent and brutal sadist without religion or honour. Yet Aslan teaches Ivan an essential truth: that strong and hard men are needed in times of war and that the Russians are doomed as long as they are led by incompetents and cowards who fail to understand the true nature of military conflict.

Anthony Anemone

Our Own

Svoi

Country of Origin:

Russia

Language:

Russian

Studio:

Slovo

Director:

Dmitrii Meskhiev

Producers:

Viktor Glukhov
Sergei Melkumov
Elena Iatsura

Screenplay:

Valentin Chernykh

Cinematographer:

Sergei Machil'skii

Art Directors:

Aleksandr Stroilo
Zhanna Pakhomova

Composer:

Sviatoslav Kurashov

Editor:

Marina Vasil'eva

Duration:

111 minutes

Genre:

War Film

Cast:

Konstantin Khabenskii
Sergei Garmash
Mikhail Evlanov
Bogdan Stupka
Anna Mikhalkova
Fedor Bondarchuk
Natalia Surkova

Year:

2004

Synopsis

Set in German-occupied territory in the early months of World War II, *Our Own* begins with a Nazi attack on a Red Army unit. A Russian NKVD officer (Garmash) and a Jewish Commissar (Khabenskii) change out of their uniforms and into peasant clothes to avoid being shot. They are captured and meet up with a third man from their unit, a peasant sniper named Mit'ka (Evlanov). When their prison column nears the sniper's village, the three escape. They end up in Mit'ka's father's barn. Mit'ka's father (Stupka) spent years in the Gulag and has returned to become village headman. His village is occupied by Nazi soldiers and collaborators. Mit'ka and his comrades threaten the delicate balance that the father has helped to maintain in difficult circumstances. Eventually, the soldiers attempt to escape and to join up with the Red Army.

Critique

Our Own appeared as part of a wave of movies and television series that revisited the Great Patriotic War's significance in the Putin era. The film explores one of the central issues of wartime – the way in which populations are divided into 'ours' and 'theirs'. Meskhiev does not settle for simple definitions of these terms and uses his wartime setting to expose the ways that the Stalinist system worked. He sets his film in a town occupied by the Nazis, a place where the local population must choose between resistance and collaboration, passivity or action, life and death. These choices force the characters in the film to confront the issue of who exactly is 'our own'. In the case of the village headman this choice divides his family. The tension that the film depicts revolves around the headman and his choices – who, ultimately, is *svoi*? His son, whose escape leads the Nazi occupiers to ratchet up searches in the village? His daughters, whose frontline husbands' actions also threaten to destroy the peace? His fellow villagers, including Mit'ka's girlfriend Katia (Anna Mikhalkova), who has also learned how to survive under Nazi occupation? The two escapees and Red Army members, who represent the system that sent him to the camps? Or his occupiers, some of whom are friends also upset with Soviet power? Meskhiev's film blurs the lines between 'our own' and 'them', categories that Stalinist culture attempted to define clearly. Moreover, none of the characters represent an officially approved 'ours' in the Stalin era: POWs, kulaks and anti-Soviet collaborators are not part of the ideal Soviet society.

The subtitle of Meskhiev's film offers a clue into the way in which the film plays with the existing myths about the war – *Holy War, Usual Story (Sviashchennaia voina, obychnaia istoriia)*. The story told in *Svoi*, however, is far from the 'usual' one about the war. While the Germans remain enemies, the film suggests that the 'real' enemies are as likely to be 'your own' people. The end of *Svoi* expresses these debates quite clearly. The village headman, after his son has killed the local police chief, turns to the NKVD officer and points his gun. The officer, thinking he will be killed, cries out 'I'm one of yours, one of yours (Ia zhe svoi, svoi)'. The headman answers: 'no one is going to hurt you', then watches as the officer runs way. However, the headman tells his son to follow the NKVD man, imploring him 'to go and defend the

Dmitrii Meskhiev, *Our Own* (2004).

motherland'. Despite his hatred for the regime, the old man accepts that he does have a homeland and that it does represent something important for him. *Our Own* therefore sheds light on a Soviet taboo topic: the experience of occupation. It ultimately offers a tense, believable story about patriotism and heroism in the face of invasion that expands Soviet-era cinematic narratives.

Stephen Norris

Company 9

9-aia rota

Country of Origin:
Russia

Language:
Russian

Synopsis

Company 9, set during the final two years of the Soviet-Afghan War (1987–1989), tells the story of a group of young Soviet soldiers whose wartime experience bonds them together. The first half of the film concentrates on the soldiers' physical and psychological training at boot camp. The second half of the film, based on actual historical events, takes place in Afghanistan and focuses on Company 9, into which five of the soldiers from boot camp enter. As the group endeavours to secure a safe mountain passage into the Khost province, they reach the height of 3234 metres; the number comes to signify the locale of the definitive battle that defeated the company.

Studios:

Art Pictures

1+1

Matila Rohr Productions

Slovo Production

Company:

STS

Ukraine Media Group

Director:

Fedor Bondarchuk

Producers:

Fedor Bondarchuk

Elena Iatsura

Sergei Mel'kumov

Aleksandr Rodnianskii

Screenplay:

Iurii Korotkov

Cinematographer:

Maksim Osadchii

Art Director:

Grigorii Pushkin

Composer:

Dato Evgenidze

Editor:

Igor' Litoninskii

Duration:

135 minutes

Genre:

War Film

Cast:

Fedor Bondarchuk

Aleksei Chadov

Ivan Kokorin

Konstantin Kriukov

Artem Mikhalkov

Mikhail Porehenkov

Irina Rakhmanova

Artur Smol'ianinov

Year:

2005

Critique

Five years in the making and with a budget of 9 million dollars, the highest of any Russian film ever made at the time of its production, *Company 9* was conceived to be a blockbuster. The film is packed with Russia's best male actors, both newcomers (Chadov, Smol'ianinov and Kriukov) and veterans (Bashirov and Govorukhin). No expense was spared: the latest cameras, top-quality special effects and sound editing done by the London studio Pinewood Shepperton combine to make a professional feature film with undeniable mass appeal – it grossed $23.47 million in its first month on the big screen. The grandiose scale of this debut film hints at the director's privileged position within the post-Soviet film industry. Son of Sergei Bondarchuk, who directed the Soviet classics *Fate of a Man* (1959) and *War and Peace* (1966–1967), Fedor Bondarchuk's access to stars, technology and funds is a rarity.

Fedor Bondarchuk's experience directing television advertisements can be sensed in *Company 9*, which focuses less on the historical causes and repercussions of the Afghan War, and, instead, makes emotional appeals to nostalgia, patriotism and friendship. In a sense, with *Company 9* Bondarchuk is selling something: he 'rebrands' the Soviet-Afghan War by looking back at it with a positive retrospective glance. Use of dreamlike slow-motion shots of soldiers hugging and cheering after successfully accomplishing a training mission conveys the sense of sentimentality that pervades the film. Intimate displays of friendship – for example a scene of the boys sweaty and in various stages of undress lying on one another as they pass a joint and take turns making love to a mythical village girl before being deployed to Afghanistan – constructs the soldiers into a legend about the formative experience of war. Importantly, this wartime camaraderie is linked to patriotic goals. As the soldiers graduate from boot camp, the camera, level with a waving Soviet flag, peers down on the rows of young men through the red flag. The metaphor is clear: Bondarchuk's film is filtered through a patriotic Soviet perspective.

The celebration of the soldiers' strong bonds to one another and the dignity ascribed to the Soviet mission in Afghanistan pairs strangely with the film's visual and narrative quotations taken from American films about the Vietnam War. The first half of *Company 9* borrows liberally from Stanley Kubrick's classic *Full Metal Jacket* (1987). Bondarchuk, following Kubrick, opens his film in the military barbershop as the young soldiers get their heads shaved. In both films the soldiers are given nicknames: in *Full Metal Jacket* the monikers include Private Joker, Private Pyle, Private Cowboy and Private Snowball; in *Company 9* there is Liutyi (Fierce one), Chugun (Iron), Vorobei (Sparrow) and Gioconda (i.e, the artist). The drill sergeant of *Company 9* is visually modelled on the sergeant of Oliver Stone's *Platoon* (1986) – he, too, has a distinguishing scar on his right cheek. In his behaviour, he's reminiscent of Sergeant Hartman (R. Lee Ermey) from *Full Metal Jacket*: the Soviet drill sergeant (an atypical character in the Russo-Soviet war film tradition), following the example of Hartman, greets his soldiers with insults and punches to the stomach. However, whereas the Vietnam War film employs biting satire to critically comment on war, Bondarchuk's film does not ridicule the Soviet campaign in Afghanistan and does not wonder whether the young soldiers lost their lives for a legitimate cause. The goal of *Company 9* is to sustain the myth of the Soviet soldier within the post-Soviet culture industry. Ironically, it takes a Hollywood-sized budget, British sound editing and reference to the American Vietnam War film to perpetuate this Soviet legend.

Dawn Seckler

COMEDY/ COMEDY COMEDY MUSICAL COMEDY

Since its very early years, Russian film has enjoyed a rich and diversi-
fied tradition of comedy, and some of the best pre-Revolutionary
films were comedies. Evgenii Bauer's *Cold Showers* (1914), and *The
Thousand and Second Ruse* (1915), are both very funny early examples of the genre, combining bedroom farce (including cross-dressing)
with portrayals of the 'modern' woman. But it was with the birth of
the Soviet cinema industry that film comedy really developed its own
identity, and created its own stars. One of the most accomplished
films of the so-called 'Golden Age' (1924–1930) of Soviet cinema was
Lev Kuleshov's *The Extraordinary Adventures of Mr West in the Land
of the Bolsheviks* (1924), which combined political satire – the West's
ignorance of the new Soviet reality – with knockabout farce, including car chases, a cowboy running amok in Moscow and mistaken
identity. Kuleshov's nod to Hollywood was noted and criticized. The
decade also produced satirical comedies by Iakov Protazanov, such
as *The Trial of the Three Million* (1926), with its easy NEP targets such
as thieves, clergy and businessmen, *Don Diego and Pelageia* (1929),
a clever send-up of petty bureaucracy and *St Jorgen's Feast* (1930),
which similarly ticks the right boxes in its mockery of religion.

Protazanov not only made comedies that were popular, but also
ideologically 'safe'. He helped launch the career of perhaps the Soviet
Union's greatest comic film actor, Igor' Il'inskii, who would later create
some of Soviet cinema's most durable comic characters. But as the
criticism of Kuleshov had shown, comedy was a problematic genre
with its potential for subversive laughter and social satire, and the film
comedies of the succeeding decades were required to support state
objectives.

Those who set the ideological agenda during the predominance
of socialist realism wished to direct humour into acceptable channels,
so it is no surprise to learn that the comedies of the 1930s and 1940s
were rarely laugh-out-loud funny. But they did not need to be, and the
function of comedy became defined as serving the state in showing an
optimistic and 'life-affirming' view of the world, especially life in Stalin's
Soviet Union. A last hurrah is Grigorii Aleksandrov's *Jolly Fellows*

Leonid Gaidai, *The Diamond Arm* (1968).

(1934), with its (literally!) knockabout slapstick and celebration of jazz as the expression of the sheer exuberance of life. One of the first 'musical comedies', it is distinctive in that it is at least funny (though it proved controversial on its release).

Aleksandrov's subsequent comedies, such as *The Circus* (1936), *Volga-Volga* (1938), *The Radiant Path* (1940) and *Spring* (1947), all light-hearted vehicles for his wife Liubov' Orlova, feature music by Isaak Dunaevskii and predictably cute outcomes. But they also embed the twin narratives of Stalinist culture: life is good and getting better, and individual drive and commitment to the cause can bring success and happiness. The life-as-fairytale motif reaches its epitome at the climax of *The Radiant Path*, where Tania Morozova (Orlova) is whisked into an aerial motor tour of the country by her fairy godmother.

Ivan Pyr'ev's collective farm musicals, such as *The Rich Bride* (1937), and *Tractor Drivers* (1939), posit the village as an astonishingly cultural habitat, especially in terms of musical ability, a motif that reaches its apogee in *Kuban Cossacks* (1949), where the village shop has a grand piano for sale. These films all starred Pyr'ev's wife, Marina Ladynina, another singing blue-eyed blond, and were intended to celebrate the recent collectivization of agriculture as an unequivocal triumph for the peasants' way of life. *Kuban Cossacks* was singled out for criticism by Khrushchev after Stalin's death for its blatant 'falsification' of reality.

Comedies of the 1930s and 1940s were popular, and justified the regime's desire to make 'cinema for the millions'. These were films that people wanted to see, and the musical comedy was the most popular genre of the Stalinist period. They also embedded a narrative of inclusivity and participation, where apparently ordinary folk could achieve social advancement. In Aleksandr Ivanovskii's *A Musical Story* (1940), a taxi driver becomes an opera singer (though he is played by the outstanding tenor Sergei Lemeshev), and Ivanovskii focuses, too, on the everyday life of people living in communal apartments. Konstantin Iudin's *A Girl with Character* (1939), and *Four Loving Hearts* (1941), are light-hearted narratives set among ordinary townsfolk and the military. An interesting facet of the Stalinist comedy is the admission, in Tat'iana Lukashevich's *The Foundling* (1939) and Iudin's *Twins* (1945), of homeless children, but in these films, of course, children are returned to their parents.

The death of Stalin saw the re-emergence of film satire. Though not a satire as such, Mikhail Kalatozov's *Loyal Friends* (1954) tells its audience that the 30 years of Stalin's rule were not happy times, and that real happiness was to be experienced in the 1920s, and again, hopefully, since the death of Stalin. It also reminded Soviet filmgoers that film could actually be funny as it depicted the various mishaps encountered by three childhood friends who meet up after 30 years and, all pillars of the Soviet establishment, decide to take a river trip and recapture the fun and enjoyment of their youth.

The Thaw years also saw the emergence of the two major figures in post-war film comedy: El'dar Riazanov and Leonid Gaidai, both of whom would dominate film comedy for the next two decades. Riazanov's first major success was *Carnival Night* (*Karnaval'naia noch'*, 1956), with Igor' Il'inskii reprising his persona from *Volga-Volga* as an obstructive administrator who, in one brilliant scene, totally deconstructs a proposed sketch to anaemic absurdity. Riazanov's subsequent comedies proved very successful and struck a chord with a responsive audience as they addressed topical social issues, be it car ownership, women in the workplace, the increasing impersonality of big cities or the black economy that was becoming more and more of a necessity amid the wholesale *deficit* of 'advanced socialism'. *The Unbelievable Adventures of Italians in Russia* (1973) was highly unusual in that it was a Soviet-Italian co-production that featured well-known Italian and Soviet comic actors (Andrei Mironov, Ninetto Davoli), but also managed to pull of some impressive visual stunts. *Irony of Fate, or Enjoy Your Sauna!* (1974) continues to be shown on Russian TV on New Year's Eve, and in 2007 most of the original cast (including Riazanov himself in a cameo) were reassembled for a sequel, though not directed by Riazanov. *The Garage* (1979) is almost a call to arms, showing the rebellion and chaos that ensues when the weakest and most vulnerable citizens reject the platitudes and coercion of those in authority.

Riazanov was able to cast some of the country's best-loved actors in his films, including Valentin Gaft, Andrei Mironov, Andrei Miagkov, Alisa Freindlikh and Liudmila Gurchenko. Leonid Gaidai also had his own 'stable', especially the trio of 'ViNiMor', Georgii Vitsin, Iurii Nikulin and Evgenii Morgunov, in a phenomenally popular series of films in the 1960s, depicting the hapless adventures of these three Soviet stooges as they engage in various anti-social and illegal activities (poaching, brewing home-made vodka, kidnapping). *The Diamond Arm* (1968) was voted in 1995 the best Soviet comedy ever, starring Iurii Nikulin, Andrei Mironov and Anatolii Papanov in a hilarious story of smuggling and mistaken identity. *Ivan Vasil'evich Changes Profession* (1973) achieves the difficult task of eliciting pity for a time-travelling Ivan the Terrible as he encounters the barriers of Soviet bureaucracy. Whereas the best comedies of Riazanov relied on witty verbal exchanges and satirical undertones immediately understood by a knowing Soviet audience, Gaidai's comedy was less socially concerned and more physical, with much use of trick photography.

Soviet film comedy fell into decline in the late 1980s as directors were able to address topics from the recent past or social ills of the present that were far from funny. In the post-Soviet period directors such as Dmitrii Astrakhan, Aleksandr Rogozhkin and Iurii Mamin have tried to persuade an impoverished and demoralized population that there is comedy in their troubled times. These are narratives that emphasize the goodness of ordinary Russians and their endurance of social ills, where excessive vodka drinking is celebrated as a national virtue, rather than the killer of thousands of middle-aged men every year. However, Valerii Todorovskii's *Hipsters* (2008) offers an exhilarating and liberating celebration of youth culture in the early 1960s with a clear post-modern wink that removes the deadpan seriousness of 'history'.

Film comedy was at its most popular in the otherwise dark years of Stalinism, and again in the period of economic and social 'stagnation' of Brezhnev's rule, and this can be no coincidence. In both periods, the political leadership needed narratives to legitimize their authority, and to persuade the citizenry that society was stable, progressive and just; but the citizenry, too, needed to be persuaded, and occasionally they wanted to laugh.

David Gillespie

The Cigarette Girl from Mosselprom

Papirosnitsa ot Mossel'proma

Country of Origin:
Soviet Union

Language:
Russian

Studio:
Mezhrabpom-Rus

Director:
Iurii Zheliabuzhskii

Screenplay:
Aleksei Faiko
Fedor Otsep

Cinematographer:
Iurii Zheliabuzhskii

Art Directors:
Vladimir Balliuzek
Sergei Kozlovskii

Duration:
79 minutes

Genre:
Comedy

Cast:
Igor' Il'inskii
Iuliia Solntseva
Nikolai Tsereteli

Year:
1924

Synopsis

An old chestnut – a film about film – with an even older scenario – three men competing for the attention of an attractive young woman. Yet, historically and geographically, the story is clearly set in contemporary Moscow, with ample footage of streets, trams, carriages, shops, monuments, the river and a racecourse. The casting of one of the eponymous heroine's admirers as a portly bespectacled and bow-tied American businessman, Oliver MacBride, sets the action against Russia's New Economic Policy. An office clerk, Mitiushin, of a foolishly romantic disposition, similarly fixes upon the heroine, Zina Vesenina, as his object of affection, despite his being averse to smoking, making even the camera sway queasily. Meanwhile, a film director temporarily takes a shine to Mitiushin's long-suffering, buxom neighbour. Zina's third suitor is the film director's cameraman, Latugin. *The Cigarette Girl* leaves the viewer in little doubt, ever, as to where Zina will eventually bestow her favours. But it is fun to find out just how, one fine day, she finally comes to see herself on screen, from a theatre box above stalls occupied by enthusiastic fellow cigarette sellers.

Critique

Against a setting of New Moscow, Latugin's affection for Zina (Solntseva) is confirmed by her omnipresence in the rushes screened of his footage of 'New Moscow': Zina smiling on a bridge; at a fountain; on the street (and, again, with flowers); at the university; at the river; in a park and ushering children in a parade. Having once discovered her by chance, Latugin (Tsereteli) proceeds obsessively to pose test shots of Zina, who, in turn repeatedly rebuffs MacBride's lascivious advances and his invitation that she work as a model for him. Zina is keen to return to him the change from an enormous note with which he has paid for a packet of *papirosi*. For MacBride, Zina is the equivalent of the dumb painted mannequin that he transports in one of the numerous hampers and cases accompanying him on his visit. (The carriage from the station collapses under the combined weight of its passenger and his luggage.) Meanwhile, the hapless clerk (Il'inskii) mistakes a stunt dummy thrown from a bridge for Zina herself: elaborately crossing himself and nervously procrastinating at the water's edge, he finally launches himself into the shallows and doggy-paddles towards the body – only to be disappointed before managing to topple his rescuers' boat. The director resuscitates Mitiushin's neighbour.

Such 'tricks' of the cinema were commonly reported in 1920s popular Soviet cinema journals. Similarly, the rude rejection of the clerk's unsolicited, hand-penned film script was an experience with which a number of film fans and viewers of *The Cigarette Girl* could, perhaps, blushingly share. Many fans dreamed of being 'discovered', just as American stars were reputed and reported to have been found by chance. The bossy director shouts instructions through a megaphone and wields measuring sticks to position his actors in correct focus. In the film's slapstick and chase sequences there was yet more to amuse a popular audience, even if, on its release, it failed to satisfy Moscow's more serious critics. Much of the entertainment is supplied by Il'inskii who, from 1920, worked as an actor in Meyerhold's Theatre. His set-piece turns here provide a case study for the application of bio-mechanical technique and broadly drawn caricature (abetted by a prosthetic nose, affected boater and cane, and, after a visit to the barber's, a swaggeringly worn, impressively waxed moustache). When MacBride offers the clerk his fat paw, Il'inskii continues to shake through his entire body for moments afterwards; a drunken encounter with a lamp post sends him reeling backwards and forwards across the street; at dinner he downs not only his own glass but every glass on the table; frightened by a knock on the door, Il'inskii's feet fail to find his slippers.

This physical humour is offset by Zina's tenderness and Solntseva's more naturalistic performance. She gently lays a rose on the hidden stash of cigarette packets that Matiushin has bought from his favourite vendor. Solntseva becomes self-consciously amateurish for Latugin's footage of his amateur inamorata.

Amy Sargeant

The Girl with a Hatbox

Devushka s korobkoi

Country of Origin:
Soviet Union

Language:
Russian

Studio:
Mezhrabpom-Rus

Director:
Boris Barnet

Screenplay:
Valentin Turkin, Vadim Shershenevich

Cinematographers:
Boris Frantsisson
Boris Fil'shin

Art Director:
Sergei Kozlovskii

Duration:
68 minutes

Synopsis

Wide-eyed and spirited Natasha Korosteleva makes hats with her grandfather in their small cottage near Moscow. Each morning, Natasha fends off the clumsy advances of the love-struck Fogelev as she travels to the city to bring her hats to the pretentious Madame Irène, who owns a millinery shop and cheats the Housing Committee by falsely registering Natasha as the resident of her spare room. One day on the train, Natasha encounters the strapping, big-footed Il'ia, who has come to Moscow to study and cannot find a place to live. A series of mishaps keeps Natasha wary of Il'ia, but she soon takes pity and schemes to marry him in order to grant him legal entitlement to Irène's spare room. Irène and her husband Nikolai are angered and attempt to expose Natasha and Il'ia's marriage as fraudulent. They even fire Natasha, but in place of Natasha's earned wages, Nikolai pays her with one of his lottery tickets. After that ticket wins a 25,000-ruble jackpot, madcap frenzy ensues as Nikolai tries to reclaim his ticket, while Il'ia and Natasha discover and try to prove their love for each other.

Critique

The Girl with a Hatbox both embodies and lampoons many of the contradictions in Soviet society during the era of the New Economic Policy (NEP). The New Economic Policy allowed small-scale privatization to exist within the state-run economy throughout most of the 1920s in order to re-energize and grow the decimated post-Civil War economy, yet those who participated in this government-sanctioned capitalism were prone to ridicule as NEPmen and NEPwomen. In

Genre:

Comedy

Cast:

Anna Sten
Vladimir Mikhailov
Vladimir Fogel'
Ivan Koval'-Samborskii
Serafima Birman
Pavel Pol'
Eva Miliutina

Year:

1927

the film, Nikolai conforms to the physical stereotypes attributed to a NEPman, analogous to the typage of a western capitalist: a pudgy build, dressed in a suit and wearing a bowtie and pince-nez spectacles. Irène is similarly depicted as westernized, with her foreign name, boyish figure and flapper-esque layered skirts. She puts on airs and feigns a delicate constitution, all the while haranguing and bullying everyone around her. She and Nikolai trick members of the Housing Committee into believing that Natasha lives with them so that they can use their spare room to host dinner parties for their hoity-toity, effete friends. They even have a maid, Marfushka, who seems content to serve them, despite the heightened sense of class consciousness that should have accompanied the Revolution. Although these characters are sketched broadly for laughs, they also serve as the antagonists of the film and exhibit behaviour to be shunned and condemned in Soviet society.

The film also mocks absurdist aspects of everyday life, no doubt recognizable to contemporaneous audiences. Il'ia endures the Moscow housing shortage and is forced to sleep outside in the snow for want of a room. After Natasha cleverly secures Il'ia the spare room of Irène

Boris Barnet, *Girl with a Hatbox* (1927).

and Nikolai, he faces the tensions of communal living: he is spied upon during his vigorous morning workout and is shown navigating confusedly through rows of hanging laundry while attempting to locate the washroom sink. Fogelev is seen struggling to maintain his footing on icy pathways through the snow, and passengers waiting at Fogelev's station must chase after a suburban train that overshoots the boarding platform. The physical comedy pervading the film was carried out by actors trained in Kuleshov's studio and the Meyerhold theatre.

The Girl with a Hatbox represents the kind of Soviet filmmaking that was often considered to be in opposition to montage filmmaking. It is 'popular cinema', seemingly devoid of an overt ideological message and made expressly to entertain rather than educate its audiences. As a comedy, the film draws upon the widely practised conventions of its genre. The narrative is configured around a love triangle, and its consequent romantic entanglements result in an entirely predictable happy ending that nevertheless is framed as having arisen due to chance. These generic norms were viewed by critics as emblematic of the film's western and bourgeois sensibility. Just as the Soviet economy under NEP could be seen as a compromise of questionable ideology, a film such as this was deemed similarly questionable, an unjustified compromise with capitalist filmmaking practices that irredeemably permeated the very content and style of the film. In fact, the film itself served as an extended promotion for the state lottery system. Still, despite the film's supposed lack of ideological rigor, it is admittedly often witty and thoroughly zany. The Girl with a Hatbox is a testament to the diversity to be found in Soviet filmmaking of the 1920s, and it certainly lives up to its professed goal of entertaining its audiences.

Vincent Bohlinger

St Jorgen's Feast Day

Prazdnik sviatogo Iorgena

Country of Origin:
Soviet Union

Language:
Russian

Studio:
Mezhrabpom

Director:
Iakov Protazanov

Screenplay:
Iakov Protazanov
Vladimir Shveitser

Synopsis

The Cathedral of St Jorgen is preparing for its celebration of the saint's feast day, a major profit centre for the church. In order to extract even more money from the people, the church is preparing an historical film on St Jorgen's life and miracles. Pilgrims flood the town with their offerings; the priests sell relics. The bishop and bankers count their loot. In the meantime, a notorious criminal, Michael Korkis has escaped from prison, with the help of his trusty sidekick. The police discover the two men on their train out, but they manage to escape again, dressed as nuns. Hearing of the riches the church collects on the feast day, the two men (dressed as themselves again) join the pilgrimage to the cathedral. After numerous diversions and chases, Korkis finds himself locked in the cathedral he planned to rob. His only way out is to impersonate the saint. Miracle! Miracle! He forgives the people's sins without payment, to the horror of the priests. 'St Jorgen' beckons his sidekick to be 'cured', marries the saint's 'bride', a woman he had flirted with earlier, and the happy trio escapes across the border, loot in hand.

Cinematographer:

Petr Ermolov

Art Directors:

Sergei Kozlovskii

Vladimir Balliuzek

Anatolii Arapov

Composer:

Sergei Boguslavskii

Duration:

80 minutes

Genre:

Comedy

Cast:

Igor' Il'inskii

Anatolii Ktorov

Mariia Strel'kova

Igor' Arkadin

Mikhail Klimov

Year:

1930

Critique

St Jorgen's Feast Day appeared in the third year of the Cultural
Revolution that accompanied Stalinization. The Cultural Revolution
called for the arts to be 'in the service of the state', and the film
served the campaign against religion, one of the cornerstones of
the cultural upheaval of the late 1920s and early 1930s. The alliance
between the clergy and capitalists in extorting the masses is clearly
shown.

Protazanov, who was one of early Soviet cinema's most prominent
popular directors, displays his light touch for weighty issues; the
bishop and his cohort are stereotyped as money-grubbers and con
men, but amusingly so. They merely dupe people who are eager
to be duped, sedated as they are by the 'opiate' of religion. His
two crowd-pleasing stars – Anatolii Ktorov as the suave Korkis, and
Igor' Il'inskii, as his bumbling accomplice – bring established comic
personas to the shenanigans. (The sight of the knobby-kneed Il'inskii
being examined by a team of doctors called by the church must
have resulted in audience mirth.) As the object of Korkis's affections,
and the beautiful bride of the saint, Mariia Strel'kova provides some
amusing moments; she enjoys being in on the confidence game. As a
result, the film seems a high-spirited romp rather than a hate-monger-
ing diatribe.

The film is also important as an example of the way the early Soviet
sound film combined silent film aesthetics with sound. (Soviet cinema
had a great deal of difficulty making the transition to sound.) The
sound track (added in 1935) mainly consists of naturalistic effects –
bells ringing, hymn singing, dogs barking – but also puts incidental
music to good use. There is also some talking, as the bishop recounts
the tale of the miracle in the framing story that punctuates the film.
Certain scenes employ intertitles and sound together.

Protazanov is not generally remembered as a master of the mass
scene, but in this film, he displays a flair for moving crowds and
individualizing them. He uses crane shots to tower over the masses
of people converging onto the roads leading to the town and then
to the cathedral. The streets gradually fill with pilgrims, whose class
background is evident in the close-ups of their pinched and wrinkled
faces. Their eyes are vacant as they shout hosannas. There is an example of associative montage when the film cross-cuts from the crowd to
a herd of cows being whipped across the road. The film was received
by critics of the time as being 'valuable' and 'well made'.

Denise J. Youngblood

Happiness

Schast'e

Country of Origin:
Soviet Union

Language:
Russian

Studio:
Moskinokombinat

Director:
Aleksandr Medvedkin

Screenplay:
Aleksandr Medvedkin

Cinematographer:
Gleb Troianskii

Art Director:
Aleksei Utkin

Duration:
66 minutes

Genre:
Comedy

Cast:
Petr Zinov'ev
Elena Egorova
Lidiia Nenasheva

Year:
1935

Synopsis

Happiness tells of Khmyr' and his wife, Anna, impoverished peasants in pre-Revolutionary Russia. Khmyr' dreams of being a wealthy man with great riches and property. This dream is almost realized when he finds a purse full of money and is able to buy property and a horse. However, a combination of thieves, a kulak (rich peasant) and various representatives of the state gradually expropriates his new-found wealth. In a state of despair Khmyr' decides that he is going to die, yet even this desire is thwarted by religious and military figures who tell him that, given his role as a food producer for the country, he has no right to kill himself. He is taken away by tsarist soldiers and suddenly finds himself in the 1930s, in the context of communal farming. Khmyr' does not conform to the demands of the collective and still harbours individualistic dreams. Meanwhile, the kulak Foka starts to sabotage the farm and tries to burn horses to death in their stable. Khmyr' prevents this from happening and suddenly becomes a hero. This acts as the catalyst for an apparent change of heart as Khmyr' discards his old peasant costume and looks towards a new future.

Critique

Happiness is a truly remarkable film, particularly when one considers the context in which it was produced. By the mid-1930s Soviet cinema, oriented toward mass audiences, was already making films that often, if not always, followed uninspired narrative formulas, featuring political heroes or class enemies. Yet there is little about Medvedkin's film comparable to the typical cinema product of the time. Like his previous work, *Happiness* gives a humorous and honest portrayal of country life. It focuses on individual experience and shows the harsh realities of this life as an endless struggle for resources and survival. Although the film is a statement against greed (the original title was *Stiazhateli, The Possessors*), the viewer is, to some extent, supposed to sympathize with Khmyr' and the true aspirations of the Russian peasant. Medvedkin later pointed out that he aimed to expose Khmyr''s dream and idea of happiness as unrealistic and, although Khmyr' seems to change his attitude towards the collective farm at the end of the film, there is an element of ambiguity and, overall, an absence of the cliché of coming to political consciousness.

The film is extremely imaginative, adopting a mise-en-scène and narrative that are reminiscent of the witches and country bumpkins of Russian folklore and the visual codes of the lubok (woodcut). This setting combines with a dark satirical humour which, by the 1930s, was the exception rather than the rule in Soviet cinema. Khmyr''s failure 'to die' and lie in his coffin and the desperate nun's failed attempts to commit suicide on a revolving windmill are among the humorous moments that stand in stark contrast to the toothless comedy of state-approved works of literature and film.

Indeed, *Happiness* raises the question of the function of comedy and satire in the USSR. It has been suggested that Medvedkin's strategy of satirical exposure as a means of persuading people to improve their approach to work or social life may have been intended to work in favour of the Soviet regime, but the director's biting comedy, allied to his eccentric filmmaking style, also threatened to undermine that regime, especially in the eyes of many Bolsheviks. It was this very ambiguity in *Happiness* that led to its eventual withdrawal from cinemas.

Jamie Miller

Circus

Tsirk

Country of Origin:
Soviet Union

Language:
Russian

Studio:
Mosfilm

Director:
Grigorii Aleksandrov

Screenplay:
Il'ia Il'f
Evgenii Petrov
Grigorii Aleksandrov
Valentin Kataev

Cinematographers:
Vladimir Nil'sen
Boris Petrov

Art Director:
Georgii Grivtsov

Composer:
Isaak Dunaevskii

Lyrics:
Vasilii Lebedev-Kumach

Duration:
94 minutes

Genre:
Musical

Cast:
Liubov' Orlova
Evgeniia Mel'nikova
Vladimir Volodin

Synopsis

Marion Dixon, an American star performing at the Moscow circus, falls in love with Russian performer Ivan Martynov, who introduces her to the values of Soviet society. Franz von Kneischitz, Dixon's abusive manager, tries to foil the romance by implying, through an intercepted letter, that Marion loves the amateur inventor Skameikin, and ultimately attempts to ruin Dixon by revealing her secret: she has an illegitimate mulatto child. However, the Russian circus audience welcomes the child without prejudice, Kneischitz is disgraced and possibly arrested, and Skameikin in reunited with his true love, the circus director's daughter, Raechka. Dixon remains in the land of the Soviets, marching with Martynov and the other circus performers in the May Day parade on Red Square.

Critique

The plot of *Circus* is based on Il'f and Petrov's play *Under the Big Top* which Aleksandrov saw at the Moscow Music Hall, quickly deciding on a film adaptation as his next project. The director transformed Il'f and Petrov's comedy about Soviet circus life, which satirized the political fashions of the day, into a musical comedy film with elements of melodrama, embodying the core myths of High Stalinism and the ideals of the new Stalinist constitution: the Soviet New Man, the Great Family, the spontaneity-consciousness paradigm of socialist realism, the archetype of the Leader, racial equality, international solidarity of workers, state support for mothers and children. After the success of Aleksandrov's first musical comedy film, *Happy Guys*, the cinema leadership was so enthusiastic about Aleksandrov's new project that he was permitted to begin work without the usual schedule and budget plan required by the studio, an exception that later caused production problems and delays. *Circus* was the director's most stylistically imaginative and tightly structured film, largely due to his collaboration with Vladimir Nil'sen, who had just returned from the United States with a thorough understanding of American production practices and technology. In *Circus*, the film's composer, Isaak Dunaevskii, formulated the musical model which was to govern his work in cinema for the rest of his career: a central song to be elaborated throughout the film, one that would be popular outside the movie theatre; musical leitmotifs for major characters; extensive use of illustrative music to convey central plot peripeteias to the viewer. The musical centrepiece of the film, 'Song of the Motherland', with its memorable melody and patriotic message quickly became a second Russian national anthem.

Sergei Stoliarov
Pavel Massal'skii
Aleksandr Komissarov
Emmanuil Geller
N. Otto
Jim Patterson
Fedor Kurikhin
Aleksandra Panova
Solomon Mikhoels
Lev Sverdlin

Year:

1936 (restored 1970)

During World War II the song preceded announcements of official orders and later, the call sign with which Radio Moscow began its morning broadcasts was the first line of 'Song of the Motherland'.

In *Circus* the semantics of the circus plot overlay the syntax of the show musical, combined with elements of the folk musical in its Stalinist iteration. Making a show (the development of the Soviet circus act 'Flight to the Stratosphere') parallels the making of a couple identified with differing cultural and ideological values: the American artiste Marion Dixon and the Soviet performer Ivan Martynov. The secondary comic couple, one of whom is a rival to the hero or heroine, is also present in Skameikin and Raechka. Elements of the folk musical, in which the making of the couple parallels the formation of a community at the local and national levels, enter the plot as Martynov teaches

Grigorii Aleksandrov, *Circus* (1936). Martynov, Dixon and Jimmy.

Grigorii Aleksandrov, *Circus* (1936). Marion Dizon in a solo number.

Marion the 'Song of the Motherland', realizing through a song rather than a kiss both the couple's declaration of love and patriotic devotion to the USSR. The musical's traditional dual focus on a central hero and heroine is diminished because Liubov' Orlova, the pre-eminent movie star of the Stalin era, is the narrative focus of the film. Nevertheless, the dual focus still manifests itself in secondary oppositions: the home-grown hero vs a foreign heroine; communist vs capitalist ideologies; Martynov's ethic of socialist collectivity vs Dixon's focus on individual life experiences; social stability and order vs chaotic passions and deviation from conventional norms of morality (Dixon's past). *Circus* concludes with multiple finales à la Aleksandrov: the conclusion to the romantic plot with the reunion of Dixon and Martynov, the conclusion to the social narrative in the acceptance of Dixon's black baby by the circus audience, and the conclusion that opens out into the greater (and real) Soviet world of the May Day parade on Red Square.

Rimgaila Salys

Anton Ivanovich Gets Angry

Anton Ivanovich serditsia

Country of Origin:
Soviet Union

Language:
Russian

Studio:
Lenfilm

Director:
Aleksandr Ivanovskii

Screenplay:
Evgenii Petrov
Georgii Munblit

Cinematographer:
Evgenii Shapiro

Art Directors:
Abram Veksler
Semen Mandel'

Composer:
Dmitrii Kabalevskii

Editor:
Aleksandr Ivanovskii

Duration:
80 minutes

Genre:
Musical comedy

Cast:
Nikolai Konovalov
Liudmila Tselikovskaia
Pavel Kadochnikov
Tat'iana Kondrakova
Sergei Martinson
Vladimir Gardin

Year:
1941

Synopsis

Anton Ivanovich Voronov is a highly respected professor at the Moscow Conservatoire, who places the music of Bach above everything else and regards it as the ultimate yardstick by which other musical accomplishments must be measured. His daughter, Serafima, is an aspiring singer with great potential, and her father's anger is aroused when she begins singing in the operetta composed by Aleksei Mukhin, thus abandoning what he considers the higher calling of opera. Mukhin's work, however, demands a high level of ability from his soloist, and Anton Ivanovich is persuaded of the legitimacy of operetta as a musical genre when, in a dream, he is visited by Johann Sebastian Bach himself, who tells him that 'people need all kinds of music'.

Critique

A film that begins by contrasting and then ends with reconciling the elevated genre of classical music with the more prosaic operetta. It is also a narrative of social inclusivity in which the finale includes all the major characters. Otherwise, this is a light-hearted comedy of manners, here reduced to musical tastes. There is a budding romance between Mukhin and Serafima, but it takes second place to the compatibility of their musical gifts. The guiding motivation of both Anton Ivanovich (Konovalov) and Mukhin (Kadochnikov), the operetta composer, is quality: both strive for the best and recognize only the best, refuse to compromise their principles and recognize in each other kindred spirits only at the very end. The film therefore demonstrates that opera and operetta can live alongside each other in Stalin's Russia. The opulence of Anton Ivanovich's home environment (with servants) is worthy of note, a sign of old-worldly grandeur that can be achieved in the 'new' world by those with talent and drive. Whereas elitism is eschewed, stratification according to talent and worth are affirmed.

However, the most interesting character in this otherwise cheery and sun-blessed story is the hack composer Kerosinov (Martinson), who works not to satisfy his inner Muse but simply for money, and who reveals himself to be venal, cynical and manipulative, willing to exploit others for his personal gain. Unmasked as a 'tale-teller', 'ignoramus' and 'rogue', he is every bit the opportunist who would thrive on denunciation and strife. But this danger cannot be confronted in musical comedy, and at the end of the film Kerosinov even plays in the orchestra that performs the 'symphonic poem', an intermediate genre that unites both feuding composers and family members of different generations. The film is also noteworthy in that it was the first starring role for Liudmila Tselikovskaia, and for the cameo appearance (as Bach) of the pre-Revolutionary director Vladimir Gardin.

David Gillespie

Kuban Cossacks

Kubanskie Kazaki

Country of Origin:
Soviet Union

Language:
Russian

Studio:
Mosfilm

Director:
Ivan Pyr'ev

Screenplay:
Nikolai Pogodin

Cinematographer:
Valentin Pavlov

Art Directors:
Boris Chebotarev
Iurii Pimenov
Georgii Turylev

Composer:
Isaak Dunaevskii

Editor:
Anna Kul'ganek

Duration:
111 minutes

Genre:
Musical comedy

Cast:
Marina Ladynina
Sergei Luk'ianov
Vladimir Volodin
Aleksandr Khvylia
Sergei Blinnikov
Klara Luchko
Ekaterina Savinova
Vladlen Davydov
Andrei Petrov
Iurii Liubimov
Boris Andreev
Valentina Telegina
Konstantin Sorokin

Year:
1949 (restored 1968)

Synopsis

The film is set in the fertile Kuban' area of Southern Russia where peasants from several collective farms converge for the post-harvest fair. The youthful romance of widowed Galina Peresvetova, chair of 'Lenin's Precepts' kolkhoz, and Gordei Voron, chairman of the 'Red Partisan' farm, is rekindled when they meet at the fair. The romance of a young couple – the agricultural worker Dasha from 'Red Partisan' and the horse breeder Nikolai from 'Lenin's Precepts', also blossoms at the fair, but the couple become pawns in the rivalry between the quarrelling kolkhoz chairmen whose pride, hot temper and competitiveness, along with a series of comic misunderstandings, stand in the way of their reconciliation. Nikolai wins the horse race, the culminating event of the fair, thereby forcing Voron to honour his agreement and allow him to marry Dasha. In the chairmen's horse-and-buggy race, Peresvetova initially takes the lead, but seeing Voron's distress, holds back her horse, allowing him the satisfaction of winning the race. When Voron demands that Nikolai move to his kolkhoz as another condition of marriage, the couple marry without his blessing and move to Peresvetova's kolkhoz. The two chairs quarrel again over the young couple, but are reconciled through the mediation of the regional Communist Party leader.

Critique

Kuban Cossacks is Ivan Pyr'ev's last, technically most accomplished and ultimately his most controversial musical comedy film. Much of its success was due to the music of Isaak Dunaevskii, whom Pyr'ev was able to recruit as composer for the film, after Aleksandrov, Pyr'ev's rival in the genre, cut his ties with Dunaevskii during the anti-Semitism campaign of 1948. The kolkhoz musical is a sub-genre characteristic of Soviet Russia as a largely agrarian society. The structure of *Cossacks* conforms to the paradigm of the folk musical, in which the making of a couple – here two couples – parallels the task of creating community and doing the work of the nation. In fact, *Cossacks* has congruence with Rodgers and Hammerstein's folk musical *State Fair* (1945), in which a farming family also leaves its routine occupations for the holiday world of the Iowa State Fair, where the parents compete for blue ribbons and their children find romance. Both films strive to create an optimistic scenario of recovery and prosperity after the national traumas of World War II.

In *Cossacks* the traditional pattern of a primary, serious romantic couple and secondary comic couple is modified, as the middle-aged Peresvetova and Voron constantly quarrel in the manner of screwball comedy and in contrast to the harmonious courtship of the secondary couple. Other secondary male characters from the two kolkhozes enhance both the comedic flair and folk flavour of the film through verbal jousting in their roles as matchmaker and resistant senex figures. When the kolkhoz chairs are romantically reunited with the help of the state, represented by the local Party leader, they are also doing the work of the country, as the modernizer (read politically conformist) Peresvetova changes the backward economic-social ways of the

Ivan Pyr'ev, *Kuban Cossacks* (1949).

Cossack traditionalist Voron. In accord with the folk musical paradigm, the female harnesses and transforms the potentially destructive but societally necessary energy of the wandering male, as the reconciled Peresvetova and Voron are shown riding quietly in her buggy at the end of the film. The marriage of the young couple, Dasha and Nikolai, will further the advancement of their specialties, agriculture and horse breeding, two crucial areas of collective farming in the Kuban'. The finale literally unites all in community as the film's actors greet each other and march toward us, singing in unison.

The embedded show, a performance of amateur kolkhoz talent which includes female and male folk dancing, brilliantly performed *chastushki* (satiric folk couplets) and weight-lifting by a kolkhoz strong-man framed as folkloric *bogatyr'* (Russian knight), is both organic to the folk fair chronotope and responds to the renewed ideological initiative in favour of melodic folk music. The music and lyrics of *Cossacks* are characteristic of more sophisticated unified musicals in conveying through song what is not verbalized in dialogue: Peresvetova's rueful love for the dashing but temperamental Voron, Dasha's as yet unspoken love for Nikolai and the affirmation of nation and future happiness in a much stronger key than in the comic-romantic narrative. The first two songs were composed in the folk style and quickly entered the popular repertoire, enhancing the popularity of the film.

Although Khrushchev initially liked the film, he later made it the poster child for 'lacquering', the falsification of reality in Stalinist cinema, part of his de-Stalinization campaign of 1956. During perestroika, the debate over *Cossacks* resurfaced as a three-sided argument among those who viewed it as base falsehood, those who saw it as a life-affirming idealization that helped the Russian people survive the difficult post-war years, and those who viewed the film as consistent with their own life experiences in prosperous kolkhozes. With the passage of time, *Cossacks* has become a classic of Soviet cinema and a prime example of the kolkhoz musical comedy genre.

Rimgaila Salys

Carnival Night

Karnaval'naia noch'

Country of Origin:
Soviet Union

Language:
Russian

Studio:
Mosfilm

Director:
El'dar Riazanov

Screenplay:
Boris Laskin
Vladimir Poliakov

Cinematographer:
Arkadii Kol'tsatyi
Art Directors:
Konstantin Efimov
Oleg Grosse

Composer:
Anatolii Lepin

Synopsis

A group of enthusiastic students plans songs and skits for a New Year's ball. Two of them, Grisha and his sweetheart Lena, struggle against the bureaucratic meddling of the club's director, Ogurtsov. Against the background of Ogurtsov's constant posturing and dogmatic utterances, Grisha also tries hard to tell Lena of his affection. Ogurtsov censures all these innocent, heartfelt acts of ardour and their comedy kits as 'indecency', though an undaunted Cupid also strikes some of the elder members of the club's organizers. The director's ideological zeal is inspiring nobody, to the point where he is actually kidnapped and locked away during the show itself. Only then is the real, original programme of song and dance quickly reinstated. An aged, respectable band of pensioners hired by the director immediately reveals itself as disguised students and light-hearted jazz fills the hall. Grisha unexpectedly becomes compère, thus boosting his confidence to tell Lena he loves her. Ogurtsov is now utterly ignored as balloons and lovers spin across the dance floor.

Critique

This film is famous for sounding the importance of light entertainment and comedy after Stalin's death, both in terms of a new, cheerful community and a satirical critique of the old. Innovative social potentials are evoked in the imagined conflict between some young people and an aging, intolerant bureaucrat: hardly, it must be said, the stuff of comic blockbusters, but a dangerous theme in 1956, nonetheless. Any risks inherent in criticizing the recent past were lessened by setting

El'dar Riazanov, *Carnival Night* (1956); Grisha and Lena finally dance tog

Editor:

A. Kamagarova

Duration:

78 minutes

Genre:

Musical comedy

Cast:

Igor' Il'inskii
Liudmila Gurchenko
Iurii Belov
Georgii Kulikov
Sergei Filippov
Ol'ga Vlasova
Andrei Tutyshkin
Tamara Nosova
Gennadii Iudin
Vladimir Zel'din
Boris Petker

Year:

1956

the film on New Year's Eve, a time traditionally associated with hopes for 'unbelievable' metamorphoses. Another turn to tradition came from the film's recourse to an old, if not pre-Revolutionary art form: the cabaret or *estrada* revue, as staged by the students. A heritage of multiple, multifarious performers and genres on one stage all helped to bring variety back to the silver screen in a tale of mass inclusion. Joyful multiplicity and the unexpected, impulsive behaviour of wise-cracking students would replace the staid, predictable poses of their elders.

When the film was tested before a small, yet influential audience in Moscow, members of the film crew were nervous about the degree of mockery permissible. Legend has it, however, that midway into the screening, director Riazanov saw one bureaucrat fall from his chair, another guffaw, a third smile broadly and a fourth wipe tears of mirth from his eyes. Permission to print and distribute the film seemed assured. Indeed, the movie would go on to garner several state prizes and even enjoy popularity overseas. *Carnival Night* has thus become a legendary critique of elders' 'concern and suspicion' at everything unfamiliar. As a story applicable to any generation, it is still a guaranteed fixture in New Year's TV schedules today.

Most famously, the film offered young drama student Liudmila Gurchenko her first onscreen role, as Lena, and the chance to crown the movie with its theme song, entitled 'Five Minutes'. Millions of Russians still know the words by heart, telling both of hopes for the future that 'will never leave you' and the equally permanent possibility that life can change for the better in five minutes, if one can simply muster the magic ingredient of a 'good mood'.

Lena's good mood emerges as the result of her romance with fellow student Grisha, whose initial shy approaches come to nothing. In fact, on several occasions she specifically upbraids him for both 'bashfulness and equivocation'. Although these qualities were ineffective in the brave new Moscow, Grisha announces his love only when out of sight, in disguise or over an intercom. He does so anonymously and in such a staid, awkward way that Ogurtsov thinks (wrongly) that these amplified speeches are, in fact, quotes from the world of histrionic English drama. Natural, spontaneous emotion had not been seen for a long time.

In *Carnival Night*, love is gently, if not coyly proposed in a manner that hopes to transform the collective from within. Although disagreement emerges between the new society of the students and that of Ogurtsov, viewers are given no indication that he intends to *leave* it. The students' love and laughter are both within and ultimately respectful of Ogurtsov's 'other' collective, hence the prevalence in the screenplay of a withdrawn shyness, not sadness. The joy and security of post-Stalinist society, left intact by romance, allow Grisha eventually to overcome his bashfulness at the film's close – when everybody sings and dances together. Thus began the Thaw.

David MacFadyen

The Diamond Arm

Brilliantovaia ruka

Country of Origin:
Soviet Union

Language:
Russian

Studio:
Mosfilm

Director:
Leonid Gaidai

Screenplay:
Leonid Gaidai with Moris
Slobodskoi
Iakov Kostiukovskii

Cinematographer:
Igor' Chernykh

Art Director:
Feliks Iasiukevich

Composer:
Aleksandr Zatsepin

Editor:
Valentina Iankovskaia

Duration:
100 minutes

Genre:
Comedy

Cast:
Iurii Nikulin
Andrei Mironov
Anatolii Papanov
Nina Grebeshkova
Nonna Mordiukova
Svetlana Svetlichnaia

Year:
1968

Synopsis

Semen Gorbunkov (Nikulin), an ordinary, hardworking family man, takes a cruise, visiting ports in the Mediterranean. Unbeknownst to him, his friendly cabin-mate Kozodoev (Mironov) is a member of a criminal gang smuggling precious stones and bullion into the Soviet Union. Kozodoev's task is to pretend to break his arm while visiting Istanbul. His local accomplices are to pack precious jewels in a plaster cast on his arm – the 'diamond arm' of the film title. However, in a case of mistaken identity, the goods end up in a cast on Gorbunkov's arm. On his return home, Gorbunkov is alerted to the scam and persuaded to take part in a sting operation. Kozodoev and Lelik (Papanov), another gang member, are charged with recovering the goods, but each of their comically hapless attempts at retrieval fails. Gorbunkov's increasingly uncharacteristic behaviour – drunkenness, taxi rides in the dead of night, a hotel liaison with a beautiful woman – arouse the suspicions, not only of his poor wife, but of the housing superintendent of his apartment block (Mordiukova). The gang finally manage to kidnap Gorbunkov, but the goods have already been removed by the authorities. A police helicopter hooks the gang's get-away car. The unfortunate Gorbunkov falls out of the boot, breaking his leg, but is otherwise unharmed and is reunited with his family.

Critique

The chef d'oeuvre of Leonid Gaidai's unique comic genre – encompassing an adventure or detective plot, fast pace, carefully crafted visual gags and a highly polished script full of clever jokes, ironic punning and light satire – *Diamond Arm* is regarded by many as one of the best popular Soviet films ever made. Gaidai takes the huge gamble of dispensing entirely with the most successful comic elements of his previous films featuring Nikulin, the famous circus clown of the late Soviet period. In Gaidai's short comic films of the 1960s and in *Prisoner of the Caucasus*, Nikulin had been cast as the coarse, clowning ex-con Balbes ('dolt' or 'chump'), one-third of a hugely popular troika of miscreants. Though still afforded plenty of clowning sequences, in *Diamond Arm* his character is that of the upstanding Soviet everyman, as honest and trustworthy as the day is long. Nikulin had not trained as a professional actor and his performance was criticized as uneven: the more outrageous clowning sequences involving the hugely enjoyable hamming of Papanov and Mironov are punctuated by more restrained comic interludes of domesticity featuring the charmingly uncomplicated physical and ethical presence of Nikulin. It is often said that Gaidai's films are loved as much for the sense of period nostalgia and popular cultural communion they provoke as the comedy, the physical aspects of which have not aged quite as well as the verbal. But it is probably the very unevenness of the central role, a warm and generous performance by Nikulin, along with his accomplished clowning, that has done most to contribute to the film's undiminished popularity. *Diamond Arm* is so successful because, for the first time, Gaidai is given enough room to manoeuvre in filmic time and space, enough of a large scale cinematic canvas to realize his vision of an all-encompassing comic world: swans glide on an indoor pond in a chic restaurant (a Mosfilm studio set) as Nikulin sings his famous nonsense 'Song about a Hare', his dish of grouse coming to life and flying up into the chandelier; endless fun is poked at Varvara Sergeevna, the despotic house manager, and the uneasy experience of the Soviet citizen abroad. The inquisition he receives on return from his peers about 'life over there' is given a suitably ironic treatment. In *Diamond Arm*, Gaidai gives full reign to his comic fantasy and creates one of the few truly democratic, popular-taste films of the Soviet period.

Jeremy Morris

The Irony of Fate

Ironiia sud'by, ili S legkim parom!

Country of Origin:
Soviet Union

Language:
Russian

Studio:
Mosfilm

Director:
El'dar Riazanov

Screenplay:
Emil' Braginskii
El'dar Riazanov

Cinematographer:
Vladimir Nakhabtsev

Art Director:
Aleksandr Borisov

Composer:
Mikaèl Tariverdiev

Editor:
Valeriia Belova

Duration:
155 minutes

Synopsis

On New Year's Eve four friends gather at the public baths in Moscow to celebrate the impending departure of one of them to Leningrad. The ensuing drunkenness makes it impossible to say which of them should make the flight. After much discussion at Moscow airport, the wrong man, Zhenia Lukashin, flies off. Due to the complete uniformity of Soviet cityscapes, he is able to give a taxi driver his street, building and apartment number, all of which exist in Leningrad, too. Even his key fits the lock… He falls asleep on a stranger's bed. When the flat's owner, Nadia, returns, she is horrified to discover the inebriated visitor, but eventually realizes his incredible mistake. Her fiancé (Ippolit), however, is less than understanding when he arrives, and thinks Nadia guilty of infidelity. As Lukashin sobers up, he begins to defend Nadia's innocence and is attracted to her. This attraction grows over the night of 31 December, to the point where Zhenia and Nadia see the failings in their current relationships. Lukashin and Nadia fall in love before breakfast, which leads to a return journey to Moscow. Zhenia's stunned mother and friends are introduced to this new, remarkable woman, who has transformed two lives over the course of twelve hours.

Critique

When this film debuted on 1 January 1976 at 6pm on central Soviet television, as many as 100 million people turned on their television sets. The film was later released in cinemas, where another 20 million people saw it. Cinema posters around provincial Russia proclaimed the story as 'a virtual fantasy – the New Year's adventures of two of our contemporaries'. Even in the year of that initial broadcast it was shown three more times on television, something unheard of for any dramatic work, old or new.

Nonetheless, as the drunken scenes suggest, there were a few reasons for the state to feel uneasy about the production, since some criticized the speed and whimsy of its central romance as problematic, verging on immorality, even. When, for example, the screenplay had already been performed in 110 Soviet dramatic theatres prior to being

Genre:

Comedy

Cast:

Andrei Miagkov
Barbara Brylska
Iurii Iakovlev
Aleksandr Shirvindt
Georgii Burkov
Aleksandr Beliavskii
Liubov' Sokolova
Liubov' Dobrzhanskaia
Ol'ga Naumenko
Liia Akhedzhakova
Valentina Talyzina
Gotlib Roninson

Year:

1975

filmed, it had not then, for these same reasons, played in Moscow. The story seemed a bit flippant, tending with little concern towards the cheeky traditions of bedroom farce. The film muddled its emphases and intentions, being both a 'document of social psychology' and 'a comedy with a slightly sad smile, a kind, gentle sense of humour'. This picture, suggested another equally confused definition, 'is not a musical, though it has a lot of songs, not a satirical comedy but rather a film-dialog which begins very funnily and ends in great seriousness'. If that were not puzzling enough, one finds even less assurance in the film's classification as a work 'in which a sense of fatigue is combined with a passing, light festivity. It's a mix of buffoonery with drama'. The very fact that the film contained so much and was so varied in its designs was itself an expression of hope, change and plurality. For embodying precisely that hope, Miagkov became Actor of the Year and the film was awarded Film of the Year, too. *The Irony of Fate* still plays (endlessly) on Russian television as 31 December approaches.

This feature film has become arguably the quintessential 'sad comedy', the genre for which Riazanov is best known. As can be seen from the plot synopsis, these particularly Russian comedies concerned quiet, unassuming members of society who often found themselves in saddening situations. In a land where the emphasis was always upon grand, impersonal projects of national significance, little time or attention was given to the (often more pressing) concerns of falling in love, starting a family, handling a break-up and so forth. The fact that such dilemmas are often managed in silly, if not laughable ways – ending with resignation rather than triumph – allowed Riazanov to create a rich vein of bitter-sweet humour for Russian cinema. The muddled definitions of his genre are reflected in the indecisive behaviour of his protagonists.

Riazanov shot this film on multiple cameras simultaneously, with some takes lasting half an hour. His goal was to catch the unstudied, small-scale and normal emotions that were more familiar to his audience than any barrel-chested hero of socialism. For this very reason, the shy, bespectacled Lukashin and his cold, but lonely love-interest have gone on to be national heroes for over three decades. Singing quiet songs in noiseless living rooms, they continue to symbolize the smallest opportunity for happiness, come what may.

David MacFadyen

The Sentimental Policeman

Chuvstvitel'nyi militsioner

Country of Origin:

Ukraine

Language:

Russian

Synopsis

The policeman Tolia finds the baby Natasha in a cabbage patch and brings her to the police station. He manages to calm her by wrapping her in his shirt. After being examined by a woman doctor, Natasha is placed in an orphanage. All of a sudden Tolia realizes that he loves the baby and decides to adopt her. At the orphanage, while he is told that Natasha has already been adopted by the woman doctor, Tolia discovers that Natasha is still there, but has been promised to the woman doctor. Tolia and his wife, Klava, try to win the case of Natasha's adoption in court. But in the middle of the trial the doctor's first adopted child makes an appearance, thus winning the judges over. After the trial Tolia and Klava talk about their mutual love and Klava announces to Tolia that she is pregnant.

Kira Muratova, *The Sentimental Policeman* (1992).

Critique

The film is based on a script written by Kira Muratova in 1976 (*Treasure* or *The Sentimantal Policeman*) during one of her long periods of forced inactivity as a film director. The idea of the plot came from an article by Iurii Usichenko about an adoption trial. But at the time the script was refused by Soviet television, since 'there were no abandoned children in our country'. Muratova decided to shoot the script after finishing what she herself calls her 'encyclopaedic film', *The Asthenic Syndrome*. Audience and critics were surprised by this apparently light film, disconnected from historical and social reality (though it was shot during the coup in August 1991). The director describes it as a 'kitsch bazaar icon'; it is indeed clearly influenced by popular visual arts. With its frontal, symmetrical and colourful imagery, the film presents itself as a falsely naïve anecdote.

The Sentimental Policeman, Muratova's only co-production with a western country, got a tepid reception from international audiences. Western festivals lost interest in the film when they discovered that it dealt with existential problems rather than engaging the moral and economic chaos in Ukraine at the time. The film was not unanimously acclaimed in post-Soviet space either. Even some of Muratova's strongest supporters found the film artificial and the characters schematic and mechanical.

Studios:

Primodessa-Film (Odessa)
Parimédia-film (France)

Director:

Kira Muratova

Producers:

Iurii Kovalenko
Aleksandr Andreev
Hughes Borgia

Screenplay:

Kira Muratova, assisted by
Evgenii Golubenko

Cinematographer:

Gennadii Kariuk

Art Directors:

Evgenii Golubenko
Aleksei Bokatov

Composers:

Peter Tchaikovsky

Aleksandr Vertinskii

Editor:

Valentina Oleinik

Duration:

119 minutes

Genre:

Comedy

Cast:

Nikolai Shatokhin

Irina Kovalenko

Natalia Ralleva

Leonid Kushnir

Iurii Shlykov

Uta Kil'ter

Year:

1992

Contrary to her previous films, here Muratova counts on a solid narrative structure to hold the film together. *The Sentimental Policeman* repeats the structure of a fairy tale: it contains not only a tripartite composition with a final combat, but is intentionally anti-psychological and characters' emotions are expressed by concrete metaphors. Thus, Tolia's love for baby Natasha and his desire to adopt her are the splinter in his palm; when he loses her in trial, his grief is physically represented by a nosebleed. Another feature of the fairy tale is the use of magic formulae. But Muratova also suggests an important inversion of the traditional fairy tale structure: as a rule, the itinerary of the hero takes him from consanguinity bonds (initial family) to alliance bonds (marriage). Here, Tolia starts off in a world where no one has consanguinity bonds (Klava is an orphan, just like baby Natasha), but ultimately attains a consanguinity bond: Klava is going to give birth.

This clear inspiration through the fairy tale can be found again in Muratova's film *Melody for a Street Organ* (2009). But just as in *The Sentimental Policeman*, the codes of the fairy tale are broken to present a unique Muratovian universe obeying non-magic rules. No miracle will rescue the abandoned children in *Melody*, but a magically found baby will make its way to a true birth in *Policeman*.

Finally, in her first film released after the fall of Soviet Union, Kira Muratova establishes a direct link with the legendary Soviet film shot in Odessa, Sergei Eisenstein's *The Battleship Potemkin* (1925). But if for Eisenstein the famous stairs were the site of a struggle for power, for Muratova they are a site for love.

Eugénie Zvonkine

Window to Paris

Okno v Parizh

Countries of Origin:

Russia

France

Language:

Russian

Studios:

Fontan

Troitskii Most

Ineks

Films du Bouloi

Sept Cinéma

Director:

Iurii Mamin

Synopsis

Nikolai, a music teacher in a post-Soviet business high school, discovers in his room of a communal apartment a magic portal to Paris, which is open only periodically. He and his neighbours try to get as much from the foreign city as possible, each in his own way: while Nikolai glimpses the other life and even considers work there as a musician, the neighbours snatch as many material goods as possible. Facing the startling contrast between the uplifting life in Paris and the bleak existence in a devastated post-Soviet Russia, every character – Nikolai, his neighbours and his pupils, whom he takes for a tour of Paris – has to make a decision: on which side of the window they will stay when it closes. Nikolai's choice is especially difficult because of the romance between him and Nicole, a French taxidermist-artist. In the end, having decided in favour of their motherland and returned to Russia, the characters continue to try to break the wall between two worlds – an equivalent of the Berlin wall.

Critique

Mamin's social, fantastic comedy explores the ethical as well as aesthetic implications of emigration from post-Soviet Russia. The parable builds on the idiom 'window to Europe', referring to Peter the Great,

Producers:

Guy Séligman, Lavrentii Emrashvili

Screenplay:

Iurii Mamin
Arkadii Tigai
Vladimir Vardunas
Viacheslav Leikin

Cinematographers:

Sergei Nekrasov
Anatolii Lapshov

Art Director:

Vera Zelinskaia

Composer:

Iurii Mamin
Aleksei Zalivalov

Editor:

Ol'ga Adrianova

Duration:

120 minutes

Genre:

Comedy

Cast:

Sergei Dontsov (Dreiden)
Agnès Soral
Viktor Mikhailov
Nina Usatova
Andrei Urgant

Year:

1993

who opened the passage to the Baltic sea for Russia by building St Petersburg: the new window directly connects the St Petersburg communal apartment with Paris. On the one hand, Russia and France of the early 1990s are explicitly shown as contrasting poles, and their representations dwell grotesquely on national stereotypes: the outrageous drinking of the Russians, the mysterious Russian soul, the brutal yet friendly French obsession with sex and decadent French art for art's sake. But the whole structure of the film suggests that this is an opposition of doubles, each world a mirror reflection of the other. Mirroring is present on all levels of the film, starting from the initial scenes when an idyllic picture of Paris on the wall dissolves to a carnivalized street scene of Petersburg with exaggerated stereotypical signs of the time, including a long vodka queue. When Nikolai and his neighbours first get to Paris through the magic portal, drunk as they are, they do not even realize at first that they are in a foreign country: 'If it was not for the TV tower, I wouldn't even have recognized the town', notes one of them, failing to identify the Eiffel Tower. First enchanted with the city, Nikolai eventually discovers that Paris cares for his music no more than does St Petersburg: soon after he finds a job in an orchestra, he realizes in horror that he is expected to play without his trousers. Nikolai and his French counterpart Nicole not only have similar names, but discover darker sides of each other's world in parallel. Mamin complicates the choice that his characters have to make by blurring the binaries between the two worlds. Similarly, he points to the deep inner affinity of socialism and capitalism: Nikolai claims that the same people who have been nurturing the builders of communism are now bringing up the young builders of capitalism. Mamin previously created images of dubious historical cycles in his film *Sideburns*. But *Window to Paris* is not at all pessimistic. Hope emerges through images of the new generation: Nikolai's pupils finally agree to return to 'their wretched country' and try to change it. Mamin also uses the liberating potential of carnival, transforming the bleak scenes of Russian aggression into bold buffoonery.

Music is an indispensable part of this carnival. Mamin combines sources that are iconic references for Russian audiences, but that are stylistically incompatible, ranging from Tchaikovsky to Revolutionary songs. The recurrent tune of the film is an old French song. All the characters have their own relation with music, which becomes an ironic measure for character assessment: they play and sing for joy and for money, they refuse to subvert music or cheat with the help of music, and even use pianos as storage cupboards. Like the Hamelin piper, Nikolai makes the children obey him and follow him from Paris to St Petersburg; in a similar way, a band playing the 'Internationale' leads the angry paupers away from the liquor store.

The rich audio-visual texture of the film, its theatricality and broad use of mass festivities are the director's trademark: even though they have been compromised by the official Soviet mass holidays (Neptune's Day), such holidays still preserve the spirit of the Rabelaisian carnival.

Milla Fedorova

Peculiarities of the National Hunt

Osobennosti natsional'noi okhoty

Country of Origin:
Russia

Language:
Russian

Studio:
Lenfilm

Director:
Aleksandr Rogozhkin

Producer:
Aleksandr Golutva

Screenplay:
Aleksandr Rogozhkin

Cinematographer:
Andrei Zhegalov

Art Directors:
Valentina Adikaevskaia
Aleksandr Timoshenko

Composer:
Vladislav Panchenko

Editor:
Tamara Denisova

Duration:
96 minutes

Genre:
Comedy

Cast:
Ville Haapasalo
Aleksei Buldakov
Viktor Bychkov
Semen Strugachev
Sergei Russkin
Sergei Kupriianov

Year:
1995

Synopsis

In *Peculiarities of the National Hunt (in Autumn)* the Finn Raimo, who is researching the traditions of the Russian hunt from the time of the tsars to the present, joins a group of Russians, including a general, a businessman, a gamekeeper and a policeman, in the hunt. The drinking bouts the Russians associate with hunting, however, are not what Raimo expects. He initially refuses to drink, while dreaming of the imperial hunting party of the late nineteenth century as they hunt down a fox with their dogs, elegantly ride on their horses and, of course, converse in French. In the meantime, the non-Russian speaker is marginalized as the Russians indulge in alcohol. The Finn is an outsider, misunderstood and displaying utterly non-Russian manners: he tidies up, cares for the environment and waits for the hunt, not realizing that it has already begun – at least, *à la russe*.

Critique

The film explores the Russians' notorious love for vodka through a series of anecdotes. Rogozhkin merges situational comedy (bureaucrats and officials who do not behave like serious citizens and are helpless in matters of everyday life) with the eccentricity of character induced by vodka consumption and isolation from the world of 'normalcy'.

Rogozhkin draws on the Russian tradition of drinking captured so well in Venedikt Erofeev's *Moscow to the End of the Line* (1973). More important still is the impact of advertising campaigns for vodka as broadcast on Russian television in the mid-1990s, especially the commercials for the vodka label 'White Eagle' (Belyi Orel, 1994–1995), produced by designer Iurii Grymov, known for his extravagant style that knows no border between the beautiful and the vulgar. The White Eagle campaign centred on the delirious hero reaching a state of absolute freedom from social conventions and restrictions thanks to the influence of alcohol. The beautiful images of delirium contrast with the images of a sober reality. Similarly, an early 1990s ad for Smirnoff vodka presented the idea of a clearer reality that can be perceived under the influence of alcohol. The 'clearness of sensations' achieved through alcohol consumption allows the protagonist to unmask reality: he sees the things hidden under the glossy surface. The guests no longer wear elegant party dresses, but look like wild animals from a horror movie. It is a frightening, but certainly a more interesting view than the dull party seen without vodka.

This function of vodka as a stimulant for the clear perception of reality, together with the structural principle of ads as a series of clips, without beginning and end, underlies Rogozhkin's film. The fragmentary structure, the anecdotal character of the dialogue, and the lack of logic replicate the incoherent speech of a drunkard. His hunters repeat the same absurd action over and over again.

The characters are representative of the new, no longer classless Russian society: the military, the new Russian, the state official, the policeman. However, beneath their social image they hide their authentic selves: the love of animals, humans and nature. Under the influence of vodka they reveal their true identities and values: the

Aleksandr Rogozhkin, *Peculiarities of the National Hunt* (1995).

good and honest demeanour of a Russian folk hero, who kills no animal, who helps his fellow human beings and who is at one with nature. Therefore, the general 'Mikhailych' Ivolgin deploys his skills to organize a party or a hunt; the state official Lev Soloveichuk is a pitiable creature when it comes to practical matters; the policeman Semenov is always helpful; the businessman Sergei Olegovich has problems at home; and the forester Kuzmich meditates instead of clearing forests and hunting animals. Rogozhkin removes all negative attributes and marks of power from these social types and replaces them with positive and vulnerable qualities.

Russian life fails to coincide with the Finn's imagination. The military and the police hardly reinforce order: a military aircraft is used to transport vodka and animals, and the police vans facilitate a visit to some prostitutes. The breakdown of social order in contemporary Russia is treated with self-irony. Drinking may have no purpose, but it is a habit that makes social and national differences disappear, that lifts temporal boundaries by bringing together past and present, and annihilates the borders between animals and humans. The world returns to its purest form, devoid of boundaries or limits. What matters in the hunt is not the result, but the time spent in good company.

Birgit Beumers

The Irony of Fate: A Continuation

Ironiia sud'by: Prodolzhenie

Country of Origin:
Russia

Language:
Russian

Studio:
Pervyi kanal

Director:
Timur Bekmambetov

Producers:
Konstantin Èrnst
Anatolii Maksimov

Screenplay:
Aleksei Slapovskii

Cinematographer:
Sergei Trofimov

Composers:
Iurii Poteenko
Mikaèl Tariverdiev

Editors:
Dmitrii Kiselev
Il'ia Lebedev

Synopsis

As its title suggests, this film 'continues' the basic structure of Èl'dar Riazanov's classic comedy The Irony of Fate (1975). Kostia, the son of Riazanov's original hero, Evgenii, gets drunk in a bathhouse on 31 December – just as his father had more than 30 years ago. Horribly intoxicated, Kostia wakes up in the bedroom of a strange woman (Nadia). She, it transpires, is the daughter of Nadezhda Vasil'evna, whom Kostia's father almost married three decades earlier. A jealous young businessman, Iraklii, worsens Kostia's predicament and is very keen to get rid of him before the New Year celebrations begin. Kostia, however, manages to outsmart Iraklii and return to this unknown, yet alluring young woman. As the plot develops, viewers are also informed of what has happened to the older characters since 1975: Nadezhda had actually married Ippolit, Nadia's father, though she subsequently got divorced; Evgenii had also married after the affair with Nadezhda, but could never completely forget her. New love in the present and old passions from the past conspire to bring two generations of sweethearts together, leaving them in a shared state of promise. Maybe these two couples will find a happiness that – as we now know – eluded them in 1975.

Critique

This film plays the triple role of a sequel, a remake, and – at the same time – a complex back-story, imagining all manner of events that befell the characters from Riazanov's classic. Given the almost legendary fame of that 1975 feature, which enjoys the status of Frank Capra's It's a Wonderful Life (1946) or B.D. Hurst's Scrooge (1951) in Russia, public interest was assured. An enormous advertising campaign ran nationwide in the months before the film's release, emphasizing several reasons to see it: the movie would reveal the truth about Evgenii and Nadezhda; it was officially endorsed by Riazanov himself; and had been shot by Timur Bekmambetov after his success with the sci-fi blockbusters Night Watch (2004) and Day Watch (2006). The

Duration:

113 minutes

Genre:

Comedy

Cast:

Andrei Miagkov

Iurii Iakovlev

Barbara Brylska

Sergei Bezrukov

Konstantin Khabenskii

Elizaveta Boiarskaia

Year:

2007

campaign paid off and the movie became the most profitable film of 2008, grossing $50 million domestically.

Critics of this fiscal success condemned the film, not only because it turned a universally adored story into a cash cow, but also because it was full of crude product placements for telephone companies, cars, mayonnaise, cosmetics, beer, vodka, canned fish, chocolate and airlines. Fearing this kind of commercial conceit beforehand, screenwriter Aleksei Slapovskii had been extremely wary of taking part in the project. Similarly, not all the actors from 1975 signed on for a second tour of duty. Riazanov himself had been offered the chance to direct the work but, like Slapovskii, worried about spoiling an almost timeless movie. Nonetheless, in a more modest capacity, he did agree to reappear in his fleeting onscreen role from the original.

The biggest changes, over and above any plot twists, were Bekmambetov himself and his celebrated style of grand, crowd-pleasing computer generated images. As the magic of New Year allows for all manner of transformations, both public and private, so Bekmambetov was able to include a wide range of special effects; some of them, rather strangely, were based upon visual gags taken straight from *Night Watch*. In other words, a few of the CGIs used for this quiet tale of love unfulfilled came directly from a loud and violent vampire flick. In some ways, though, these changes just reflected the radically different nature of post-Soviet society and what was needed to make any depiction thereof convincing in 2008. Here one might point to the casting of Sergei Bezrukov as Iraklii; as a decidedly non- or post-Soviet figure, he comes to the screen in 2008 as the high-ranking executive of a cell-phone company.

In essence, *The Irony of Fate: A Continuation* reflects the worldview of the man credited with the project's inception – Konstantin Ernst, head of Channel One. An air of stately order pervades the film, with then-President Putin appearing briefly on a television set. The president's speechwriter was even responsible for the lyrics to one of the film's newer songs, performed by Alla Pugacheva and her daughter, Kristina Orbakaite. As some commentators pointed out, another facet of this 'ideological' aspect was evident in the lessening role of destiny. Despite remaining in the title, 'fate' is sidelined by the importance of free will and intelligent choices, be they in the workplace (Iraklii), or in moments of difficulty (Kostia). Craftiness trumps chance and, as a result, this sequel and/or remake is much more positive than the original, which is coloured by an enduring air of melancholy. Bekmambetov's contemporary and positive outlook, replete with thrilling effects, make the 'continuation' a film of greater western inclination, as a result of which (and with no sense of irony) it outperformed all American blockbusters of the same holiday season.

David MacFadyen

Valerii Todorovskii, *Hipsters* (2009).

Hipsters

Stiliagi

Country of Origin:
Russia

Language:
Russian

Studio:
Krasnaia Strela

Synopsis

In 1955, the stilyagi, or style-hunters and dandies, who imitate western fashion, are attacked by the Soviet youth organization, the Komsomol. One evening the Komsomol member Mels chases a stilyaga girl through a park and finds himself attracted to her. He begins to challenge Soviet conformity and turns into a stilyaga himself, even learning how to play the sax. Eventually Mels meets Pol'za, the girl from the park. When Pol'za discovers she is pregnant, they marry; however, the child is not from Mels, but from a one-night stand Pol'za had with a black man. In the meantime the stilyaga Fred, the son of

Director:

Valerii Todorovskii

Producers:

Valerii Todorovskii
Leonid Iarmol'nik
Leonid Lebedev
Vadim Goriainov

Screenplay:

Iurii Korotkov

Cinematographer:

Roman Vas'ianov

Art Director:

Vladimir Gudilin

Composer:

Konstantin Meladze

Editor:

not known

Duration:

136 minutes

Genre:

Musical Comedy

Cast:

Anton Shagin
Oksana Akin'shina
Maksim Matveev
Sergei Garmash
Oleg Iankovskii
Irina Rozanova
Leonid Iarmol'nik

Year:

2008

a diplomat, has the opportunity of making a career as a diplomat with a posting in the United States. Fred immediately relinquishes his stilyaga antics and marries a girl from a diplomat's family. When Fred returns to Moscow for a visit, he sees Mels and tells him that their idea of a western lifestyle is nothing but a figment of the imagination. Mels and Pol'za are joined by a crowd of all nationalities and colours, from past and present on Tverskaia Street as they wander towards the central square of today's Moscow.

Critique

Hipsters revives the genre of the musical film and offers a distanced approach to the 1950s, or more precisely the period preceding Khrushchev's secret speech in 1956 but following Stalin's death in 1953. Todorovskii characterizes this period by a feeling of suppression of otherness and a tendency to create uniformity, which is opposed by the stilyagi in their imitation of western fashion.

The film's style, with its close-ups and crane shots, musical interludes and colourful dresses – that could never have been captured on Soviet colour film stock so brightly – deliberately sets itself apart from the style of the 1950s in order to underline the artificial quality of the historical setting and thereby emphasize the performative and glossy nature of the film. Furthermore, songs distance the action from the present; they are used both for the portrayal of the stilyagi and the komsomol, ridiculing the komsomol as a dull chorus. The musical form itself undermines the komsomol's ethos as a serious ideological organization.

Mels – the name being made up of the first letters of Marx, Engels, Lenin and Stalin – drops the 's' in his name when he becomes the stilyaga Mel. This simple act turns into an ideological scandal, since it means disloyalty to Stalin: Mel has to surrender his Komsomol membership card. The brutal chopping of the stilyaga's clothes in the first Komsomol raid is exaggerated, and the personal rather than ideological motivation for Komsomol leader Katia's campaign against Mel (frustrated love rather then ideological conviction) also contradict the spirit of the time.

Mel remains a loyal friend and almost conforms to normalcy in his support of Pol'za and her black child, conceived in a one-night stand she had with a negro visiting Moscow – for the sake of exoticism and the encounter with otherness. The reference to Aleksandrov's *The Circus* (1934) is obvious: Marion Dixon and her black child are integrated into the Soviet collective represented by the circus audience. Pol'za becomes an average Soviet mother, concerned with the child and household chores rather than her outfits. Mel's ideals are shattered when Fred tells him that the stilyaga would stick out in the crowd even on Broadway. Otherness is an invention, a myth. The film's finale sings a song of praise to the present – rather than the past – for allowing genuine multi-culturedness, otherness and difference – ideals promulgated in Soviet propaganda. Only now, in present-day Moscow, on Tverskaia Street, can the stilyaga Mel – the flawed predecessor of multi-culturedness – be joined by a crowd of different people, from skinheads to punks, who populate contemporary Moscow. In this sense, the film debunks the stilyaga myth as an illusion and shows the time and place for genuine variety as the Moscow of today, playing into the hands of liberal and democratic ideologies.

The film treats the past as an aesthetic phenomenon rather than exploring social or historical issues. Therefore, the musical numbers, from the jazz gigs played by Mel and his friends, underline the literally and figuratively dissonant voice of the stilyaga, which contrasts with the threatening and monotonous chorus of the Komsomol.

Birgit Beumers

MELODRAMA

Initially a distinct theatrical genre that emerged during the after-math of the French Revolution, melodrama is now understood more broadly as 'a mode of heightened dramatization' and a 'certain fictional system for making sense of experience', to use Peter Brooks's terminology. The melodramatic mode of expression can manifest itself in a variety of genres and art forms, ranging from early modernist novels to pulp fiction, and from soap operas to the 'staged' funerals of national celebrities. In short, melodrama can be understood as a genre, as well as a style and a specific aesthetic category.

While some of its characteristics may stand out more prominently than others, it is commonly agreed that melodrama is based on the aesthetics of excess, presenting its characters and their environment in an exaggerated way. Visually, this penchant for excessiveness may find expression in sumptuous sets, interiors jam-packed with luxurious objects and flamboyant dresses intended to enhance the characters' sex appeal; psychologically, it comes to the fore in the characters' inability to control themselves and the 'melodramatic' way in which they express their emotions (high-pitched voices, wild gestures). Hence, melodrama's predilection for scandal scenes and improbable plot turns that tax the characters to the limit, while simultaneously keeping the viewer emotionally enthralled. Because melodrama deals primarily with such basic human emotions as love, hatred and jealousy, the plot can be situated in any social environment. Its typical setting, though, is the private or domestic sphere, and its main character is usually female.

The earliest melodramas, especially those penned by the genre's spiritual father, René-Charles Guilbert de Pixérécourt, were designed to satisfy the audience's need for poetic justice. Relying on an anti-thetical understanding of good and evil, de Pixérécourt and his fol-lowers made sure to offer dénouements that had the villain punished and the fair maiden rescued. This tendency to reduce the story to a battle between virtue and vice, and to identify the former with the existing order, has earned melodrama a reputation as a conservative genre. Rather than challenging the status quo, classical melodrama resolves conflict by restoring and affirming traditional hierarchies.

Abram Room, *Bed and Sofa* (1927).

In the course of the nineteenth-century, however, and especially with the onset of modernity, the genre's moral rigour considerably decreased. Modern scholars have questioned the notion of melodrama's inherent conservatism, pointing out that the restoration of the status quo does not necessarily imply that all problems have been overcome. Once considered a form of 'escapist' entertainment, melodrama is now regarded as an ambiguous and ideologically more complex genre with a potential for problematizing, rather than reinforcing existing hierarchies.

Russian film melodrama emerged almost immediately after the national film industry had taken root in the 1900s. Even if it endured fierce competition from historical films and screen adaptations of classical literature, silent movie melodrama enjoyed enormous popularity, reaching its heyday between 1913 and 1917 when directors like Nikolai Larin and Evgenii Bauer quickly rose to prominence. Set in milieus as divergent as the merchant class and the aristocracy, the films of these directors can best be understood as '*domostroi* dramas', as Louise McReynolds has described them: their fictional worlds recall the sixteenth-century manual for good house-keeping (*Domostroi*) which asserted the authority of the father, while demanding complete obedience from other family members. The plot revolves around a heroine's attempt to free herself from the stultifying atmosphere of the patriarchic home. This attempt usually provokes a reaction from the patriarch (father or possessive husband) who denies her claim to independence: she is callously married off in order to cement relations with a business partner, sexually abused or otherwise mistreated. The heroine may then be granted some form of revenge (killing the perpetrator, starting an independent and successful life as an actress); the ending, however, is not entirely happy because it leaves the heroine marked for life and often involves bloodshed (e.g., suicide of the male antagonist).

While this sort of closure has been regarded as a common preference among pre-Revolutionary Russian directors for 'tragic endings' (as opposed to the happy endings more typical of Western melodrama), the labels 'ambiguous' and 'conservative' may be more appropriate. In films like *Drama on the Volga* (1913), *Twilight of a Woman's Soul* (1913) and *A Life for a Life* (1916) conflict is not resolved in a 'conservative' fashion by the restoration of old power relations; rather the heroine challenges and undermines these relations, which may result in her own destruction. In contrast to the women characters, the men in these melodramas leave anything but a favourable impression. Weak, ineffective or morally corrupt, they desperately and vainly try to hold on to the 'old ways'.

For obvious reasons, the first two decades of Soviet power were not conducive to melodrama in its 'purest' form, although melodramatic elements can easily be pointed out in a variety of early Soviet films, even in the experimental films by Grigorii Kozintsev and Leonid Trauberg (*The Devil's Wheel*, 1925; *The Overcoat*, 1926). Melodrama's traditional focus on private, rather than public life, as well as its preoccupation with personal emotions, made it an inappropriate vehicle for conveying the collectivist worldview of communism. Profound changes in the organization of everyday life, ranging from setting up communal apartments to publicity campaigns urging women to cast off the yoke of housekeeping and calling for the destruction of the stuffy bourgeois home, also contributed to the genre's demise. Characteristically, in Abram Room's *Bed and Sofa* (1927), one of the very few melodramas produced during this period, the heroine literally walks out on both her husband and her lover, leaving them behind in their cluttered private apartment. Like the strong and independent women in Evgenii Bauer's films, this new Soviet woman tries to assert herself by fleeing an oppressive and male-dominated world that already belongs to the past.

Even if the 1930s saw the return of more traditional gender stereotypes that relegated women back to the family as the site of their primary responsibility, films dealing with family life as such were considered suspect. The nuclear family, though partly restored as the bedrock of the nation (as evinced by the institution of 'maternity medals'), was deemed irrelevant to the 'Great Family', which consisted of the Soviet people and 'father' Stalin. This situation began to change during World War II when the nuclear family was allowed to occupy a modest place in films showing life on the home front. Yet although these movies centre more on the vicissitudes of an individual couple separated by the war and less on heroics performed in combat, the characters' private concerns remain subordinated to the great cause. Married or engaged, what really unites the couple is their staunch patriotism. Consequently, the hero's safe return from the front and his reunion with the heroine, as in Aleksandr Stolper's *Wait For Me* (1943), do not so much signify the preservation of the nuclear family, as the survival of the great family of the Soviet people. Only towards the late 1950s do we see a significant reversal of this situation. In Mikhail Kalatozov's *The Cranes Are Flying* (1958), it is the heroine's personal experience of the war that propels the plot forward. Thus starting in the first years of 'developed socialism', the family drama takes precedence over the social (or national) drama, even if the latter does retain some relevance.

Two developments mark the evolution of melodrama during the Stagnation era under Brezhnev: first, its gradual disconnection from traditional associations with 'low' culture and its recognition as a legitimate and commercially lucrative genre. For all the undeniably melodramatic ingredients operative in Soviet film of the 1950s and 1960s, melodrama's existence in contemporary Soviet cinema had always been denied. That situation changed dramatically in the early 1970s, and by the end of the decade the genre figured prominently in the production plans of Goskino. Second, in comparison with the melodramas of the Thaw era, in Brezhnevite melodrama the balance between public and private life tipped even further in favour of the latter. In Vladimir Men'shov's *Moscow Does Not Believe in Tears* (1979), for instance, professional success is shown to be insufficient or even counterproductive for attaining personal fulfilment.

With the exception of Nikita Mikhalkov's and El'dar Riazanov's forays into historical melodrama (*Slave of Love*, 1976; *A Cruel Romance*, 1984), over the past 30 years, the genre has addressed contemporary issues by refracting them through the lens of personal relationships and family life. Melodramas of the late 1990s and the new millennium tend to focus on the disintegration of the family, in particular on the figure of the ineffective or failing father (Ivan Vyrypaev's *Euphoria*, 2006; Katia Shagalova's *Once Upon a Time in the Provinces*, 2008). At the same time, a number of directors appear eager to suggest a way out of Russia's family crisis, concluding their films with the reconstitution of the nuclear family (Pavel Lungin's *Wedding*, 2000) or the reconciliation of a generational conflict (Aleksei Popogrebskii's *Simple Things*, 2007). Especially for this last category of filmmakers, the option of a 'conservative' or 'happy' dénouement seems more attractive than the alternative of an ambiguous or 'tragic' ending.

Otto Boele

The Merchant Bashkirov's Daughter (Drama on the Volga)

Doch´ kuptsa Bashkirova (Drama na Volge)

Country of Origin:
Russia

Language:
Russian

Studio:
Grigorii Libken's Volga Co.

Director:
Nikolai Larin

Producer:
Grigorii Libken

Screenplay:
Nikolai Larin

Cinematographer:
Ianis Dored

Duration:
43 minutes

Genre:
Melodrama

Cast:
Unknown

Year:
1913

Synopsis

Natalia, the title character, has fallen in love with Egorov, a young clerk who works in her father's shop. The patriarchal Bashkirov, however, has already arranged her marriage to one of his colleagues; the two men sign the formal agreement, and then toast with vodka shots, to the evident distress of the merchant's wife. When her mother arranges a few moments for the young lovers to be alone in Natalia's room, the father returns home unexpectedly. The women hide Egorov under Natalia's mattress, accidentally suffocating him. They enlist a brawny peasant to hide the corpse, which he nails into a barrel and then unceremoniously dumps into the Volga. When the body is discovered, the wily peasant then realizes that he has leverage over the women, and he blackmails Natalia into coming to his hut, where he rapes her. He then pressures her to meet him in a bar, where she keeps pouring the vodka until he and his buddy pass out. Natalia sets fire to the place after blocking the exits, and then dissolves into hysteria as she watches the flames.

Critique

Produced by a small provincial film company in 1913, this movie was quickly purchased by the Pathé Frères Company, which maintained an office in Moscow. Supposedly based on a true story, the plot had been staged for the theatre in 1894 as *The Murderess: The Merchant Osipov's Daughter*. A merchant family named Bashkirov objected to the film's title, prompting it to be distributed as *Drama on the Volga*. The thematic intertwining of the conflicts between generation and gender keeps this movie fresh today as a window to the past. Costumes code the class structure: the patriarchal merchants in their caftans wear beards and part their long hair down the middle, in sharp contrast to the stylish Egorov. The mother is also particularly interesting, as she tries to help her daughter despite her inability to challenge her husband's authority. The peasant-rapist contradicts any possible nostalgia for the provincial sublime, despite several evocative outdoor shots of the river. Nor does he inspire socialist sympathies, reminding viewers instead of the visceral and brutal anger that fuelled many from the underclasses. Politics aside, this film also fits into the growing popularity of cinematic violence. Natalia's collapse into a hysterical fit in the last scene was at the time also becoming a familiar trope of feminine frustration. Director Larin did not move far professionally after this in Russian cinema; his last known film was *The Father-in-Law Killer and Nastia, the Beauty* (*Svekor-dushegub i krasotka Nastia*, 1916), based on a novel by Aleksei Pazukhin, one of the most prolific writers of serialized sensational novels published in the tabloid press. After emigrating in 1920, Larin continued as a filmmaker in Bulgaria and Germany.

Louise McReynolds

Evgenii Bauer, *Life for a Life* (1916).

A Life for a Life

Zhizn' za zhizn'

Country of Origin:
Russia

Language:
Russian

Studio:
Khanzhonkov & Co.

Director:
Evgenii Bauer

Producer:
Aleksandr Khanzhonkov

Screenplay:
Evgenii Bauer

Synopsis

Two daughters of a wealthy, and female, factory owner (Rakhmanova) fall in love with the same Prince Bartinskii (Polonskii). One of the daughters, however, Nata (Kholodnaia), is adopted and therefore without a dowry. The prince marries the biological daughter, Musia (Koreneva), and Nata is forced to marry a businessman (Perestiani), who is as kind and wealthy as he is older than she. The prince, an utter cad, seduces the willing Nata, and then steals from her husband by forging his signature to a promissory note. Although he treats her coldly, Musia still loves her husband and begs her brother-in-law not to prosecute the prince. The irate mother, aware of the prince's deceptions, can tolerate him no longer. She shoots him, and then stages his murder to look like suicide. Both distraught daughters rush to his corpse.

Critique

A Life for a Life was rightfully heralded as Russia's contribution to the large-scale international productions of the era. Its stars were the

Cinematographer:

Boris Zavelev

Duration:

66 minutes

Genre:

Melodrama

Cast:

Vera Kholodnaia
Lydia Koreneva
Vitol'd Polonskii
Ol'ga Rakhmanova
Ivan Perestiani

Year:

1916

brightest, and its director, Evgenii Bauer, boasted a cinematic eye as innovative as any of his western peers. For this film he finally received the budget capable of funding his opulent visuals. Based on Georges Ohnet's potboiler *Serge Panine* (1885), which the author had only recently adapted for the French cinema and which was subtitled 'A Tear for Every Drop of Blood', the film was re-titled for its American release *Her Sister's Rival* – a rhetorical manoeuvre that reflected a different theme than that emphasized by Bauer. This was a distinctively Russian film, the epitome of the culture's melodrama both thematically and aesthetically. Bauer artfully contrasted noble decadence to bourgeois morality, one of the genre's commonplaces. Virtue triumphs, but only ambiguously, as both daughters clearly prefer the decadence that their mother destroyed in order to save them. Renowned for his uses of mise-en-scène, Bauer staged the scenes to evoke the emotional despair with which the film ends. Rather than rivals, the sisters are victims, each overwhelmed by spacious sets and furniture that renders them too small to assume a stance equal to the prince's. The lavish sets are also multi-layered to emphasize the mutual implications of every relationship. Poignantly, Nata can only drape herself across the back of a bedroom chair when her cuckolded husband discovers her with her lover. Musia sits even more dejectedly, dwarfed by a fireplace in their connubial apartment. In his signature film, Bauer projects the political culture of the age, the inability of Russians to wrest themselves from the stranglehold of a social and political system, even when they themselves could recognize its decay.

Louise McReynolds

The Devil's Wheel

Chertovo koleso

Country of Origin:

Soviet Union

Language:

Russian

Studio:

Leningradkino

Directors:

Grigorii Kozintsev
Leonid Trauberg

Screenplay:

Adrian Piotrovskii

Cinematographer:

Andrei Moskvin

Synposis

Originally entitled *The Sailor from the Aurora*, the film shows the NEP-era misadventures of a young sailor assigned to the revolutionarily iconic cruiser *Aurora*. Vania finds himself in Leningrad's 'Narodnyi Dom' amusement park, where he is distracted from his revolutionary zeal by the beauteous delinquent, Valia. The *Aurora* leaves without him and, overwhelmed by his deserter's guilt, Vania comes with his damsel-in-distress to a den of the NEP criminal element. Leningrad's lower depths are depicted with imaginative gusto; and admiringly, especially owing to the figure of the charismatic gang leader 'Human Question'. In a disproportionately aggressive operation, the police exterminate the gang and its leader, and this grandiose finale overwhelms whatever attention the viewer might pay to Vania's melancholic return to the *Aurora* in the dim Leningrad morning.

Critique

The plot of this film bears an uncanny resemblance to Veniamin Kaverin's 1924 novella *The End of the Gang*, though all the parties involved denied any immediate borrowing or influence. Playing as it does with the concept made famous by Kozintsev's teacher/

Art Director:

Evgenii Enei

Editor:

Boris Shpis

Duration:

76 minutes

Genre:

Melodrama

Cast:

Petr Sobolevskii
Sergei Gerasimov
Ianina Zheimo
Liudmila Semenova
Andrei Kostrichkin
Sergei Martinson

Year:

1926

rival Sergei Eisenstein, *The Devil's Wheel* can be described as a 'montage of distractions', though attractions, including those of Narodnyi Dom park, also play a crucial role in this rich and ambivalent work. While the protagonist is distracted from his duty by his libido and by the picturesque chaos of the Leningrad underworld, the audience in turn is distracted from the sailor's ideological tribulations, and whatever lesson these may convey, by this mesmerizing underworld, 'another' world normally excluded from the conception of the Soviet city.

The great magnetic force of the plot lies in its witty inclusion of the elements required by the urban melodrama, particularly the Dickensian species thereof: the 'angelic' protagonist Vania (Sobolevskii), lured by dark forces; the quasi-prostitute Valia (Semenova) with a heart of gold; and the irresistibly attractive villain, the 'Human Question' (Gerasimov). Trauberg and Kozintsev moreover appropriate the main vector of the melodramatic plot – that of the fall, which the film instantiates in Vania's descent from the heights of ideological chastity into the embrace of a 'delinquent' girl and her way of life. But in order for this metaphor to take hold of the audience, the cinematography of Moskvin (who joined Kozintsev on this film) had to embody a dizzying roller-coaster ride thrilling to audience and character alike, and to take the notion of the fall to its full, vertigo-inducing realization. Surviving several collapses of his still less-than-perfect movie camera, Moskvin made the combination of technical virtuosity with the realization of metaphor his signature.

Also symptomatic is the episode in the park's dance-hall, which Moskvin, searching for the perfect opportunity to indulge his interest in drastic chiaroscuro lighting, insisted on shooting at night. Kozintsev recalls: 'we drew a rope over the crowd's heads and asked everyone to smoke as much as they possibly could. The beam of a strong searchlight was aimed in such a way that only heads could be seen. Moving slowly, the searchlight exposed silhouettes of the heads, the transparent smoke backlighting the fragile figure of the ropedancer...'

Moskvin's technique exposes, as is typical for his style, not just the heads of Leningrad idlers but the underlying pathos of the film: the desire to peek into the dark but attractive world of social marginals. Contemporary critics reacted to this pathos with unanimous hostility: they sensed (rightly) that instead of lauding the *Aurora* and her sailors, the Factory of the Eccentric Actor (FEKS) had staged an expressive farewell to the wild spirit of the 1920s and to the idea, threatened by rising Soviet homogeneity, of Petersburg's otherness.

Polina Barskova

Bed and Sofa

Tret'ia meshchanskaia
(Liubov' v troem)

Country of Origin:
Soviet Union

Language:
Russian

Studio:
Sovkino Moscow

Director:
Abram Room

Screenplay:
Abram Room
Viktor Shklovskii

Cinematographer:
Grigorii Giber

Art Directors:
Vasilii Rakhal's
Sergei Iutkevich

Duration:
74 minutes

Genre:
Melodrama

Cast:
Nikolai Batalov
Liudmila Semenova
Vladimir Fogel'

Year:
1926

Synopsis

One morning in July 1926 a young print worker, Volodia (Fogel'), arrives in Moscow to look for work. A husband and wife, Kolia (Batalov) and Liuda (Semenova), go about their usual routine in their tiny apartment in Third Meshchanskaia Street. Volodia finds a job, but has nowhere to live; he bumps in to his old army friend, Kolia, who suggests he stay on their sofa. Liuda is not consulted and not pleased. However, Volodia is attentive and helpful to Liuda, in marked contrast to her husband, and when the latter goes on a business trip (he is a construction worker), they embark upon an affair and Volodia exchanges the sofa for the matrimonial bed. Upon Kolia's return he is told the truth and leaves, only to come back later and occupy the sofa. Before long Liuda finds that Volodia is as flawed a partner as Kolia and, feeling sorry for her husband, allows him back in to the matrimonial bed, sending Volodia back to the sofa. When Liuda realizes she is pregnant, but unsure who the father is, both men decide she should have an abortion. Liuda decides against the men's wishes and leaves them, her home and Moscow. Kolia and Volodia share a momentary pang of guilt, but ultimately remain unchanged.

Critique

Bed and Sofa is a beautifully crafted, engaging and intellectually provocative film, which still exudes the energy and enthusiasm poured into it by its makers. Room's film was initially entitled *Ménage à trois* (*Liubov' v troem*), but this wording was considered too explicit in the late 1920s.

The key themes touched upon in this film are very much of their time: on the one hand there is the issue of social change and the role of women in society, as represented by Liuda's initial stifling role as a bourgeois housewife and her eventual escape; on the other the theme of people like Volodia coming to the capital to start new lives. The latter idea is neatly subverted by Liuda's leaving Moscow at the end of the film, leaving her destination, fate and many other questions deliberately unresolved.

The plot is merely the framework upon which Room has piled detail upon detail, and it is these minutiae that make the film a work of art. The subtle precision of the acting reveals the characters' psychological states. The finely tuned variations of lighting (by Grigorii Giber) add meaning and aesthetic integrity to the film. Stylistically, as otherwise, *Bed and Sofa* is a highly skilful work, and it is noteworthy that the lattice-effect shadows cast on Volodia and Liuda at different moments (thereby linking them symbolically) prefigure and pre-date Aleksandr Rodchenko's famous *Girl with a Leica* by seven years. The density and richness of the textures and surfaces within the film, almost at times to the point of overload, convey the oppressive nature of the cramped space within the apartment, or the relative spaciousness of the world outside, especially as perceived by Liuda. In historical terms, the film leaves a lasting legacy, as the aerial views of Moscow include shots of the original Church of Christ the Saviour, which are significant documentary records as well as pure art.

Room explicitly directed the camera to look at the world through the eyes of the protagonists, particularly in shots from Liuda's point of view, whether with semi-obscured views of the legs of passers-by from the window, conveying her sense of being an imprisoned observer, or panoramic scenes from the aeroplane Volodia takes her on, or the cinema he takes her to (where she is again an observer). Volodia briefly takes her away from it all, literally and figuratively, and these scenes are clear examples of Room's love of spectacle (which feature in most of his films in some form). However, Liuda soon returns to a reality even more oppressive than before Volodia's arrival. By contrast, Kolia has been escaping from the domestic environment daily when he goes to work, where he is able to look down upon Moscow from the top of the Bolshoi theatre, which he is restoring. In Room's film the city is visually striking, but also highly symbolic; Moscow looks impressively modern, yet by restoring that particular building, Kolia is preserving an element of the pre-Revolutionary past, which reflects his attitude to family life. Liuda's rejection of this attitude is revealed in an equally symbolic act, as she wrenches her photo from its restrictive frame and leaves for good; the frame on the wall is shown poignantly empty.

Room's film has enduring appeal; there are academic studies of *Bed and Sofa* from various decades and countries, but different kinds of tributes have also been made to the work: in 1997 the opera *Bed and Sofa. A Silent Movie Opera* was staged in New York and later released on CD. In 1998 the director Petr Todorovskii filmed an odd 're-make' of the film, set in contemporary Russia, called *Retro vtroem*.

Milena Michalski

Wait for Me

Zhdi menia

Country of Origin:
Soviet Union

Language:
Russian

Studios:
Central United Feature Film Studio (TsOKS)
Alma-Ata

Directors:
Aleksandr Stolper
Boris Ivanov

Screenplay:
Konstantin Simonov

Synopsis

In Moscow, at the home of pilot Nikolai Ermolov, friends and family gather to mark his imminent departure for the front. Ermolov's wife, Liza, insists on spending the last hour alone with her husband. Soon afterwards, Nikolai's plane is shot down by the Germans; Nikolai and his friend, war correspondent Mikhail Vainshtein, survive and manage to escape, albeit separately: Mikhail saves valuable documents, whereas Nikolai joins a guerilla unit. Back at home, Liza helps digging trenches while keeping her firm belief that Nikolai is alive. She chastizes her friend Sonia who no longer thinks that her husband, Andrei, will ever come back. When Andrei does return, he is heartbroken over Sonia's betrayal; he feels dead long before his actual death from an exploding bomb. Liza keeps waiting, and finally Nikolai opens the door to their apartment.

Critique

Konstantin Simonov, the most celebrated Soviet World War II correspondent, wrote his legendary poem 'Wait for Me' in 1941. It brought

Cinematographer:

Samuil Rubashkin

Art Directors:

Artur Berger
Vladimir Kamskii

Composers:

Nikolai Kriukov
Iurii Biriukov

Editor:

Evgeniia Abdirkina

Duration:

87 minutes

Genre:

War Melodrama

Cast:

Mikhail Nazvanov
Valentina Serova
Elena Tiapkina
Boris Blinov

Year:

1943

him instant fame and the gratitude of countless men and women in the military. Simonov turned the poem into a play and later a screenplay. Director Aleksandr Stolper, whose *Lad from Our Town* (1942) had demonstrated his ability to combine patriotic optimism with intimate melodrama, was assigned to direct *Wait for Me* together with Boris Ivanov. Given the still precarious situation of the Red Army in 1942–1943, encouragement and optimism were expected from feature films above all. Not surprisingly, Simonov's script is relatively simplistic, juxtaposing the 'positive' Liza who maintains an unshakeable faith in her beloved's survival to the 'negative' Sonia who gives up on her husband and enjoys the benefits of an extramarital affair. However, there are a number of elements that soften the moral lecturing so typical of Stalinist cinema. Already in the first scene, Liza's insistence on being left alone with Nikolai in the hour of farewell is a violation of traditional collectivist standards. Indeed, the actress portraying Liza, Valentina Serova, was the ideal choice for conveying such a surprisingly independent attitude – she owed her stardom to the title role in *A Girl with Personality* (1939). Stolper, a reliable craftsman, did his best to visualize the harsh reality of war to the maximum degree tolerated at the time. *Wait for Me* skilfully contrasts the warmth and protection of Moscow interiors – designed by the experienced Artur Berger – against the wildly inhospitable winter storms in which the men have to fight. The interior scenes convey an uncommon atmosphere of intimacy, condensed in several excellent close shots, while the exterior episodes emphasize Soviet fighters' heroism. It is peculiar for this melodrama that the fighters' selflessness in the open sphere is motivated by the protectiveness of the private space that they are leaving behind. Although *Wait for Me* contains some declamatory elements, too, their number is noticeably limited, and not once do the characters mention 'comrade Stalin' or 'our Communist Party'. Instead, their conversations deal with everyday problems in war conditions, not the macro-political purposes of their struggle. It was this sense of civility, love, friendship and trust that endeared *Wait for Me* to millions of viewers. Communist watchdogs disliked its central metaphysical message, which normally would have been seen as incompatible with the Marxist-Leninist materialist dogma, but allowed it since its positive effect on soldiers' motivation was undeniable.

Some external factors, too, have to be taken into consideration in order to explain the film's unusual emotional impact on contemporaries. Many viewers were familiar with Valentina Serova's story: her first husband, pilot and hero of the Soviet Union Aleksandr Serov (1910–1939), had fought in the Civil War in Spain and later perished in a plane crash. Konstantin Simonov, Serova's second husband, dedicated his 'Wait for Me' to her and wrote the screenplay with her in mind. Moreover, the role of Nikolai Ermolov was the last performance of Boris Blinov who had portrayed Chapaev's commissar Furmanov with charm and reserve – he died of typhoid fever in Alma-Ata at the age of thirty-four. And yet, the film's intrinsic qualities are far more important than contextual factors, primarily the convincing performances by Serova, Blinov, Lev Sverdlin, Mikhail Nazvanov and Elena Tiapkina, who provide their rank-and-file characters with a blend of strength and tenderness, humour and melancholy, down-to-earth rationality and hope against all odds. While the film's emphasis on the vital connection between the front and the rear made it a useful tool for propaganda, its focus on the human dimension of a horrific war endeared it to rank-and-file Soviet citizens.

Peter Rollberg

Red Guelderbush

Kalina krasnaia

Country of Origin:
USSR

Language:
Russian

Studio:
Mosfil'm

Director:
Vasilii Shukshin

Screenplay:
Vasilii Shukshin

Cinematographer:
Anatolii Zabolotskii

Art Director:
Ippolit Novoderezhkin

Duration:
108 minutes

Genre:
Literary adaptation

Cast:
Vasilii Shukshin
Lidiia Fedoseeva-Shukshina
Georgii Burkov
Lev Durov

Year:
1973

Synopsis

The film begins in a 'corrective labour facility' with an evening concert given by the inmates. Those about to be released sing the 'Bom-bom' chorus in the popular ballad 'Vechernii zvon' ('Evening Bells'). Among them is Egor Prokudin (Vasilii Shukshin), a career criminal. On his release his attempts to re-establish links with his former gang and girlfriend result in disappointment, and Egor travels to the village of Iasnoe ('Clear'), where he hopes to make a fresh (and honest) start. While in prison he had been in correspondence with a resident of the village, Liuba Baikalova (Lidiia Fedoseeva-Shukshina), and while living with her and her parents he works first as a chauffeur and then a tractor-driver. It becomes clear that the reason Egor has chosen Iasnoe is because his mother lives nearby. Though he has not seen her since he was sixteen, he refuses to make himself known to her when he and Liuba visit. Egor is found by his former gang, and shot by Guboshlep, their leader (Georgii Burkov). Egor dies in a field. Liuba's truck driver brother Petro rams the gang's car and pushes it into the river, then waits for the police to arrive.

Critique

One of the most popular films of the 1970s, it was written for the screen by Shukshin and published as a novella (*povest'*) in 1973. Shukshin himself died shortly after its release the following year. On the level of plot the film was sensational on its release, as it was the first to show prison life in (admittedly sanitized) detail, and not only acknowledged the existence of the criminal underground but even showed its workings. Guboshlep is a charismatic leader, but beneath his surface charm he is a psychopath who thinks nothing of killing.

The character of Egor Prokudin spoke to an entire generation, men and women uprooted from their rural communities through the tumultuous social and political processes of the 1930s and 1940s, but unable to adapt to urban life. Despite his criminal past, Egor is essentially an honest, even innocent soul looking for some purpose and identity, which he hopes to find through an emotional release he formulates as a 'festival of the soul' (*prazdnik dushi*). When he arrives in Iasnoe he is struck by the wide-open expanses that can provide an inner sense of freedom (*volia*). Liuba offers him not so much a romantic relationship as a mother-figure providing the security and home he left as a teenager. Prokudin's personal tragedy is framed as the symbolic death of the Russian peasant, surrounded by gleaming

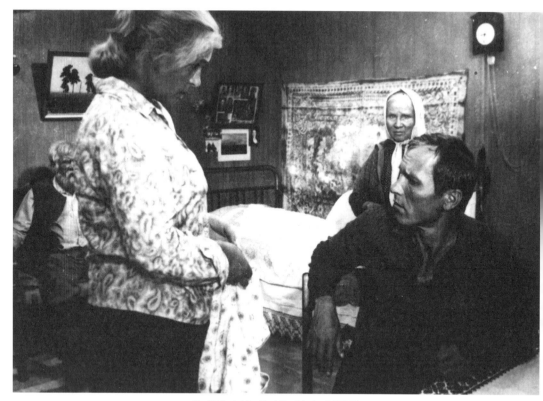

Vasilii Shukshin, *Red Guelderbush* (1973).

church cupolas and with a choral soundtrack accompanying his last minutes. His death is associated with Sergei Esenin, the 'last poet of the Russian village', whose poem 'Pis'mo materi' ('A Letter to Mother') is sung diegetically in the last minutes before Egor is shot. Prokudin has abandoned his mother and his roots, and he knows nothing about village life, throwing hot water onto Petro rather than on the bath-house coals. Whereas the spiritual wholesomeness of village life is signified by Liuba's white dress, the town is associated with crime and loose morals. Egor's attempt to organize a 'debauch' proves farcical. Only in death is Egor reunited with the Russian earth, and he dies 'a peasant'. The film, therefore, offers a significant development of the thematic concerns of 'village prose' of the 1960s and 1970s. Here the link of man and nature is broken, Russian life is dominated not by the 'soft' feminine principle but by the hard and violent masculine ethos of gangsterism and prison. Significantly, Guboshlep equates his own brand of violence with that administered by the Soviet state during the purges: 'when you cut down the forest, wood chips fly' (*les rubiat, shchipy letiat*). Rather like Elem Klimov's *Farewell*, *Red Guelderbush* shows the very human cost of Russian social and political history in the twentieth century.

David Gillespie

A Slave of Love

Raba liubvi

Country of Origin:
Soviet Union

Language:
Russian

Studio:
Mosfilm

Director:
Nikita Mikhalkov

Screenplay:
Andrei Mikhalkov-Konchalovskii
Fridrikh Gorenshtein

Cinematographer:
Pavel Lebeshev

Art Directors:
Aleksandr Adabashian
Aleksandr Samulekin

Composer:
Eduard Artem'ev

Editor:
Liudmila Elian

Duration:
94 minutes

Genre:
Melodrama

Cast:
Elena Solovei
Rodion Nakhapetov
Aleksandr Kaliagin
Oleg Basilashvili
Konstantin Gregor'ev

Year:
1975

Synopsis

In the midst of Civil War, in an unnamed resort town in Southern Russia, a Moscow film company is working on a new picture starring a famous actress, twenty-eight-year-old Ol'ga Voznesenskaia. She becomes interested in Viktor Pototskii, a cameraman, who also secretly films war documentaries for Bolsheviks. After she helps him to hide one of his films, he invites her to a secret night screening of his footage. The footage shocks her and she decides to go back to Moscow, but is convinced to stay. Once again Ol'ga helps Pototskii. She also admits her love to him and realizes that he loves her back. However, when Pototskii is driving off with a promise to come by that evening, he is blown up in front of her eyes. In search of Pototskii's film, the White Army officer Captain Fedotov invades the studio and Ol'ga shoots him, but misses. Seconds later, the Bolsheviks storm the studio, kill the captain and save Ol'ga, by putting her on a tram that goes to town. However, the tram's driver jumps off the moving tram and abandons her to the Whites as a Revolutionary. The film ends with the White officers chasing after horrified Ol'ga in an empty tram.

Critique

Essentially, Nikita Mikhalkov's A Slave of Love is a love story. In the centre of the film is a nascent feeling between Ol'ga Voznesenskaia and Viktor Pototskii. In a way, following tradition of a pre-Revolutionary melodrama, where no happy end is possible, Pototskii dies before he gets a chance to have an affair with Voznesenskaia. As to Voznesenskaia, her death is implied at the end as well, as she left alone in a tram exclaiming to the Whites, 'You are animals, gentlemen; you will be cursed by your country'.

With that said, A Slave of Love is about love for that wealthier, carefree life that is slipping away. Famous Chekhov's 'to Moscow, to Moscow' is the film's leitmotif. Moscow – so desirable but impossible to come back to – represents that lost life. For the film's crew the past is irrevocable, and the only way to live it is through cinema. Mikhalkov manages to express the feeling of those, who are left behind; it is the feeling found in The Cherry Orchard. In general, Chekhovian motives and influences are quite obvious in the film, and just like in Chekhov's plays, the old wealthier classes here are quite often funny in their absurdity and oblivion. The film recreates the atmosphere of this general confusion and loss both visually and contextually. Kaliagin, the film's director, is not sure how to proceed filming without his male lead. Voznesenskaia is repeatedly shown as lost and restless. Significantly, at the film's basis is a figure of the silent screen queen Vera Kholodnaia, here Ol'ga Voznesenskaia. Kholodnaia, just like Voznesenskaia, was a symbol of that leisured life, so glamorous and tragic at the same time. Quite often Mikhalkov films her moving away from the camera and disappearing. This could be read as a loss of that glamorous life, for which the figure of Voznesenskaia (and Kholodnaia) stands for.

Nikita Mikhalkov, *Slave of Love* (1976); Elena Solovei and Rodion Nakhapetov.

Nevertheless, *A Slave of Love* is also about love for film and art in general. The film revolves around a melodrama production, in which Voznesenskaia stars. The issue that arises and is carried throughout is the one of an adequacy of such a production during the Civil War. Both Voznesenskaia and Kaliagin find their art empty and pointless. At first, the filming seems not to be going well because Voznesenskaia's partner, Maksakov, is still in Moscow. However, as Mikhalkov seems to suggest, it is not about Maksakov. Maksakov stands for something bigger, it is not just a lack of a male lead – Maksakov represents that purpose, that ideal that this bourgeois art lacks. It becomes especially obvious when the rest of the crew arrives and brings a newspaper, which announces Maksakov's acceptance and support of the Revolution (and with that, his choice to remain in Moscow). Lacking a purpose and a male lead the film cannot be completed successfully, which implies that this art cannot survive in its old 'bourgeois' form.

Thus, Voznesenskaia embodies this loss: she cannot function without the male lead and an idea (as it quite often happens in

Mikhalkov's films, a male figure is connected to the ideological in the film). As soon as she finds her own a male lead (Pototskii) and with that a purpose (helping Bolsheviks), she loses them both to the war, thus proving the impossibility of being in between, or trying to keep the old life style in this new order, of being a 'bourgeois' actress in the Revolutionary film. Mikhalkov's ability to express this atmosphere of melancholy and nostalgia, of a life that is slipping away, stresses not only the ideological, but also humane attitude toward those who have lost their past, and have no place in the present.

Mariya Boston

Moscow Does Not Believe in Tears

Moskva slezam ne verit

Country of Origin:
Soviet Union

Language:
Russian

Studio:
Mosfilm

Director:
Vladimir Men'shov

Screenplay:
Valentin Chernykh

Cinematographer:
Igor' Slabnevich

Art Director:
Said Menial'shchikov

Composer:
Sergei Nikitin

Editor:
Valeriia Belova

Duration:
150 minutes

Genre:
Melodrama

Synopsis

The film follows the destinies of three friends – Ekaterina, Antonina and Liudmila – from the late 1950s to the late 1970s. Originally living together as students in the same dorm room, they subsequently make very different life-choices. The three girls represent three character types: one is dedicated to her career, the second to a simpler life with her husband and the third to nothing in particular, eventually falling victim to her own laziness. Ekaterina begins her career on the noisy floor of a factory, but works her way up to senior management; Antonina is attracted by the idea of marriage and a family early on and soon retreats to something of a rustic idyll. Liudmila is most attracted to Moscow but she fares worst of all. Enamored with glamour and stardom, she never applies herself after graduation. Adulthood brings her nothing more than a drunken spouse and wretched domestic life. Meanwhile Ekaterina – the most socially mobile character – overcomes difficulties caused by an early pregnancy to reach the upper flight of socialist society. Ironically, though, when she finally meets a suitable lover, Gosha, he is unnerved by her remarkable (or non-traditional) success. Only through a compromise between her careerism and his class-related anxieties does the couple find harmony and happiness.

Critique

The story of this film's creation begins in 1978 when the screenplay was first under consideration at the state studios of Goskino. The project was approved with relative speed, but one particular problem arose during casting. Director Vladimir Men'shov had difficulty finding a suitable male actor for the role of Ekaterina's ultimate companion, Gosha. After some debate, the role was offered to Aleksei Batalov, already well known as the hero of some rather dated dramas such as *A Grand Family* (1954) or *The Rumiantsev Case* (1955). Nonetheless it was precisely because of these old-world associations that Batalov was chosen. The director was looking for the embodiment of a working-class 'slogger', as he put it, the kind of man who embodied a certain constancy in Soviet values, no matter how petty a modern

Vladimir Men'shov, *Moscow does not Believe in Tears* (1980); Katia leaves the maternity ward.

Cast:

Vera Alentova
Aleksei Batalov
Irina Murav'eva
Aleksandr Fatiushin
Raisa Riazanova
Boris Smorchkov
Iurii Vasil'ev
Natal'ia Vavilova
Oleg Tabakov
Evgeniia Khanaeva
Viktor Ural'skii
Zoia Fedorova
Liia Akhedzhakova
Valentina Ushakova
Innokentii Smoktunovskii

Year:

1979

family movie might seem. Rather than bow to the modishness of a bourgeois melodrama, he wanted *Moscow Does Not Believe in Tears* to 'capture the Russian popular spirit'.

That phrase speaks directly to the most commonly debated aspect of the film: whether it does indeed surrender political purpose to a kitchen-sink drama, or whether the sub-plots such as Ekaterina's workplace success prove exactly the opposite, that the movie celebrates a greater potential for advancement enjoyed by Soviet women, especially when compared to their western counterparts. Ironically these issues arose more overseas than in Russia, where the film was seen as blissful escape from archetypal Soviet moviemaking, burdened with heavy-handed politicking. Given that the feature affords much time to widespread, yet arguably trivial problems – such as the life of a single mother – *Moscow Does Not Believe in Tears* was referred to in the Soviet press as a work of 'consoling realism'. It brought comfort to people in their private difficulties, without necessary reference to a loud and public ethos.

Even though the film was shortlisted in Hollywood for the 1980 Best Foreign Film Oscar, many US papers prior to the awards dismissed it as throwaway twaddle. The *New York Times*, for example, called it 'hackwork' in comparison to Truffaut's submission (*The Last Metro*) or Kurosawa's *Kagemusha*. Critics saw little originality in the movie, comparing it to the 'flabby comedies' of 1930s Hollywood, thus – ironically – offering a variation on Men'shov's own love for Russian film of the same period. The Hollywood tropes stolen by so many Stalinist classics remained recognizable for American critics, but they took on an inverted significance in another country. Rarely were these Hollywood parallels treated kindly.

Nonetheless, *Moscow Does Not Believe in Tears* won the 1980 Oscar. At the peak of its social significance, this sprawling family saga ran simultaneously in twenty Moscow cinemas and would eventually be seen by 85 million people across the Soviet Union. It even enjoyed great popularity among American audiences, reflecting perfectly the workings of Cold War détente: Ronald Reagan would subsequently feel that this film could help him 'know' the desires of Soviet delegates at a Cold War summit. Despite any presidential wish for happy universality, though, public suspicion endured in America that Katia, Tonia and Liuda were 'loose, whining characters'. Whatever they were trying to do, it looked more like a sad, sorry melodrama or unfunny spoof than romantic comedy. Only in Russia did the political context remain in the background, where the film is loved to this day.

David MacFadyen

ASSA

Country of Origin:
Soviet Union

Language:
Russian

Studio:
Mosfilm

Director:
Sergei Solov'ev

Screenplay:
Sergei Livnev
Sergei Solov'ev

Cinematographer:
Pavel Lebeshev

Art Director:
Marksen Gaukhman-Sverdlov

Composer:
Boris Grebenshchikov

Editor:
Vera Kruglova

Duration:
153 minutes

Genre:
Melodrama

Cast:
Sergei Bugaev (Africa)
Tatiana Drubich
Stanislav Govorukhin
Aleksandr Bashirov
Boris Grebenshchikov
Viktor Tsoi

Year:
1987

Synopsis

ASSA is a nonsense word suggested by the rock musicians starring in the film. ASSA is the first film in the trilogy, followed by Black Rose is a Symbol of Sorrow, Red Rose is a Symbol of Love (1989), and House Under the Starry Skies (1991); there is also a sequel, 2 ASSA 2 or the Second Death of Anna Karenina (2009).

The film is set in the resort town of Yalta in winter. A young woman, Alika, comes to town to meet with her older lover, a mobster named Krymov. While he is delayed, she meets young rock-musician, Bananan, who plays in the restaurant with his rock band. Alika reunites with Krymov, but her friendship with Bananan grows and she begins to spend more time with him, while Krymov is busy plotting the theft of an antique violin. Krymov and his accomplices are secretly watched and investigated by the police. Krymov becomes suspicious and jealous of the relationship between Alika and Bananan. At first he warns Bananan, then tries to bribe him to leave the town. When the young man refuses, Krymov murders him. Alika in turn shoots Krymov when she finds out about Bananan's death.

Critique

ASSA is considered one of the most important films of the perestroika period. ASSA was the first Soviet film to feature Russian underground rock music. In 1988 this meant public recognition for underground art and public acceptance of the youth subculture as an agent of change. The young generation was an important subject in perestroika cinema that produced a corpus of youth-oriented films that described it either as a lost generation (Little Vera, Vasilii Pichul, 1989) or as the generation of hope and change (Is it Easy to be Young?, Juris Podnieks, 1987). ASSA's reception made it a cult film among young people in the late 1980s. The screenings were accompanied by an 'art rock parade' – live concerts of banned rock groups, exhibits of contemporary underground artists and fashion designers. ASSA became the embodiment of the spirit of change, drawing unprecedented numbers of viewers. It captured the hopes and aspirations of the late perestroika era, which produced a sense of individual and public empowerment, when a free society seemed to be within reach and the old taboos could be done away with overnight. This message is especially evident in the end of the film, when Viktor Tsoi, leader of the group Kino, sings 'We Wait for Change' (My zhdem peremen), and the scene that starts as a rehearsal at the restaurant turns into a concert with thousands of fans.

However, the final song with its hard rock beat and straightforward rebellious message contrasts with the tone that ASSA sets. ASSA mostly features music by Boris Grebenshchikov and Aquarium, known for subversive tongue-in-cheek texts and experimental musical forms. This choice compliments pastiche style, formal experimentation and an absurdist touch characteristic for ASSA. The film's formal sophistication starts with art direction that fills the scenes with the strange objects that seem to come straight from a conceptual installation.

Solov'ev also uses his signature techniques, such as the use of graphics and text within visual material. Bananan's dreams are presented as film stock with bright abstract pictures painted on it, and the film is interrupted with onscreen text commentary explaining the meaning of the youth slang.

In terms of genre, *ASSA* is eclectic, combining melodrama with a criminal thriller about cops and gangsters; fantasy sequences about a *coup d'état* against Paul I that comes to life as Krymov reads about it in a book; and a social message brought in by Russian rock. None of the genres is entirely functional: the cops and gangsters story seems not only irrelevant but is openly mocked in the end, when long onscreen text describes all the financial scams perpetrated by Krymov. Life, death and mafia power boil down to dull description in the Soviet ideolect. The heart of the film is obviously with youth subculture, whose absurd lyrics and crazy stunts are positioned as more meaningful than an elaborate heist or Mafiosi brought to justice. Russian rock has a long tradition of cultural resistance that manifested itself in the kind of absurdity and irony that Sergei Solov'ev uses in the film. However, the budding relationship between Alika and Bananan is depicted with utmost tenderness and seriousness.

The incongruence of genres adds to the film's compartmentalized nature. The different stories exist as different worlds – a commentary on the radical changes that befell Russia with the advent of perestroika. Solov'ev's visual and narrative techniques emphasize the divide between the old and new. The sunny southern Yalta is covered in snow and mud. The young couple go on a mountain lift and the background song tells about a golden city under the blue sky, while the camera pans and reveals the unkempt, grey city underneath. The cops, gangsters, lovers and rock musicians exist in parallel universes, and when they meet the results are either frightening – as in the gruesome death of Bananan, or grotesque – as in the final triumph of the police. The fantasy sequences about the murder of Paul I during the *coup d'état* suggest a parallel both to the martyred Bananan and the fading of the old generation, the death of Krymov, in the name of the future that bursts onto the scene with the end song, demanding change.

Volha Isakava

The Wedding

Svad'ba

Countries of Origin:
Russia
France
Italy
Germany

Language:
Russian

Studios:
CDP
Arte France Cinema
Mosfilm
WDR
Lichtblick Cologne
Cine B

Director:
Pavel Lungin

Producers:
Catherine Dussart
Erik Waisberg

Screenplay:
Aleksandr Galin
Pavel Lungin

Cinematographer:
Aleksandr Burov

Art Director:
Il'ia Amurskii

Composer:
Vladimir Chekasin

Editor:
Sophie Brunet

Duration:
99 minutes

Genre:
Melodrama
Comedy

Synopsis

Tania, a model living in Moscow, returns to her home town to marry her earlier love Mishka Krapivin, now a miner. When Mishka at last receives his wages, he still has no money to buy his bride some eye-drops. With his friend Garkusha he tries to sell knives to make some money, but Garkusha would rather exchange knives for vodka, so they both end up totally drunk. When they come across a rich Ukrainian woman on a staircase, Garkusha steals her eye-drops and gives them to a dead-drunk Mikhail. The police arrive at the scene and identify Mishka as the perpetrator and arrest him. In exchange for a wedding invitation, the police officer releases Mishka for two hours so that he can get married. At the wedding party, Tania's ex-boyfriend shows up, the rich Muscovite Mafiosi Vasilii Borodin. He tries to win Tania back, but to no avail. However, when the wedding party is over, Mishka has to go back to prison. While Garkusha pilfers a gun from the police officer, Mishka and Tania manage to escape. Borodin leaves for Moscow and the guests at the wedding party, including the police officer, continue to celebrate.

Critique

After several darker films, such as *Taxi Blues* (1990) and *Luna Park* (1992), Lungin wrote and directed the comedy *The Wedding* (2000). In the same vein as Hollywood comedies, the film depicts the events before and after a wedding and contains the usual characters of a good and bad guy vying for the love of a beautiful girl. However, in essence, the film explores the specificities of Russianness. *The Wedding* shows a rural community with high unemployment figures, where people try to find some relief in the copious consumption of alcohol. The social realism is enhanced by the documentary style of the film, which is shot with a hand-held camera, using no special effects and no additional soundtrack. In spite of their poverty, everyone does their very best to help Mishka and his parents organize a good wedding party. Mishka's colleagues from the mine give him their salaries, the market vendor gives him a bunch of flowers for free and a truck driver sells his cement and gives Mikhail the money. Verbally, the Russians' generosity is related to their utter humaneness. Donating a big fish, the grocery shop owner states, 'Please, take this fish as a present. We are human beings too'. The police officer is the only person in town to be shown as inhumane. He refuses to close the case against Mishka, although people ask him to be human. At the very end of the film, then, the police officer finally shows mercy and refuses to arrest Garkusha for his crimes. Instead, he takes a glass of vodka, embraces Garkusha and starts the after-party. The humane features of the townspeople, and to a wider extent Russians, are contrasted with the lack of humaneness in the rich Muscovite Borodin. He is a 'New Russian', a man with loads of money and arrogance, but no moral values. Moscow here symbolizes the bad side of Russian life, underlined by the fact that the successful and beautiful Tania decides to leave the glitter and glamour of the capital for a

Cast:

Marat Basharov

Mariia Mironova

Andrei Panin

Natal'ia Koliakanova

Marina Golub

Year:

2000

rural, but essentially Russian town. In this respect, the film conveys a message about the present state of Russia: by choosing Mishka instead of Borodin, Tania installs hope for a better future for Russia that can be found by returning to the roots. The wedding itself is a culmination of Russian traditions: guests drink litres of vodka, propose toasts to the married couple and dance to traditional wedding songs. The film draws on the happiness of parties and gatherings. It is the film's happy end, the celebratory atmosphere and the smiling faces that make it a real feel-good movie.

Jasmijn Van Gorp

LITERARY ADAPTATION

The history of Russian cinema is inseparable from that of the film adaptation. From its inception, Russian film engaged in a dialogue with literature, first modelling itself upon theatre and classical fiction in order to consolidate its own cultural status, then attempting to establish itself as 'high art' in its own right. Many early Russian films were adaptations of nineteenth-century Russian fiction. The birth of cinema coincided with a surge of national feeling and adaptations of the quintessentially Russian works of Lermontov and Dostoevsky exploited the new medium to promote a revitalized Russian self.

Literature's influence on cinema continued to reverberate within revolutionary avant-garde cinema through the involvement of leading formalists, Viktor Shklovskii and Iurii Tynianov, in *ekranizatsii* during the 1920s and 1930s. One reason for formalism's prominent role in cinema was the ability of many of its protagonists to compensate for the lack of good scenario writers who would also be ideologically sound (a recurrent problem in Soviet cinema history). For this reason, following Stalin's clampdown on avant-garde culture, film provided both writers and critics with a refuge from the ravages of the repressions.

For a while, formalist notions of the essential differences between film and literature coincided with Bolshevik sensibilities. Formalist technique and radical Marxism merged in one of the most important early Soviet films: Pudovkin's adaptation of Gor'kii's novel, *Mother* (1926). Pudovkin's striking use of montage and cinematic synecdoche, and his presentation of the characters as expressionist archetypes mark the film as a conscious visual reinterpretation of a source whose revolutionary message it distils into stark blocks of cinematic meaning.

As the utopian experimentation of the early 1920s waned, the purpose of the *ekranizatsiia* changed as it became ever more subordinate to the demands of a repressive state apparatus desperate to consolidate its still precarious hold on power.

The same contradiction emerged in what became the chief rationale for the Stalinist screen adaptation: its ability to reinforce the dogmas of socialist realism. With a remit to furnish a middlebrow culture capable of appealing to the masses, cultural policy makers placed a premium on accessibility. Bridging the divide between highbrow literature and popular film, the *ekranizatsiia* was ideally suited to this purpose. It facilitated the rapid canonization of key texts. Aleksandr Fadeev's *The Rout* and Mikhail Sholokhov's *And Quiet Flows the Don*

Nikita Mikhalkov, *Unfinished Piece for a Mechanical Piano* (1976); Sashen'ka and Platonov.

Literary Adaptation   169

were adapted as early as 1931, *Chapaev* in 1934, with Nikolai Ostrovskii's *How the Steel Was Tempered* following later in 1942. The *ekranizatsiia* also legitimated socialist realism by demonstrating its links with pre-Revolutionary literature and with progressive world culture as a whole. Nineteenth-century classics featuring criticism of the old tsarist order were milked for all they were worth.

Early twentieth-century works which openly embraced the coming Revolution (such as Gor'kii's autobiographical trilogy), and Soviet fiction set in the pre-Revolutionary period, were prominent amongst 1930s and 1940s adaptations. Such adaptations offer a convenient solution to the representational paradox of how to demonstrate the immanence of the socialist utopia within an everyday reality stubbornly resistant to the optimistic paradigm imposed upon it.

The 1930s and 1940s also saw a steady stream of *ekranizatsii* of judiciously selected world classics (predominantly those dealing with social themes or popular uprisings), providing socialist realism with organic roots in world history. However, the *ekranizatsiia* was compelled to engage with some of the tensions entailed in managing the relationship between the verbal and the visual, the official and the popular. Film's visual regime entails a subjectivization of experience at odds with the pseudo-objective rhetoric of the narrative voice it translates into cinematic language. In classic socialist realist adaptations like *And Quiet Flows the Don* and *The Rout*, the camera frequently adopted the viewpoint of the leading character, subjectivizing viewer experience in a manner subversive of the official rhetoric of the transcendence of 'spontaneity' by 'Party consciousness'.

In the later Stalin period, the *ekranizatsiia*'s allegiances with the new rhetoric of the outstanding individual accorded more readily with official discourse which was, by now, fully engaged with fostering the Stalin personality cult. One of the most important films of the late 1930s was Vladimir Petrov's adaptation of Aleksei Tolstoi's historical novel, *Peter the Great* (1937). While the novel evoked favourable comparisons between Stalin and Russia's first iron-willed reformer, Petrov ensured that the parallels conformed to contemporary ideological orthodoxies.

The dual tendencies observed in the *ekranizatsiia* of the 1930s intensified during and after World War II. On one hand, they continued to serve as a means of popularizing, canonizing and 'correcting' key texts. On the other hand, during the war the rigid dogmas of socialist realism began to splinter under pressure from twin imperatives: the need to unite the Soviet people under the banner of a revived Russian national spirit, and the need to celebrate individual acts of heroism. Here, too, with its grounding in native literary tradition, the screen adaptation was a useful tool. An interesting example is Aleksandr Stolper's 1948 adaptation of Boris Polevoi's socialist realist paradigm, 'Tale of a Real Man' (1946). Polevoi's text centres on the true story of Aleksei Mares'ev, a double amputee who, overcoming bureaucratic hurdles to his desire to fly again, finally takes to the air in battle again. The tale's theme of resistance to impersonal, institutional obstacles is at odds with socialist realist convention and is omitted in the film. However, by expanding on a brief scene in the novella in which Mares'ev dances to a folk song in his new prostheses, the film underscores the Russian nationalist theme.

In the early 1950s, film adaptations returned to more conventional Stalinist themes. Films were made of some of the most trenchantly socialist realist novels. Thus, Vsevolod Kochetov's production novel, *The Zhurbins* was adapted by Iosif Kheifits in 1954 as *The Big Family*. Kheifits's reworking of Kochetov is unsurprising in the context of the infiltration into post-Stalinist cinema of the concerns of the individual and private. Two of the main characteristics of early Thaw film adaptations were a reshaping of the literary canon to include some previously ignored or suppressed works; and a re-interpretation of canonical texts to reflect the shifting of values away from the tenets of Stalinist collectivism. Thus, Ivan Pyr'ev used his position at the summit of the Soviet film hierarchy to rehabilitate the works of Dostoevsky. Meanwhile, 1958 saw a new version of Fadeev's

The Rout retitled as *The Youth of our Fathers* in a manner indicative of the wave of early Thaw-era nostalgia for the purity of Leninist principles.

At the same time, cinema itself was advancing in new directions and, rather than fade into insignificance, screen adaptations often spearheaded these innovations. For example, the career of Tarkovskii, who achieved world recognition for articulating a pure cinematic vision inspired by his veneration of his father's poetry, began with a highly impressionistic interpretation of the tale of a war orphan, *Ivan's Childhood*.

Experimentation ground to a halt with Khrushchev's demise. The new, repressive atmosphere accounted for the banning or shelving of several groundbreaking *ekranizatsii*. Nonetheless, the increasing premium placed on 'culturedness' (*kulturnost'*), reflecting anxiety over the influences of Western mass culture, meant that there remained a place for tasteful adaptations of the Russian classics, a number of which appeared in the Brezhnev period.

Another approach to the issue was to cast popular media stars in serious literary adaptations. Vladimir Vysotskii, who had attained popularity of mythical proportions through his guitar poetry and appearances in war films, is one example. An unanticipated consequence of this phenomenon was that it contributed towards the growing trend towards interpretations of *ekranizatsii* which stressed parallels between the represented literary past and the Soviet present, making it difficult to avoid the sense that these films were replete with hidden, allegorical meaning.

The *ekranizatsiia* also became the locus for a revitalized Russian nationalism which could now be grounded in nostalgia for the lost splendour of the pre-Revolutionary years, as evidenced in the lush cinematic landscapes favoured by the early film adaptations of Nikita Mikhalkov.

With the coming of glasnost, coded allegorizations were replaced by open polemic, as film began to reflect the ideological challenges posed to communist orthodoxy mounted across the breadth of Soviet culture. Adaptations of the late 1980s were a key forum for the re-evaluation of Soviet history. Thus, Evgenii Tsymbal's 1988 adaptation of Il'ia Zverev's short story 'Defence Attorney Sedov' deals with the manipulation of an honest attorney by the Stalinist regime during the 1930s purges.

The introduction under Gorbachev of market forces inspired an awareness of cinema's commercial potential, resulting in adaptations of contemporary crime thrillers, both Russian and Western. However, few non-commercial Russian writers of the glasnost period were adapted for screen in the 1980s, or the 1990s. The early post-communist period was marked by a prolonged financial crisis throughout the arts and resource-hungry cinema was particularly harshly affected.

In the post-Soviet period, the removal of state subsidies for cinema and television entailed a significant reduction in the number of film adaptations. Nonetheless, large-scale literary adaptations are not extinct. The early 1990s witnessed a number of provocative post-Soviet reinterpretations of nineteenth-century classics, including the cinematic transposition of Tolstoy's *Prisoner of the Caucasus*, set in the tsarist Caucasus, onto latter-day Chechnya. However, in a reprise of Stalinist policy, but to reverse ideological effect, established literary classics are now screened to bolster an officially sanctioned Russian national identity. With state-controlled television now spearheading the Russian national identity project, the *ekranizatsiia* has once again emerged as a key cultural form. Money is abundantly available, provided it is spent on the (re)canonization of approved texts. Ambitious television serials based on Dostoevsky's *Idiot*, Bulgakov's *Master and Margarita* and Tolstoy's *Anna Karenina* have been shown in the first decade of the twenty-first century.

In short, reports of the death of Russian literary culture are premature. This is thanks in no small part to the vitality of the *ekranizatsiia*, whose dialogue with its verbal sources, with the cinematic art whose fraught relationship with literature it mediates, and with the official culture to which it so often lends support will continue long into the twenty-first century.

Stephen Hutchings

The Queen of Spades

Pikovaia dama

Country of Origin:
Russia

Language:
Russian

Studio:
Ermol'ev

Director:
Iakov Protazanov

Producer:
Iosif Ermol'ev

Screenplay:
Fedor Otsep
Iakov Protazanov (based on Aleksandr Pushkin)

Cinematographer:
Evgenii Slavinskii

Art Director:
Vladimir Balliuzek

Composer:
Rafal Rozmus

Duration:
63 minutes

Genre:
Melodrama

Cast:
Ivan Mozzhukhin
Vera Orlova
Tamara Duvan
Nikolai Panov
Pavel Pavlov
Elizaveta Shebueva

Year:
1916

Synopsis

The film opens with a group of military officers playing cards, save one, German (Mozzhukhin), who only observes. One of the players then tells of his grandmother (Shebueva), a compulsive gambler, who wagered her fortune on a particular sequence of cards. German becomes obsessed with this story, to the point of seducing the grandmother's ward (Orlova) to gain access to the now elderly countess. Desperate to learn her secret, one night he threatens the old woman with a pistol. She dies of fright, but reappears to him later and confides the sequences: three, seven and ace. German plays the game, *chemin de fer*, and wins handsomely the first two nights, playing the

Iakov Protazanov, *Queen of Spades*, 1916.

first two cards. On the third night, thinking that he has played the ace to win the final pot, German sees that he has laid down the Queen of Spades, and loses everything. The face on the card is that of the countess. German goes mad.

Critique

Based on a popular short story by Aleksandr Pushkin, *The Queen of Spades* was filmed twice by the pre-Revolutionary movie industry. The first version, directed by noted director Petr Chardynin in 1910, appeared before narrative cinema had become sufficiently sophisticated to capture the psychological nuances of obsession and insanity that make the plot so compelling. Where Chardynin filmed the flatness of a staged production, director Protazanov and actor Mozzhukhin used cinematic innovations in transferring Pushkin's ideas onto the silver screen. Protazanov pioneered in flashbacks, dream sequences and crosscutting to tell the secondary story of the countess gambling in her youth within the dominant narrative arc of German's growing obsession. Mozzhukhin, the most popular actor of his age, demonstrated remarkable range, from haughty to haunted. His final scene, played in a mental institution, depends upon facial features to expose mental collapse. Ironically, most reviewers in 1916 were unimpressed with both director and actor, failing to recognize how far the pair had advanced Russian filming techniques. The negative reception can be attributed to rivalries among the major studios, and the problems any beloved fiction faces when adapted to another medium. A viewing of the two versions side-by-side serves as a history lesson in the development of the Russian cinema before the combined political and artistic revolutions that followed.

Louise McReynolds

The Mother

Mat'

Country of Origin:
Soviet Union

Language:
Russian

Studio:
Mezhrabpom-Rus

Director:
Vsevolod Pudovkin

Screenplay:
Natan Zarkhi (based on the novel by Maksim Gor'kii)

Synopsis

Somewhere in Russia, 1905: a dissolute peasant father is persuaded by Tsarist agents to provoke strikers at a factory – including his own son, Pavel. A fight ensues and the father is shot dead. While the tired and beleaguered widow watches over the laid-out body, troops arrive to restore order. An initial police search of the house produces nothing, but a second visit scares the mother into revealing the cache of guns hidden by Pavel, in the hope of saving him from retribution. She is wrong. Pavel is hit in the face and arrested. At Pavel's perfunctory trial, his mother cries out for justice. During Pavel's imprisonment, she is helped and comforted by his friends, subsequently abetting his escape. Pavel and his mother join a May Day procession, with the red flag passing forwards and upwards through its ranks. When Pavel falls, she seizes the flag; when she, too, falls, the flag is passed on.

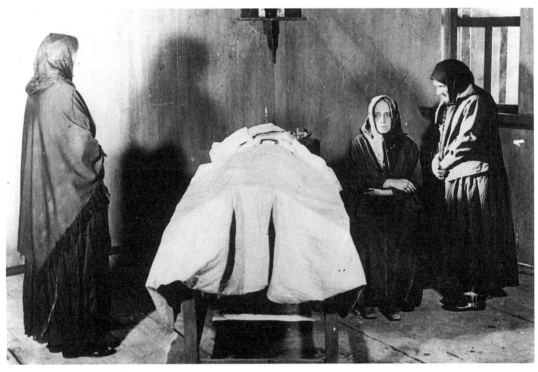

Vsevolod Pudovkin, *The Mother* (1926).

Cinematographer:
Anatolii Golovnia

Art Director:
Sergei Kozlovskii

Composer:
David Blok (Tikhon Khrennikov)

Editor:
Mikhail Doller

Duration:
66 minutes

Genre:
Literary adaptation

Cast:
Vera Baranovskaia
Nikolai Batalov
Aleksandr Chistiakov
Anna Zemtsova

Year:
1926

Critique

Maksim Gor'kii's novel, *The Mother*, and Natan Zarkhi's screenplay for Pudovkin's film, drew on newspaper reports of events contributing to the 1905 Revolution. Furthermore, Gor'kii's novel, a casualty of Tsarist censorship, had been endorsed by the Soviet leader, Vladimir Lenin.

A first film version of *The Mother*, directed by Aleksandr Razumnyi, had appeared in 1919, but had been judged ploddingly episodic by the Commissariat of Enlightenment, Anatolii Lunacharskii. Indeed, it still seems so. Zarkhi responded by purposefully expanding the role of the father (Aleksandr Chistiakov – also cast in Pudovkin's 1933 *The Deserter*), in order to set him all the more forcibly against Pavel (Nikolai Batalov) and his friends (Pavel, even asleep, carries a hammer in his pocket in order to defend his mother against his father's drunken attacks). The thrift and resourcefulness of the mother (played by Moscow Art Theatre star Vera Baranovskaia – similarly cast in Pudovkin's *The End of St Petersburg*, 1927) are set against the father's weakness when he steals the clock-weight in the hope that it will barter him vodka. An older generation is set against the aspirations of a younger generation (into which the mother is initiated). Zarkhi economically conveys the long span of Gor'kii's novel by means of significant events: Pavel's arrest; trial; death; sublimation and the mother's journey from passivity to action (or, as contemporary critics suggested, a plot defined by treachery, judgement and flight).

The mother sheds 'dull' tears at her husband's death, displaced to shots of a constantly dripping trap. Old women warn her against her rebellious son – but she learns to know better. At Pavel's arrest, a friend willingly volunteers himself in his place; during Pavel's imprisonment, various friends support and (implicitly) enlighten her – including the love interest (here, as in Pudovkin's 1925 *Chess Fever*, played by Pudovkin's wife, Anna Zemtsova). Golovnia's starkly lit, closely framed shots prompt the viewer to endorse the mother's growing distrust of authority: a police officer (played by Pudovkin himself) looks askance through wire spectacles, while Pavel, brightly smiling and wide-eyed, looks constantly ahead – towards the sun. At the trial, while the mother arrives early and wrings her hands, the judges exchange photos of 'fine fillies', doodle racehorses on their blotters and cast surreptitious glances at their watches. Acknowledgly, this scene owes as much to Tolstoy (Pudovkin's favourite author) as it does to Gor'kii.

Pudovkin and Golovnia here establish a vocabulary of shots drawn from nature to which they return in *The End of St Petersburg* and *Storm over Asia* (1928): water; shivering trees; slavering horses and dogs. Pavel's escape over the melting ice-floes seems indebted to D.W. Griffith's 1920 *Way Down East*, but here snow flakes on water are adeptly deployed by Pudovkin to reflect the accumulation of demonstrators marching towards their goal. Pudovkin interjects humour and humanism, with a bourgeois boy cadet receiving a clipped ear for his spontaneous cheering of the May Day procession. Significantly, Pudovkin cuts the smooth kid gloves of the factory master (who will not sully his own hands) against the knuckle-dusters of his hired lackeys and the 'pillars of justice and honour' of the court are intercut with cropped shots of heftily booted guards and mounted policemen.

Despite the expediency of its commissioning – for a particular purpose, at a particular time – the impact of *The Mother* has proved long-lasting and far-reaching. In the 1960s, Pier Paolo Pasolini cited the 'Spring' sequence, which greets the mother's return home from her son's prison cell, in support of his own understanding of poetic realism. Here, as in Pasolini, the poetry, and the realism, reside as much in the duration of performances as in individual shots.

Amy Sargeant

The Overcoat

Shinel'

Country of Origin:
Soviet Union

Language:
Russian

Studio:
Leningradkino

Synopsis

The Overcoat opens with a peculiar collage of story elements borrowed by screenwriter Iurii Tynianov from two other novellas of Gogol's Petersburg cycle: 'Nevskii Prospect' and 'How Ivan Ivanovich quarreled with Ivan Nikiforovich'. The film's second half faithfully follows Gogol's celebrated tale about the meek bureaucrat Akakii Bashmachkin who falls in love with the dream of having a new overcoat that could protect him from the icy abysses of Petersburg. He subsequently is deprived of his beloved overcoat in a robbery, loses the remains of his dignity in a visit to a Very Important Person, dies and turns into a deranged vindictive ghost.

Directors:

Grigorii Kozintsev

Leonid Trauberg

Screenplay:

Iurii Tynianov

Cinematographer:

Andrei Moskvin

Evgenii Mikhailov

Art Director:

Evgenii Enei

Composer:

Aleksei Shelygin

Editor:

Boris Shpis

Duration:

66 minutes

Genre:

Literary Adaptation

Cast:

Andrei Kostrichkin

Sergei Gerasimov

Ianina Zheimo

Aleksei Kapler

Year:

1926

Critique

Using the mosaic method, Tynianov and directors Grigorii Kozintsev and Leonid Trauberg create a contextualizing prelude for this story of the meek bureaucrat Akakii Bashmachkin (Kostrichkin). By reframing Gogol's 'Overcoat', they hint at the continuity of the motif of the fragility of individual identity in the face of Petersburg-wrought dehumanization: in their treatment, Bashmachkin has as a young man been the victim of a mysterious con artist, a languid prostitute, and their savvy client/co-conspirator (who will later become the VIP). Humiliated and confused, the protagonist embarks on a path leading ultimately to an empty, 'ghostly' existence, and to madness.

The Overcoat is arguably the most conceptually ambitious adaptation in the Soviet film canon, conceived as it was at the height of the collaboration between FEKS (Factory of the Eccentric Actor) and the formalist school, in which Tynianov among others championed the view of art as a system of devices. Tynianov explains the principles governing his adaptation of Gogol' thus: 'Illustrating literature for the cinema is a difficult and inauspicious undertaking, as the cinema has its own methods and devices, which do not coincide with those of literature. Film can only attempt to reincarnate and interpret literary characters and literary style in its own way. This is why this film represents not a tale from Gogol', but a cinema-tale in the Gogolian manner.'

Most important to Tynianov in his source-text are the themes of carnal lust, temptation and the unavoidable punishment that befalls one who dares to entertain desires outstripping social status. Building on Gogol's playful coinage of the overcoat as 'Bashmachkin's pleasant mistress', the screenwriter conjures from the texture of 'Petersburg Tales' the persona of the Nevskii Prospect femme fatale, an embodiment of its lascivious mirages. For the purposes of the plot, she is needed to confuse Bashmachkin and lure him into professional error (in his dreaming, the clerk miscopies 'retired major' as … 'heavenly creature'). Bashmachkin, who thus fails in his primary function in the bureaucratic universe, is severely punished by a public humiliation that Tynianov codes in his script as castration: 'He suddenly started to blink, clutched his trousers with his hands, and sat down.' This devastation propels the protagonist into a realm of entities of emptiness, a hollow world Kozintsev, Tynianov and cinematographer Andrei Moskvin endeavour to translate from the pages of Gogol' to the screen. The most important body of emptiness in this regard is the city of Petersburg itself, which Tynianov defines as a 'huge void' bereft of meaning, depth or any trace of humanity. This monster (an alluring one) becomes one of the central characters of the film. A defining characteristic of such a void, moreover, is that its utter lack of essence is concealed; thus, following Gogol's lead, Tynianov and Kozintsev carefully construct various devices to stand in for reality: dolls/automata, masks, signboards, surreal dreams. This poetics might have come across as superficial were it not for Moskvin's exquisite camerawork, which relies on the device of depiction via silhouette – as portraiture, highly popular in Gogol's time – highlighting the contrast between three- and two-dimensionality, the animate and inanimate, motion and stillness.

The film leaves the intrigue that undoes Bashmachkin rather vague: though Tynianov stubbornly endeavours to explicate it in an introduction to his 'libretto', we still wonder why the bribery/forgery sub-plot is not further developed. It seems that the filmmakers are interested not in a particular crime per se, but in that web of provocation that has served since Dostoevskii and Belyi as the fulcrum of the 'Petersburg tale' genre. A young Sergei Gerasimov was cast as the agent-provocateur, a charismatic figure of fluid, dangerous identity. *The Overcoat* became Kozintsev's main contribution to the Petersburg text: neither his dreamed-for *Bronze Horseman* (proposed in 1927) nor, conceived much later, his *Gogoliad* (1973), were allowed to come to fruition.

Polina Barskova

The Lady with the Lapdog

Dama s sobachkoi

Country of Origin:
USSR

Language:
Russian

Studio:
Lenfilm

Director:
Iosif Kheifits

Screenplay:
Iosif Kheifits

Cinematographers:
Andrei Moskvin
Dmitrii Meskhiev

Art Directors:
Isaak Kaplan
Bella Manevich

Composer:
Nadezhda Simonian

Editor:
E. Bazhenova

Duration:
83 minutes

Genre:
Literary adaptation

Synopsis

Dmitrii Gurov (Batalov) is a Moscow banker spending his vacation alone in Ialta, as he has for years, when he makes the acquaintance of Anna Sergeevna (Savvina), a married woman from the provinces in Ialta for the first time. Gurov has a world-weary, rather cynical attitude to women and short-term romances, and treats this current liaison as not much more than one of the many flings he has had in the past. Their relationship develops into a sexual one, and as the holiday season comes to an end they depart, seemingly never to see each other again. Back home in Moscow Gurov is troubled by his memory of Anna, and resolves to travel to the town of S* to try to see her. There he comes across her and her husband in the theatre, much to her amazement and fear, and Anna agrees to visit him in Moscow. This she does, and the film ends with she and Gurov continuing their clandestine relationship and aware that 'the most difficult time of their lives was only just beginning'.

Critique

Based on one of Chekhov's best-known short stories, Kheifits's film was admired both at home and abroad not only as a faithful adaptation, but also as an indicator of the new emphasis on 'human' values and individual experience that characterized the post-Stalin Thaw. Indeed, Chekhov was the in many ways the ideal writer to adapt for the new 'humanism' of the Thaw, with his interest in the individual and the uniqueness of human experience. Kheifits remains faithful to the text's theme of the essentially duplicitous nature of human life, the inner privacy each person needs and protects, and the complexity of human relationships. Similarly, the film reflects Chekhov's use of landscape to suggest human emotion. But Kheifits nevertheless provides a more explicit ideological critique than is evident in the original. Scenes set in Moscow emphasize social deprivation and desperate poverty, and Gurov's social circle is shown as dissolute and beset by domestic disharmony. These are motifs absent in the Chekhov text but included by Kheifits the scriptwriter. Chekhov's realism is thus

Cast:

Iia Savvina
Aleksei Batalov

Year:

1960

'adapted' to claim the writer as a man of great foresight, pinpointing the social inadequacies that would eventually lead to revolution. The added ideological dimension, however, should not detract from the aesthetic qualities of the film. Both Savvina, in her first film role, and Batalov are nothing less than convincing as, respectively, a wide-eyed innocent who sees in Gurov a good man, and a middle-aged roué who falls in love for the first time in his life. Similarly, Ialta and its surrounding landscape provide an evocative background for burgeoning emotions and emerging human closeness. Chekhov's eye for the telling detail is also well realized visually, conversations are rendered faithfully and narrative asides become part of Gurov's internal monologues. In technical terms, Kheifits's film provides a master class in the art of literary adaptation. But it also reminds us of that in the Soviet Union the transfer of text to screen always required a clear ideological direction.

David Gillespie

Iosif Kheifits, *Lady with a Lapdog* (1960).

Grigorii Kozintsev, *Hamlet* (1964).

Hamlet

Gamlet

Country of Origin:
USSR

Language:
Russian

Studio:
Lenfilm

Director:
Grigorii Kozintsev

Screenplay:
Grigorii Kozintsev

Cinematographer:
Jonas Gricius

Synopsis

Hamlet, Prince of Denmark, is distraught following the death of his father, the King, and the subsequent marriage of his mother Gertrude to the King's brother, Claudius, who has assumed the throne. The father's Ghost tells Hamlet that he has been murdered and impels the Prince to take revenge. Hamlet reflects on what he should do. The King's chamberlain Polonius thinks Hamlet is mad when he brutally rejects Ophelia, his love. When a group of visiting players visits the court at Elsinore, Hamlet persuades them to enact a scene of murder. Claudius's reaction persuades Hamlet of his guilt. Claudius decides to send Hamlet to England in the company of his childhood friends Rosencrantz and Guildenstern, in a plot to have Hamlet killed. Hamlet returns to kill Polonius, thinking it is Claudius. Ophelia commits suicide. Her brother Laertes takes revenge on Hamlet for his father Polonius's death. In the ensuing duel, Claudius provides Laertes with a sword with a poisoned tip, and also prepares some poisoned wine. Hamlet is mortally wounded, Gertrude drinks the poisoned wine, and a dying Hamlet then kills Laertes and Claudius. All four lie dead as the Norwegian prince Fortinbras arrives to assume the throne, and orders a military funeral for Hamlet.

Art Directors:

Evgenii Enei

Grigorii Kropachev

Simon Virsaladze

Composer:

Dmitrii Shostakovich

Editor:

Evgeniia Makhan'kova

Duration:

140 minutes

Genre:

Literary adaptation

Cast:

Innokentii Smoktunovskii

Mikhail Nazvanov

Iurii Tolubeev

Anastasiia Vertinskaia

Year:

1964

Critique

Regarded by many as the best film adaptation of Shakespeare's most famous play, Kozintsev's version succeeds in being a film very much of its time, while conforming to accepted ideological requirements. It both reflects the anti-authoritarian ethos of the Thaw by showing a society dominated by fear, suspicion and denunciation, and makes of the Prince of Denmark a socialist realist positive hero, complete with the far-seeing gaze that perceives the future vistas of a world without conflict. Filmed in black and white, the film is heavily influenced by Laurence Olivier's 1948 version, but with significant departures (not least in removing the suggestion of incest between Hamlet and Gertrude). Looming shadows and huge portcullises reinforce Hamlet's assertion that 'Denmark is a prison', and when Ophelia is encouraged to inform on Hamlet's intentions by her father, then the analogy with the recent Soviet past is clear. Smoktunovskii's Hamlet is above all a man not of words but of action, his 'To be or not to be' speech, like much of Olivier's, filmed as interior monologue and set against the crashing waves of the sea that signify his own internal turmoil. Indeed, this pivotal moment is shown not so much as an indication of Hamlet's indecision, based on an awareness that to avenge a murder he will have to commit a murder himself, as of his resolution. Hamlet may be out for personal revenge, but by righting a wrong he also becomes an agent of social justice. Both Smoktunovskii and Olivier wear white shirts, beacons of moral probity amid the corruption of the 'unweeded garden' all around them. Hamlet dies, but his death, like that of the 'positive hero', is a sacrifice that helps sweep away the old order, to be replaced by the new world represented by the 'fair Fortinbras'. Kozintsev's achievement is in adapting a classic text for the demands of his society and his time, removing Shakespeare's key ideas from the confines of a family melodrama and enriching them with an awareness of history in the making (and not a little ideology).

David Gillespie

War and Peace

Voina i mir

Country of Origin:

USSR

Language:

Russian

Studio:

Mosfilm

Director:

Sergei Bondarchuk

Synopsis

Bondarchuk's four-part epic follows Lev Tolstoy's novel closely in breadth if not in depth. Part I, 'Andrei Bolkonsky' introduces several prominent St Petersburg and Moscow families. Prince Andrei Bolkonsky's wife is pregnant and he takes her to his stern father's country estate. Andrei's friend Pierre Bezukhov, an outsider in the high society and an admirer of Napoleon, leads a dissolute life. When his adoptive father dies, Pierre suddenly becomes one of the richest men in the empire and marries the beautiful, but immoral Ellen. In 'Natasha Rostova', Andrei joins the army to fight Napoleon in Austria; during the disastrous campaign he is wounded. Upon his return he learns of his wife's death in childbirth. At a ball he meets the young and charming Natasha Rostova and falls in love with her. Yet the impulsive Natasha is under the influence of Pierre's scheming wife and her brother. The

Screenplay:

Sergei Bondarchuk
Vasilii Solov'ev, based on the
novel by Leo Tolstoy

Cinematographer:

Anatolii Petritskii

Art Directors:

Mikhail Bogdanov
Gennadii Miasnikov
Said Menial'shchikov

Composer:

Viacheslav Ovchinnikov

Editors:

Tat'iana Likhacheva
Elena Surazhskaia

Duration:

431 minutes

Genre:

Literary adaptation

Cast:

Sergei Bondarchuk
Liudmila Savel'eva
Viacheslav Tikhonov
Boris Zakhava
Anatolii Ktorov
Oleg Tabakov
Vasilii Lanovoi

Year:

1965–1967

latter plans to elope with Natasha but the plan is thwarted. Andrei
is heartbroken and leaves again for the war. '1812' tells the story of
Napoleon's invasion of Russia, with the epic battle of Borodino taking
up the bulk of the film. The final part, 'Pierre Bezukhov', recounts
Pierre's attempt to kill Napoleon in Moscow, Pierre's imprisonment
and the French retreat from Russia. On his deathbed, Andrei forgives
Natasha. After the war, Pierre meets Natasha again.

Critique

War and Peace is one of the most ambitious Soviet film projects and
certainly the most costly. The film took seven years to produce and
cost about $100 million. Adjusted for inflation, this comes to $700
million, making *War and Peace* one of the most expensive films ever
made, as well as one of the most elaborate in production design.
It is one of only few Soviet films shot in 70mm format. In short, *War
and Peace* was designed as a Soviet prestige object, demonstrating
the superiority of Soviet cinema. It won both an Oscar and a Golden
Globe Award for Best Foreign Language film and was nominated for
Best Art Direction by the Academy Awards and BAFTA.

Bondarchuk combines epic scale, an unlimited budget and readily
available human resources (the Battle of Borodino scene involved
20,000 soldiers, all dressed in impeccable period garb), with art
cinema devices. Virtually every shot claims aesthetic value. There are
dozens of complicated aerial tracking shots, elaborate use of montage
in superimpositions and split screen shots, deep focus and point-of-
view shots and so forth. The several-minute long take of the grand
ball, shot by an extremely mobile camera that now follows Natasha,
now slides along the dancers or swoops up, is a worthy predecessor of Aleksandr Sokurov's *Russian Ark*, without the perks of digital
technology and the steadicam. This visual cornucopia testifies to the
technical achievement of *War and Peace*.

Yet human relationships and Tolstoy's profound insights into human
nature are either absent or rendered formally, with Tolstoy's text in
voice-over as an excuse. Simply speaking, Bondarchuk is much better
at portraying epic battles and spectacular balls than at capturing
individuals. Clearly, even eight hours is not enough to pay full tribute
to Tolstoy's epic. Secondary characters and plot lines are drastically
reduced: Nikolai Rostov's engagement to Sonia and his marriage to
Bolkonsky's sister are missing. Andrei Bolkonsky's journey, so important to Tolstoy's critique of romanticism, is rendered in a combination
of monumental shots of Tikhonov and a voice-over conveying his
dreams of personal glory. With its overwhelming focus on war at the
expense of peace and community, one way to approach the film is as
a literal, visual illustration of Soviet high-school reading of Tolstoy's
novel. The episodes chosen by Bondarchuk for an extensive treatment
follow the Soviet ideological clichés. The most important one is peo-
ple-mindedness, exemplified by the scenes of Andrei Bolkonsky and
the 'simple soldier' Tushin, Natasha's 'people's dance' at her uncle's
country house and Pierre's meeting with Platon Karataev in the burning Moscow. And, as every Russian schoolchild can testify, the end of
Tolstoy's novel always gets scrambled. So it is in Bondarchuk's film.

After the epic burning of Moscow and the voice-over (Bondarchuk's own) solemnly delivering Tolstoy's words that good people should unite, Pierre comes to Andrei's estate where he meets Natasha. Here the film abruptly ends.

Tolstoy's anti-war message clashes with the film's relishing of battle scenes. The camera repeatedly soars over the field of Borodino and the majestic palaces, portraying people as part of an elaborate mosaic. It is no accident that in the part '1812', the opening credits roll against the background of Franz Rubo's majestic Borodino Panorama: much of this film seems to consist of animated pictures from the latter. But even if *War and Peace* falls short of Tolstoy, it remains a spectacular monument to Soviet cinema's ambitions and achievements.

Elena Prokhorova

Uncle Vania

Diadia Vania

Country of Origin:
Soviet Union

Language:
Russian

Studio:
Mosfilm

Director:
Andrei Konchalovskii

Screenplay:
Andrei Konchalovskii

Cinematographers:
Georgii Rerberg
Evgenii Guslinskii

Art Director:
Nikolai Dvigubskii

Composer:
Alfred Schnittke

Editor:
Liudmila Raeva
L. Pokrovskaia

Duration:
104 minutes

Synopsis

The retired professor Serebriakov and his young and beautiful wife Elena spend the summer on Serebriakov's estate which is run by his daughter Sonya and Serebriakov's brother-in-law by his first wife, Uncle Vania. They are in the frequent company of the country doctor Astrov, who is passionate about nature and trees. Uncle Vania feels that he has wasted his life, and drinks vodka with Astrov. Sonya loves Astrov, but is too meek to tell him and when Elena tries to find out whether Astrov reciprocates Sonia's feelings, he misunderstands and they end up kissing. Serebriakov announces he wants to sell the estate and settle in Finland – leaving his daughter and Uncle Vania with nowhere to go. Angrily, Uncle Vania fires a shot at the professor. Eventually, Serebriakov and Elena leave and everything returns to its status quo.

Critique

Uncle Vania hardly goes beyond a theatrical approach as the action remains largely confined to the inside. There is another world outside the house, which is visible through the windows and the open doors: the real space of the Russian fields. Instead, Konchalovskii concentrates on the emotional relationships between characters and makes elaborate use of colour, style of costumes and decor.

The film begins with a series of documentary photographs of scenes from Russian life in the 1890s: pictures from Chekhov's photo album show the writer in the company of friends and actors; pictures that could have been taken on Chekhov's journeys to the distant and deprived regions of Russia, showing dying children; historical photographs of the tsar and his family, the tsar on the hunt with a shot deer; and photographs documenting the famines of 1891–1892, revealing newspaper reports and images of a starving population, of barren fields and thinned woods. These photos are interspersed with the opening credits and set to the cacophonous music of Alfred Schnittke, which

Andrei Konchalovskii, *Uncle Vania* (1970).

Genre:

Literary adaptation

Cast:

Innokentii Smoktunovskii
Sergei Bondarchuk
Irina Kupchenko
Vladimir Zel'din
Irina Miroshnichenko

Year:

1971

integrates sounds diegetic to the photographs (crying of a child, train, chorus, marches, bells). Later in the film Astrov looks at these pictures and pins some of them onto the wall; he also shows them to an uninterested Elena Sergeevna, almost interrupting the film's narrative with these illustrations that accompany his speech on nature. The pictures reveal Astrov's disillusionment: he may plead for nature, for the importance of flora and fauna, but he knows only too well the reality that surrounds the estate. The scenes of the exploitation of the earth shown on the photos forebode in an apocalyptic vision the end of an era, the end of the Romanovs, the end of nature, the end of mankind. Konchalovskii uses photos as a document of the real – as opposed to the artificial – world in the house, thus referring subtly to the absurdity of the situation that the play creates: the frivolity of everyday melodrama is set against a backdrop of the end of an era. Russia's historical reality of the photos is more tangible than the family's emotional reality; the aesthetic realities (set, nature) have a more serious quality than the trifles and psychological entrapments of the characters. Nothing changes for the characters, but Russia stands on the brink of an abyss.

The drama proper begins with black-and-white shots of the interior of the house, which gradually becomes inhabited. Every act starts off with a black-and-white sequence before moving to colour, and even then colour is restricted to a blue-green-white palette. The film shifts to colour when the Serebriakovs arrive; when Elena has rejected Voinitskii's love; when Voinitskii catches Elena and Astrov in an embrace. In each act, the shift to colour occurs when the dull life acquires a different twist: the arrival; the refusal to rekindle an old love; and attempted seduction. These are all attempts, doomed to failure, to breathe new life into the dull existence of the estate. In the final act Konchalovskii operates the same principle in reverse: after the Serebriakovs' departure (in colour) the film switches back to black and white as Sonia, Voinitskii and Astrov carry on with their dull lives. The dullness and boredom of their existence is associated with a warmly tinted black and white, while the unrest brought about by the Serebriakovs brings cold hues of colour into the house.

Birgit Beumers

An Unfinished Piece for a Mechanical Piano

Neokonchennaia p'esa dlia mekhanicheskogo pianino

Synopsis

An Unfinished Piece for a Mechanical Piano is an adaptation of a little known play by Anton Chekhov, written in his youth (rejected for stage performance by the theatre director Mariia Ermolova) and commonly known as *Platonov* (draft 1878–1979, completed 1883), which raises many themes of his later major plays in an unwieldy dramatic form. The script also draws on several of Chekhov's short stories, such as 'The Literature Teacher', 'On the Estate', 'Three Years' and 'My Life'.

At the Voinitsevs' estate, the landlady Anna Petrovna has invited guests for dinner, including the Platonovs. They spend the afternoon in the open and adjourn inside the house for dinner. As tensions rise between the old landowners and the new merchant class and

Country of Origin:

Soviet Union

Language:

Russian

Studio:

Mosfilm

Director:

Nikita Mikhalkov

Screenplay:

Aleksandr Adabashian

Nikita Mikhalkov

Cinematographer:

Pavel Lebeshev

Art Directors:

Aleksandr Adabashian

Aleksandr Samulekin

Composer:

Eduard Artem'ev

Editor:

Liudmila Elian

Duration:

103 minutes

Genre:

Literary Adaptation

Cast:

Aleksandr Kaliagin

Elena Solovei

Evgeniia Glushenko

Antonina Shuranova

Iurii Bogatyrev

Oleg Tabakov

Nikolai Pastukhov

Pavel Kadochnikov

Nikita Mikhalkov

Anatolii Romashin

Natal'ia Nazarova

Kseniia Minina

Sergei Nikonenko

Serezha Gur'ev

Year:

1977

between masters and servants, a performance on the mechanical piano is supposed to diffuse the atmosphere. Yet instead another conflict erupts, between past and present, as Platonov relives his youth romance with Sof'ia, young Voinitsev's wife, and regrets the loss of his potential to effectuate change – in life and in society, as he is stuck in a marriage that stifles any potential activity through overwhelming love. He makes a farcical attempt at suicide before surrendering and returning to the status quo.

Critique

Mikhalkov's film begins with a scene in the open: Anna Petrovna Voinitseva, the widow of a general and landlady of the estate, is playing chess with Triletskii while a conversation between Voinitseva's stepson Sergei and family friend Glagol'ev can be heard. The opening establishes Mikhalkov's favourite scene: the open field bordering on a river; an old stone mansion with steps leading up to it; stucco-decorated windows and an ornate stone banister along the balcony.

Glagol'ev returns from a boat trip with Sergei's wife, Sof'ia (Solovei), and soon after the Platonovs arrive – in a prelude to the meeting between Sof'ia and Platonov (Kaliagin), old lovers who are now both married to other partners. Sof'ia remembers Platonov, but fails to recognize him. They have not met in seven years, since he was a student; now he is a schoolteacher, although he never graduated. Platonov introduces his wife Sashen'ka, with whom he has a son. He is uncomfortable in the confrontation with his old love, reminding him of unrealized potential, and resorts to playing the fool. Mikhalkov structures the film around Platonov as a series of carnivalesque interludes interspersed with more serious dialogues.

Anna Petrovna's suitor Shcherbuk arrives with his daughters and proclaims his belief in natural historical selection, in the primacy of aristocracy over the peasants and in the impossibility for the peasants to achieve anything. Mikhalkov parodies his noble status by dressing both daughters in green dresses – a colour Chekhov considered tasteless.

Meanwhile, the conversations between Platonov and Sof'ia set a serious counterpoint to the grotesque. Sof'ia refuses to remember the past, while Platonov recalls their meetings in great detail. Sof'ia holds it against Platonov that he never transformed his plans into actions, words into deeds, while she herself verbosely presents her vision of Russia's future. The situation intensifies as the number of cynical and grotesque moments increase. In order to release tension Anna Petrovna reveals the mechanical piano and asks her servant to perform a piece by Chopin. The servant 'plays' before stepping back to leave the piano to play on its own. Sashen'ka is so impressed that she faints, leaving Platonov both concerned and embarrassed.

During a dinner scene in a dark and gloomy room, the characters' real faces emerge: the doctor, Triletskii, has no sense of responsibility and refuses to attend to a patient; Petrin, the son of a worker, announces that he paid for the dinner, because Anna Petrovna is bankrupt; Shcherbuk, convinced of the nobility's superiority, leaves the table, while Anna Petrovna proposes a toast to Petrin, who has enabled her to keep the estate at the price of her honour. Platonov tells a story, which faintly disguises his past affair with Sof'ia when they were students; then Sof'ia left for St Petersburg and he waited for her, abandoning his studies. Realizing his unfulfilled potential, Platonov attempts suicide, but this is turned into a farce as he jumps into the lake at its shallowest spot. In the finale Sashen'ka swaddles him in her scarf, underscoring visually his inability to take meaningful action: all he, and the other characters, are capable of is to create absurd and ridiculous scenes without taking any action.

Critics have addressed the issue of the film's fidelity to Chekhov, of his ambivalent attitude towards the old order and an admiration for the new, noting the farcical tone of the film, but they have largely failed to infer the significance of the critique of inactivity to contemporary Soviet society.

Birgit Beumers

Lonely Voice of a Man

Odinokii golos cheloveka

Country of Origin:
Soviet Union

Language:
Russian

Studio:
Lenfilm

Director:
Aleksandr Sokurov

Screenplay:
Iurii Arabov

Cinematographer:
Sergei Iurizditskii

Art Director:
Vladimir Lebedev

Composers:
Irina Zhuravleva
Vladimir Persov

Editor:
A. Bespalova

Duration:
82 minutes

Synopsis

Based on Andrei Platonov's story 'The River Potudan'' (with elements from his novel *Chevengur*) Sokurov's first feature film depicts a soldier's difficult re-adjustment to civilian life after he returns home from the battlefields of the Russian Civil War ca. 1921. Nikita Firsov is re-united with his sweetheart, the orphan Liubov' (Liuba) Kuznetsova. During their courtship Liuba loses her close friend Zhenia to typhus, and Nikita also survives a bout of the illness. After his recovery Nikita and Liuba marry and he moves in with her. Crushed by his impotence, Nikita abandons home to wander the market of a nearby town, whence he is fetched home by his father, who tells him that Liuba had attempted to drown herself. The narrative scenes are interspersed with documentary sequences, still photographs and lyrical interludes, particularly of the colourful moment of the lovers' first meeting after the war. Two sequences – of Nikita eating with a monk and of two men in a boat discussing the afterlife – are relatively independent insertions.

Critique

Sokurov cuts Platonov's already meagre dialogue to a bare minimum, using photographs, documentary footage and an array of distorting lenses and filters to compensate for the loss of Platonov's dizzying verbal (il)logic. The film begins with old documentary footage in slow motion: a river, lumber floating on water and (twice) a huge wooden wheel being turned by workers. After the initial credits a series of colour shots (interspersed with more credits) show a young man walking across the steppe, each one at closer distance and at a different angle. This sequence ends with an enigmatic long shot of him jumping off a river bank. A shot of his home is then followed by four more documentary shots in slow motion, showing industrial workers, after which domestic scenes alternate with old photographs, some of them

Genre:

Literary adaptation

Cast:

Tat'iana Goriacheva
Aleksandr Gradov
Vladimir Degtiarev
Liudmila Iakovleva
Nikolai Kochegarov
Sergei Shukailo
Vladimir Gladyshev
Ivan Neganov
Evgeniia Volkova
Irina Zhuravleva
Viktoriia Iurizditskaia

Year:

1978 (released 1987)

examined with tracking shots and close-ups. The film is obviously less interested in telling a story than in examining the distances that separate us as viewers from the historical, emotional and technologi-cal conditions of the time. As with Platonov's prose, the meaningful development occurs less in the narrative content than in its constantly changing texture.

Nikita is usually at the centre of the camera's attention, but he is precisely its object, not its subject. The non-professional actors behave as if their world has just been illuminated after 50 years of hibernation. The snippets of clumsy Platonovian dialogue are pro-nounced woodenly, giving little insight into the characters' subjective states. In the story the reader is informed of Nikita's sparse memories and thoughts, but the film refrains from associating the documentary footage or family snapshots directly with Nikita's or Liuba's conscious-ness; indeed, some of them look more like Platonov himself, as if the author and his style are being made the subjects of representation. There are drastic shifts of perspective, a technique characteristic of Platonov, where familiar characters are suddenly encountered as if they are strangers; thus the watchman at the market discovers a mute vagrant who turns out to be Nikita, while Nikita encounters a man who turns out to be his father. Sokurov marks these sudden shifts visually; the scene of the mute Nikita at the market is in high-contrast black and white, and slow motion, approximating the visual qualities of the documentary sequences. This multiplicity of perspectives is not informed by any obvious hierarchy; the perspectival shifts reveal less about Nikita as a character than about our evolving vision of him and his world. Nikita's final illumination comes when he declares to Liuba that he 'has got used to being happy' with her. This recovery of love in the depths of abandonment is analogous to the viewer's rediscovery of vision amidst a world that is constantly slipping into obscurity and inscrutability. It is an intimacy possible only in the cinema.

Both in narrative and in visual style Sokurov draws heavily on the cinema of Andrei Tarkovsii, even to the point of presenting Nikita's home village in the style of Brueghel's *Hunters in the Snow* (which Tarkovskii cited in *Solaris* and *Mirror*). Sokurov's cameraman has recalled how he tried to reproduce the inverse perspective of Kuz'ma Petrov-Vodkin's painting and the orthodox icon.

Sokurov's film was submitted as his degree project at VGIK, but it was rejected by the administration and left on the shelf until it was restored and released by Lenfilm in the midst of perestroika. It is not entirely clear to what degree Sokurov changed the film in 1987; there is at times a marked discrepancy between the dialogue and the visu-als. In any case *Lonely Voice of a Man* marks a high-point of Soviet art cinema and can usefully be contrasted to Andrei Konchalovskii's *Maria's Lovers* (1984), which is based on the same Platonov story. It is widely regarded as one of Sokurov's finest films.

Robert Bird

Lady Macbeth of Mtsensk District

Ledi Makbet Mtsenskogo uezda

Countries of Origin:
Soviet Union
Switzerland

Language:
Russian

Studios:
Mosfilm
Sovinfilm

Director:
Roman Balaian

Producers:
Sovexportfilm
Mediactuelle SA (Switzerland)

Screenplay:
Roman Balaian
Pavel Finn

Cinematographer:
Pavel Lebeshev

Art Directors:
Said Menial'shchikov
Aleksandr Samulekin

Composer:
Evsei Evseev

Editor:
Polina Skachkova

Duration:
80 minutes

Genre:
Literary adaptation

Cast:
Natal'ia Andreichenko
Aleksandr Abdulov
Nikolai Pastukhov
Tat'iana Kravchenko

Year:
1988

Synopsis

Katerina Izmailova is a young woman married to the elderly merchant Zinovii. She is unhappy and bored in her childless household until the new farm worker, Sergei, arrives. Katerina and Sergei become lovers. When the husband unexpectedly discovers the lovers, a brawl ensues and Katerina kills her husband. She and Sergei start living together almost openly, but their plan to take over the estate is disrupted, since the husband had a distant male relative who is considered an heir. The boy and his elderly caretaker move in with Katerina, who is genuinely happy to have the child around. Sergei, however, expresses concerns that their rights and privileges will be taken away by the underage heir. Katerina's initial reaction to the possibility of violence against the child is negative, but she is quickly overpowered by the displeasure and discontent on Sergei's part. When the boy is left alone in the house, Katerina and Sergei suffocate him, with Katerina initiating the murder. Their crime is discovered and both are sentenced to prison. During their transfer to another prison, Sergei abuses Katerina, and starts having an affair with another female prisoner. During a river crossing Katerina throws herself and her rival into the frozen river, where both women drown.

Critique

Lady Macbeth of Mtsensk District is based on the physiological sketch by the nineteenth-century Russian writer Nikolai Leskov. *Lady Macbeth* quickly became a culturally significant narrative, touching on many issues of nineteenth -century Russian culture and literary tradition. The story has been the subject of different artistic adaptations, notably Dmitrii Shostakovich's opera. Another adaptation is *Moscow Nights* (1994) by Valerii Todorovskii, set in contemporary Moscow and stylized as a film noir rather than a naturalist sketch. The original literary text presents Katerina as a cold-blooded murderess, meticulously narrating all the gruesome details of the crimes she plans and commits. The story describes Katerina as a kind of monster from the unconscious, governed by a drive for pleasure, with no capacity for self-reflection or moral judgment. Shostakovich's opera emphasizes the naturalist element in the story – Katerina becomes a victimized figure: unhappily married, a product and a prisoner of her social milieu, reflecting another position in the long-standing debate of whether evil is the product of individual will or society's pressure.

Roman Balaian's adaptation stands somewhere in-between, endowing Katerina with monstrous and redeeming characteristics. Visually the film is done in the tradition of the 'picturesque style' movement (*zhivopisnyi stil'*, a term coined by the critic Valentin Mikhailovich in 1978) – a trend in Soviet cinema of the 1970s that brought new poetic and lyric qualities to cinema via beautifully and carefully constructed mise-en-scène, reminiscent of painting; an aesthetically self-conscious and nuanced vision that focused on environment and technique rather than story and character motivation. This style was attributed to such directors as Sergei Solov'ev, Nikita Mikhalkov and cinematographer Pavel Lebeshev (who worked with Balaian on *Lady Macbeth*). *Lady Macbeth of Mtsensk District* is beautifully done: with intricate play of light and shadows, soft colours and idyllic landscapes, where Katerina and Sergei spend their romantic dates, feeding horses and playing games. There is an intentional discrepancy between the love scenes in the bright open air, bathed in sunlight, and the dimly lit interiors where lust and murder emerge as the driving force of the film.

Katerina is presented as a paradoxical character – a caring tender lover and a brutal murderess, a bored idle wife who yawns and stretches with remarkable regularity and a strong-willed woman who turns her life around for herself. The film has an obsession with mirrors: Katerina is reflected in multiple wall and hand mirrors that she intently looks into, examining her face. The film starts and ends with the image of Katerina as a little girl looking in the mirror in the sunlit background, examining her teeth; then, the child's image turns into an image of Katerina as an adult in shackles in the winter, looking in the mirror with the same intensity and curiosity. Katerina is like Caliban who does not see 'his face in the glass' – her identity is obscured primarily from herself. She cannot see that she is a monster – which in itself becomes a redeeming quality for the film's heroine. Admittedly, Katerina is not indifferent to taking others' lives – the film positions her more as confused about ethics, succumbing to her desires, rather than indifferent to morality altogether as in the original story or defiant of society's norms as in Shostakovich's opera. That is why Balaian's Katerina hangs on to the only thing she knows for certain, her attachment to Sergei. In the end she sacrifices her life and that of another woman for this feeling of certainty. The film's contrast between visual beautification of Katerina's environment and the dark subject matter underscores this confusion, pointing out that Katerina's love for Sergei is a happy joyful feeling and a dark murderous passion, and that she cannot discern where one ends and the other begins. The music in the film, composed by Evsei Evseev, comprises chiefly piano and music box melodies that play over and over again, reflecting the vicious circle that the film perpetuates – love and murder, morality and identity being blurred together not in a fatal fusion of passion and crime, but in a petrifying state of confusion.

Volha Isakava

Katia Izmailova/ Evenings around Moscow

Katia Izmailova/
Podmoskovnye vechera

Countries of Origin:
Russia
France

Language:
Russian

Synopsis

Katerina Izmailova (Ingeborga Dapkunaite) works as secretary to Irina Dmitrievna (Freindlikh), a romantic novelist. She begins an affair with the carpenter Sergei (Mashkov), with whom Irina Dmitrievna may also be romantically involved. When her mistress discovers the affair she becomes very angry, and Katerina allows her to die by not giving her access to her medication. Katerina's husband Mitia also finds out about the affair, and Sergei kills him. Katerina confesses to the police chief Romanov (Iurii Kuznetsov), but he dismisses her confession and seeks evidence. Katerina and Sergei take Irina Dmitrievna's latest novel and give it a happy ending, but it is rejected by the publisher. Sergei revives his interest in the nurse Sonia (Shchukina), with whom he had already been emotionally involved. Katerina offers to drive them to the railway

Studios:
Les filmes du rivage
TTL Films

Director:
Valerii Todorovskii

Producers:
Marc Ruscar
Igor' Tolstunov

Screenplay:
Alla Krinitsyna, with François Guérif
Cecile Vargaftig
Marina Sheptunova
Stanislav Govorukhin

Cinematographer:
Sergei Kozlov

Art Director:
Aleksandr Osipov

Composer:
Leonid Desiatnikov

Editors:
Elen Gagarin
Alla Strel'nikova

Duration:
96 minutes

Genre:
Literary Adaptation

Cast:
Ingeborga Dapkunaite
Vladimir Mashkov
Alisa Freindlikh
Aleksandr Feklistov
Iurii Kuznetsov
Natal'ia Shchukina
Avangard Leont'ev

Year:
1994

Down House

Daun Khaus

Country of Origin:
Russia

Language:
Russian

Studio:
Poligon

station, and on the way devises a pretext for Sergei to get out of the car. She then drives the car off a bridge with herself and Sonia inside.

Critique

A loose adaptation of Nikolai Leskov's 1865 novella 'Lady Macbeth of Mtsensk', with the subject matter brought forward to the post-Soviet present, with stylish clothes, fast cars and opulent interiors. Leskov's work foregrounds the sexual attraction and capacity for violence of the main characters, and Todorovskii does not let his expectant audience down. But his ambition is much greater than simply updating an accepted if controversial classic of Russian literature. Rather, the theme of the film is not the ravages of uncontrolled passion but literature and the force of the written word. As she is about to allow herself to be seduced by Sergei while sitting at her typewriter, she tells him 'I am not writing, I am retyping'. By then attempting to rewrite Irina Dmitrievna's novel she wants to be able to write her own happy end, but, as in life, this does not convince. Katia wishes her life to be part of an accepted literary convention, but life does not provide conventions. Indeed, as Sergei's subsequent behaviour shows, life is far from simple and happy. The police chief Romanov is obviously based on the figure of Porfirii Petrovich from Dostoevsky's *Crime and Punishment*, thus providing an extra literary reference point. But Todorovskii confounds cultural expectation by showing the police chief as incompetent, unwilling to accept a confession as proof of guilt and thus unable to secure a conviction for the murders. Life and literature, the director tells us, are very different. Todorovskii also litters the narrative with telling references to Russian literature, French and Hollywood film noir, especially with regard to the popular plotline of unfaithful-wife-and-lover-kill-husband (cf. *The Postman Always Rings Twice*, *Les Diaboliques*, *Blood Simple*). The film is a successful literary adaptation that remains faithful to the spirit of the original text while making the book's central idea relevant and interesting to a modern audience well versed in western and Russian literary and cinematic traditions.

David Gillespie

Synopsis

On a highway, Count Myshkin is picked up by a bus. Travelling from Zurich to Moscow, Myshkin meets Rogozhin, a New Russian millionaire, who has broken his leg in a skiing accident. Myshkin is returning to Russia for the first time and is to meet up with his only relative, the wife of General Epanchin. The general is attempting to marry off Nastas'ia Filippovna, Rogozhin's beloved, to his trusted employee Gania Ivolgin. Intrigued by the story of Nastas'ia Filippovna, Myshkin enters the race to marry her. Rogozhin wins, but Nastas'ia Filippovna runs away from the registry at the last minute. Myshkin seeks Rogozhin to comfort him and the two exchange crosses as a sign of brotherhood. However, Rogozhin tries to kill Myshkin, who is rescued

Director:

Roman Kachanov (Jr)

Producers:

Sergei Chliiants

Iurii Tiukhtin

Screenplay:

Roman Kachanov

Ivan Okhlobystin

Cinematographer:

Mikhail Mukasei

Art Director:

Ekaterina Zaletaeva

Composer:

Evgenii Rudin (DJ Groove)

Editor:

Natal'ia Sazhina

Duration:

95 minutes

Genre:

Literary Adaptation

Melodrama

Cast:

Fedor Bondarchuk

Ivan Okhlobystin

Anna Buklovskaia

Aleksandr Bashirov

Jerzy Stuhr

Juozas Budraitis

Year:

2001

by Aglaia, General Epanchin's daughter, on a red scooter. The two prepare to get married, but on the wedding day, Nastas'ia Filippovna turns up and Myshkin is again won over, only for her to quickly leave him again. Rogozhin invites Myshkin to dinner, where they feast, to Myshkin's surprise, on Nastas'ia Filippovna, whom Rogozhin has just killed. Myshkin walks into a sun setting over a desert.

Critique

The fact that *Down House* is an adaptation is evident from the beginning: the first words uttered are 'Idiot, idiot …', as Myshkin boards the bus to Moscow. Furthermore, as the title *Down House* appears (derived from Down's Syndrome), a small picture of Dostoevsky appears in the background, but quickly fades away, suggesting that the film has a connection to the famous novel. True, this is not an 'ordinary' adaptation. However, the film is very close to Dostoevsky's novel *The Idiot*; for example, all the names and plot are kept, yet the setting changes completely to both contemporary and futuristic exploits. The dichotomy between materialism and spiritualism is also present in the film. Even stories told within the main narrative are given prominence in the film, as small clips are inserted to visualize characters' storytelling. At the beginning of the film Myshkin is uninterested in sex (true to Dostoevsky's character), but Aglaia awakens his sexuality: he almost marries her, turning the saintly figure into a human character of flesh and blood. Thus, rather than saintly or foolishly, he has just taken too many drugs and therefore constantly hallucinates, which is magnificently put to use in the cinematography: Myshkin jumps through paintings, Moscow is experienced as a sci-fi city, his landlady transforms into atoms, and desert sand with neon flashing light confine the space for Myshkin's final scene. The film takes Myshkin seriously by making him human, but retains his characteristic features of exposing the corruption, vulgarity and absurdity of (post-Soviet) Russia. 'Sarcasm hits harder while in laughter' could be the motto of the co-authorship that Kachanov and Okhlobystin establish. In *Down House* their combined skills of mindless silliness and a Monty Python-esque fusion of moving images and drawn cartoons gives the classical story a makeover that has no equal – where else would one find 'beauty will save the world' in neon lights. The beauty of Kachanov and Okhlobystin will not save anything other than a few laughs brought about with the absurd realization that history repeats itself – which rings true for both the postmodernist and post-communist spirit.

The iconoclastic features of Kachanov's and Okhlobystin's film are everywhere and could be in themselves the aim of the film. The whole point of taking on a classic and turning it on its head shows that a re-examination is taking place. On the other hand, the film is also about the metaphorical killing of the master-writer, or at least the death of the celebration of the writer. Russia does not kill authors (any more), but China does, as Myshkin narrates in a vignette about the execution of a Chinese writer. While the story about the Chinese writer might serve as a new border where artists are executed or not (Asians as incomprehensible Others), it is more pertinent to view this within the overall effort of getting rid of elitism and logocentrism. Rather than proclaiming the 'death of the author', *Down House*, and subsequently Kachanov and Okhlobystin, give birth to a new future for Russia without the author/prophet guiding people to become saints or demons.

Lars Kristensen

BIOPIC

The genre designation 'biopic' (short for 'biographical picture') refers to an acted (i.e., non-documentary) film with a real-life historical figure as the protagonist and a narrative based, with a widely varying degree of verisimilitude, on that person's own actual experiences. It is sometimes considered a sub-category of other genres, such as the historical epic or costume drama, and also frequently overlaps with genres such as the war film and even the comedy and the romance. Biopics have accounted for many of the best-known works of world cinema, especially Hollywood cinema, many of whose biopics have been among the most acclaimed and prize-winning films: Milos Forman's *Amadeus* (1984), Richard Attenborough's *Gandhi* (1982), Ron Howard's *A Beautiful Mind* (2001), Stephen Spielberg's *Schindler's List* (1993), Martin Scorcese's *Raging Bull* (1980) and Mel Gibson's *Braveheart* (1995), to name just a few. (This representative list of American and British biopics, when contrasted with the Russian examples of the genre discussed below, underscores how often Western biopics depict subjects outside the country of the films' production, and how seldom Russian film did so.)

In Russia and the Soviet Union the biopic has been primarily a sub-category of the historical film and, from the 1930s until the early 1980s, of that most distinctly Soviet genre, the historical-Revolutionary film. The very first Russian acted film, Vladimir Romashkov's *Stenka Razin* (1908) was technically a biographical picture; the protagonist – the Cossack leader of an anti-tsarist uprising in the seventeenth century – was an actual person, although the film is based more immediately on a folksong about him than any historical or biographical documents. Still, that film established the Russian film industry's self-reflexive interest in the nation's historical personalities that would continue, especially during the Soviet period.

After 1917, and especially after the institution of socialist realism as the officially prescribed mode of cultural production in the early 1930s, the Soviet state cultural industries strove to populate the newly created national mythology with real-life heroes. This process involved, of course, enshrining the feats of the Revolutionary leaders

(Lenin, Stalin, etc.) on film, but also re-presenting and redefining the role of pre-Soviet historical figures. Tsarist military men and explorers such as the hero of the Napoleonic Wars Marshal Kutuzov, for example, enjoyed lionization on screen (Vladimir Petrov's *Kutuzov*, 1944), as did the geographer Nikolai Przheval'skii (Sergei Iutkevich's *Przheval'skii*, 1951). The obvious monarchist loyalties of these past figures were deemed secondary to the importance of their role in defending and expanding the Russian empire. Sergei Eisenstein's *Ivan the Terrible* (Part I, 1944; Part II, 1946, rel. 1958) is another example of this strategy, albeit a much more complex and idiosyncratic one, as is Vladimir Petrov's two-part biopic *Peter the Great* (Part I, 1937; Part II, 1938).

Pre-Soviet cultural figures also became the protagonists of Soviet-era biopics intended to draw a clear connection between contemporary Soviet society and forward-thinking artists and writers of the imperial past. One of the earliest and most popular subjects of the Russian biopic has been the 'national poet' Aleksandr Pushkin, who was featured even before the Revolution in Ivan Goncharov's *Life and Death of A.S. Pushkin* (1910), and several times during the Soviet period, most notably in Vladimir Gardin's *The Poet and the Tsar* (1927) and Abram Naroditskii's *Youth of the Poet* (1937); the latter was part of the Stalinist state's elaborate celebrations of the 100th anniversary of the poet's death. The Stalin period especially produced numerous biopics about Russian cultural giants, including composers (Lev Arnshtam's *Glinka*, 1946; Grigorii Roshal's *Mussorgskii*, 1950), poets (Vsevolod Pudovkin and Dmitrii Vasil'ev's *Zhukovskii* (1950)) and scientists (Roshal''s *Academician Ivan Pavlov*, 1949). The contemporary 'national author', Maksim Gor'kii, was himself the subject of a trilogy of biopics (based on his own autobiographical trilogy) produced a mere two years after his death: Mark Donskoi's *Gorky's Childhood* (1938), *My Apprenticeship* (1939) and *My Universities* (1940).

Another popular choice for depiction in Russian biopics was, and still is, the twentieth-century military hero (and occasionally heroine). The film often credited with being the first successful manifestation of socialist realism in Soviet cinema, Georgii and Sergei Vasil'evs' *Chapaev* (1934), is based on a 'biographical novel' about Vasilii Ivanovich Chapaev, martyred peasant-general of the Russian Civil War. Lev Arnshtam's *Zoya* (1944) tells the story of Zoia Kosmodemianskaia, a teenaged partisan killed by the Nazis.

Soviet cinema in the late 1950s and early 1960s saw a relative paucity of biopics, as the film industry, like other cultural media, turned to more lyrical and 'everyday' themes in the wake of Khrushchev's liberalizing de-Stalinization policies. The emphasis on the 'great man' theory of historical progression that seemed to characterize Stalinist cinema, especially late Stalinist cinema, was also giving way to a new concern with collectives that did not lend itself as well to the biopic genre. Khrushchev and his successors as general secretary were not portrayed on screen as was Stalin (for example, in Mikheil Chiaureli's *The Vow*, 1946) and Lenin (for example, Mikhail Romm's *Lenin in October*, 1938).

Although in Russia as elsewhere in the world the biopic most commonly overlapped with popular, 'mainstream' genres such as the costume drama or the war film, some of the leading Russian *auteur* directors have also tried their hands at biographical (including autobiographical) filmmaking. Most notable in this regard has been Aleksandr Sokurov, who has finished three of a planned four films about powerful men. *Moloch* (1999) is about Hitler and Eva Braun. *Taurus* (2001) is a highly stylized glimpse of a frail Lenin in 'retirement' after a series of strokes at a remote country estate with his wife, Nadezhda Krupskaia. *The Sun* (2005) is about the Japanese emperor Hirohito, and the fourth film of the tetralogy is a planned adaptation of the Faust story (not technically a biopic). Two of Andrei Tarkovskii's films – *Andrei Rublev* (1966) and *The Mirror* (1975) – are in the biographical tradition, although again with a strong *auteur* signature. The latter film is a non-linear narrative that uses autobiographical elements from the director's life.

Russian cinema during perestroika (1985–1991) certainly had a keen interest in historical events, but not in the sub-genre of the biopic, which had been so important to the

Soviet filmmaking that many directors in the new, open atmosphere were eager to reject. Historical films during the Gorbachev years most often dealt with the effect of historical forces and events on anonymous and often fictional Soviet citizens. There were also several revisionist portrayals of such Soviet personae non grata as Leon Trotsky (Leonid Mariagin's *Trotskii*, 1993) and Nikolai Bukharin (*Bukharin, Enemy of the People*, also directed by Mariagin, 1990). The Revolutionary and Stalinist past were also re-examined in such films as Karen Shakhnazarov's *Assassin of the Tsar* (1991) and Andrei Konchalovskii's *Inner Circle* (1991), both of which focused on real-life but non-famous people present at historically significant moments in Russian history.

After the first post-Soviet decade, which saw not only a sharp decline in film production generally but also the dominance of the crime film, the biopic and other varieties of the historical film have once again come to the fore. The ascension of Vladimir Putin to the Russian presidency in 2000 saw the beginning of the reassertion by the sate of keen interest in, if not direct control over, cultural production. Lenin's famous characterization of cinema as 'the most important of arts' was certainly still operative, as state financing (often via state-controlled television channels) again became a major factor in the film industry. Some of the resulting films have been revisionist historical (including biographical) epics. Vladimir Khotinenko's *1612: A Chronicle of the Time of Troubles* (2007), for example, portrays the future Romanov tsar, Mikhail, as a romantic hero and a great liberator of the Russian land from the pernicious interference of Poles. Vitalii Mel'nikov's *Poor, Poor Pavel* (2003) treats the life of one of Russian most neglected rulers, Tsar Pavel I. The perestroika-era impulse to expose the villains of the Soviet past has recently seen its converse enacted on the screen, with a highly laudatory biopic about one of the most notorious enemies of the Revolution, Admiral Kolchak (Andrei Kravchuk's *Admiral*, 2008).

Putin's own biography was the inspiration for a film that should certainly be included among Russian biopics, even though none of the characters are named Putin: Ol'ga Zhulina's *A Kiss – Not for the Press* (2008). The film is a love story depicting the acquaintance of a young woman with an up-and-coming Leningrad politician who is eventually elected president.

Seth Graham

Peter the First (Part I)

Petr pervyi

Country of Origin:
Soviet Union

Language:
Russian

Studio:
Lenfilm

Director:
Vladimir Petrov

Screenplay:
Nikolai Leshchenko
Vladimir Petrov
Aleksei Tolstoi

Cinematographers:
Viacheslav Gardanov
Vladimir Iakovlev

Art Directors:
Vladimir Kaliagin
Nikolai Suvorov

Composer:
Vladimir Shcherbachev

Editor:
N. Kerstens

Duration:
103 minutes

Genre:
Biopic

Cast:
Nikolai Simonov
Nikolai Cherkasov
Mikhail Zharov
Alla Tarasova

Year:
1937

Synopsis

Peter the First (Part I) depicts Russia's war against Sweden over the outlet to the Baltic Sea and the initiation of Peter's reforms. After the defeat against the Swedish army at Narva, Tsar Peter resolves to make great changes to strengthen Russia against her enemies. He puts pressure on the boyars and merchants to contribute financially to the war effort, sends their sons to Europe to learn shipbuilding, orders church bells to be taken down and made into cannons and recruits serfs into the army. With these reforms his troops prove victorious against King Charles XII. Peter founds the new capital, St Petersburg, along the banks of the Baltic. Falling ill after a flood, the tsar realizes that his heir Aleksei is hostile towards his reforms and will not continue his deeds. The narrative concludes with the birth of Peter's son with new wife Ekaterina.

Critique

At the time of writing the screenplay for *Peter the First* with the director Vladimir Petrov, Aleksei Tolstoi had published two instalments of his novel documenting the life of Peter the Great. His work with Petrov carried on from the point where the novel had ended – the Russian army's defeat at Narva. The film initiated the cycle of historical biographies of the late 1930s and 40s, including *Alexander Nevsky* (1938), *Suvorov* (1940), *Kutuzov* (1943) and *Ivan the Terrible* (1944), which took on the task of rehabilitating figures from the Russian past as national heroes. The film creates a close analogy between Peter's progressive reforms of Russia and the restructuring of Soviet society under Stalin. In portraying the strengthening of Russia against external enemies, the growth of cities, industry and self-sufficiency, and the battle against internal saboteurs, the film reflects many of the concerns of the late 1930s. 'We used to live like pigs in dirt and now have built a paradise', the emperor declares at the film's finale.

The struggle for modernization forms the central narrative line of the film. The contrast between Peter's determined strive forward and his deeply religious, weak-willed son Aleksei symbolizes the battle of progressive tendencies against the backwardness, autocracy and superstition of the old world. Showing no regard for the established authority of the church, Peter orders the taking down of church bells when it proves necessary to put the metal to use in the defence of the country. Depicted as a 'Bolshevik before his time', he values ability and dedication above inherited status, ruthlessly overturning traditional hierarchies and undermining accepted codes of 'royal' behaviour. Characterized throughout by means of antithesis, whereas Aleksei is shown surrounded by priests and boyars, the tsar's closest associate Menshikov is a former street pie seller, his wife Ekaterina a former servant girl. While the cowardly Aleksei shuts himself away from the needs of the people and the demands of the epoch, Peter takes all manner of tasks into his own hands in the service of Russia. Presenting his unity with the will of the Russian *narod* (people), the film introduces the narrative line of Fedka, the former serf everyman (and by analogy the 'Soviet New Man'), whose story develops along-side Peter's reforms.

Nikolai Simonov's dynamic incarnation of the monarch as a larger than life, tempestuous force of nature won high praise from contem-porary critics. The image of the tsar created onscreen demonstrates the 'king's two bodies' duality characteristic of portrayals of lead-ers in the Stalin era. At the same time as the film celebrates Peter's simplicity, humanity and oneness with the people, it shows him to be set apart by the great force of history that moves through his tower-ing body. Although susceptible to illness and human errors, Peter's otherworldly *bogatyr'* (epic hero) spirit is personified in his boundless energy and impulsiveness, his characteristic bellowing laugh threat-ening to tear itself away from mere materiality. His battle to defend Russia against external threats and internal conspiracies continues in the second part.

Anna Toropova

Lenin in October

Lenin v oktiabre

Country of Origin:
Soviet Union

Language:
Russian

Studio:
Mosfilm

Directors:
Mikhail Romm
Dmitrii Vasil'ev

Screenplay:
Aleksei Kapler

Cinematographer:
Boris Volchek

Art Directors:
Boris Dubrovskii-Eshke
Nikolai Solov'ev

Composer:
Anatolii Aleksandrov

Editor:
Tat'iana Likhacheva

Synopsis

October 1917. Lenin arrives in Petrograd by train from Finland. Despite being pursued by agents of Kerenskii's Provisional Government, he attends a meeting of the Bolshevik Party Central Committee where it is decided to launch an armed uprising against the Provisional Government. Announcing this decision on 10 October, Lenin also criticizes fellow leaders Trotsky, Zinov'ev and Kamenev for their 'sheer idiocy and treachery' for not supporting the immediate seizure of power. As the Petrograd workers prepare for the uprising, arming themselves for the struggle, the Mensheviks and Socialist Revolutionaries attempt to wreck the revolutionary activities of the workers and help Kamenev and Zinov'ev in their plans to stop the uprising. On the night of 25 October Lenin arrives at the Smolnyi Institute and takes command of the Bolshevik uprising. Petrograd's revolutionary workers, sailors and soldiers, carrying out Lenin's plan, take the central telegraph. The Bolsheviks' militant supporters storm the Winter Palace, the 'last stronghold of Russian capitalism', and arrest the members of the Provisional Government. Lenin and the other Bolshevik leaders then enter the great hall of Smolnyi, where he pronounces to the masses assembled for the Second All-Russian Congress of Soviets that 'the Workers' and Peasants' Revolution has been accomplished'.

Critique

In its full, original version, Romm's film clearly sets out to show the closeness of Lenin and Stalin during the critical days of the Bolshevik seizure of power. By 1937, the Stalin cult was reaching its pre-war height, and the film essentially represents a cinematic version of the Revolutionary history presented in the 'definitive' *Short Course of the History of the All-Union Communist Party,* the ultimate Stalinist history

Duration:

103 minutes

Genre:

Biopic
Historical-Revolutionary

Cast:

Boris Shchukin
Nikolai Okhlopkov
Vasilii Valin
Elena Shatrova

Year:

1937

of the Revolution, published in the year of the film's release. Each of the film's key scenes of Revolutionary activity serves to construct the myth of Stalin's unique 'link' with Lenin. Upon his arrival in Petrograd, the Bolshevik leader goes straight to a meeting with Stalin 'on the very next day', a discussion which lasted 'four hours'. At the 'critical' 10 October meeting, Stalin stands behind Lenin as he speaks, a visual manifestation of the 'natural' succession from one man to another, and one which is echoed in the film's iconic final scene. As Lenin proclaims power, arm outstretched, Stalin is once again seen standing directly behind him.

Stalin is also protective towards Lenin, which intrinsically puts him in a superior position. He tells the worker Vasilii to take care of Vladimir Il'ich and not let him out onto the street. Lenin asserts during the 10 October meeting: 'as Comrade Stalin absolutely rightly says, we must not wait'. Not only is this crucial phrase of Lenin's transferred to Stalin, but his rectitude is contrasted with the 'idiocy or total treachery' of Kamenev, Zinov'ev and Trotsky, whose disgrace by 1937 was total. Just as it was important to show that Stalin had been crucial to the Revolution from the very beginning, it was also essential to show how the 'enemies of the people' of the late 1930s had been traitors all along. For the audience of 1937, Stalin is thus present at all the film's key 'historical' moments.

The 1963 version of the film represents one of the starkest examples of 'de-Stalinization' in Soviet cinema. Using various techniques ranging from new voiceovers, to 'blocking' Stalin's image with the use of a newly added head of a Central Committee member, to cutting many scenes completely, any image or mention of Stalin was expunged from the film. Upon its re-release, audiences were not shown that Lenin met Stalin alone upon his arrival in Petrograd, or that Stalin ordered the worker Vasilii to keep Lenin safe. Stalin is seemingly absent from the critical 10 October meeting, his hip just visible for those 'in the know' behind the enormous superimposed head of an anonymous Central Committee member. Lenin no longer asks Vasilii to urgently get hold of Stalin and Sverdlov upon reading of Kamenev's treachery; instead a voice which impersonates that of Shchukin simply asks the worker to fetch Sverdlov. Lenin's old comrade Kamenev, along with his 'accomplices' Trotsky and Zinov'ev, is, however, in full accordance with the limits and contradictions of Khrushchev's 'de-Stalinization' programme, still very much described as a traitor to the cause.

Romm's film thus acts as a demonstration of the turbulent and contested mythmaking of the world of Soviet history cinema, making its own journey, along with the rest of Soviet society, from the extreme heights and distortions of the 'cult of personality' to the selective iconoclasm and 'renewed truth' of the 'Thaw'. All commercial editions of the film, even now, are of the re-edited 1963 version, making it very difficult for viewers to gain access to Romm's original cinematic dramatization of Stalin's *Short Course*.

Daniel Levitsky

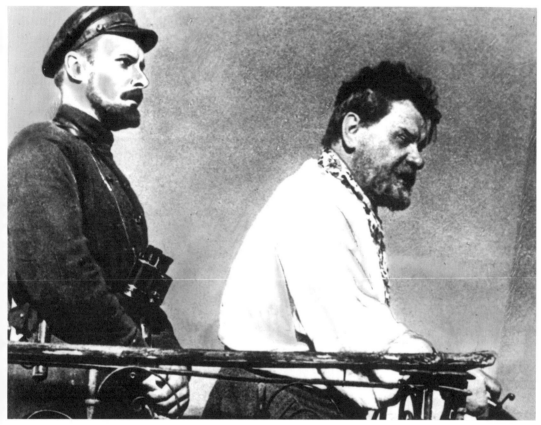

Aleksandr Dovzhenko, *Shchors* (1939).

Shchors

Country of Origin:
Soviet Union

Language:
Russian

Studio:
Kiev Film Studio

Directors:
Aleksandr Dovzhenko
Iuliia Solntseva

Producer:
Kiev Film Studio

Screenplay:
Aleksandr Dovzhenko

Synopsis

The year is 1919, and during the Civil War Ukraine is occupied by German and Polish forces. The Reds also do battle with Ukrainian nationalists under the leadership of Semen Petliura who occupy Kiev. Bolshevik forces under the leadership of the charismatic and iron-willed Nikolai Shchors march on Kiev, capturing some cities but losing others on the way. Inspired by the personal courage of Shchors, the Bolsheviks capture Kiev. At the end Shchors greets the massed ranks of marching soldiers in a final affirmation of the link of Ukraine and Bolshevism.

Critique

Dovzhenko was one of the great directors of the 'golden age' of Soviet silent cinema in the 1920s, his lyrical film-poem *Earth* (1930) being both its pinnacle and culmination as sound cinema began to take hold. *Shchors* is of interest, therefore, primarily as a record of how an innovative director with an original, poetic vision was

Cinematographer:
Iurii Ekel'chik

Art Director:
Morits Umanskii

Composer:
Dmitrii Kabalevskii

Editor:
O. Skripnik

Duration:
118 minutes

Genre:
Biopic
Historical

Cast:
Evgenii Samoilov
Ivan Skuratov
Luka Liashchenko
Nina Nikitina

Year:
1939

drummed into the service of Stalinist cinema, and forced to legitimize the Stalinist interpretation of recent history. Stalin himself suggested that Dovzhenko, a Ukrainian himself, make a film about the Revolutionary leader Nikolai Shchors (1895–1919), and the film was closely supervised at every turn. But rather than make the hero into a Ukrainian Chapaev, Dovzhenko created a type who was to become a staple figure in the biopic sub-genre. Dovzhenko's Shchors is a man without feelings, without human passion, and, as played by Evgenii Samoilov, without any facial expressions. He is an embodiment of pure ideology. We know that he is the repository of truth because several times he announces 'Lenin himself told me'. He has a wife, we learn, but he communicates with her only by telegram, and then dryly and without betraying any emotion. As he declaims: 'The revolutionary goal is always victorious over personal interests.' Because of his heroic status even brides-to-be show their attraction, but he does not respond. Shchors's mission, and that of the film, is to prove that the future of the Ukrainian people lies not as a separate national entity, but in a united state under Bolshevik leadership. There is some condescension in the portrayal of Ukrainians themselves, who wear quaint flowery national dress and speak with the thick accent that native Russians find so amusing. But even in showing a Revolutionary hero who would provide the model for future national heroes – emotionless, entirely devoted to the cause, neglecting his family (if he has one) – Dovzhenko allows some glimpses of his former artistic self. The film begins with shots of sunflowers, an immediate reminder of the opening of *Earth*, and then partisans seem to rise from the earth to attack the foreign invader. The Ukrainian land itself becomes an active participant in the battle for national sovereignty. Dovzhenko has made a film to order, and one that consciously denigrates Ukrainian national culture and history, but he leaves at least a residue of equivocation. In real life Shchors was killed in 1919 but, unlike Chapaev, he is allowed to survive in the film version.

David Gillespie

Ivan the Terrible

Ivan Groznyi

Country of Origin:
Soviet Union

Language:
Russian

Studios:
Mosfilm
TsOKS

Synopsis

Eisenstein's unfinished trilogy follows Tsar Ivan IV (1530–1584) from his traumatic childhood through his efforts to establish a modern, centralized state against the opposition of the Orthodox Church, the ruling boyars and hostile neighbours. Eisenstein chose events from Ivan's life to explain both his achievements and his methods: intimidation, demagoguery, deception and terror. This treatment challenges the audience to consider whether the ends (imperial conquest, national power) justify the means. After his wife is poisoned and his friend Kurbskii turns traitor, Ivan forms an ominous band of royal servitors. When the church, represented by another friend, Filipp, threatens to oppose him, Ivan has Filipp's family executed. When the boyars, led by Ivan's relatives, Efrosinia and Vladimir Staritskii, threaten to assassinate him, Ivan tricks Vladimir into getting murdered instead. And

Director:

Sergei Eisenstein

Producer:

Sergei Eisenstein

Screenplay:

Sergei Eisenstein

Cinematographers:

Andrei Moskvin

Eduard Tissé

Art Directors:

Sergei Eisenstein

Isaak Shpinel'

Composer:

Sergei Prokofiev

Editors:

Sergei Eisenstein

Esfir Tobak

Duration:

99+85 minutes

Genre:

Biopic

Historical

Cast:

Nikolai Cherkasov

Liudmila Tselikovskaia

Serafima Birman

Pavel Kadochnikov

Mikhail Nazvanov

Andrei Abrikosov

Mikhail Kuznetsov

Mikhail Zharov

Year:

1944

1946

when (in Part III), the *oprichnik* leaders Aleksei and Fedor Basmanov seem to betray him, Ivan has the son Fedor kill his father Aleksei. The only friend Ivan can count on is Maliuta Skuratov, his spy and executioner. By the end of Part III, Ivan achieves his goal of reaching the Baltic Sea. He is at the height of his powers but utterly alone and Russia is in ruins, everything sacrificed for the Great Russian State.

Critique

Eisenstein's legendary trilogy consists of Part I, completed in 1944 and released in 1945; Part II, completed 1946 and released in 1958; Part III unfinished.

Ivan the Terrible is a haunting treatment of power and violence, with an eccentric form that emphasizes dialectical conflicts at the heart of Ivan's persona, processes of historical change and the nature of visual perception and signification – this is not a typical biopic. The duality at the heart of Eisenstein's thinking, the film's visual style and the political conditions of its making, have made *Ivan* difficult to interpret: was Eisenstein praising or condemning Ivan, or both, or neither? Some believe Eisenstein made a politically orthodox film because he cared more about aesthetics than politics or because he had to follow the party line. Some believe that authorial intent is irrelevant and analyse the film in relation to other philosophical, psychological or aesthetic texts. Others see the treatment of Ivan as a visionary leader in Part I and a murderer in Part II as evidence that Eisenstein eventually gained the nerve to criticize the ruler. These approaches, while valuable, underestimate the film's complexity, production history, multitude of sources, many-layered structure and its linkage of history, politics, psychology and aesthetics.

Eisenstein was interested in how Ivan became Terrible. This coincided with his curiosity about his own biography; how the human develops, nations evolve, history proceeds and how we come to understand our own individual and collective pasts through art. He explores contradictory perspectives on Ivan, modelling him variously on himself, his father or his mentor Vsevolod Meyerhold, and on Stalin. There are aspects of Eisenstein's portrait that are unmistakably Stalinist, scenes that are clearly rooted in Soviet experiences of terror, compliance, resistance and corruption; and there are archival documents that demonstrate that while Eisenstein admired Ivan and his vision for Russia, he did not approve of the methods used to materialize that vision. He viewed Ivan's fate, however, as tragic because Ivan suffered remorse and begged for forgiveness, while Stalin suffered no such pangs, eventually telling Eisenstein in person that he considered the film's Ivan insufficiently ruthless and overly prone to self-doubt. The larger tragedy to be found in Eisenstein's Ivan resides in the historical inevitability of betrayal and violence, the cyclical paths of history and the human capacity for self-delusion and destruction, the only reliable relief from which is the pleasure found in art.

For many, the passion Eisenstein invested in *Ivan* is obscured by cinematic strategies that distance the viewer: inscrutable gender characterizations, expressionistic and melodramatic acting, symbolic usage of lighting and sets, contradictory storylines and a profusion of

Sergei Eisenstein, *Ivan the Terrible* (1944, 1946).

visual details that led Roland Barthes to develop his theory of visual 'excess'. The historical context and the director's intent help us make sense of the film and its lasting significance.

Ivan raises questions that still matter about politics, individual responsibility and human nature. Eisenstein's treatment of these issues derive from his wide reading, but also from his personal experience of Stalinist hypertrophied power, with its unpredictable judgements, uncertain boundaries between public and private and its corrupt and corrupting forces in everyday life. Eisenstein believed that all people, even tyrants, are divided by contradictory impulses for power and compassion, revenge and friendship, feeling and thinking, and the film's emphatic contrariness asserts the artist's right to ask hard questions instead of offering consoling solutions. This strategy produced the opposite of amoral relativism: it denied viewers a neutral vantage point and challenged them to reclaim their own authority to make meaning from observation and experience. *Ivan the Terrible* is difficult film because it denies us a hero to identify with or to judge, but it is a great film because it offers us an artist working at the height of his powers to create a portrait of evil that resists simplification. In a world that preferred its heroes simple and its enemies undiluted, this was a courageous project.

Joan Neuberger

Academician Ivan Pavlov

Akademik Ivan Pavlov

Country of Origin:
Soviet Union

Language:
Russian

Studio:
Lenfilm

Directors:
Grigorii Roshal'

Screenplay
Mikhail Papava

Cinematographers:
Viacheslav Gordanov
Evgenii Kirpichev
Mikhail Magid
Lev Sokol'skii

Art Directors:
Abram Veksler
Evgenii Enei

Composer:
Dmitrii Kabalevskii

Editor:
Valentina Mironova

Duration:
98 minutes

Genre:
Biopic

Cast:
Aleksandr Borisov
Nina Alisova
Nikolai Plotnikov
Marianna Safonova
Fedor Nikitin
Grigorii Shpigel'

Year:
1949

Synopsis

Russia, 1875: In Riazan', Dr Pavlov is summoned to a landowner who refuses to accept the inevitability of his death; to Pavlov's dismay, he orders the destruction of a beautiful apple orchard. 1894: Experimenting on dogs, Pavlov tries to comprehend the interaction between nerves and external signals governing digestion. In 1904, he formulates the principles of conditional reflexes. When Zvantsev, an opponent of Pavlov's materialist worldview, leaves the laboratory, the scientist hires Varvara Ivanova who becomes his most reliable assistant. 1912: Pavlov receives an honorary doctorate from Cambridge University. 1917: Despite Pavlov's political scepticism, the Bolshevik administration treats him with great respect. Maksim Gor'kii pays a visit to inquire about his needs, revealing that Lenin personally sent him. On tour in the United States, Pavlov is attacked by a racist and defends his view of the equality of all human beings. Communist hack Sergei Kirov oversees the creation of a large centre for physiological research. At the Fifteenth World Congress of Physiologists, Pavlov gives a passionate speech in support of world peace. Shortly before his death in 1936, he sends an inspiring letter to the komsomol congress.

Critique

The most famous Russian scientist of his time, Ivan Petrovich Pavlov (1849–1936) presented a ticklish subject for Stalinist cinematic hagiography. Pavlov was an outspoken critic of the Soviet government and remained an unabashed Christian believer to the end who used his immense authority to protect people in danger. But in the late 1940s, with the Cold War atmosphere worsening, Pavlov's international reputation and his well-known insistence on staying in the Soviet Union were useful ingredients for a prestige biopic, as was his pride in the achievements of Russian science that could be misinterpreted so as to corroborate the vicious campaign against 'cosmopolitanism'.

Mikhail Papava's screenplay is structured in a linear chronological manner, selecting situations in which Pavlov makes grandiose statements or demonstrates personal features such as compassion with simple folk, tenacity in pursuing scientific hypotheses and a principled stance against reactionaries of various persuasions. Roshal''s direction gives Aleksandr Borisov ample opportunities to shine, portraying Pavlov's hot temper, stubbornness, charming eccentricity and dry humour. The result is a largely convincing character portrait, with secondary characters functioning as mere pawns, including Nina Alisova's assistant Ivanova and Fedor Nikitin's Zvantsev.

From a historical point of view, the film's falsifications are considerable. Thus, on several occasions Pavlov states that he does not believe in a soul, accusing a disagreeing colleague of cowardice and implying that he himself is an atheist. Gor'kii, as portrayed by Nikolai Cherkasov, expresses his dismay over not being a member of the Bolshevik Party – at a time when his actual criticism of Lenin and the destruction of cultural values led to serious conflicts with the Bolsheviks. In accordance with Roshal''s ultra-rationalist concept of Pavlov, Evgenii Enei's interiors are kept deliberately geometrical and simplified, never even trying to achieve realistic effects. The exteriors are filmed in an emphatically poetic style, pointing toward the scientist's love for the motherland.

In many respects, Academician Ivan Pavlov is a replica of *Baltic Deputy* (1937), featuring an idiosyncratic, world-famous intellectual who willingly co-operates with the Soviet state. In both cases, Lenin is personally concerned about the wellbeing of the central character; to support Pavlov, the government releases a decree elevating his physiological research to a national priority. The main difference between the two films lies in their depiction of the scientific community: while the fictitious biologist Polezhaev in the earlier picture is an outsider shunned by his colleagues, Pavlov enjoys the admiration of a majority of scientists, especially the young generation. The Russian intelligentsia is shown as intrinsically democratic and gregarious while invariably maintaining high intellectual standards. Another indisputable strength of Roshal''s film is its apt visualization of scientific truth-finding. Thus, an episode depicting a public experiment on canine salivation generates genuine suspense. On the whole, the anti-western paranoia typical of the Stalinist biographical genre is kept to a minimum; the Cambridge scenes even contain some benevolent humour, and while Pavlov's appearance in the United States emphasizes – quite realistically – the presence of racist views, that episode also features a crowd of American admirers of the Russian's work. Although openly didactic and artistically pedestrian, Roshal''s biopic nonetheless describes intellectual work with unequivocal respect and conveys this attitude to the viewer.

Peter Rollberg

Mirror

Zerkalo

Country of Origin:
Soviet Union

Languages:
Russian
Spanish

Studio:
Mosfilm

Director:
Andrei Tarkovskii

Screenplay:
Aleksandr Misharin
Andrei Tarkovskii

Synopsis

A prologue shows a stuttering boy undergoing successful speech therapy, at the close of which he announces: 'I can speak'. There follow approximately twenty sequences which comprise the invisible protagonist Aleksei's memories of childhood (from ca. 1936 and 1942) and experiences as an estranged husband and ineffectual father in present-day Moscow (ca. 1969), interspersed with documentary sequences relating these experiences to historical events (most notably Stalinist celebrations, the Spanish Civil War, World War II and the Sino-Soviet conflict). The soundtrack features extracts from numerous classical compositions and three poems by Tarkovskii's father Arsenii. The voice of the protagonist is supplied by Innokentii Smoktunovskii. In the final frame the two dimensions of memory and vision coalesce into a single image.

Critique

Mirror represents Tarkovskii's most ambitious and experimental film both in its narrative structure and in its cinematic style. At

Cinematographer:

Georgii Rerberg

Art Director:

Nikolai Dvigubskii

Composer:

Eduard Artem'ev

Editor:

Liudmila Feiginova

Duration:

108 minutes

Genre:

Biopic

Autobiography

Cast:

Margarita Terekhova

Filip Iankovskii

Ignat Danil'tsev

Nikolai Grin'ko

Alla Demidova

Iurii Nazarov

Anatolii Solonitsyn

Innokentii Smoktunovskii

Larisa Tarkovskaia

Mariia Tarkovskaia

Year:

1974

first screening it can be very difficult to work out the connections between the sequences, which Tarkovskii claimed to have rearranged many times before settling on the right order. Complicating matters is the fact that the same actress plays the protagonist Aleksei's mother and his estranged wife, while the same young actor plays Aleksei at the age of about ten and his son Ignat. Though Aleksei quickly points out that he always remembers his mother with his ex-wife's face, many of Tarkovskii's colleagues at Mosfilm – and countless viewers since – have wondered, in the words of Marlen Khutsiev, 'Who is who?' The confusion underscores the interrelatedness of all images and their inseparability from the imagination which engenders them.

The intersection between this personal imaginary and the broader social imaginary is explored in the documentary sequences. On one

Andrei Tarkovskii, *Mirror* (1975).

level the Spanish footage is a kind of flashback to explain the presence in Moscow of a Spanish family which finds itself tugged in the conflicting directions of nostalgia and assimilation. However this is but one function of the footage, which does not so much authenticate the fictional narrative as it fills in the history of the protagonist's vision. The film might even be seen to be arresting the authenticity of the documentary footage, questioning whether it might not be even more subject to the pressure of the imaginary than the authorial record of personal experience.

A similar ambiguity pervades the scenes of supernatural intervention, which might just be a figment of the characters' imagination. The visitation of the mysterious guest is prefaced by a long take featuring the boy Ignat and his mother Natalia which situates the supernatural in the everyday. In her haste Natalia drops her handbag, and Ignat eagerly begins to help pick up the spilled coins from the parquet floor, pressing them into his palm and tracing their design with his finger. When he reaches for another coin he quickly pulls his hand away, explaining that he had received an electric shock; he then smirks and remarks that he is experiencing déjà vu: 'It's as if all this has already been once, though I've never been here before.' Natalia answers: 'Give the money here. Stop imagining things [*Perestan' fantazirovat'*], I implore you.' Throughout the shot Eduard Artem'ev's electronic score features a harsh crescendo that prepares the viewer for the irruption of outside forces; however this discontinuity is embedded within the fluid continuity of Tarkovskii's signature long takes. The complex confluence of temporalities and dimensions of reality within the shot is analogous to the way the coins conduct multiple dimensions of physical and psychic reality: material history and electrical charge converge with the less tangible currents of memory, fantasy and vision in a single imprint of currency.

Tarkovskii uses film to show the friction caused by the imaginary coming into contact with time. Though it is not a direct critique of the Soviet imaginary, *Mirror* seeks to redefine the viewer's very attitude towards images not as the storehouse of the past, but as a condition for experiencing the world.

Robert Bird

Rasputin

Agoniia

Country of Origin:
Soviet Union

Language:
Russian

Studio:
Mosfilm

Synopsis

Russia 1916. Nationwide discontentment threatens the monarchy with collapse, but Tsar Nicholas II ignores the impending danger. Deeply concerned about his haemophiliac son, he puts all his trust in faith healer Grigorii Rasputin, thus allowing him to assume an unassailable position. Rasputin has Prime Minister Goremykin replaced by the incompetent Slavophile Boris Stürmer and gets away with sexually assaulting a baroness in public. Meanwhile indignation over Rasputin's behaviour is growing. Prince Iusupov, whose wife has aroused Rasputin's sexual appetite, and Grand Duke Dmitrii Pavlovich discuss the possibility of his elimination. A mysterious woman calls Rasputin

Director:
Elem Klimov

Screenplay:
Semen Lungin
Il'ia Nusinov

Cinematographer:
Leonid Kalashnikov

Art Director:
Shavkat Abdusalimov

Composer:
Alfred Schnittke

Editor:
Valeriia Belova

Duration:
151 minutes

Genre:
Biopic
Historical drama

Cast:
Aleksei Petrenko
Anatolii Romashin
Velta Line
Alissa Freindlikh
Aleksandr Romantsev
Iurii Katin-Iartsev
Leonid Bronevoi

Year:
1975

on the phone and invites him over, but the rendezvous is a trap organized by the Orthodox Church. Exiled from Petrograd, Rasputin forces his way into the palace at Tsarskoe Selo where he manipulates Nicholas into launching the so-called Baranovichi operation (one of Russia's worst defeats in World War I). News that the offensive has failed reaches Rasputin in his native Siberia. After his return to Petrograd, Iusupov, the Grand Duke and Duma-member Purishkevich, carry out the assassination. A burial scene featuring the tsar, the empress and Rasputin's family, is followed by a cut to black-and-white imagery of Bolsheviks saluting the October Revolution.

Critique

Originally entitled *The Antichrist* and shown in the West as *Rasputin*, *Agonia* (Death Throes) is as much about the last convulsions of the Russian monarchy as it is about the assassination of its central character. With its many references to the inevitability of revolution, the film recalls (and borrows from) such epic movies as Pudovkin's *The End of St Petersburg* and Eisenstein's *October* (both 1927). This tribute to the montage school is not accidental, as *Rasputin* was initially intended for release to mark the 50th anniversary of the October Revolution in 1967. Yet the message of Klimov's film is considerably less straightforward than that of the anniversary movies of the 1920s. Nicholas II is shown as a weak, yet cultured man capable of feeling remorse over Bloody Sunday (9 January 1905). Rasputin, too, is a more complicated character than the lecherous fraud he was traditionally made out to be. The film contains an episode in his native Siberia illustrating his complicated relationship with his family and fellow villagers. Despite a new title and a number of changes in the script, KGB chief Iurii Andropov remained dissatisfied with the final result, arguing that the film paid too much attention to the personal lives of Rasputin and the imperial family. Completed in 1974 and immediately 'shelved', *Rasputin* was shown in Venice in 1982 and released in the USSR only in 1985.

Rasputin is structured as a double narrative that unfolds through the alternation of (authentic) black-and-white footage and acted sequences in full colour. The documentary images offer a harrowing panorama of the people's suffering, accompanied by a voice-over spelling out all the woes under the last tsar, while the acted scenes predominantly feature members of Russia's corrupted elite. These two storylines eventually merge when a frantic Rasputin runs into a demonstration and discovers one of his future assassins. The scene is shot alternately in black and white, and colour, suggesting that the morally depraved in-crowd of pre-Revolutionary Russia, epitomized by Rasputin, is doomed to be crushed by the course of history.

Throughout Klimov employs Eisenstein's concept of intellectual montage, particularly the device of the non-diegetic insert. For example, the scene that features a frenzied Rasputin stammering the word 'Baranovichi' in the presence of Nicholas and his wife Alexandra is intercut with black-and-white images of running sheep (*barany*), alluding to the catastrophic outcome of the battle at Baranovichi. The same scene contains a flash cut to Rasputin dressed as a groom and carrying a woman in his arms (a metaphor for Russia). This particular image, which echoes the age-old idea of the monarch being wed to his country, illustrates that Rasputin, not the tsar, is ruling Russia.

Based on meticulous archival research, *Rasputin* pays due attention to historical figures who tried to use Rasputin for their own goals. This adds to the psychological complexity of Rasputin who gradually becomes aware of being a pawn, rather than an agent. Yet perhaps the most telling sign of the film's unorthodox approach is the fact that Rasputin is shown in different roles and capacities: he is simultaneously a shrewd manipulator, a loutish womanizer, a (lacking) father and a social outcast in his native village. Even if the sceptical reception by his countrymen is intended to 'prove' that Rasputin is not a man from the people (as the empress believes), his apparent frustration over this rebuke makes him almost human; more human than Soviet censorship could possibly allow.

Otto Boele

Taurus

Telets

Country of Origin:
Russia

Language:
Russian

Studio:
Lenfilm

Director:
Aleksandr Sokurov

Producer:
Viktor Sergeev

Screenplay:
Iurii Arabov

Cinematographer:
Aleksandr Sokurov

Art Director:
Nataliia Kochergina

Composer:
Andrei Sigle

Editor:
Leda Semenova

Synopsis

Unfolding over two days in 1924, the film depicts the dying Lenin, world revolutionary and father of the USSR, now powerless and isolated at his Gorki estate. Cared for by his wife, Nadezhda Krupskaia, sister Maniasha, his German doctor and several attendants, Lenin raves about his diminishing faculties, discusses the deaths of great figures (including Marx), rides a car to a picnic in a meadow and ponders his historic legacy. In a key scene the 'great leader' interacts with a visitor, his eventual successor Joseph Stalin, asking for poison to hasten his demise. At film's end, Lenin is left alone in his wheelchair while Nadezhda rushes off to answer a long-awaited telephone call from the Party Central Committee. His cries are answered only by the distant lowing of a cow. The once-all-powerful despot, at the end of his life, stares longingly at clouds in a bottomless sky. A storm looms.

Critique

Like the other works in Sokurov's 'Men of Power' tetralogy – *Moloch* on Hitler (1999), *The Sun* (2005) on Hirohito and a planned adaptation of Goethe's *Faust* – *Taurus* utilizes unconventional cinematography, unorthodox performances, slow pacing and a highly imaginative approach to its subject for a meditation on the dehumanizing effects of absolute power. While some critics fault Sokurov for the film's rambling script and 'stagy' shots, others highlight the comedic potential of a once-towering figure like Lenin diminished to a sick, ranting old man (seen naked more than once). Still others accuse Sokurov of over-humanizing his dictators, glossing over their crimes in pursuit of some a-historical 'universality' of mortal existence. In evoking compassion for Lenin's death agonies, so goes this critique, the film risks betraying the many victims of his policies. On the other hand, *Taurus* hardly heroicizes its subject. Deprived of the telephone, even

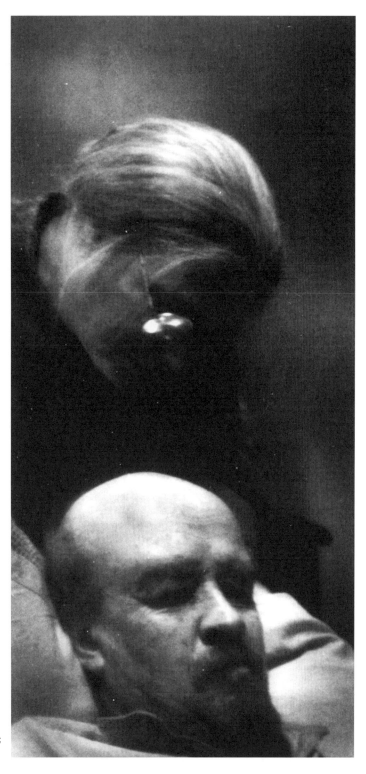

Aleksandr Sokurov, *Taurus* (2001);
Lenin and Krupskaia.

Duration:

94 minutes (cinema)
104 minutes (video)

Genre:

Biopic
Drama

Cast:

Leonid Mozgovoi
Mariia Kuznetsova
Sergei Razhuk
Nataliia Nikulenko
Lev Eliseev
Nikolai Ustinov

Year:

2000

a newspaper (rudely snatched away by an orderly), Lenin knows the Party he founded has abandoned him; explosions of rage alternate with a muted resignation and transient pleasures of the natural world (birdsong, thunder, sunlight through a window). While based on accounts of Lenin's final days (following a series of strokes), the film's idiosyncratic representation of historical figures renders them by turns sympathetic and grotesque – perhaps a corrective to the many Soviet-era cine-panegyrics to the 'dear leader' such as Mikhail Romm's *Lenin in October* (1937). The petty, whining Lenin of *Taurus* could not be further from the strong, avuncular figure of Stalinist propaganda.

Still, at times the film seems fascinated by the iconicity of its subjects: one shot in particular lingers on the just-arrived Stalin in his greatcoat, standing like a predator beside his car. These images enact a haunting 'resurrection' of the dead; from such a distance the illusion of a living Stalin seems disturbingly convincing. Yet Sokurov will often deflate such apotheosizing imagery; for example, the meeting between Stalin and Lenin includes shot-reverse shot extreme close-ups of the two leaders, revealing (through his facial expressions and eyes) Lenin's craven baseness as he begs for poison, and Stalin's deceitful, pock-marked, mannequin-like visage. Here the director most blatantly strips the legend from the man.

For *Taurus*, Sokurov served for the first time as his own cinematographer; his dark, saturated, oft-blurred images flirt with inscrutability. The estate often appears in fog, its interior a labyrinth of murky, green-tinted rooms; even when the sun breaks the imagery recalls day-for-night photography. As in *Mother and Son,* many shots hark back to the silent era. As pointed out by several critics, the film's greenish, gloomy palette makes it appear as if the action is occurring underwater. As in much of Sokurov's work, these atypical visual strategies reference European art, in this case Vermeer and – in part through the colour scheme and repeated mentions of an approaching storm – Giorgione's 'The Tempest' (1506–1508).

Like many films of its time, *Taurus* focuses on themes of death and decay, in part as a means of exorcising Soviet-era ghosts. In this sense one may compare it to Nikita Mikhalkov's *Burnt by the Sun* (1994) as a re-examination of the Stalinist past, albeit in an unorthodox manner. Similarly, like Andrei Zviagintsev's *The Return* (2003) and other recent films, *Taurus* ironicizes the theme of paternity through the figure of a decrepit father whose 'progeny', the Soviet Union, is itself now defunct.

Taurus seems to be a sustained meditation on illness, the body and the universality of the dying process, the loss of control at the end of life – regardless of one's earthly achievements. Yet some have seen in Sokurov's dying yet stubbornly atheistic Lenin a perverse parody of the communist fixation on materialism.

José Alaniz

Russian

Russkoe

Country of Origin:
Russia

Language:
Russian

Studios:
Sinemafor
Trial Blok
Pygmalion Production, with the support of the Cinematography Section of the Russian Ministry of Culture

Director:
Aleksandr Veledinskii

Producers:
Aleksei Aliakin
Sergei Chliiants
Maksim Lagashkin
Aleksandr Robak

Screenplay:
Aleksandr Veledinskii, based on Eduard Limonov

Cinematographer:
Pavel Ignatov

Art Director:
Il'ia Amurskii

Composer:
Aleksei Zubarev

Editor:
Tat'iana Prilenskaia

Duration:
112 minutes

Genre:
Biopic

Cast:
Andrei Chadov
Ol'ga Arntgol'ts
Evdokiia Germanova
Mikhail Efremov

Synopsis

Eddie is a working-class teenager in 1959 Kharkov. He hangs out with shady characters, but is also a gifted poet, albeit one who uses his talent to distract crowds while his friend picks pockets. He pursues a local beauty, Sveta, promising her a date in a restaurant with the implicit assumption that she will repay him sexually. When he catches Sveta kissing his friend, Ed shows up at her flat with a knife, but runs off before she opens the door. He wanders the snowy streets and nearly commits suicide before his mother finds him and has him put in the Saburka, an infamous psychiatric hospital whose patients had included the artist Mikhail Vrubel' and the futurist poet Velimir Khlebnikov. There Ed bonds with the other maltreated patients, one of whom introduces him to the richness of Russian literature. After a brief escape, during which he climbs a church tower and prays for 'an interesting life', Ed is recommitted to the asylum, which prompts his mates to stage a 'storming' of the hospital (à la the storming of the Winter Palace in October 1917) in protest. When he is finally released, he has learned hard truths about his place in the world as a son and an artist.

Critique

The title of *Russian* in the original is *Russkoe*, which refers not to 'a Russian person' or the Russian language, but something closer to 'Russianness' or 'things that are essentially Russian' (indeed, one suggested English translation is *It's Russian*). 'Russkoe' is the title of an early poem by the Russian author and (more recently) radical nationalist political figure Eduard Limonov, on whose autobiographical novels Veledinskii's film is based. Despite the title's seeming nod, however ironic, to idealistic Russian soul-searching and abstract values, the film is nevertheless also firmly in the realist tradition. The tight, disciplined narrative remains focused on its hero's negotiation of the social reality that surrounds him and discovery of his potential place within it. Yet *Russian* is by no means a straightforward biographic film of Limonov. It is also a largely unsentimental contemplation of the East vs West, Spirit vs Flesh dilemma that is every Russian's celebrated and accursed birthright.

Poetry in the film is represented as both divine and visceral, the coin of a value system that Russia has traditionally posited as an alternative, a way out of the messy world of material values. Veledinskii's attempt at reconciling the filth, viscera and squalor of modern Russian life with both a sense of 'higher values' and an engaging, marketable film product is ultimately more honest than other such attempts, and does not resort to crude juxtaposition with an Other to define a Russian Self.

Someone once said that there are four escape routes from reality: into crime, into art, into madness and into religion. In *Russian*, what we have is a struggle among the four for the fate of the young protagonist. The material reality of a late 1950s Soviet city is, on the surface, dominant. Even before the narrative begins, during the credits, each name we see projected on the screen is accompanied and

Vladimir Steklov
Aleksei Gorbunov
Dmitrii Diuzhev

Year:
2004

represented by an object. Poverty and squalor dominate the mise-en-scène. The plot itself, especially before Ed enters the Saburka, is driven by exchange, barter and transfer of things of value: a knife, a razor, a ring, a book, a maidenhead, souvenir badges, a notebook, a photograph, eyeglasses, nylons, mandarin oranges, vodka, roubles. Ed's sole motivation in the beginning of the film is the achievement of a physical act (sex with Sveta) by material means (buying her dinner in a restaurant). Sveta's calculating promiscuousness is mitigated, however, by the fact that she will trade her physical affection not only for material wealth and status, but also as a token of her appreciation for good poetry and for the company of a true poet. In a film in which there is no shortage of mentors (which can be seen as a nod to the classic mentor-initiate model of Soviet socialist realism), Sveta's lesson for Ed (which he misses, tragically, the first time she offers it, when he comes to her door with the knife) may be the most relevant to his personal arc: that poetry is a useful tool for negotiating reality, especially in Russia, where the line between art and reality has so often been blurred.

Seth Graham

The Admiral

Admiral

Country of Origin:
Russia

Languages:
Russian
French

Studios:
Channel One
Film Direction
Dago Productions

Director:
Andrei Kravchuk

Producers:
Dzhanik Faiziev
Anatolii Maksimov
Dmitrii Iurkov

Screenplay:
Vladimir Valutskii
Zoia Kudria

Cinematographer:
Igor' Griniakin

Synopsis

We are introduced to Admiral Aleksandr Kolchak (1874–1920) relatively late in his career, in 1916, when he is in command of a Russian ship in the Baltic Sea during World War I. Thanks to his calm and quick thinking under fire, a more powerful German warship is sunk. At a celebration soon thereafter in Finland, he meets and falls in love with Anna Timireva, the wife of one of his subordinate officers. She reciprocates, and the two maintain a chaste, long-distance affair as the tumultuous events of the day send them to various places inside and outside the crumbling Russian empire. Kolchak, sent into exile by the head of the Provisional Government in mid-1917, returns to Russia after the October Revolution to fight the Bolsheviks. He appoints himself supreme ruler of Siberia, the base for his campaign against the Reds in the Russian Civil War. Anna finally leaves her husband and joins Kolchak permanently in Siberia, but the Whites suffer defeat after defeat. Kolchak is arrested by the Bolsheviks and shot in 1920. An epilogue shows Anna as an extra on the set of Fedor Bondarchuk's film *War and Peace* in 1964, looking wistfully at a ballroom scene.

Critique

Five years in the making, sophomore director Andrei Kravchuk's *The Admiral* is a well-produced mix of epic history and romantic melodrama that recalls David Lean's *Dr Zhivago*, with its wartime trains, constantly re-separated lovers and anti-Bolshevik message, and, ultimately, James Cameron's *Titanic*, with its fatefully truncated romance and epilogue showing the woman's life decades after her lover's

Art Directors:

Mariia Turskaia

Aleksandr Zagoskin

Composer:

Gleb Matveichuk

Editor:

Tom Rolf

Duration:

124 minutes

Genre:

Biopic

Historical

Cast:

Konstantin Khabenskii

Elizaveta Boiarskaia

Sergei Bezrukov

Vladislav Vetrov

Year:

2008

watery demise. Unlike those two blockbusters, however, *The Admiral* is also a biopic, and one that flirts with hagiography even before Admiral Kolchak's martyred body is thrown into a cross-shaped hole in the ice (conveniently left over from a recent church baptism ceremony) by his godless Bolshevik executioners. In part the thoroughly uncritical portrait of Kolchak is compensatory; for so long, and for obvious ideological reasons, White Army leaders could only be pilloried in the Russian media, especially cinema, the main vehicle for populating the official dramatis personae of historical heroes and villains. The few detectable character flaws in Kravchuk's representation of Kolchak come at moments when the admiral's penchant for self-aggrandizement comes to the fore. For example, his repeated assurances that the city of Irkutsk – effectively already firmly in the hands of the Reds – will be secure the moment he personally arrives, suggest that he views himself as the ultimate repository of Russian imperial sovereignty. The scene in which he takes a solemn and religiously toned oath before his troops, as 'Supreme Ruler of Russia', at a time when the Whites' eastern front was thousands of kilometres east of Moscow, similarly suggest an unjustifiably inflated self-image. Most of the battle scenes showcase his own bravery, rather than that of his sailors and soldiers (an exception is the scene in which the White soldiers, having run out of ammunition, attach their bayonets and charge out of the trenches directly towards the Red machine guns).

Yet criticizing the film's lack of nuance and dramatic license is, in a way, not entirely fair. The biopic genre arguably lends itself to such one-sided portrayals, and *The Admiral* is certainly less revisionist and nationalistic than other post-Soviet Russian historical epics such as Nikita Mikhalkov's *Barber of Siberia* (1998) or Vladimir Khotinenko's *1612: A Chronicle of the Time of Troubles* (2007). It is also important to remember that Russian filmmakers are still in the process of creating a profitable, popular national cinema, a project in which watchable, mainstream films are essential. In this respect, Kravchuk's film was a success, as it represented another benchmark hit in the resurgent Russian film industry, which began recovering from a dismal decade (both financially and artistically) early in the new millennium. *The Admiral* had a budget of $20 million, extremely large by Russian standards, and earned an impressive profit. Much of the budget was spent on CGI, which certainly shows in the impressive naval-battle scenes. The wide-screen potential of the Siberian countryside, staple of so many Russian films before and after the fall of the Soviet Union, is also used to full effect.

Konstantin Khabenskii plays Kolchak with a reserved propriety, even in the romantic scenes, which adds to the sense of Kolchak as a force of history rather than a human character. Khabenskii has become a sort of Russian Harrison Ford, having starred in no less than four of the largest-grossing Russian films of the new millennium, all of which, except for *The Admiral*, directed by Timur Bekmambetov: *Night Watch* (2004), *Day Watch* (2006) and the sequel to the 1970s favourite *The Irony of Fate* (2007).

Seth Graham

ACTION/RED WESTERN

The cinematic genre of action films reveals a high degree of crossover with the genre of the adventure film (not covered in this volume). While both rely upon a juxtaposition of good and evil, the 'action flick' is arguably more concerned with physical conflict and violence, while filmic adventures frequently align their chase sequences or rescue scenes with travel-related plots.

According to Hollywood's conventions, action and adventure films are usually those in which movement is more important than speech. In the early days of Soviet cinema, this concern with movement is reflected in such films as Lev Kuleshov's *Mr West* (1924), which draws on a number of devices taken from Los Angeles: continuity editing (which Kuleshov called 'American montage') or chase scenes between characters modelled on the stars of American cinema (such as Harold Lloyd and Douglas Fairbanks). In addition there is a shift towards acrobatic stunts instead of the psychological characterization so distinctive in pre-Revolutionary theatre. All this speaks to Soviet cinema's attempts at creating adventure or action films in order to match the fiscal benchmarks of their US counterparts, which flooded Soviet distribution in the 1920s.

Indeed, Russian cinema has long struggled with a range of terms for the action or adventure film: while the label 'adventure film' (*prikliuchencheskii fil'm*) can be frequently found in genre classifications of Soviet and Russian movie making, alongside it there existed the 'thriller' (*ostrosiuzhetnyi fil'm*, or *triller*) and the 'action film' (*boevik*); under the influence of post-Soviet shoptalk the phonetic transcription of 'action' as *èkshn* has also gained currency. Given this wavering, it is telling to look at ways in which the Russian action/adventure tradition developed.

The action or adventure film often placed the prowess of a lone hero against a collective enemy, a principle which lent itself to the portrayal of ideological clashes between Reds and Whites during the Civil War, widely used as a historical backdrop for films in the 1920s and 1930s. Both historical and biographical films were popular, such as the famous *Chapaev* (1934), but a specifically Soviet variant of the genre of the action/adventure film would only emerge decades later.

Blessed not only with great physical skill, but also moral justification, the male pro-tagonist of the Western adventure/action genre would typically overcome great odds at sea, upon land or even high in the clouds. These swashbuckling Hollywood traditions, often set in distant times and very formulaic, would subsequently be given new life by the real-life events of World War II. The resulting camouflaged heroes, in turn, would slowly transform into the more debonair spies of Cold War escapades.

In the same American context, by the 1970s and 1980s this kind of generic purity was lost to a series of expensive and profitable blockbusters. Such testosterone-fuelled films, meagre in terms of screenplay, almost always bore their central message through visible, visceral deeds. Heroes *showed* what mattered, often through direct and violent conflict with the representatives of opposing worldviews. The morality of these well-built matinee idols was grounded in certain assumptions: heroism is often a lonely calling and champions of any laudable cause will rarely have many friends or meaningful relatives. Such was the life of an adventurer.

This kind of movie would become a genuine artistic and commercial force in Russia thanks to the hugely popular tradition of 'Red Westerns' or so-called 'Easterns'. Pre-saging their themes of perilous uncertainty – and therefore audience exhilaration – is Vladimir Motyl''s *White Sun of the Desert* (1970), in which a Red Army soldier during the Civil War is unexpectedly caught up in haphazard action along the Caspian Sea. This apparent formulaic clarity is distinctly undercut by our hero's (comedic) need to spend more time defending a local harem than Moscow's value-system. Increasingly, Motyl''s viewers are left with a sense of unpredictability, both in terms of filmic plot and social causality; almost anything can happen. Nonetheless, both profits and viewer satisfaction increased as a result; *White Sun of the Desert* remains a cult film of the Stagnation era to the present day.

This use of illogicality – based upon vigorous subversions and plot twists – adopts a more serious quality in those Red Westerns produced by Central Asian film studios. The significance of random chance is evident in Shaken Aimanov's *End of the Ataman* (Kazakhfilm, 1970), or Ali Khamraev's *Seventh Bullet* (Uzbekfilm, 1972), both set in capricious times and places. Closely involved with film production in the same region, the young Moscow intellectuals and Film Institute graduates Andrei Mikhalkov-Konch-alovskii and Nikita Mikhalkov would contribute to scripts of some local Red Westerns. More precisely, Mikhalkov later drew on his experiences with this genre – and the clas-sic westerns of American cinema – for his debut feature *At Home among Strangers...* (1974). Despite the fact that these Soviet films employed – successfully – the same brooding sexuality of their American forerunners, they would fall out of fashion in the 1980s. To a large degree, tales of daring loners lost ground to special effects and the 'disaster movie'.

This territory is notably opened by Aleksandr Mitta's grandiose feature, *Air Crew* (1980); despite the recourse to loud explosions and noisy chaos in such movies, a certain conservatism returned to adventure features of the 1980s. In action or catastrophe-driven movies of the same decade in the West, elements of conformist consolation are almost always evident, in that virtuous characters survive – no matter the apocalyptic ravages of storms, war or disease. *Air Crew* works to similar effect: unforeseen earthquakes conspire to severely damage a Soviet airliner en route to Moscow. All ensuing, potentially awful dangers are overcome thanks only to the bravery of the aircrew, who rise above their personal problems in order to give everything – for the passengers. Mikhalkov's doubts over ideological zeal among Revolutionary troops become for Mitta a similar reliance among a steadfast, intrepid minority, but here that comradeship is tempered in the more institutional environment of a state airline crew. Thus the social tedium of Brezhnev's era starts to create action movies at the expense of peril. The 'right' people always make it through.

Hence, perhaps, the brief return to irony and jesting under Gorbachev as a means to challenge narrative certainty and reinstate the risky/risqué value of unpredictability. Alla Surikova's *Man from the Boulevard des Capucines* (1987) coincided with the erratic faltering of the Soviet grand narrative after perestroika by looking at the ability of cinema to create – and even falsify – reality. This story of silent movies in the Wild West almost becomes an action film not by virtue of its cowboys and bar brawls, but because we never know what new realities or worldviews will be shaped – and manipulated – by film itself.

It seems possible, therefore, to speak of different kinds of Soviet action movies over the course of the twentieth century. The first exists on a sliding scale – back and forth – between severe peril and an ideological interpretation thereof, where disaster never truly looks likely. The degrees to which actuality might be under threat are sometimes assessed in between conservative assurance and genuine unease, in realms where only small, dependable enclaves of friends might offer resistance against unpredictability. If so, then a second type of 'action' also appears. Films styled along the lines of Surikova's goofball adventure, emphasizing the arbitrarily fictive nature of film – the fact it can build any reality – suggest that bona fide jeopardy, which cannot be remade or redirected, is in the outside world.

The more commercialized post-Soviet film industry has seen a return to the action genre in its 'pure' form, without ideological strings attached. Indeed, some of Russia's more recent action movies suggest – in a dead-end, documentary manner – that the nastiness of an unsafe reality is all around us. Aleksei Balabanov, Sergei Bodrov Jr and Petr Buslov have all portrayed a world dark enough to make viewers lose their faith in several nationwide institutions or time-honoured places of refuge. Buslov's *Bimmer*, for example, turns the entire idyll of the Russian countryside into an impulsive realm of unrestrained crime and cruelty.

This, perhaps, gives us the Manichean balance of Timur Bekmambetov's action blockbusters, *Night Watch* (2004) and *Day Watch* (2006). Here good and evil both exist with equal influence. Any thrilling action – any danger – comes from not knowing which of the two will have the upper hand, or when: Heaven only knows – quite literally. Since these two movies are, to some degree, a slightly consoling response to the unbalanced, disastrous action of Russian lawlessness in the1990s, it comes as no surprise that the conservative politics of Putin's period in office produced a return to the 'managed' action feature – to controllable degrees of peril, held in check by some greater force.

David MacFadyen

The Extraordinary Adventures of Mr West in the Land of the Bolsheviks

Neobychainye prikliucheniia mistera Vesta v strane bol'shevikov

Country of Origin:
Soviet Union

Language:
Silent

Studio:
Goskino

Director:
Lev Kuleshov

Screenplay:
Nikolai Aseev
Vsevolod Pudovkin

Cinematography:
A. Levitskii

Art Director:
Vsevolod Pudovkin

Editor:
Aleksandr Levitskii

Duration:
86 minutes

Genre:
Action comedy

Cast:
Porfirii Podobed
Aleksandra Khokhlova
Boris Barnet
Vsevolod Pudovkin
Sergei Komarov

Year:
1924

Synopsis

The naïve American Mr West sets off to visit the USSR, having been warned that Bolshevik savages run the country. He is accompanied by his bodyguard, the cowboy Jeddy. Upon arriving in Moscow, Mr West falls into the clutches of a gang of Russian thieves. In an elaborate extortion scheme, they prey on his fears of Bolshevism and trick him into turning over his American dollars. Meanwhile, after a series of misadventures in Moscow, Jeddy is brought into contact with Soviet authorities, who turn out to be quite civilized and conscientious. They rescue Mr West from the criminals and then show him that Soviet Russia is actually an enlightened and progressive nation.

Critique

Lev Kuleshov's *Mr West* can be seen as an elaborate student project, a diploma film of sorts. From 1920 to 1924 Kuleshov taught at the State Film School in Moscow, working with a remarkably talented circle of students, the so-called Kuleshov workshop. Included in the group were Vsevolod Pudovkin, Boris Barnet, Aleksandra Khokhlova and Sergei Komarov, all of whom were destined for stellar film careers. The group's film education was initially constrained by a shortage of available film stock in the early 1920s, and students had to learn about cinema without enjoying the opportunity to shoot much original footage. Kuleshov innovated 'films without film', staged plays that imitated cinematic technique. He also encouraged his students to study extant feature films, including the many foreign films that were entering the Soviet exhibition market in the early 1920s. The majority of the imports were Hollywood features, and Kuleshov and his students took particular interest in those American movies which seemed to offer a dynamic style and sophisticated editing. Kuleshov posited that Hollywood film techniques could and should be adopted by Soviet filmmakers. He and his students did exactly that in *Mr West*, a feature project they were able to undertake through Moscow's Goskino studio in 1924 when film stock finally became available. Kuleshov directed and his students played the lead roles.

The film pays homage to its American source material in a number of ways. The title character resembles Harold Lloyd, and the acrobatic Jeddy is based on Douglas Fairbanks, both of whom were quite popular with Russian audiences. The film is a political comedy, but it draws on other genres that Kuleshov identified with Hollywood, including Westerns, action-adventure films and slapstick. Kuleshov and his group also tried out many of the techniques they had studied in the class. For example, *Mr West* utilizes a variant of Hollywood continuity editing – what Kuleshov called 'American montage' – in action scenes. Specific devices practiced in the workshop were also given a filmic incarnation in *Mr West*. In the eye-line matches at the film's end, when the title character looks out on scenes of the 'real Russia' and registers his approval, one sees an application of the famed Kuleshov effect.

Lev Kuleshov, *The Extraordinary Adventures of Mr West...* (1924).

The film's main comic target was the political divide between Soviet Russia and the United States, caused, Kuleshov suggests, by international misunderstandings. Although many Americans in the 1920s may have feared the intentions of Revolutionary Russia, Kuleshov saw around him a Russian population that embraced America's cultural exports, especially its movies. It is telling that Kuleshov applied an American model of filmmaking to a Soviet movie that he hoped might help bridge the political gap between the United States and the USSR.

Vance Kepley, Jr

Thirteen

Trinadtsat'

Country of Origin:
Soviet Union

Language:
Russian

Studio:
Mosfilm

Director:
Mikhail Romm

Screenplay:
Iosif Prut
Mikhail Romm

Cinematographer:
Boris Volchek

Art Directors:
Vladimir Egorov
Mikhail Kariakin
Andrei Nikulin

Composer:
Anatolii Aleksandrov

Editor:
Tatiana Likhacheva

Duration:
86 minutes

Genre:
Adventure
Revolutionary drama

Cast:
Ivan Novosel'tsev
Elena Kuz'mina
Aleksandr Chistiakov
Andrei Fait

Year:
1936

Synopsis

Red Army commander Ivan Zhuravlev accompanies ten honourably discharged soldiers on their way to the city. With them are Zhuravlev's wife, Masha, and an old geologist, Postnikov. Amidst the Karakum desert, they stumble upon a hidden well located near an ancient tomb. They also find brand new weapons belonging to Shirmat Khan and his anti-Bolshevik insurgents, the so-called *basmachi*. Zhuravlev gives order to wait for Shirmat Khan and fight him until regular Red Army troops arrive. Eager to get to the well, Shirmat Khan's men attack the group relentlessly. One by one, the Soviet soldiers are killed. However, Private Muradov, sent out as a messenger, is able to lead a Red Army battalion to the embattled well; he and the last survivor, Iusuf Akchurin, are honoured as heroes – while Shirmat and the remnants of his gang are arrested.

Critique

Thirteen is one of the most remarkable Civil War thrillers in the Soviet cinema. Dedicated to the twentieth anniversary of the founding of the Red Army, its story was inspired by John Ford's *The Lost Patrol*. Ironically, neither Romm nor screenwriter Iosif Prut had seen Ford's epic, yet their boss, Boris Shumiatskii, then in charge of the Soviet film industry, had related the story verbally. This was Romm's second feature after a silent Maupassant adaptation, *Boule de Suif* (1934). The film's well paced adventure plot, narrative stringency, overall economy and psychological plausibility meet the highest international standards.

Thirteen is largely free of the ideological verbosity and demagoguery that burden Romm's Stalinist pictures. From the very first scene, the film generates suspense and human interest. The dominating visual motif – ever-changing wave patterns across the endless desert sands – serves as a constant reminder of the one element that is vital to friend and foe: water. The way in which each group member handles water, negotiating the rations, drinking, sharing or saving it, characterizes them as individuals. Water is the main theme of their conversations and also the underlying reason for the clash with the Islamic rebels (although Zhuravlev makes it clear that the Red Army forces have been trying to capture Shirmat Khan for some time).

Romm creates a desert realm that is infinite yet claustrophobic; although there are no visible boundaries, there is also no alternative to staying together since the surrounding desert means certain death for anyone trying to find a way on their own. Water's status as the most precious commodity of all becomes obvious when one of the soldiers climbs into the hidden well for the first time, watching a small cup slowly filling up. Both the process of observing the dripping water and waiting for the arrival of Shirmat Khan's troops determine the film's temporal structure during its first third.

For the remaining two thirds, it is a sequence of deaths that both form a tense rhythm and convey a sense of tragic inevitability. All the same, the group accepts this inevitability. Consisting of representatives of various nationalities – Russians, Ukrainians, Tatars – each member is marked by a specific speech pattern and accent, sometimes in a humorous way. Military and civilians stand by each other, sharing a sense of genuine mutual care and common civic duty. These ten soldiers, so recently anticipating a return home, agree with Zhuravlev that neither the discovery of the well nor the chance to capture Shirmat should be dismissed lightly.

Only one soldier breaks rank when, in a feverish fit, exhausted and hysterical, he hopes to save his life by switching sides. Not surprisingly, his comrades finish him off. All the others remain loyal to the cause, meeting their death in a quiet, deferential manner. Even an undisciplined, quarrelsome old scientist takes up a gun, quickly learns the basics of shooting and begins to kill *basmachi*. Likewise Masha, the commander's wife, initially stays behind the frontline, but when the fighters are shot in rapid succession, including her beloved husband, she takes a rifle and joins the fight – until she, too, is killed. Collective interests trump those of the individual. Likewise a higher cause – defeating the enemy of a Bolshevik state – enables these individuals to transcend any brute survival instinct.

The heroism in Romm's picture is of an unspectacular kind – no wounds are shown, no cries are heard. Moreover, there are no political sermons, and the instructions and orders of the commander are calm, pragmatic and to the point. This understated pathos is unusual for Soviet cinema in the 1930s and has secured the film its freshness and enduring appeal alone.

Peter Rollberg

White Sun of the Desert

Beloe solntse pustyni

Country of Origin:
Soviet Union

Language:
Russian

Studio:
Mosfilm

Director:
Vladimir Motyl'

Screenplay:
Valentin Ezhov
Rustam Ibragimbekov
Mark Zakharov

Synopsis

At the close of the Russian Civil War, Red Army officer Fedor Ivanovich Sukhov is finally making his way home after years of fighting in the deserts of Central Asia. As he strides the shifting sands, he dreams of his verdant homeland and beautiful wife. His journey is interrupted, however, when he finds himself first called upon to protect a harem from their husband – the notorious bandit Black Abdullah. Sukhov leads the wives to a town on the edge of the Caspian Sea where they set up a dormitory and he attempts to teach them to be liberated Soviet women. With the help of a young Russian soldier, an embittered local man (Sayid) a Tsarist excise man, and a museum curator (Lebedev), he mounts a desperate defence against the bandits. In the ensuing bloody action, the bandits are killed to a man, and Sukhov emerges from the final standoff with Abdullah wounded but victorious. However, victory has come at a price: one of the wives has been murdered, and all of his allies, except for Sayid, are dead. At the film's conclusion, Sukhov and Sayid part ways amicably, and Sukhov continues his journey home.

Cinematographer:

Eduard Rozovskii

Art Directors:

Valerii Kostrin

Bella Manevich-Kaplan

Duration:

85 minutes

Genre:

Action

Adventure

Cast:

Raisa Kurkina

Anatolii Kuznetsov

Spartak Mishulin

Pavel Luspekaev

Kakhi Kavsadze

Tatiana Fedotova

Tatiana Denisova

Nikolai Godovikov

Year:

1969

Critique

White Sun of the Desert was to be the Soviet answer to the popular Western. Yet, while clearly drawing on Western cinematic tropes, the film undoubtedly spoke to Soviet audiences regarding issues of nation and empire, since it promulgates nationalist ideals of a Russian-dominated Central Asia. Since the film's release, however, screenwriter Rustam Ibragimbekov has vehemently denied such intentions. Indeed, looking closely at how Motyl' visually constructs the film, it becomes clear that he emphasizes the incompatibility of Soviet and Central Asian cultures, plus the failure of the Soviet project in the East. This was an interesting cinematic stand to take at a time when the idea of the 'brotherhood of nations' was still very much alive in Soviet rhetoric.

The core narrative revolves around a love triangle, so to speak. Sukhov is torn between a love for his wife, Katerina, and his attraction to the harem. Within this structure, Sukhov is a model of Soviet strength, ingenuity and virtue. Sukhov's wife, who becomes the visual embodiment of Russia, represents 'Home'. Abdullah's harem is associated with a generic, decaying and unassimilated Central Asia. Thus, perhaps, Motyl' portrays the Soviet involvement in Central Asia as a betrayal of the homeland.

Sukhov's uniform clearly identifies him with Soviet military power. He is not the only Red Army soldier in the film, but whereas other soldiers' uniforms become sweaty and tarnished in the heat and the sand, Sukhov's uniform is almost always pristine, as if he is a mythic Soviet soldier, unaffected by the weather or general conditions around him. Furthermore, Sukhov is always filmed either in the foreground or silhouetted on top of a dune, standing out sharply against the sky. In this way, Motyl' establishes both Sukhov's power and his foreignness. By contrast, the wives are often shown as emerging from behind the sand dunes, or enclosed in ancient decaying buildings. They are further associated with the foreign, unassailable East by their heavy horsehair veils which cover them entirely. All is hidden.

While Sukhov is placed outside the desert, the woods and grasslands of Russia envelop Katerina. Moreover, Katerina strongly resembles Soviet images of Mother Russia. The camera pans slowly up her legs in order to focus on her pelvis; the folds in her red dress underscore both her sexuality and her fertility. By sexualizing Katerina in this way, Motyl' emphasizes Sukhov's uncomplicated visual possession of her body and, by extension, the motherland as a whole.

The resulting narrative of betrayal, enacted in the East, is most obviously enunciated in the scene in which Giuchitai attempts to seduce Sukhov. Sitting up late, preparing for battle, Sukhov suddenly hears the tinkling of bells as Giuchitai – unveiled – dances provocatively towards him. As Giuchitai attempts to explain the advantages of polygamy, Sukhov honourably refuses to look at her. An image of lovely Katerina flashes up before him and Sukhov sends Giuchitai away. This scene establishes that the film's central question, perhaps, is not whether Sukhov, the embodiment of Soviet military power, *can* possess Giuchitai and Central Asia, but whether he *should*.

Vladimir Motyl', *The White Sun of the Desert* (1970).

This moral hazard for Russia is illustrated not only through the theme of infidelity, but also through the real physical danger in which various Russian characters find themselves. By the end of the film, all of Sukhov's Russian allies in the village have been killed: the priest, the Tsarist excise man and the young soldier. Furthermore, Sukhov's potential wife Giuchitai is murdered by her husband, the bandit Abdullah. Her death is directly a result of her own 'betrayal', a result of living under Sukhov's protection. Ultimately we are lead to consider the possibility that Russia's presence in Central Asia not only endangers Russian purity, but also destroys an engaging, exotic, traditional Eastern culture, represented by Giuchitai.

Emily Hillhouse

The End of the Ataman

Konets Atamana

Country of Origin:
Soviet Union

Language:
Russian

Studio:
Kazakhfilm

Director:
Shaken Aimanov

Screenplay:
Andrei Konchalovskii
Eduard Tropinin

Cinematographer:
Askhat Ashrapov

Art Director:
Viktor Lednev

Duration:
146 minutes

Genre:
Action
Red Western

Cast:
Asanali Ashimov
Viktor Avdiushko
Gennadii Iudin

Year:
1970

Synopsis

In 1921, at the height of the Civil War, the Red officer Chadiarov is assigned a special task: to kill the ataman Dutov, a collaborator of the Whites. During this operation Chadiarov discloses the spy in the Red Army headquarters in his Kazakh hometown. In order to fulfil his mission, Chadiarov, who is a Chinese prince, has to get himself arrested as a spy by the Soviet commander; then he escapes and crosses the border to China, where he pretends to side with the ataman who resides there. Chadiarov fulfils his secret mission successfully while its full scale and significance of his action transpire only at the end.

Critique

The film's director Shaken Aimanov (1914–1970) was an actor and director at the theatre in Alma-Ata before he made the first genuine Kazakh feature film, *A Poem About Love*, in 1954. The film studio in Almaty is named in honour of this first ethnic Kazakh filmmaker.

The film is part of a trilogy about the Revolution: *The End of the Ataman* was followed by *Trans-Siberian Express* (1977) and *The Manchurian Version* (1989). Andrei Konchalovskii wrote the script for this film together with Eduard Tropinin, which earned him a Kazakh State Prize in 1972.

The theme of the Civil War raging in the southern and eastern borderlands of the Soviet empire offered a most suitable subject matter for adventure or action films, genres that were in early Soviet cinema tied closely to the Revolutionary struggle, translating in ideological terms into the opposition of the Red vs White Army to match the classical Hollywood opposition of the action/adventure between good vs evil. Cavalry chases, escapes, hide-outs in the steppe made this film a true gem in the tradition of the 'Eastern', or 'Red Western', but even more significantly this was a film which showed that support for the Red Army extended way beyond ethnic Russians, showing the Chinese prince Chadiarov as a Soviet hero, thus reflecting the full Sovietization of Central Asia.

The second film in the trilogy, *Trans-Siberian Express*, follows secret agent Chadiarov to the Manchurian city of Kharbin, where in 1927 he resides under the pseudonym of Fan and poses as manager of a cabaret. Fan is blackmailed by a banker to travel to Moscow with a Chinese passport and in the company of his 'wife' Sasha. He soon discovers a plot to kill the Japanese businessman Saito, travelling on the same train to offer economic collaboration to the Soviet regime. A criminal gang – composed of Sasha, Saito's bodyguard and a journalist – intend to blame the murder on Fan, who will appear as a Soviet secret service agent. Thus, the counter-Revolutionaries will prevent economic collaboration with Japan, while the blame will fall on the Soviet Union. As the train travels through Mongolia and Siberia Fan works out the plot and, continuing to play the foolish and silly cabaret owner Fan, he sows suspicion among the enemy. Once Fan has debilitated the gang and prevented the crime, the Red officers arrive to arrest the criminals. The film adopts the style of a detective story, with clear references to a Soviet version of the 'Orient Express'.

The three films represent an attempt to create, in the popular genre of an 'Eastern' action film, the story of a secret agent's life, bringing out his commitment to the communist cause and underscoring the unity in Central Asia with the Soviet Empire during the 1920s. The choice of a spy story further aligns the film with genre cinema at a time when spy films flourished both in Russia and abroad. The entire project of the trilogy made at Kazakhfilm is significant for the Eurasian theme, the links between the centre and the periphery, between Asia and Europe. In the context of Soviet cinema of the 1970s Central Asia was an attractive location for the adventure genre, and the popular film *White Sun of the Desert* (1970), directed by Vladimir Motyl' and scripted by Rustam Ibragimbekov, further underpins the popularity of these exotic settings.

Birgit Beumers

The Seventh Bullet

Sed'maia pulia

Country of Origin:
Soviet Union

Language:
Russian and Uzbek

Studio:
Uzbekfilm Studio

Director:
Ali Khamraev

Screenplay:
Fridrikh Gorenstein
Andrei Konchalovskii

Cinematographer:
Aleksandr Pann

Art Director:
Emonuel Kalantarov

Composer:
Rumil' Vil'danov

Editor:
V. Makarova

Synopsis

Uzbekistan in the 1920s: Bolshevik commander Maksumov returns to the Uchkurgan settlement after spending a few days in the regional capital. He finds the place devastated and depopulated. His opponent, Hayrullah, a leader of the anti-Soviet *basmachi*, has not only defeated the Red Army troops but also convinced more than a hundred of them to switch sides. Maksumov decides to go to the lion's den on his own in order to confront the enemy. With him is Aigul, a young woman who has been bought by Hayrullah as his new wife. Maksumov joins a caravan on its way to the *basmachi* camp. Tied up, humiliated and harassed by Ismail who claims that Maksumov killed his brother, the Bolshevik commander is brought to Hayrullah, who tries to corrupt him. After Maksimov's refusal to serve the *basmachi*, Aigul frees him from prison. During the ensuing struggle, Maksumov is victorious and kills Hayrullah, yet Aigul also loses her life.

Critique

Ali Khamraev's *The Seventh Bullet* belongs to a peculiar sub-genre, sometimes referred to as the 'Eastern', a Western-type action flick with an explicit pro-communist propaganda message, usually taking place during the 1920s Civil War. The Eastern typically features a Bolshevik superman as its central character, a man just as apt in delivering ideological arguments as in handling guns and martial arts. Commander Maksumov in *The Seventh Bullet*, ably portrayed by Kyrgyz star Suimenkul Chokmorov (1939–1992), is a stony-faced, fearless hero with a highly controlled body language; his physical prowess and strategic aptitude ultimately convince the doubting natives to rejoin his military unit. On several occasions, he recalls his suffering at the hands of the tsarist police, which provides motivation for his staunch pro-Soviet position.

Duration:

84 minutes

Genre:

Psychological thriller

Cast:

Suimenkul Chokmorov
Dilorom Kambarova
Khamza Umarov
Bolot Beishenaliev

Year:

1972

Maksumov's opponent, Hayrullah, come across as a mere stock character – a ruthless, brutal, one-eyed patriarch in the service of British imperialists, whose airplanes he is impatiently expecting. Somewhat questionably, Fridrikh Gorenshtein's and Andrei Mikhalkov-Konchalovskii's script also repeats a clichéd constellation from the latter's *The First Teacher* (1965), with a virile Bolshevik leader and a teenage girl who is erotically attracted to him. Among the film's strengths is a credible evocation of impending doom during the opening episodes, created by Aleksandr Pann's camera – with wide, dust-filled vistas of devastation and hopelessness. Rumil' Vil'danov's dramatic, dissonant score is dominated by drums and trumpets and adds to the suspense. The film, as with many other Easterns, uses the exotic nature of Central Asia to impressive visual effect. The chase and fight scenes are staged in a professional manner, arguably to the standards of international cinematography.

Interestingly, both the habits and rituals of the native population are depicted with similar degrees of authenticity and respect. Noteworthy is the film's ambiguity in regards to Islam. While Maksumov states at the beginning of the feature that 'Right now, a Red Islamic unit is more important than Russian troops' and quotes the Koran in an affirmative manner, one of his opponents later observes that 'The men are beginning to believe in the Bolsheviks more than in Allah'. The film's dark, anti-climactic ending adds to this air of instability, both standing in contrast to Maksumov's military victory and giving the viewer at least some indication of Civil War's widespread, tragic destruction.

Peter Rollberg

The Red Poppies of Issyk-Kul

Alye maki Issyk-Kulia

Country of Origin:

Soviet Union

Languages:

Russian, Kyrgyz

Studio:

Kyrgyzfilm Studio

Director:

Bolotbek Shamshiev

Screenplay:

Iurii Sokol
Vasilii Sokol

Synopsis

Somewhere in Kyrgyzstan in the 1920s, a pro-Soviet guard Karabalta – his name means 'black axe' – detects secret paths in the mountains used by smugglers to transport opium across the Soviet border. Meanwhile, a strange man named 'Golden Mouth' offers to accompany a patrol unit led by Russian commander Kondratii, promising to help find these smugglers and their camp. He claims to know a location where hundreds of pounds of opium are stored. When Kondratii goes on a mission to find the opium storage, smugglers attack the Soviet camp and take Karabalta and Kondratii's wife hostage. Karabalta finally encounters the leader of the gang, Baidak, and challenges him to fight Kyrgyz-style, one on one, resulting in Baidak's defeat. The natives are told by the victorious Soviet troops to go home and till their land – the new government will protect their peaceful work.

Critique

The literary source for Shamshiev's thriller, Aleksandr Sytin's novella *The Smugglers of Tian-Shan*, provided a plot in accordance with the basic formula of the Soviet Western (the so-called 'Eastern', or

Cinematographer:

Viktor Ovsennikov

Art Director:

Aleksei Makarov

Composer:

Mikhail Marutaev

Duration:

99 minutes

Genre:

Historical action
Red Western

Cast:

Suimenkul Chokmolov
Sovetbek Dzhumadylov
Eleubai Umurzakov

Year:

1972

'Red Western'): a larger-than-life Bolshevik superman fights a violent native gang operating under the leadership of a cunning and ruthless criminal patriarch. In *Red Poppies of Issyk-Kul*, an ascetic, quiet superman – as usual – embodies the film's positive moral core, but this time he is not fully in charge. The Russian commander repeatedly appears as a competitor for leadership, resulting in miscommunication and, ultimately, a loss of life. Tellingly, Karabalta is forthcoming only in the company of his fellow countrymen, whereas he remains guarded with the Russians. Almost until the end, his personality remains hard to read, which adds not only to the film's suspense, but also to the Russians' suspicions. Karabalta indicates that, years ago, he was imprisoned by the tsarist authorities, then escaped to China and later found a safe haven at the border, taking his family to an inhospitable mountain region. Although the Russian Bolsheviks and their Kyrgyz allies work together, there still is a certain amount of mutual distrust.

In particular, the lifestyle of the natives is not fully comprehensible to the Russians. However, when the normally reserved Kyrgyz people are among themselves, they do reveal a broader, clearer emotional register. Thus, on one occasion, Karabalta even sings a ballad to the *dombra*, enchanting the native community (the song's various stanzas are illustrated with a montage of poetic images). The Soviet forces are depicted as promoters of a necessary modernization against the resistance of patriarchal, backward Kyrgyz forces, whose purported spirituality is mere hypocrisy and whose patriotism just a means to manipulate the native population. The rank-and-file Kyrgyz are torn between tribal loyalty toward their leaders and the new powers that treat them more humanely.

Interestingly, Baidak loses the people's support not because he fights the Soviets, but because he kills the winner of a horserace, violating ancient national law. At the end, however, the Kyrgyz masses march in close togetherness and wash their faces in the river – a symbol of cleansing the traces of the past and looking forward to the future.

Shamshiev's contribution to the historical action genre that enjoyed particular popularity in the late 1960s–1970s carries a strong national flavour. Unlike other directors, he seems to have appropriated the action-filled and suspenseful plot as a means to capture cultural peculiarities, rather than for mere entertainment or propaganda. The film is distinguished by superb camerawork, praising the beauty of Kyrgyzstan's wild nature in lavish widescreen images. This beauty, too, is of conceptual relevance, since nature is a de facto 'ally' of the natives. Thus, Shamshiev's sensitive treatment of seemingly trivial subject matter elevates *The Red Poppies of Issyk-Kul* to a remarkable artistic level.

Peter Rollberg

At Home among Strangers, a Stranger at Home

Svoi sredi chuzhikh, chuzhoi sredi svoikh

Country of Origin:
Soviet Union

Language:
Russian

Studio:
Mosfilm

Director:
Nikita Mikhalkov

Screenplay:
Eduard Volodarskii
Nikita Mikhalkov

Cinematographer:
Pavel Lebeshev

Art Director:
Aleksandr Adabashian

Composer:
Eduard Artem'ev

Editor:
Liudmila Elian

Duration:
97 minutes

Genre:
Adventure
Red Western

Cast:
Iurii Bogatyrev
Anatolii Solonitsyn
Sergei Shakurov
Aleksandr Porokhorshchikov
Nikolai Pastukhov
Aleksandr Kaidanovskii
Konstantin Raikon
Aleksandr Kaliagin
Nikita Mikhalkov

Year:
1974

Synopsis

In the early 1920s, five friends bound together by the Revolution are building a new life as Communist Party officials in a small, southern border town. While the war has almost ended, there are still gangs of outlaws and scattered groups of pro-tsarist Whites operating in the region. When one of the friends, Egor Shilov, is ordered to bring expropriated gold to Moscow, his mission is not unanimously endorsed because his brother had once fought for the Whites. The night before the journey he is kidnapped and drugged, returning home only after the gold has been removed from the train by an enemy faction. Then the train is attacked for a second time, now by the gang of the Cossack captain Brylov. Shilov becomes the prime suspect and can only exonerate himself by finding both the money and a turncoat. While Shilov pursues Brylov, the Cheka is looking for the traitor. In the meantime the gold has been hidden by the Tatar Kayum, who first tries to kill Shilov but helps him when the latter saves him from drowning. Together, they follow Brylov and in a shoot-out Kayum and Brylov are killed. Brylov's gang is destroyed by the Reds, the traitor is discovered – he is none of the old friends who finally meet among the barren hills, celebrating a new victory over the enemies of the state.

Critique

This directorial debut of the popular actor Nikita Mikhalkov represents, perhaps, the most successful marriage of the traditional Soviet and Revolutionary adventure film and the equally traditional American genre of Westerns; here they are transformed into the so-called 'Eastern', or 'Red Western' of Eastern European cinema. Mikhalkov's feature, though, was not the first attempt. Five years earlier, Vladimir Motyl' made *White Sun of the Desert* (1969), a highly successful Eastern set in the 1920s, in a desert near the Caspian Sea. This would be followed by *The Seventh Bullet* (1972) by Ali Khamraev, based on a script by Friedrich Gorenstein and Mikhalkov's elder brother, Andrei Konchalovskii. Konchalovskii, coincidentally, also co-authored the script of yet another Soviet Eastern, *The End of the Ataman* by Shaken Aimanov (1970).

Having decided to make this feature himself, Nikita Mikhalkov took the most basic conventions of the Western and Eastern; he then combined and contrasted them. In *At Home among Strangers…* the 'iron' communists of the 1920s are remarkably similar to the lonesome heroes of classic Westerns. There is an avenger whose personal issues (of suspect honesty and political adherence) force him to fight for a civic purpose; and there is the revelation of a traitor and discovery of stolen gold. Then there are horseback chase sequences, train robberies, shoot-outs, issues of greed or violence, brooding silences and moments of comic relief. While it is true that the money is dutifully dispatched to Moscow – to help with famine relief – and all the main characters are staunch members of the Communist Party, there is talk here of both Marx and God. Contemporary reviewers,

Nikita Mikhalkov, *At Home among Strangers…* (1974), Nikita Mikhalkov as Brylov.

while noticing such thematic daring, also criticized the film's frequent recourse to narrative clichés, saved only occasionally by some formal inventiveness.

Mikhalkov transformed a very simple, sometimes implausible story into a complex plot full of ellipses, flashbacks and time-distortions. The film embodies these with jump-cuts, unmotivated crane- and tilt-shots that have no foundation in the narrative, along with switches from scorched-like sepia frames to monochromes. Some of these transformations were later explained by film crew members as the result of economic factors rather than conscious artistic decisions.

Pavel Lebeshev's fluid camera movements are interlaced by heart-rending melodies written by Eduard Artem'ev. Previously Artem'ev had composed the score for Andrei Tarkovskii's *Solaris* and would subsequently do the same for *Mirror* and *Stalker*. Likewise, some of Mikhalkov's actors were also connected with Tarkovskii: Anatolii Solonitsyn was known for his roles in *Andrei Rublev* and *Solaris*, while Aleksandr Kaidanovskii would go on to play the role of Stalker. All of these contributors transform a genre exercise into a bold parable and a striking credo that friendship trumps political alliances, personal needs and even the needs of the state.

Natalia Riabchikova

Air Crew

Ekipazh

Country of Origin:
Soviet Union

Language:
Russian

Studio:
Mosfilm

Director:
Aleksandr Mitta

Screenplay:
Iulii Dunskii
Valerii Frid
Aleksandr Mitta

Cinematographer:
Valerii Shuvalov

Art Director:
Anatolii Kuznetsov

Composer:
Alfred Schnittke

Editor:
Nadezhda Veselevskaia

Duration:
144 minutes

Genre:
Action

Cast:
Georgii Zhzhenov
Aleksandra Iakovleva
Leonid Filatov
Elena Koreneva
Ekaterina Vasil'eva

Year:
1980

Synopsis

Andrei Vasil'evich, a reserved and laconic veteran of the skies, heads the crew of an international Aeroflot aircraft. Valentin, a helicopter pilot, has tried for several years to save his failing marriage. After a difficult divorce, he joins Andrei Vasil'evich's flight crew. Igor', a flight engineer, is a sociable and carefree ladies man who becomes enamored with Tamara, a flight attendant. The second half of the film details what begins as a routine flight. The crew is to deliver emergency supplies to an unnamed country, suffering from the aftermath of an earthquake. Upon arrival, a tremor shakes the earth, damaging the runway. Despite unstable conditions the plane, filled with children, women and injured passengers miraculously takes off. However, it is discovered that the plane was damaged on takeoff, making it unlikely that the aircraft will reach its destination. Igor' and Valentin are sent to the exterior of the plane to repair a crack in the body. After extreme turbulence, the flight successfully concludes, despite the loss of the plane's tail on landing. After the flight, Andrei Vasil'evich gets used to life on the ground as he is forbidden to fly due to his health. The personal strife that Valentin and Igor' experienced in the first half of the film is resolved.

Critique

Although many films in the Soviet era were shown in two sections, *Air Crew* actually changes genres between Parts I and II. Aleksandr Mitta, previously known for low-key melodramas, possibly could not resist the slow and methodical drawing-out of the heroes' personal lives in the first half, which is practically the length of a feature film. The result is that one feels as if two separate feature films are on display.

The first half is a quirky Soviet comedy drama, detailing the personal lives of the three main members of the crew who lead separate, although sparsely interconnected lives. Andrei Vasil'evich's health is declining and after returning from a flight, the first thing his wife does is check his blood pressure. His teenage daughter, now pregnant, causes him much grief, reminding him that soon he will stop flying and can raise a grandchild. Valentin is trying to save his marriage, but his wife is becoming more temperamental and unpredictable. She is clearly suffering from the double burden of raising the child and working, while Valentin is away flying helicopters on disaster missions. She starts suspecting him of having affairs during his extended absences and gains custody of their son after a bitter divorce battle, accusing him of being a drunk before the judge. Igor', an unabashed bachelor, seduces women with his exotic treasures, gathered in foreign lands. Citing the progressiveness of Soviet society, he does not believe in marriage. His attitude begins to change when he falls for Tamara, a stewardess. She tells him that contrary to what he believes, all women want to get married and have children, asking him why she needs the independence and modernity he seems to be championing for the opposite sex.

Whereas the first half of the film offers gripping snapshots of the private lives of Soviet pilots, the second part turns the film into an action-adventure epic. Upon landing in the city of Bidri, the damage is apparent. When a tremor rocks the land soon after arrival, explosions light up the sky. The men of the crew immediately demonstrate their courage and decide to take off, despite the dangerous conditions. A woman cries for the men to do something; Andrei Vasil'evich stoically declares: 'We cannot take off, but we cannot stay.'

Andrei Vasil'evich quickly assumes the archetype of an older action hero, showing resolve and unflinching bravery in the midst of panic. Both Igor' and Valentin also demonstrate masculine courage, daring to repair external damage to the aircraft despite the obvious risks. Their daring contrasts with images of frightened female passengers, hiding in blankets underneath the shadows. Upon landing, the women aboard the plane mob the captain, lavishing him with kisses and praise. The modest Andrei Vasil'evich calls his wife. Not wanting to worry her, he explains that poor weather had caused their delay.

Andrei Vasil'evich does not pass his next health test and takes his 'grounding' hard. Whereas Igor' and Valentin were seemingly punished in the first half of their film for their apparent selfishness, now they are rewarded for their valour. Igor' and Tamara get back together; she forgives him for his infidelity, being clearly overcome with respect for his bravery and resolve. The affable Valentin also finds love and is soon free from the tyrannical memory of his first wife.

While *Air Crew* was perhaps the most ambitious action-adventure film shot in the Soviet Union, the special effects are by today's standards primitive and unconvincing. Many of the action scenes rely on decelerated or sped-up motion sequences, plus countless explosions, in order to disguise the inadequacy of a Soviet studio's technical capabilities. While the action scenes remain improbable, the sub-plot of Soviet virility is entirely convincing. All of the men suffer bruised egos and this fated flight grants them an opportunity to permanently regain any machismo lost in the first half. Viewed as a two-part or double feature, however, *Air Crew* is a strange marriage of genres.

Joe Crescente

A Man from Boulevard des Capucines

Chelovek s bul'vara Kaputsinov

Country of Origin:
Soviet Union

Language:
Russian

Synopsis

Johnny First, an early cinema entrepreneur, arrives in a forlorn Western settlement where he begins to screen silent films at a local saloon. A firm believer in the educational potential of cinema, Mr First soon transforms rowdy cowboys into sober and polite moviegoers and gains the love of Ms Diane Little, a local cabaret star. Their engagement upsets Pastor Adams, Ms Little's unlucky suitor. The saloonkeeper harbours a grudge against Mr First as well: with no more drunken brawls, his income radically drops. To top it all, additional free screenings are held for women and Indians, both reaffirming First's democratic view of art. As these conflicts escalate, the Pastor and the saloonkeeper hire Black Jack to gun down this recently arrived missionary of cinema, but the latter miraculously survives. Nevertheless, anything resembling calm is quickly destroyed by

Studio:

Mosfilm

Director:

Alla Surikova

Screenplay:

Eduard Akopov

Cinematographer:

Grigorii Belen'kii

Art Director:

Evgenii Markovich

Composer:

Gennadii Gladkov

Editor:

L. Gorina

Duration:

99 minutes

Genre:

Musical Comedy
Western
Melodrama

Cast:

Andrei Mironov
Aleksandra Iakovleva
Mikhail Boiarskii
Oleg Tabakov
Nikolai Karachentsev
Igor' Kvasha

Year:

1987

Mr Second, another travelling entrepreneur who, during First's short absence, begins to screen morally degrading films, and the town descends back into violence. The film ends with Mr First, his fiancée and Black Jack all leaving the town in hopes of penning splendid new pages for the future history of cinema.

Critique

Released during perestroika, *A Man from Boulevard des Capucines* transposes a Soviet image of the Wild West, formed during the previous decades, onto the canvas of a late-Soviet musical comedy par excellence. This universe of merry drunken brawls, ruthless gunfights and capitalist 'spiritual decay' would enter Russia's collective imagination as one of the last Soviet blockbusters. Similarly, the death of Andrei Mironov before the film's release marked the beginning of the end of Soviet cinema.

One of the film's awards was granted 'for a truthful depiction of the Wild West in the equally wild conditions of Soviet filmmaking'. Besides a few items borrowed from studios in Czechoslovakia, all film props, including the cowboy hats, were domestically produced, thus creating the film's distinctly Soviet-Western atmosphere. Another obvious example of these 'wild conditions' was Gorbachev's simultaneous anti-alcohol campaign of 1985–1987. Resulting censorship on the depiction of spirits resulted in absurd big-screen images of cowboys sipping milk while watching their first silent shorts.

Surikova's movie focuses upon the collision between different systems of image production and dissemination. From the film's opening seconds the viewer is immersed in a universe so remote that modernity itself makes an entrance not via the traditional use of locomotives, but merely a delayed image thereof: Lumière's *Arrival of the Train*. Encountering these new, enticing tableaux of civilization, the saloon-dwellers give up their cheerful, booze-addled self-destruction and approach instead the unknown realm of onscreen emotional experiences geared to educate their human sensibilities. As the audience for this pedagogical enterprise gradually expands to include minorities, control is seemingly lost over the population according to economic or religious factors. This loss brings new problems: with the advent of 'lowly mass entertainment', the very same audience, hoping for visual enlightenment, seems easily swayed by decadent images as it begins feeding on high art's corpse. Ironically, it is now an outlaw who comes to the defence of culture's lost cause.

Despite the celebratory comic mode of the film, its grim message foreshadowed future developments in Soviet cinema. Vasilii Pichul's *Little Vera*, a blockbuster produced one year later, exposed these latent processes of moral degradation and civic disintegration. Highly entertaining on the surface, *A Man from Boulevard des Capucines* resists making any subversive political statements. Instead, we see a star-studded cast of Soviet actors playing with onscreen alternative identities only four years before the collapse of the Soviet Union.

Sasha Razor

Brother

Brat

Country of Origin:
Russia

Languages:
Russian
English
French

Studio:
CTB

Director:
Aleksei Balabanov

Producer:
Sergei Sel'ianov

Screenplay:
Aleksei Balabanov

Cinematographer:
Sergei Astakhov

Art Director:
Vladimir Kartashov

Composer:
Viacheslav Butusov

Editor:
Marina Lipartiia

Duration:
96 minutes

Genre:
Crime
Action

Cast:
Sergei Bodrov Jr
Viktor Sukhorukov
Svetlana Pismichenko
Mariia Zhukova
Iurii Kuznetsov
Viacheslav Butusov
Irina Rakshina

Year:
1997

Synopsis

Brother introduces a young man, Danila, who has just finished his military service in southern Russia. His mother sends him to St Petersburg to live with his older brother, Viktor, who, viewers soon discover, is a hit man. Without any hesitation or scruples, Viktor involves Danila in the criminal world, causing him to risk his life. Danila, however, having just returned from war, cannot be easily trapped in Viktor's plan and effectively deals with his assassins. After discovering that his brother has set him up, Danila spares Viktor's life, gives him some money and sends him to live with their mother before himself leaving for Moscow.

Critique

Brother created a new type of hero in post-Soviet film: the hit man who follows his own moral standards in deciding whom to kill and whom to spare. He protects the poor and delivers justice, yet upholds no coherent moral principles and kills callously. Viewers of *Brother* know nothing of Danila's past with certainty. He claims to have served at 'the Headquarters', but his skills in assembling hand-made guns make one question the accuracy of this information. One may argue that Danila seeks guidance and is even concerned with existential and philosophical questions. In *Brother*, the story takes place almost entirely in St Petersburg and only once shows Danila's hometown in the provinces. St Petersburg is marked in the Russian imagination as the Russian 'window to the West'. Embarking on the crucial process of westernization of Russian culture, history and identity, in 1703 Peter the Great built the city with western architectural style and ambience. In this city, the window to the West, Danila meets Kat, who hangs out at McDonald's and takes him to a party with foreigners.

On his first day in the city, Danila befriends an ethnic German, Hoffmann, living in Russia. Here Danila also encounters Hoffmann's friends at a Lutheran cemetery, a reminder of the other in the Russian predominantly Orthodox tradition; here his brother has acquired the nickname 'the Tartar'. Contrary to such exposure to otherness, Danila declares that he is 'not wild about Jews', refuses to have anything in common with Southerners and despises Americans and the French, recognizing no difference between the two. Unlike the somewhat enigmatic characterization of the male protagonist, the female characters bear uniformly negative portrayals: Danila and Viktor's mother still lives in the past, unaware of her sons' real lives; Sveta, one of Danila's girlfriend, opts to remain in an abusive relationship; Kat, another girlfriend, is a junkie, who hangs out at McDonald's. Balabanov somewhat deviates from the rules of the action genre, and, through periodic fade-to-black, he punctuates the pace of the action and creates a unique rhythm. This technique ruptures the plot and relates to the unstructured and inconsistent character of the main protagonist. The director often uses the black screen to imply brutal violence or gratuitous sexuality without actually showing it. With the fade-to-black technique and quick cutting from one scene to another, Balabanov avoids the onscreen representation of cruelty.

Yana Hashamova

Brother 2

Brat 2

Country of Origin:
Russia

Languages:
Russian
English
Ukrainian

Studio:
CTB

Director:
Aleksei Balabanov

Producer:
Sergei Sel'ianov

Screenplay:
Aleksei Balabanov

Cinematographer:
Sergei Astakhov

Art Director:
Aleksei Giliarevskii

Composer:
Viacheslav Butusov

Editor:
Marina Lipartiia

Duration:
122 minutes

Genre:
Action
Crime

Cast:
Sergei Bodrov Jr
Viktor Sukhorukov
Sergei Makovetskii
Irina Saltykova
Kirill Pirogov
Aleksandr Diachenko
Dariia Lesnikova

Year:
2000

Synopsis

In *Brother 2* viewers follow Danila from Moscow to Chicago, where he goes to avenge the brother of a fellow soldier from the Chechen war. He hitchhikes from New York to Chicago and befriends an American trucker. In Chicago, equipped with the power of a children's poem about love for the homeland, Danila kills a number of African-Americans and climbs a skyscraper via an outside emergency staircase to confront an American business man, who has abused the trust of a Russian hockey-player. While in *Brother* he sleeps with Kat and Sveta, very opposite and yet ordinary young women, in *Brother 2*, his mere appearance is enough to infatuate the pop star Irina Saltykova (played by Irina Saltykova herself). In Chicago, he saves the Russian prostitute Dasha, who decides to follow him and go back to her country. He even has a sexual encounter with the African-American television reporter Lisa Jeffry (also playing herself). At the end, Danila and Dasha return triumphantly to their beloved homeland.

Critique

Three major characteristics define Danila in *Brother 2*: First, he loves his motherland precisely because it is his; second, he does not care about money; and third, he is a super-man. Love for the motherland is supported by a racist attack on American democracy, with its political correctness and 'hypocritical' regulations. Viktor is shocked when a policeman wants to arrest him for drinking from an open bottle in public because he has seen others drinking in front of the store. (He failed to notice that they were hiding the bottles in paper bags.) The predominant image of the United States shown to viewers is that of problematic realities subject to selective, over-emphasized and exaggerated treatment in the interests of negation. Expanding the boundaries of resentment, in *Brother 2*, Viktor does not like Filipp Kirkorov, a contemporary Russian pop singer, because he uses make-up and is Romanian. When corrected about Kirkorov's nationality (Bulgarian), Viktor answers in the usual way: 'What's the difference?' The hatred in *Brother* – directed only against such 'traditional enemies' as Jews, Chechens and westerners – spreads over in the sequel to include all non-Russians – Romanians, Bulgarians and Ukrainians, too. When Viktor runs into Ukrainians in Chicago he refers to them with a pejorative ethnic term and calls them Nazi collaborators.

In all his conquests in America, Danila aspires to obliterate the enemy's identity structure: he achieves his goal by downplaying the western belief in its supremacy, by physically eliminating his American enemies and all others who stand on his way, and by emasculating America, as he sexually conquers the African-American journalist.

These negations are also reflected in editorial techniques. Although the director continues to use the fade-to-black technique in *Brother 2*, it does not work as effectively. The practice is used less and appears only before or after an important episode. Similar observations can be made about the use of music and colours in the films, where problems relate to a loss of subtlety. In the sequel, the colours are much brighter. Along with the shades of the first film, the philosophy and mystery about the meaning of life and death soon disappear.

Yana Hashamova

Sisters

Sestry

Country of Origin:
Russia

Language:
Russian

Studio:
CTB

Director:
Sergei Bodrov Jr

Producer:
Sergei Sel'ianov

Screenplay:
Gul'shad Omarova
Sergei Bodrov Jr
Sergei Bodrov

Cinematographer:
Valerii Martynov

Art Director:
Vladimir Kartashov

Composers:
Viktor Tsoi
'Agata Kristi'

Editor:
Natal'ia Kutserenko

Duration:
80 minutes

Genre:
Thriller

Cast:
Oksana Akin'shina
Katia Gorina
Roman Ageev
Dmitrii Orlov
Aleksandr Bashirov

Year:
2001

Synopsis

A young girl, Sveta, is preparing a party to celebrate the release from prison of a man who is both her mother's new husband and her half-sister's father. She currently lives with her grandmother and is quickly disgusted by the wealth of her new family. It soon transpires that Sveta's new stepfather, Alik, is both a local mafia boss and accused of stealing from the local godfather. In order to protect his eight-year-old daughter Dina from being kidnapped, Alik tries to hide the two half-sisters in a flat, but they are immediately exposed. Sveta, nonetheless, manages to escape with her sister. First they try hiding with relatives, but these family members are too scared to house them. Consequently, Sveta breaks into a friend's dacha (or so she thinks). Alik's rivals, though, have established the girls' whereabouts and they burn down a dacha, albeit the wrong one. Without a place to stay, the sisters take off with a group of gypsies, who have been begging on a train. The next day, while working for the gypsies, the girls are taken by the police and are soon to be brought to Alik's rivals. The policeman in charge of the exchange, though, takes pity on the girls and moves them to his house on a small river island. As the rivals close in on the girls' final hiding place, Alik and his crew turn up to save the girls at the last minute.

Critique

There are several references to Bodrov Jr's own persona throughout the film; he stars in a cameo role and is accompanied by the music of rock group Bi2, which was intrinsic to the character of Danila Bagrov in *Brother 2*. The title of Bodrov Jr's directorial debut also seems to mirror that (in)famous precursor. However, despite being in the same cinematic style as Balabanov's popular films, *Sisters* is thematically richer. If we continue with the motif of music, then the blend in *Sisters* of 1980s Soviet rock and Indian Bollywood melodies makes any simplistic narrative of national identity impossible. Sveta herself is a product of diverse cultures, one Asian and the other western, which combine in order to inform a (Russian) whole.

Sveta is also contrasted with her sister, Dina, who has grown up in wealth as a gangster's child; Dina, though, has yet to face her own demons and accept the brutal reality of her father. The two sisters are marked by difference, something underscored visually through their clothing and verbally through their worldviews. Sveta wants to be a sniper in Chechnya, while Dina pretends that her hat makes her invisible. Both escape their quotidian realities through self-deception, while at the same time probing into a feared 'Real' that is hinted at through Dina's drawings and Sveta's enquiry about her real Chechen father.

On one level, the sisters' backgrounds could be interpreted as a form of class struggle (New vs Old), but this duality is complicated with the inclusion of the Gypsies. In the company of the Gypsy family, both sisters are privileged 'White' kids on the run. They lose their sense of family unity, projected through motifs of a dinner gathering that again frustrate any easy interpretations of kinship or nationhood. Bodrov Jr is – thus far in the movie – interested not so much in group membership as in its margins or edges. Thus the gangsters are predominately seen in maritime environs, yacht harbours or ferry terminals; these places suggest a

Sergei Bodrov Jr, *Sisters* (2001).

desirable locale of possible departure, without the risk of ever going away. The girls are associated with urban outskirts and suburbs. These places are full of lakes, water basins, rivers and scrubland – all barren landscapes that emphasize the loneliness and isolation of the two main characters.

The girls' final hideaway, the policeman's house, is isolated by water; it is an island from which the only retreat is through the boating or maritime sphere associated with gangsters. However, the same water becomes a space that allows the girls to change identities. It is here that Dina dances for her sister; we are shown the girls exhibiting their talents and togetherness – now *despite* their differences. They are shown dancing against the cloudless, light-blue sky. The penultimate scenes, therefore, speak of mergers.

The resulting dream of linking Asia to a Russian nationality is not without its nostalgia for the Soviet 'friendship of peoples'. After all, Dina is shown dancing to Indian motifs that speak of Soviet retro-radio broadcasts. Bodrov Jr is of course complicit in this politicized portrayal of the girls; in fact he appears as the narrative's guardian angel, even, magically promising to protect Sveta. With this type of simplified or codified conclusion, the film falls back into an easy duality of mafia-related, 'Good vs Bad' tale, despite the earlier investigations of complex identities, and social peripheries. Black and white prevail over anything grey.

Lars Kristensen

Bimmer

Bumer

Country of Origin:
Russia

Language:
Russian

Studios:
CTB
Pygmalion Production

Director:
Petr Buslov

Producers:
Sergei Chliants
Vladimir Ignat'ev

Screenplay:
Petr Buslov
Denis Rodimin

Cinematographer:
Daniil Gurevich

Art Director:
Ul'iana Riabova

Composer:
Sergei Shnurov

Editor:
Ivan Lebedev

Duration:
110 minutes

Genre:
Gangster Film

Cast:
Vladimir Vdovichenko
Maksim Konovalov
Andrei Merzlikin
Sergei Gorobchenko

Year:
2003

Synopsis

In Russian, *bumer* is the vernacular for a BMW; consequently this feature concerns a sleek, imposing BMW 750 IL that cruises the streets of Moscow. Initially, the car carries four young men who are trying to escape from the mafia. A scuffle with some bandits in a local street puts one of the main characters into a dangerous position; his friends come to his rescue. Together they head out of the Russian capital, leaving their loved ones behind. With no clear idea of their final destination, the four men start an extremely problematic journey through the Russian provinces. As they pass through a series of challenges and trials, their bond becomes stronger; the BMW, however, appears to be both their only reliable transport and the cause of their troubles. As the foursome's mistakes start to overshadow their progress, further still from Moscow, even the car will fail them.

Critique

Bimmer is one of the first important films of the new century that focuses on Russian life outside of Moscow. The friends' escape from the capital provides the director with an opportunity to explore the social and cultural order in the countryside. The journey serves as a narrative tool that brings together a series of accidents and confrontations. Each of them accentuates a specific feature of Russian rural life: for example, a clash with local bandits exemplifies issues of widespread power struggle, while an encounter with a faith healer provides commentary on the ethical nature of current social conflict. The film, as we see, presents various members of Russian society at war with each other; state authorities fail to provide them with either support or protection. The four friends, although presented in a sympathetic fashion, are in facts bandits ready both to avenge and kill, if needs be. They, too, epitomize conflict. As a result, this film makes some critical observations about the confused morality of contemporary Russian society; this is a civic realm where survival instinct, not the rule of law governs individuals. The heroes' survival depends on their solidarity, while destiny – or their own wrongdoing – continuously tests that bond.

The film presents an exploration of contemporary Russian masculinity: each member of the central foursome is unable to maintain a loving relationship with friends or family. This is embodied in terms of failed communication: a mobile phone they believe helps to connect them with their families is, in actual fact, used as a tracking device by their enemies. Though they travel as a group, each of these young men has to confront his inner conflicts individually. Thus the movie demonstrates a crisis both of friendship and of individual identities. These four hyper-masculine buddies emerge both vulnerable and unable to function in the unknown world of rural Russia. The film utilizes elements of a road movie, gangster movie and action flick. It even recalls elements of various Soviet war features that once focused on the collective heroism of groups. *Bimmer*, nonetheless, presents a process of de-heroization and emasculation by underscoring a loss of both purpose and progression.

The film was well received by Russian audiences who saw it as a symbol of the 'perestroika generation' finding its way in post-Soviet Russia. The appeal of the film was in a graphic representation of violence, together with a procession of expensive cars or mobile phones. The ringtone used frequently throughout the film has been one of the most popular among Russian men ever since. *Bimmer* thus helped to establish its leading men in Russian cinema; most of them remain primarily associated with gangster and crime movies. The film was followed by a sequel as well as a few parodies, including Dmitrii Puchkov's *Anti-Bimmer*.

Vlad Strukov

Night Watch

Nochnoi Dozor

Country of Origin:
Russia

Language:
Russian

Studios:
Pervyi kanal
Kinokompaniia Tabbak
Bazelevs

Director:
Timur Bekmambetov

Producers:
Varvara Avdiushko
Konstantin Ernst

Screenplay:
Timur Bekmambetov (based on the novel by Sergei Lukianenko)

Cinematographer:
Sergei Trofimov

Art Director:
Valerii Viktorov

Composer:
Iurii Poteenko

Editor:
Dmitrii Kisilev

Duration:
114 minutes

Synopsis

A new type of social order dominates contemporary Moscow; 'Others' who possess supernatural powers, live among normal humans. The Others fall into two groups – the Dark Ones, or 'Day Watch', who gain their power by feeding on the blood of humans, and the Light Ones, or 'Night Watch', who are supposed to protect people from their Dark opponents. This struggle dates back centuries, when an ancient conflict was instigated by an awful curse, imposed on a semi-mythical virgin who once lived in Byzantium. In the Moscow of 1992, city dweller Anton Gorodetskii seeks help from a sorceress in order to regain his unfaithful wife; he learns that she is carrying another man's child. Anton asks the sorceress to terminate the pregnancy; the Night Watch, however, intervenes and saves the child. They also bring Anton into their order. Thereafter he begins hunting vampires who attack innocent Muscovites. Twelve years later, in today's city, Anton comes across his son, Egor, on the Moscow Metro; Anton tries to re-establish his parental authority but to no avail. Egor, revealed to viewers as one of the Others, chooses the Dark side. Anton, himself under similar pressures, is simultaneously attracted to Svetlana, a very powerful member of the Night Watch.

Critique

The film documents the social and cultural changes that occurred in Russia under Putin; these are presented through elements of fantasy, horror and science fiction. By introducing the conflict between the Day Watch and Night Watch, the director attests to divisions in Russian society that, in his mind, emerged after Yeltsin's transitional period of the 1990s. The movie's fragile truce between the Dark and Light forces epitomizes the weakness of the Russian law in modern-day Moscow. The son of the main character, Egor, symbolizes the new nation: his father, Anton, had attempted his son's murder in 1992 (through abortion) but the boy survived. That dramatic salvation becomes a metaphor for Russia's difficult rebirth after the demise of the USSR.

The on-going struggle between Anton and Egor is established as the movie's narrative driving force. In fact, the majority of the film's

Timur Bekmambetov, *Night Watch* (2004); Konstantin Khabenskii as Anton Gorodetskii.

Genre:

Fantasy
Horror
Action

Cast:

Konstantin Khabenskii
Vladimir Men'shov
Viktor Verzhbitskii
Mariia Poroshina
Rimma Markova

Year:

2004

other characters merely embody variations upon this complex father-child conflict with sub-plots of parental responsibility and filial ties. Together they might be seen as an extension of the Oedipus complex, resulting in the movie's stubbornly mythological register. *Night Watch* is one of many films produced in Russia since the end of the 1990s that explores the problem of father-child relationships in depth.

The film is loosely based on a series of novels by Sergei Lukianenko, which accounts for the sometimes confusing storyline. The narrative includes multiple flashbacks that explain the reasons behind the conflict; thus the viewer gradually learns the 'new laws' that govern Moscow. Much, however, remains obscure.

The film includes many celebrities from Russia's cinematic heritage, creating a unique, post-Soviet panoply of mass entertainment. The movie is especially famous for its innovative digital effects; their wizardry matches the abandon with which Bekmambetov mixes old and new film stars. *Night Watch* engages with a new, digital culture through set-pieces inspired by computer gaming and various websites. Although visually and emotionally dark, the film contains many humorous one-liners and visual tricks that produce a rich, constantly energetic spectacle.

Night Watch was Russia's first major blockbuster after the fall of the USSR, and garnered a considerable amount of international attention. The film also propelled the career of its director, Kazakh-born Timur Bekmambetov into the limelight. He has since become one of the top producers in Hollywood.

Vlad Strukov

Day Watch

Dnevnoi Dozor

Country of Origin:
Russia

Language:
Russian

Studios:
Pervyi kanal
Kinokompaniia Tabbak
Bazelevs

Director:
Timur Bekmambetov

Producers:
Natela Abuladze
Konstantin Ernst

Screenplay:
Timur Bekmambetov (based on
the novel by Sergei Lukianenko)

Cinematographer:
Sergei Trofimov

Art Director:
Valerii Viktorov

Composer:
Iurii Poteenko

Editor:
Dmitrii Kisilev

Duration:
132 minutes

Genre:
Fantasy
Horror
Action

Cast:
Konstantin Khabenskii
Vladimir Men'shov
Viktor Verzhbitskii
Mariia Poroshina
Rimma Markova
Zhanna Friske
Aleksei Chadov
Dmitrii Martynov

Year:
2005

Synopsis

Day Watch is a sequel to Timur Bekmambetov's Night Watch (2004). Both films tell a story of the struggle between two opposing forces, the Day Watch and Night Watch. Their leaders are Zavulon and Geser, respectively. The confrontation between them is ancient; viewers learn of this history first through flashbacks to World War II, and then to the thirteenth-century Mongol occupation of Russia. Their historic, mythological and fantastic confrontation is played out in the private lives of the main characters. The central figure, Anton, tries to re-establish contact with his son Egor, and he is ultimately torn between parental responsibility and a new-found love for a troubled stranger, Svetlana. Kostia, Anton's neighbour, has to choose between the orders of the Day Watch and his passion for a mysterious female, Alisa. Kostia's father is ready to sacrifice himself in order to protect the future of his endangered son. Disaster seems inevitable. Anton manages to resolve his own conflicts – and those of others – by snatching a magical 'chalk of destiny', returning to the past and rewriting the future.

Critique

The plot of Day Watch revolves around various tactics of retribution that the Dark and Light forces employ against each other; these alternating acts of vengeance are paralleled by a strong sense of equality and ultimate justice. Alisa, for example, attempts to take revenge on the murderer of her best friend, Galina; Egor carries out a harsh reprisal against his father, and so forth. A resulting metaphor of vampirism is used as a narrative device to blur (through digital imagery) any clarity of stable characterization or enduring moral dispositions. Computer-generated imagery allows for the constant transformation of people into animals and birds, toys into destructive weapons and so forth.

The same effect is used with regard to time. The film's characters inhabit the real spaces of contemporary Moscow as well as the historical past; all events appear to be linked and governed by the flexible truce between the Day and Night Watches. Between these opposites lies the so-called 'gloom', an alternative third space where the laws of time and gravity cease to exist.

Day Watch features a greater number of characters and plot-lines than its prequel, yet it is more successful in rendering the central narrative and providing psychological characterization. Multiple storylines gain clarity because each of them develops a central issue of father-child relationships and an associated morality. In the final scene of the film these lines are brought together in a literal fashion as all forces converge for the grand, final ball sequence. Festivities soon turn to hellish fighting, full of phantasmagorical visions that refer to different cultures, myths and legends. The film overwhelms the viewer with its chaotic cultural, social and political references, providing a network of possible interpretations ranging from a biblical creation myth to the modern conflicts between the KGB and CIA. The film borrows creatively from The Matrix, The Lord of the Rings and other modern epic trilogies, resulting in a kaleidoscopic series of double entendres and other associations.

The feature benefits from a star cast that includes Russia's film, television and music celebrities. Released on 1 January 2006 (that is, on Russia's main public holiday) the film offers a feast of celebrities, special effects, mischievous humour, extraordinary stunts and melodramatic twists. The movie manages, as a result, to stretch genre boundaries, emerging as an extraordinary hybrid of Christmas fairy tale, national epos, horror film, comedy and drama. *Day Watch* broke all box-office records for Russian domestic film distribution, earning more than 30 million dollars in order to surpass the previous record holders, including Bekmambetov's own *Night Watch* (2004).

Vlad Strukov

CHILDREN'S FILMS

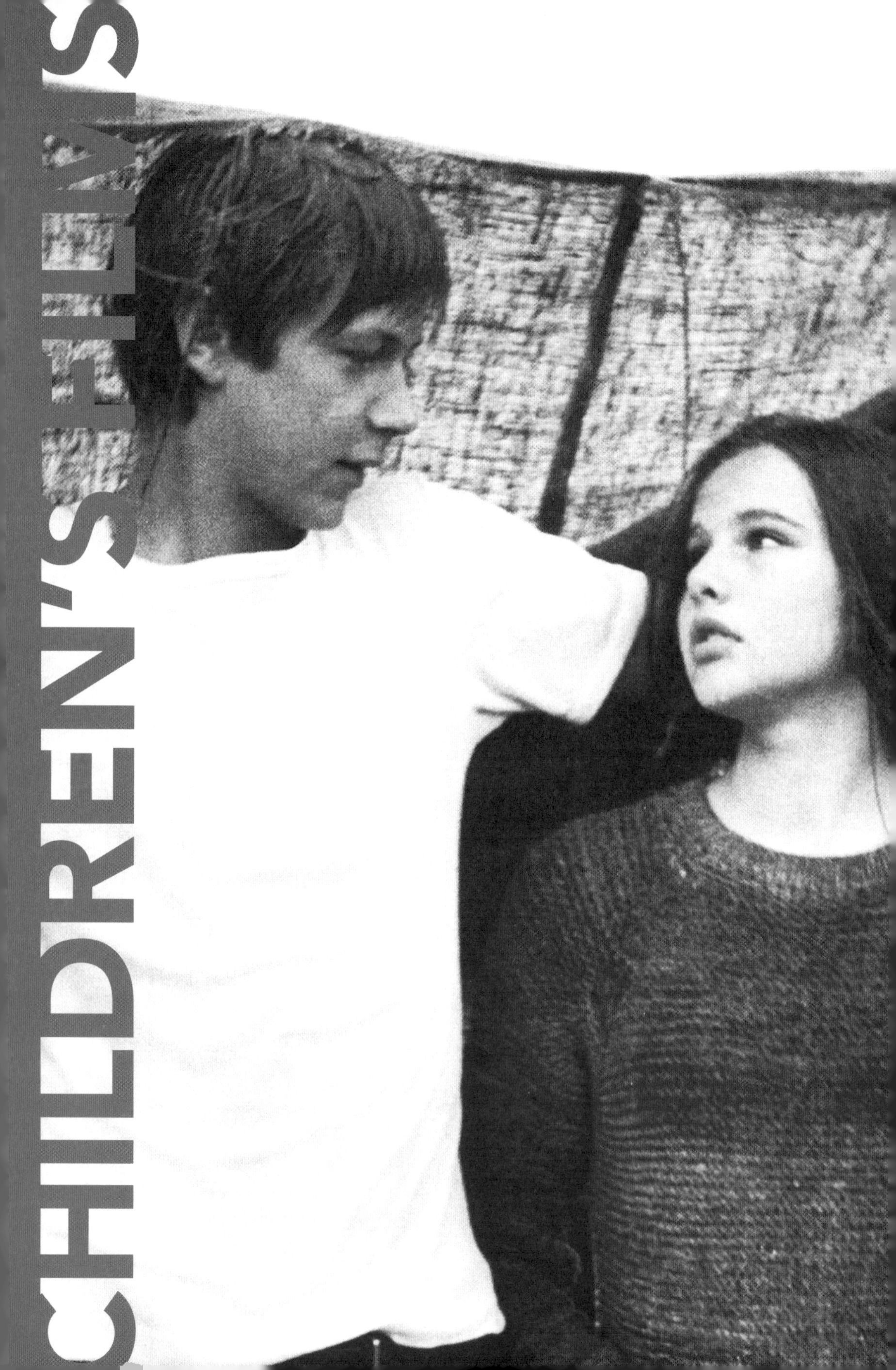

Although the first films targeting children as its prime audience appeared in Imperial Russia, it was the Soviet government that put a special emphasis on cinema as a tool of children's education and propaganda. In 1918 the government set up the Children's Cinema Section within the People's Commissariat of Enlightenment (*Narkompros*). While the Bolsheviks dreamt of pictures glorifying the Revolutionary ethos, the culture under the New Economic Policy (1921–1928) required ideological compromises with commercial culture. In literature, writers embraced Nikolai Bukharin's notion of Red Pinkerton; in cinema, directors used adventure as a vehicle for the new ideology. Ivan Perestiani's *Red Imps* (1923) became a model of successfully combining communist ideology with a Western-style story.

By the late 1920s the NEP-era compromises with commercial cinema were over, and cultural administrators established children's cinema as a special branch. By the mid-1930s Soviet children's cinema acquired institutional and aesthetic forms that it preserved until its demise in the late 1980s. The government established a special children's cinema infrastructure by creating studios dedicated to films for young audiences (Soiuzdetfilm and Soiuzmultfilm) and building special cinemas for children.

Evgenii Dobrenko notes that socialist realist literature and cinema made for adults gravitated toward cultural production for children in its simplified language, heroes and clear polarization between good and evil. Many films not specifically addressed to children became nevertheless popular with children at the time: Nikolai Ekk's *Road to Life* (1931) and the Vasil'ev Brothers' *Chapaev* (1934). *Road to Life* dealt with the resocialization of juvenile criminals and established the school film as one of the main variants of the socialist realist master plot.

Stalinist cinema also played a special role in providing visual confirmations of the utopia that was supposed to come true in the USSR. The fairy tale and the adventure film about children helping adults in their struggle for social justice became the major sub-

Sergei Solov'ev, *A Hundred Days after Childhood* (1974).

genres of cinema for children. Two filmmakers, Aleksandr Ptushko and Aleksandr Rou, were the main filmmakers engaging in fairy tale films. In 1935 Ptushko released his first fantasy, *New Gulliver*, combining live action with animation. Ptushko specialized in adaptations of Soviet fairy tales, such as *Golden Key* (1939), *Tale of Lost Time* (1964), and films based on Russian epics, such as *Sadko* (1952) and *Il'ia Muromets* (1956). Rou specialized in adaptations of Russian folk and fairy tales, with *Vasilisa the Beautiful* (1939) and *Jack Frost* (1964).

The Stalinist revival of imperialist expansionism found its representation in the adaptations of the novels by Jules Verne and Robert Lewis Stevenson. In these films, filmmakers often 'improved' the original story to suit Marxist ideology. Thus, in *Children of Captain Grant* (1936), the villain Thomas Ayrton is redeemed because his crime stemmed from the class oppression experienced in the British Navy. Finally, Aleksandr Razumnyi, and Arkadii Gaidar, synthesized Verne's adventure and Soviet ideology in their film *Timur and his Team* (1940). The story, originally titled *Duncan and his Team*, was inspired by Verne's novel about Captain Grant's children.

Vladimir Shneiderov produced ethnographic films about Soviet scientists' travels in Central Asia and the Far East: *Dzhulbars* (1935), *Golden Lake* (1935), *The Alamasts Gorge* (1937), *Gaichi* (1938). In these films, scientists and secret service agents prospect the natural resources and help the locals find the path toward the correct ideology. Shneiderov's adventures shared their vigilant spirit with numerous spy films for children (*Lenochka and Grapes* (Kudriavtseva, 1936), *Train Goes to Moscow* (Gindelshtein and Poznanskii, 1938), *High Award* (Shneider, 1939)).

An overview of Stalin-era children's cinema would be incomplete without discussing the alternative voices to Stalinist mainstream. In the 1930s, Mark Donskoi filmed his famous trilogy based on Gorky's autobiography, which anticipated neo-realist aesthetics, favouring the child protagonist and the nuclear family as the core of the protagonist's world. The 1930s is also the time of Margarita Barskaia's experiments as she sought the sources of authentic performances in children's improvisation. Her first film, *Torn Boots* (1933), featured children as lead actors, while her second film *Father and Son* (1936) depicted the Soviet family as a site of social crisis; this film was banned.

During the Great Patriotic War, Soiuzdetfilm was evacuated to Stalinabad, where the studio produced twelve films; these were fairy tale films, adventures and films about children helping adults in socialist construction. The war effort also increased a demand for the films about young heroes sacrificing their lives in the fight against the Nazis. Only two films of the 1940s challenged the aesthetics of official children's cinema: *Once Upon a Time There Was a Girl*, an understated melodrama about war orphans (Eisymont, 1944) and *Cinderella*, a self-reflexive fairy tale, evoking avant-garde acting of the 1920s (Kosheverova and Shapiro, 1947).

During the post-war reconstruction, children's cinema was a low priority for the Soviet government. In 1947 Soiuzdetfilm was reorganized into the Gorky Film Studio without any mandate of making films for children. Only in 1957 was the production of films for children increased. Mosfilm established a special children's cinema unit, 'Youth'. In 1963 Gorky Studio gained the status of a studio producing films for children and adolescents.

The revival of cinema for children was inspired by the de-Stalinization policies during the Thaw. Under the influence of neo-realism, young heroes acquired the status of paragons of innocence and integrity. The child hero became the protagonist not only in films for children but also in films for general audiences, because the child embodied anti-monumentalism as the key trope of de-Stalinization.

Thaw filmmakers also reconsidered the conventions of the school film and the collective's central role in the socialization of children. While the children's collective remained the key social unit in the films, many films emphasized the value of the individual as well. Such films as *Tale of the First Love* (Levin, 1957), *And What If This is Love?* (Raizman,

1962) raised issues of privacy and human relations, where the school as a state institution had no business whatsoever.

Thaw-era filmmakers challenged Stalinist aesthetics by invoking on screen the Revolutionary art of the 1920s. In 1966 Aleksei Batalov adapted Iurii Olesha's *Three Fat Men* (1966), while Edmond Keosaian released a remake of *Red Imps* titled *The Elusive Avengers* (1966). In the same year Gennadii Poloka created a comic adaptation of Grigorii Belykh and Leonid Panteleev's *Republic ShKID*.

In the 1960s, inspired by European art cinema, Soviet directors started making *auteur* films, which were officially listed as films for children. The 'Youth' unit, for example, started its production of children's films with Andrei Tarkovskii's *The Steamroller and the Violin* (1960). Among the *auteurs*, Rolan Bykov emerged as the filmmaker who dedicated his talent to art cinema for children: *Dolittle-66* (1966), *Attention, a Turtle!* (1970) and *The Scarecrow* (1983). In his films, children try to identify their authentic feelings against the barrage of ideological narratives foisted upon them at school.

Bykov redefined the mission of children's cinema from a tool of state propaganda to a mouthpiece of Thaw intelligentsia's ideology. The best films for children of the 1960s and 1970s were made by art cinema filmmakers (Bykov, Leonid Nechaev, Dinara Asanova, Boris Rytsarev) and promoted such values as the respect for the individual and ideological tolerance.

In the 1970s science-fiction films for children took off with the success of Richard Viktorov's *Moscow-Cassiopeia* (1973) and *Teenagers in the Universe* (1974). These films combined space adventure with a thinly veiled critique of Soviet society. At the centre of the films stood failed extra-terrestrial civilizations, where the totalitarian repression of the individual led to ecological disaster. While science-fiction films for children thus used Aesopian settings to hint at the fact that Soviet utopia had long gone astray, social problem films of the 1970s and 1980s, above all Dinara Asanova's *Tough Kids* (1983) and Bykov's *Scarecrow*, openly questioned the ideological premises of Soviet cinema for children and, in the final analysis, served a lethal blow to this branch of the Soviet propaganda industry.

The ideological crisis of children's cinema went hand in hand with the changes in the economic priorities of the Soviet film industry. The Gorky Studio switched to making B-quality detective films in order to increase revenues. From 1981 to 1985, out of 105 films released by the Gorky Studio, only seven were for children.

After the fall of the USSR, Russian screen culture for children was increasingly dominated by Hollywood and Disney products. In their turn, Russian filmmakers tried to create domestic cinema and television for children and family audiences. In 1989, Bykov established the Rolan Bykov Foundation with a mandate to create a television channel for children, produce films and hold an annual festival of children's cinema. The foundation released two civic-minded documentary series: *The Sacred War* (about war through children's eyes) and *Children of the Countryside: SOS!* (about social problems of children in rural Russia).

In the late 1990s the St Petersburg studio 'Windmill' (*Mel'nitsa*) started the production of animated features and television series for family audiences (*Adventures in Emerald City*, 1999; *The Little Long Nose*, 2002; *Alesha Popovich and Tugarin the Dragon*, 2004; *Dobrynia Nikitich and the Dragon*, 2006; and *Il'ia Muromets and Nightingale the Bandit*, 2007), while only few live-action films for children appeared in the same period, largely about poverty and street urchins (e.g. Andrei Proshkin's *Spartak and Kalashnikov*, 2002).

The immediate future of screen culture for children seems to belong to state-controlled television. In 2006 Vladimir Putin spoke to the Duma about creating specialized television channels for children, and in the following year two state-controlled media holdings, First Channel and VGTRK, launched such channels: *Telemania* and *Bibigon*.

Alexander Prokhorov

Red Imps (Little Red Devils)

Krasnye d'iavoliata

Country of Origin:
Soviet Union

Language:
Russian

Studio:
Kinosektsiia Narkomprosa Gruzii
(Goskinoprom Gruzii)

Director:
Ivan Perestiani

Screenplay:
Pavel Bliakhin
Ivan Perestiani

Cinematographer:
Aleksandr Digmelov

Art Director:
Fedor Push

Duration:
130 minutes

Genre:
Children's Film

Cast:
Konstantin Davidovskii
Pavel Esikovskii
Sofiia Zhozeffi
Kador Ben-Salim
Vladimir Sutyrin
Vitalii Brianskii

Year:
1923

Synopsis

Around 1920–1921, in a small Ukrainian village near the Crimean coast, the teenager Misha does metalwork repair on railroad cars with his father Petrov. Misha reads and fantasizes about the 'Leatherstocking Tales' of James Fenimore Cooper, while his sister Duniasha is obsessed by Ethel Voynich's *The Gadfly*. When the anarchist peasant army of 'Bat'ko' Nestor Makhno attacks the village, Petrov is mortally wounded. With his last breaths, he instructs his children to fight the enemy together with the Red Army. Misha and Duniasha set off to join forces with the First Cavalry commanded by Semen Budennyi. They soon meet a black street acrobat named Tom Jackson and become fast, dear friends. The adventurous, good-natured threesome encounters a range of wild exploits, from beatings and kidnappings to gun skirmishes and cavalry attacks. After many death-defying escapades, they finally succeed in capturing the erratic and sadistic Makhno and bring him to Budennyi. Crowds cheer enthusiastically as Budennyi kisses and bestows the Order of the Red Banner upon the three protagonists.

Critique

Originally released as a two-part serial, *Red Imps* was the first domestic box-office hit of the Soviet film industry. Although set in Ukraine and featuring Ukrainian historical figures from the Civil War, the film was produced in Georgia by the Film Section of the Georgian Commissariat for Education. Furthermore, much of the cast and crew, including director Ivan Perestiani, came from Georgia. This kind of cultural hybridity can also be found in the narrative structure and overall style of the film. As Soviet audiences strongly favoured foreign films, Perestiani incorporated various aspects of western – particularly Hollywood – filmmaking into a story that otherwise seemed distinctly local and appropriately Soviet.

The narrative design of *Red Imps* largely follows that of American serial queen melodramas and Douglas Fairbanks-style swashbuckling adventure films. The film maintains a fairly loose structure, with a series of individual set pieces linked together by a single, relatively vague but overarching goal: to defeat and/or capture Bat'ko Makhno. The narrative is driven by distinct obstacles that arise within each set piece. In each instalment of a serial such as *The Perils of Pauline* (1914) or *The Exploits of Elaine* (1914), the brave heroine would find herself facing an altogether new hazard – trapped on a runaway hot air balloon, locked in an underground tunnel flooding with water, etc. Typically, each set piece would involve yet another elaborate scheme by the antagonist to entrap the protagonist, who, surely enough, would fall haplessly for it. The protagonist would then have either the proper wits or the good fortune to overcome or be rescued from this predicament. The antagonist would once again be forced to hatch a new plot and the story would continue. Such is the narrative design of *Red Imps*: Misha is captured by Makhno's bandits, knocked uncon-scious, thrown from a cliff into the sea, and it is Tom who must save

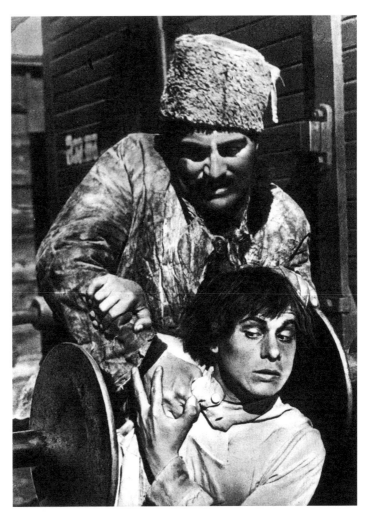

Ivan Perestiani, *Red Imps* (1923).

him; Duniasha is captured by Makhno's bandits, knocked unconscious, strung upside down from a tree, and it is Misha and Tom who must save her; Misha is captured by Makhno, forced to fisticuffs against Makhno's goliath warrior, and it is Misha who must save himself. In principle, such a structure allows the filmmaker to easily expand or contract the narrative as needed, the only required resolution being the unmasking and/or capturing of the antagonist. As the film centres on individual scenes of orchestrated action, Perestiani draws upon analytical editing traditions and accelerated editing rates – both common in the West – in order to clearly depict spatial relationships within a scene and heighten the sense of action and suspense.

Western influences are also acknowledged in the books that are read and then 'lived' by our young heroes: the fearless outdoor adventures of the American James Fenimore Cooper combined with the revolutionary fervour and romance of the British Ethel Voynich. Perestiani tellingly shies away from pre-Revolutionary Russian cinema's interest in exploring character psychology. Misha and Duniasha's father is murdered, yet throughout their supposed quest for vengeance, they consistently sport either good-humoured grins or game-faced determination. As in its Hollywood counterparts, the emphasis here is strictly on action and our plucky heroes have no time to ponder the morbid or morose.

The success of the *Red Imps* led to four sequels: *Savur-Mogila*, *The Crime of Princess Shirvanskaya*, *The Punishment of Princess Shirvanskaya* and *Illan Dilli*. These sequels were produced in 1926, directed by Ivan Perestiani and featured the same principal characters and cast as the original. A sound version of *Red Imps* was released during World War II, and in 1966 Edmond Keosaian released a colour widescreen remake under the title *The Elusive Avengers*.

Vincent Bohlinger

The Road to Life

Putevka v zhizn'

Country of Origin:
Soviet Union

Language:
Russian

Studio:
Mezhrabpomfilm

Director:
Nikolai Ekk

Screenplay:
Aleksandr Stolper
Regina Ianushkevich
Nikolai Ekk

Cinematographer:
Vasilii Pronin

Art Director:
Ivan Stepanov

Composer:
Iakov Stolliar

Duration:
95 minutes

Synopsis

The Road to Life tells of the fate of the thousands of homeless children in the USSR during the early 1920s. The film begins by showing how the children are exploited by a certain Fomka Zhigan, who forces them to trick and rob people on the streets so that they can survive. The children are eventually rounded up by a commission of social workers. One of the workers, Nikolai Sergeev, devises a plan to create a children's collective, where they will learn to be joiners, mechanics and shoemakers. Despite initial hostility on the part of the children, the collective is formed. The attempts to change the children's bad habits are not instantaneously successful; when supplies of raw materials run dry and the leadership of Sergeev is absent, they go on a spree of vandalism. Later Zhigan makes a return when he finds his income is gone and that life is difficult with nobody to exploit. He attempts to draw the boys back into his world by getting them drunk, but fails. The film ends on both a tragic and triumphant note. The boys complete their work laying a local railway which is opened with celebration. Yet this is tinged with sadness as one of the head boys, Mustafa, who has successfully moved on from his past, dies and so the celebration is also a tribute to him.

Critique

The Road to Life is deservedly considered to be a key film in the history of Soviet cinema, not just because it was the first, proper feature film with sound, but also due to the high quality of the production as a whole. The theme of homelessness among children was a matter of grave concern for the Soviet leadership, yet it also made for a dramatic, profound and entertaining story. This, alongside the fine work of the filmmakers, led to both popular and critical success at home

Genre:

Children's film

Cast:

Nikolai Batalov

Iyvan Kyrlia

Mikhail Zharov

Regina Ianushkevich

Vladimir Vesnovskii

Year:

1931

and abroad. In America the film enjoyed relative popularity and this may have been related to the problem of homelessness during the Great Depression.

At one point the film refers to the need to end homelessness among children and to make them happy citizens (accompanied by an image of Lenin). Yet the film is less about didactic preaching than it is a humane, universally applicable story. In the first place, it seeks to explain why homelessness can happen, without blaming the pre-Revolutionary era. We are shown one, initially happy, family in which the mother dies. The father then begins to drink heavily and beats his son Kolia, who then finds himself on the street. The attempts to resolve the situation through labour appears to be a fairly predictable solution to the problem. However, Nikolai Sergeev's efforts to subtly show the boys the meaning of trust, structure and the surrogate family of fellow urchins, makes for a believable and convincing narrative.

By 1931, the montage movement had already faded and this film, as with the majority of movies in the 1930s, is centred on the script and dialogue. Nonetheless, the director does have a distinctive visual style. In particular, he frequently edits together close-ups of the characters reacting to events, such as the death of Kolia's mother. Although this can be rather sentimental at times, it also effectively conveys a whole range of complex emotions among the children, including distress, confusion, anxiety and humour. This is also achieved by the superb level of acting across the board. Nikolai Batalov is outstanding as Sergeev with his charismatic inspiration, bringing meaning to the children's lives. Indeed, the child actors are also highly effective, including Iyvan Kyrlia who played Mustafa, yet had no professional training. *The Road to Life* proved to be Ekk's most famous film and it remains a classic of Soviet cinema.

Jamie Miller

Torn Boots

Rvanye bashmaki

Country of Origin:

Soviet Union

Language:

Russian

Studio:

Mezhrabpomfilm

Director:

Margarita Barskaia

Screenplay:

Margarita Barskaia

Synopsis

Torn Boots was, according to Margarita Barskaia, the first children's sound film when it was released in 1933. The story takes place in Germany as the Nazis rise to power. The dock-workers are on strike and this event is contextualized within the working-class family where there is poverty, hunger and hardship. Initially, children play at being families and doctors, but, as the plot develops, we are drawn more and more to the idea that the children are not immune to the class conflict of the adult world. Child labourers are shown working at a rubbish tip and can only dream of having the wonderful toys displayed in a shop window. The film shows the children as they become more politically aware in the school environment. Eventually, the workers' children unite to join their fathers as they protest, but a young child, Bubbi, is mercilessly shot dead by the police. The film ends with young communists defiantly marching into the future, suggesting that this terrible sacrifice has not been in vain.

Cinematographers:
Georgii Bobrov
Sarkis Gevorkian

Art Director:
Vladimir Egorov

Composer:
Vissarion Shebalin

Duration:
88 minutes

Genre:
Children's Film

Cast:
Mikhail Klimov
Ivan Novosel'tsev
Vladimir Ural'skii

Year:
1933

Critique

Torn Boots is essentially an example of political propaganda aimed at children, although it has a distinctly adult tone in many places. It replicates the coming to communist consciousness that character-ized so many Soviet films, especially during the 1930s. The children begin with their naïve games, but they experience the harsh reali-ties of everyday life, for example in school. Here they are subjected to corporal punishment, overly authoritarian teachers and relentless religious dogma, which is associated with the conservatism of Nazi politics. The school also acts as an arena of class conflict between children who are in favour of the striking fathers and those who are against. Eventually, the working-class children prevail and reach a form of class consciousness. This is particularly clear after the death of the young hero, Bubbi Slezak.

   Yet it would be unfair to dismiss *Torn Boots* as merely a crude piece of propaganda. Although this function is central, the film is made to exceptionally high standards. One of its obvious strengths is the extraordinary skill shown by the child actors. In a variety of situations the children are able to convey extremely complex emotions. In one scene, Bubbi looks through a toy shop window at the bewildering array of objects on display and reacts with the most natural expres-sions of joy, delight and surprise. The film also reveals the influence of the 1920s montage movement. Following Bubbi's death the turmoil of the situation is powerfully conveyed by rapid shots of panic-stricken crowds and a mother who is blind but hears the shot and fears for the life of her own child. Perhaps the most significant message of the film is not the obvious one we see in the narrative, but another idea that, with hindsight, seems more profound. Barskaia's film is slightly ambiguous as it also suggests that political conflict destroys child-hood: it is the necessity of coming to consciousness so early that denies the children the normal everyday joys of being children and robs them of their naïveté. This idea is of great relevance to the fate of children under the Stalinist regime.

Jamie Miller

New Gulliver

Novyi Gulliver

Country of Origin:
Soviet Union

Language:
Russian

Studio:
Mosfilm

Synopsis

At a summer camp in the Crimea, the young pioneer Petia falls asleep in the sun during a group reading of his favourite book, *Gulliver's Travels*. Petia dreams that he is Gulliver on board a sailing ship attacked by brutal pirates. Along with three others he triumphs, but the ship sinks spectacularly when it crashes into rocks. When he wakes up, he is tied up and surrounded by Lilliputians. This monarchy is strictly divided into grotesquely depraved courtiers supported by their soldiers and the oppressed workers slaving under ground in munitions factories. In this communist revisioning of Swift's story, Petia duty-bound as a young pioneer, takes a different approach to his liter-ary predecessor. The 'Man Mountain' Petia sides with the oppressed

Director:

Aleksandr Ptushko

Screenplay:

Serafima Roshal'
Grigorii Roshal'
Aleksandr Ptushko (based
on Jonathan Swift's *Gulliver's
Travels*)

Cinematographer:

Nikolai Renkov

Art Directors:

Iurii Shvets
A. Nikulin
Aleksandr Zharenov

Composer:

Lev Shvarts

Duration:

68/73 minutes

Genre:

Children's Film
Adventure
Literary Adaptation

Cast:

Vladimir Konstantinov
Ivan Iudin
Ivan Bobrov
F. Brest

Year:

1935 (restored 1960)

Aleksandr Ptushko, *New Gulliver* (1935).

workers who warn him that the king's men intend to poison him for
his suspiciously egalitarian views. Petia unites with the workers who
have started a revolution in response to the despotic king's ministers
attempt to destroy them. Together they are able to overcome the
king's armies and take over the country. However, their victory celebrations are interrupted by the laughter of the young pioneers who
have been listening to Petia talking in his sleep.

Critique

Freely adapted from Swift as a Soviet satire of capitalism, *New
Gulliver* was a groundbreaking work. Ptushko's first feature film was
not only one of the first full-length animated films made anywhere in
the world, but it also stunningly combined live action and stop-motion
three-dimensional puppet animation in an extraordinary fantasy
adventure.

Three years in the making, *New Gulliver* was a technological feat.
The Lilliputians were highly expressive with more than 1,500 (some
accounts claim 3,000) separate 'puppets' employed. They had detach-
able heads to provide the opportunity to effectively animate different
facial expressions. The king's evil ministers perform the most detailed
gestures. Some of the finest characterizations are those of the snig-
gering idiot king and his sadistic ministers – exquisitely stereotyped
capitalist monsters who stop at nothing in their lust for power. The
fight in parliament is hilarious and the continuity of the mass action
scenes is fluid and lively. For a Marxist revision, it was surprising just
how dynamic the grotesque ruling class characters were. In contrast,
the workers were made uniformly of dark plasticine with little indi-
viduality to avoid making them appear parodic. However, this denied

them revolutionary zeal by symbolically accentuating the faceless dullness of the working class.

Remarkably, this painstaking technique was combined intimately with the young Gulliver's live-action performance in powerful mass scenes. The strangest of them featured Gulliver consuming food delivered by a conveyor belt and seated opposite the king while they are entertained by a bizarre line-up of ballet dancers, love serenades and dwarf microputs. These breathtaking scenes are wonderfully staged with strong dramatic connections between Gulliver and the Lilliputians.

The cohesiveness of the action is juxtaposed against the purposeful clash of logic, styles and historical periods. The architecture is medieval but with constructivist flourishes of swinging cranes. The munitions factory is a modernist nightmare with astonishing machinery and massive spidery robots. The King's courtiers get about in ancient wigs and large cars while the soldiers wear armour and gas masks.

Ptushko's sound design was equally impressive with startling synchronized dialogue and innovative recording techniques producing the definitive squeaky, high-pitched sped-up voices forever associated with puppets. The dialogue scenes of the shrill tremolo courtier Lilliputians produced a disquieting effect that was modulated when the more sonorous Lilliput workers spoke with Gulliver. The lampooning of romantic love songs with the grimacing, toothy rendition of 'My Lilliput Girl', accompanied by a burlesque ballet, became an enduring hit. Technology is ingeniously represented through sound when the devious ministers use a record player to deliver the idiot king's lip-synched speeches while a sparsely modernist sound design sets the mood for the mechanical nightmare of the munitions factory.

The film's success was phenomenal domestically and internationally, with the critics and the general public. While the film can be seen as communist kitsch, it continues to maintain its appeal with its innocent impulse to fairness embedded in a fantastical adventure. Ptushko only made one more film (*The Golden Key*, 1939) that combined live action with animation. The success of *New Gulliver* facilitated Ptushko's considerable future experimentation in special effects and fantasy, and gave rise to the on-going popularity of stop-motion animation.

Greg Dolgopolov

Captain Grant's Children

Deti kapitana Granta

Country of Origin:
Soviet Union

Language:
Russian

Synopsis

The crew of Scottish Lord Glenarvan's yacht, the *Duncan*, finds in the stomach of a caught shark a message from shipwrecked sea captain Harry Grant. After a request from Grant's children, Robert and Mary, mediated by Glenarvan's wife, Glenarvan launches a rescue expedition – in spite of the refusal of assistance from the London authorities, which suspect him of nationalist, anti-English sentiments. On their long voyage, the rescuers are joined by the very knowledgeable, but extremely absent-minded French explorer Jacques Paganel. After many dangerous adventures in Patagonia and the Southern Seas

Studio:
Mosfilm

Director:
Vladimir Vainshtok

Co-Director:
David Gutman

Screenplay:
Oleg Leonidov

Cinematographer:
Arkadii (Abram) Kal'tsatyi
(Kol'tsatyi)

Art Directors:
Vladimir Balliuzek
Iakov Rivosh

Composer:
Isaak Dunaievskii

Duration:
83 minutes

Genre:
Children's Film
Adventure
Literary adaptation

Cast:
Iurii Iur'ev
Nikolai Cherkasov
Iakov Segel'

Year:
1936

(including captivity by a Maori tribe), the search party rescues Captain Grant from an island in the South Pacific, leaving behind the criminal Ayerton, who is to blame for Grant's troubles.

Critique

A period adventure film aimed primarily at children and adolescents, *Captain Grant's Children* remains a source of uncomplicated but enjoyable entertainment – a relative rarity among 'adult' Soviet films, but a more frequent feature of Soviet children's cinema. This phenomenon can be observed particularly during the Stalin regime, with its didactic pretensions and the wish to extend its control to all sections of the population.

The film's director Vladimir Vainshtok belonged to the second tier of Soviet filmmakers; his successes were few, but notable, not least because he belonged to that relatively small group of directors who preferred to work in cinematic genres usually associated with western 'bourgeois' cinema. While compelled to include in his films some ideological content (most notably in the 1937 adaptation of R.L. Stevenson's *Treasure Island*), Vainshtok still managed to convincingly convey the spirit of adventure – something which still makes *Captain Grant's Children* one of the most successful screen adaptations of Jules Verne's works and a real pleasure to watch and recall. Indeed, it is the sense of modest but tangible and practically uninterrupted pleasure – enhanced by a bookish pace and an archaic style in which even the technical imperfections of the soundtrack and special effects play a positive role – that allows this film to be singled out as an almost unique experience not only within Stalinist cinema but Soviet film culture in general.

The film's pleasurable mood is most strikingly conveyed by Isaac Dunaievskii's musical score and the acting of Nikolai Cherkasov. Unlike the orchestral music in many of Hollywood's adventure films, Dunaievskii's score is situational and unobtrusive. The same is true of Cherkasov's performance as the eccentric geographer Paganel: his acting is psychologically precise and only slightly self-ironic. Therefore, it is integral to the film's mix of subdued sentimentality and carefully constructed credibility (among other things, guaranteed by the expertise of the Academy of Sciences' Ethnographic Museum) called upon to relate both to the sincerity of child's fantasies and to the Stalinist concept of man's conquest of nature – in this case applied to a refreshingly and curiously broader category than the new Soviet man.

Sergei Kapterev

Vasilisa the Beautiful

Vasilisa prekrasnaia

Country of Origin:
Soviet Union

Language:
Russian

Studio:
Soiuzdetfilm

Director:
Aleksandr Rou

Screenplay:
G. Vladychina
Ol'ga Nechaeva
Vladimir Shveitser

Cinematographer:
Ivan Gorchilin

Art Director:
Vladimir Egorov

Composer:
Leonid Polovinkin

Editor:
Kseniia Blinova

Duration:
72 minutes

Genre:
Children's Film
Fairy tale

Cast:
Georgii Milliar
Sergei Stoliarov
Lev Potemkin
Nikita Kondrat'ev
V. Sorogozhskaia
Irina Zarubina

Year:
1939

Synopsis

Through a combination of impetuousness and fate, the young and immature Ivan meets the beautiful and enchanted Vasilisa, who assumes the form of a frog in public and performs chores while out of sight. Ivan's older brothers choose brides too, but choose them badly. The jealousy of these women leads to Vasilisa being kidnapped by the dragon Zmei Gorynych, and Ivan has no choice but to leave his home in pursuit of his abducted fiancée. Having cast off the provinciality of his origins, Ivan traverses the majestic Russian land, overcoming challenges and maturing into a hero. By the time he enters the dark forest where Zmei Gorynych dwells with his ally Baba Yaga, he is a mighty defender of the Russian people. Evil schemes cannot keep the destined pair apart; Ivan and Vasilisa overcome their enemies, and, their joint victory complete, they greet a glorious sunrise spreading over the Russian land where they return.

Critique

Although it shares its title with a Russian folktale, Aleksandr Rou's *Vasilisa the Beautiful* is not a filmic adaptation, so much as a synthesis of several traditional tales in a new form, which adapts some ideas for the contemporary viewer. *Vasilisa* thus occupies a middle ground between traditional folk culture, as it came to be celebrated during the Stalin period, and the new socialist realist tales composed as part of the revival of Russo-centric nationalism after Stalin's consolidation of power in the late 1920s. As might be expected from this cultural context, the film incorporates folkloric motifs into a form defined by the aesthetic and ideological demands of socialist realism.

Vasilisa begins with a frame narrative in which three epic bards, dressed in traditional Russian costumes and plucking the strings of traditional Russian instruments, inform the viewers that they are about to witness 'popular truth'. As they fade out, the main plot commences with placid nature scenes in which the youthful protagonist Ivan soon appears. These first few shots reveal many of the central themes of the film. The epic bards, situated, like Ivan, in a natural environment, already suggest the primacy of magnificent nature over insipid culture. Ivan, who is noble and graceful on his own in the forest, regresses in the company of his immature brothers, but his degradation is only partial, as he does not follow them home. In their squalid hut, the brothers expect the father to feed them, but he spills their food on the floor.

It is not altogether clear why a merchant's daughter and noble-woman condescend to marry into this family, but when they do, they introduce chicanery to the previously innocent incompetence of the familial arrangement. Only the arrival of Vasilisa adds an element of order and dignity to the family scene, as she cleans the house and harvests wheat. Unfortunately, the treachery of the upper-class brides leads to her abduction by Zmei Gorynych.

Vasilisa's kidnapping is an opportunity in disguise for Ivan, for only by leaving his home behind can he mature and become a hero. As he departs, his father tells him to seek knowledge among the people. Ivan's development will involve getting to know the people and the land – that is, acquiring a national consciousness. The process of maturation reaches its completion when the young peasant, having travelled beyond the Russian land (and therefore able to apprehend it as a whole in contrast to the dark forest he now enters) is instantaneously transformed into an epic hero.

The mise-en-scène establishes three spatial zones in the film: Ivan's village, the Russian land and the dark forest – the latter consisting of animations and sets reminiscent of the jagged, angular mise-en-scène of German expressionist films. Ivan must leave behind the confining domestic space of his village, mature as he travels the Russian land and defeat the threat emanating from the dark forest. His mission complete, Ivan cannot possibly go back to his dysfunctional village life: he is now an epic hero and a defender of a collective and national Russian space against foreign threats and domestic corruption. But Ivan is no individualist hero: he owes his victory to the power latent in the Russian land and the wisdom of its people.

Vadim Shneyder

Two Captains

Dva kapitana

Country of Origin:
Soviet Union

Language:
Russian

Studio:
Lenfilm

Director:
Vladimir Vengerov

Screenplay:
Veniamin Kaverin
Evgenii Gabrilovich

Cinematographer:
Apollinarii Dudko

Art Director:
David Vinitskii

Composer:
Oleg Karavaichuk

Editor:
Evgeniia Makhan'kova

Synopsis

In a provincial Russian town, the young Sania Grigor'ev finds a bag with letters, which, among other things, refer to a lost Arctic expedition under Captain Tatarinov. After he moves to post-Revolutionary Petrograd, orphaned Sania gets acquainted with Tatarinov's family and decides to find out the truth about the ill-fated expedition. Sania learns that the expedition was ruined by the greed and intrigues of Captain Tatarinov's brother Nikolai, now the director of the school he attends, where Sania also meets the Captain's daughter Katia and falls in love with her. The suicide of Katia's mother, for which Nikolai Tatarinov blames Sania's arrogant insensitivity, separates the two young people for several years. They meet again after Sania has become an Arctic pilot, still pursuing his search for traces of Captain Tatarinov's expedition. Neither World War II, nor the new intrigues of the perished captain's brother and his minion Romashov can prevent Sania from finding the truth about his hero's last days. During an Arctic mission against German warships, he discovers the remnants of the lost expedition.

Critique

Work on the screen adaptation of *Two Captains*, Veniamin Kaverin's *Bildungsroman* which paralleled the stories of a pre-Revolutionary Russian and a Soviet Arctic explorer, started in the Stalinist 1940s. However, the filmic version of the novel appeared only in 1956, just after the Soviet Communist Party's anti-Stalinist Twentieth Party Congress. While Vladimir Vengerov's adaptation could hardly be regarded as radical or controversial, the film's partial renunciation of

Duration:

98 minutes

Genre:

Children's Film
Literary Adaptation
Adventure

Cast:

Aleksandr Mikhailov
Ol'ga Zabotkina
Evgenii Lebedev
Leonid Gallis

Year:

1955

ideological settings in favour of psychological authenticity represented post-Stalinist Soviet culture's shift toward a less constrained model.

Vengerov's film was one of the first successful efforts to establish new cinematic conventions that would transport the still inevitable ideological message in a more palatable manner, with a nod towards international cinema as Soviet audiences got acquainted with foreign films after World War II and with a retrospective look at Russian cultural tradition. The plot-driven, eventful material of Kaverin's novel provided the basis for a cinematic narrative which efficiently discarded secondary details and concentrated on the book's dynamic components. At the same time, the avoidance of suspenseful junctures (in spite of the story's detective and melodramatic aspects and such plot turns as suicide, battlefield betrayal and the discovery of the lost expedition's last stand) subordinated narrative intricacies to a nuanced treatment of the complexities and subtleties of human relationships.

Non-emphatically but compellingly, *Two Captains* represents a transition from the cinema of the late Stalin period to more liberal post-Stalinist aesthetics: the strategy of early post-Stalin cinema, with its search for new themes and motifs, was emblematized by the balanced and transparent technique, as well as the streamlined and reserved narrative dynamic employed by the filmmaker. The aesthetic of representational and stylistic equilibrium and of subdued dynamism – in this particular case borrowed from a canonical socialist realist literary work aimed primarily at younger readers and representing officially approved, ideologically sound entertainment – rejected the static extremism of the Stalin era but, at the same time, sought to avoid conflicts with the emerging political establishment, whose inherent conservatism still demanded non-controversial, ideologically sound artistic works with transparent narratives. *Two Captains* was not only a successful interpretation of a Soviet literary classic, but also an instrument of the 'creeping' subversion of the outdated Stalinist aesthetics.

Sergei Kapterev

The Republic of ShKID

Respublika ShKID

Country of Origin:

Soviet Union

Language:

Russian

Studio:

Lenfilm

Director:

Gennadii Poloka

Synopsis

In the 1920s Leningrad, the Dostoevsky School of Social-Labour Education (ShKID) opens its doors to the first pupils. The students, homeless children from the streets of the city, have a hard time adjusting to the school's discipline and the even rebel when one of their favourite teachers is fired. However, the school's principal, Viktor Nikolaevich Sorokin (Vikniksor as students call him), finds a common language with the pupils based on absolute trust and care. He helps them organize a republic, compose a hymn and suggests self-government, in which student representatives are in charge of all the school activity. But things go wrong when bread disappears from the kitchen; however, the students learn to deal with the culprits themselves. The ShKID pupils also learn about pioneers and, when they are refused membership, they create an organization of their own. The film ends with all the students and pioneers coming together to celebrate

Screenplay:
Aleksei Panteleev

Cinematographers:
Dmitrii Dolinin
Aleksandr Chechulin

Art Directors:
Nikolai Suvorov
Evgenii Gukov

Composer:
Sergei Slonimskii

Duration:
103 minutes

Genre:
Children's Film
Comedy

Cast:
Sergei Iurskii
Pavel Luspekaev
Iuliia Burygina
Aleksandr Mel'nikov
Vera Titova
Anatolii Stolbov

Year:
1966

Mamochka, one of ShKID's ex-students who is in hospital, because he stood up for a pioneer. Vikniksor forgives Mamochka for disappearing with the money earlier and announces that students' secret organization shall be legalized from now on.

Critique

Poloka's *The Republic of ShKID* is based on the famous novella of the same title by Grigorii Belykh and Aleksei Panteleev (pen-name of Aleksei Eremeev, written in 1927). Following the novella's popularity, the film was very popular and became a major box-office success; it became a Soviet classic not only for children, but also for adults and many generations of Russians, who still incorporate quotations from the film into everyday speech, like the famous *ne shali* ('don't be naughty') that the enormous gymnastics teacher repeats to his students. The film has all the vital elements for a Soviet blockbuster: it advocates proper Soviet morals of fairness, responsibility and hard work. It tells about the birth of a nation that takes care of its youngsters, pulling them off the streets, giving them an education and eventually turning them into productive members of a socialist society. All this is accomplished with self-irony and humour, but also with seriousness regarding the difficulties of the student-teacher relationships and the purpose of education in general. Significantly, Poloka managed to convey the atmosphere of post-Civil War Leningrad: poverty and hunger are emphasized both visually and contextually throughout the film. The students have political consciousness: they stage Blok's 'The Twelve' and make 'revolutionary' posters during their 'revolt'.

Vikniksor's rejection of class prejudice for the sake of ideological tolerance represents the values of the Thaw-era intelligentsia. The film starts with the headmasters of different boarding schools rejecting an orphan; only Vikniksor takes him on condition of receiving an

Gennadii Poloka, *The Republic of ShKID* (1966).

extra pair of pants, nails and some sugar (at the orphan's suggestion). Significantly, from the start, the headmaster listens to this young man, and this theme stands at the centre of the film: to overcome prejudice and not approach the students as 'criminals', but take them for what they really are. As the film suggests, they really are intelligent (albeit tricky), energetic and even eager young people who love arts and music, who have different talents and understand honour and fairness. Significantly, it is the teachers – representatives of Russian intelligentsia – who bring forth these qualities. The old school headmaster, who does not believe in violence but in persuasion and respect, earns the students' trust by respecting them. Thus, the students learn to overcome their own preconceptions of intelligentsia. Despite her initial fear of the 'hooligans', the only female teacher at the school, Ella Andreevna Lumberg, controls the pupils in the end by the simple blow of a whistle when confronted by a pioneer leader's statement that the intelligentsia should not be trusted with these kids. Hence, on a different level, the film promulgates a sort of collaboration between the two forces or orders. *The Republic of ShKID* seems to propose not a complete rejection of experience (here embodied in the school staff), but their incorporation. Quite literally, the old intelligentsia's experiences teach a lesson to the new order, the Republic of ShKID, where each participant has his own responsibilities and where teachers are open to the students' suggestions. The film stresses that only with that collaborative effort can the new order function.

Mariya Boston

A Hundred Days after Childhood

Sto dnei posle detstva

Country of Origin:
Soviet Union

Language:
Russian

Studio:
Mosfilm

Director:
Sergei Solov'ev

Producer:
Boris Gostynskii

Synopsis

During a sojourn in a young pioneers' camp, fourteen-year-old Mitia falls in love with his classmate Lena and sets out to win her affection. Over the course of the three summer months (the 'hundred days' of the title) Mitia, inspired by his conversations about art with the charismatic camp counsellor Sergei, attempts to use literature to aid him in his quest. He tries everything from behaving like a fictional character in a novel to performing the part of a jealous, passionate husband to Lena's tragically misunderstood wife in a camp performance of a classical play. But every attempt to impress Lena is ultimately cancelled out by Mitia's vain and cynical nemesis, the teacher's pet Gleb, who turns out to be the true object of Lena's affection. After Mitia finally confronts Lena and learns of his failure, another girl, whose advances Mitia has himself ignored for some time, professes her affection for him; he is unable to return it.

Critique

A Hundred Days after Childhood was Sergei Solov'ev's first film with a contemporary setting. Until then he had only directed screen versions of works from the Russian literary canon: Anton Chekhov, Maksim Gor'kii and Aleksandr Pushkin. Entrusted with what was ostensibly a children's film on a non-controversial topic – a caption at the end

Screenplay:
Aleksandr Aleksandrov
Sergei Solov'ev

Cinematographer:
Leonid Kalashnikov

Art Director:
Aleksandr Borisov

Composer:
Isaak Shvarts

Editor:
Alla Abramova

Duration:
89 minutes

Genre:
Children's Film

Cast:
Tat'iana Drubich
Boris Tokarev
Sergei Shakurov
Irina Malysheva

Year:
1975

of the film defines the theme explicitly as 'sentimental education' – Solov'ev once again turned to the Russian literary tradition. The camp counsellor promotes, and Mitia eventually embraces, the literary cult of Mikhail Lermontov (1814–1841), the author of the novel *A Hero of Our Time*, whose awkward minor character Mitia tries to emulate by putting a fake cast on his leg and parading in front of Lena, and of the drama *Masquerade*, which the campers produce, with Mitia and Lena co-starring as the married couple whose ruin the character played by Gleb effects. The conceit of the film's setting further helps frame the story's well-worn topoi – first love, summer in the country, love triangle – as echoes of a rich and deeply meaningful but mysterious cultural tradition: the camp is housed in an eighteenth-century manor house, complete with a theatre, and cared for by an elderly woman who serves as a living link to the pre-Revolutionary world.

A few telling attributes of Soviet life are strewn about: a young-pioneer necktie here and there, an authoritarian camp director, a vintage socialist realist plot digression involving cabbage-picking that leads to a fight between Mitia and Gleb. But the film gently resists being turned into a Soviet summer-camp satire; unlike Elem Klimov's scathing *Welcome, or No Trespassing* (1964), it does not present camp life as a metaphor or microcosm. That life is instead unobtrusively marginalized, rendered seemingly irrelevant to the film's primary concerns. Klimov's black-and-white grotesque is countered by sequences that flaunt their indulgence in color and soft-focus close-ups to the accompaniment of Isaak Shvarts's poignantly excessive waltz in a minor key. Solov'ev offers no apologies. Michelangelo's sculpting technique and Leonardo's vision for Mona Lisa – however trite (especially for the film's adult viewers), these subjects, discussed breathlessly by the camp counsellor with his students, are what sustains Mitia in the end. Growing up is figured as a discovery of an alternative, though not subversive, aesthetic universe – a discovery that helps transcend rejection and humiliation.

A set of melodramatic narrative and visual clichés about adolescence gives rise to an earnestly self-deprecating statement of the central, abiding and ubiquitous fantasy of the Soviet 1970s: that acute nostalgia for an idealized inaccessible world, be it Russia's cultural legacy, the West or childhood delusions (the film puts forth its visual argument in part by rendering these equivalent), can sublimate, suspend and possibly redeem the daily, unavoidable pressures of politicized realia. The narrative is broken into a brief prologue and thirteen 'chapters', whose titles are announced by captions; while the sequencing of these episodes preserves conventional causality and linearity, the possibility of un-narrated, un-filmable gaps cultivates an illusion of intimacy, of a mythic autonomous sphere of emotion and aesthetic curiosity, on whose existence the film's story of adolescent angst depends for its own artistic redemption. In the 1980s Solov'ev returned over and over to the search for an inaccessible world – with differing degrees of cinematic experimentation, ideological cynicism and appeals to the Russian intelligentsia's famously literature-centric predilections. But the illusory boundary of that world is first charted in a children's film that seeks to educate the sentiments by suspending history.

Boris Wolfson

The Scarecrow

Chuchelo

Country of Origin:
Soviet Union

Language:
Russian

Studio:
Mosfilm

Director:
Rolan Bykov

Screenplay:
Vladimir Zheleznikov
Rolan Bykov

Cinematographer:
Anatolii Mukasei

Art Director:
Evgenii Markovich

Composer:
Sofiia Gubaidulina

Editor:
Liudmila Elian

Duration:
127 minutes

Genre:
Children's Film
Social Problem Film

Cast:
Iurii Nikulin
Kristina Orbakaite
Elena Sanaeva
Mitia Egorov
Rolan Bykov

Year:
1983

Synopsis

Lena Bessol'tseva comes to a new school in a provincial town, where she moves in with her grandfather, an art collector. On the first day of school she gets the nickname 'Scarecrow' for being a little awkward and smiling too much. The true troubles start when a class trip to Moscow is cancelled because of their skipping a class and going to the movies instead. Lena's new friend, Dima Somov, accidentally runs into Margarita Ivanovna, their teacher, and tells her where everyone is. The film then revolves around the issue of betrayal: Dima denounced his classmates to the teacher, thus everyone is punished. Lena then tells her classmates that she did it and becomes an outcast, hated by everyone. She, however, believes that Dima will eventually tell the truth, but every time he has a chance, he fails to do so. The class-mates' hatred eventually forces Lena out of town. Her grandfather goes away with her, bestowing his art collection on the town. He also gives a portrait that looks just like Lena to the school. Dima finally tells the truth, but it is too late: Bessol'tseva is gone.

Critique

'I am not afraid of anyone', says the main heroine, Lena Bessol'tseva. This sentence in a way reflects one the most important ideas in the film. *The Scarecrow*, based on Vladimir Zheleznikov's novella, tells a story of fear and bravery, honour and betrayal, true friendship and first love. The story, however, is complicated by the fact that it is twelve year olds who have to deal with all these issues. For them, there are no grey areas – one is either best friend or enemy, coward or hero, loved or hated. Just like many Western films, and unlike Soviet 'school' films, *The Scarecrow* focuses on the children's cruelty. The fire scene seems to be the epiphany of ruthlessness: the pupils burn a scarecrow dressed in Lena's clothes and make her watch it. Lena pulls down her effigy, saves her dress and thus metaphorically saves herself, taking control of the situation. This symbolical burning gives her new power. She forgives Dima 'because she was on fire', but she does not care any more, because she is not longer afraid to be judged.

As often happens, children's cruelty is influenced by the relation-ships with their parents. Marina, one of the classmates, is upset about not going to Moscow because she misses her father who lives there and because she cannot stand her mother. The 'steel button' Mironova, who never cries, always follows the rules and cannot forgive traitors, at the end of the film cries out that everyone around her is 'just like' her mother, who wants everything done hush-hush. Thus, Bykov seems to suggest that a lot of the children's problems stem from the parents, or from a lack of a relationship with them. The adults never interfere with the children's troubles, which, as it appears, poses a problem in itself. Adults never really show any interest in the children's affairs and are often presented as bystanders. This is repeat-edly emphasized visually, when the audience's attention is drawn to the adults on the screen rather than the children in the background. Raised by single mothers, alcoholic fathers and grandparents, the chil-

Rolan Bykov, *The Scarecrow* (1982). Lena.

dren are forced to create their own (cruel) rules in order to make sense of their world, to distinguish between true friends and enemies. Thus, the problem of alienation and hatred as raised in the film is social as much as psychological.

The Scarecrow gives two different parts of the story. The first one is presented through flashbacks as Lena tells her grandfather about the cancelled trip to Moscow and everything that leads up to it. The second part deals mostly with the present which, however, does not bring a true resolution. On the contrary, the film ends on a rather pessimistic note: Lena leaves the town with her grandfather, who abandons all his beloved paintings. Her classmates feel incredibly guilty and remorseful as they realize that she is a most honourable person. Nevertheless, they are not brave enough to apologize directly to Lena and can do so only when she is gone, writing 'Forgive us, Scarecrow' on the board above the lookalike portrait. Lena, on the other hand, has come to say goodbye and forgive Dima. Her grandfather, who listened to her and tried to support her, played a key role for her confidence. Perhaps this could be read as Bykov's commentary on society in general, where children feel unloved, ignored and misunderstood and where physical and emotional tortures go unnoticed.

Mariya Boston

Tough Boys

Patsany

Country of Origin:
Soviet Union

Language:
Russian

Studio:
Lenfilm

Director:
Dinara Asanova

Screenplay:
Iurii Klepikov

Cinematographer:
Iurii Veksler

Art Directors:
Natal'ia Vasil'eva
Vladimir Svetozarov

Composers:
Viktor Kisin
Vitalii Chernitskii

Editor:
Tamara Lipartiia

Duration:
97 minutes

Genre:
Children's Film
Youth Drama
Social Problem Film

Cast:
Aleksei Poluian
Valerii Priemykhov
Ol'ga Mashnaia
Ekaterina Vasil'eva
Zinovii Gerdt
Marina Levtova
Iurii Moroz
Lidiia Fedoseeva-Shukshina

Year:
1983

Synopsis

Instead of becoming a sports coach, Pavel Vasil'evich has taken on the responsibility of supervising and educating a group of teen hooligans in a rural summer camp. To the boys he is known as Pasha. He has created a commune where all the participants must contribute to the collective efforts. In the evenings all the members of the camp gather for open assemblies where issues are discussed and birthdays celebrated. In contrast to his assistant Oleg Pavlovich, Pasha does not consider himself to be an educator whose task it is to discipline the children; instead, he sees himself as an older brother to the boys. One day, when Pasha is in town, the boys stage a rebellion after an altercation with Oleg Pavlovich. In the process, they destroy much of the camp. When Pasha returns, he is undeniably angry as he feels that his trust has been broken. The boys try to rebuild what they have destroyed and earn Pasha's forgiveness. In the end, when one of the boys runs off to the city, all the boys follow Pasha to demonstrate their allegiance to him.

Critique

A classic of late stagnation-era Soviet cinema, *Tough Boys* begins with a documentary-style montage of scenes of troubled teens being asked questions about their misdeeds. The final question posed is 'Who is a kind person?' to which the boys have difficulty answering. In a juvenile court Vova Kireev is being sentenced for petty theft. Pavel Vasil'evich pleads with the judge to allow him to take Vova with him to his camp. At fifteen, Vova is malnourished, he tells the judge: he has never known a parent's love and is embarrassed about his lacks and ashamed for himself, which shows that the boy has a conscience. The judge agrees.

Nearly all of the film's action takes place on the grounds of a makeshift lakeside camp and is shot in grainy colour. Pasha encourages the children every evening before dinner by asking them to think of a good deed they have done in the course of that day. Pasha operates differently from the younger Oleg Pavlovich, a hot-headed and feared figure, who sees the children in an 'us vs them' relationship. According to him, the goal of the camp is to turn the boys into men, whereas for Pasha the goal is to 'awaken their hearts'. These are boys that must be loved, he states.

Much of the first half details preparation for a visitor's day. Many relatives and friends arrive with gifts. One boy is visited by his grandmother: when he asks where his mother is, she tells him right away that she is drinking again. Another boy is visited by his father, who is inebriated during the ceremony. The parents of one particularly troubled youth who has escaped across the river (and whom Pasha nonetheless periodically visits and feeds) arrive to see their son. Pasha rows them across the river, but the boys have moved on from their spot. These parents differ from the others, as they belong to the intelligentsia. Pasha encourages them to take their son home and raise him properly, but they seem utterly confounded as to how to deal with their child.

Valerii Priemykhov in the lead role won the USSR State Prize in 1984 for his work in the film. He is outstanding and utterly convincing in the role, capturing Pasha's compassion, disappointment and patience. While the weariness occasionally shows on his face, Pasha goes to great lengths to explain to judges, documentary filmmakers and parents why his camp is important and why the children should be loved and cared for. The children, led by Andrei Zykov as Vova Kireev, form a brilliant acting ensemble. They effortlessly portray the confusion, sadness, deviance and misplaced goodness of these tough, yet fragile and helpless youths. Dinara Asanova's brilliant direction allows the actors to shape the action. Many of the cast are non-professionals, and a number of scenes were improvised, allowing for an extremely natural feel to the film. Asanova was posthumously awarded a USSR State Prize.

Music is the centrepiece of the film, with songs (by Vitalii Chernitskii and Viktor Bolshakov) acting alternately on the sidelines and in the centre of the action. It is not a musical, however, and there is no forced importance of the music. The soundtrack seamlessly moves from the background to the foreground and fades out again. Occasionally the songs are performed by a few of the boys as an ensemble, while at other times they resemble singalongs with Pasha joining in the choruses. All the songs are communal and melancholy, and they compliment rather than upstage the action of the film. Many have become classics in their own right, among them 'I Called for My Horse' and 'Shirt of a Nettle Leaf'.

Joe Crescente

Freedom is Paradise

S.E.R. (Svoboda – eto rai)

Country of Origin:
Soviet Union

Language:
Russian

Studio:
Mosfilm

Director:
Sergei Bodrov Sr

Screenplay:
Sergei Bodrov Sr

Synopsis

In the courtyard of a special school it is announced that Sasha has escaped. Sasha boards a bus and arrives at Klava's to ask about his father's whereabouts; he wants his father to recognize him as his son. Klava, though, turns him in and Sasha is given one last warning. But Sasha escapes again, this time by hiding in a truck. He gets help from a woman whom he has just attempted to rob, but with cash in hand and travelling by train, he manages to get closer to the labour camp in Arkhangel'sk where his father is in prison. But once again, Sasha is caught. Before he is taken back, Sasha swallows a large nail and, when at the hospital for an x-ray, he runs. Back on the train, he is caught stealing, but jumps from the toilet window off the train. Now on foot, Sasha continues his journey hitchhiking. A truck takes him to a port, where Sasha boards a ship. He finally reaches the labour camp. However, his dad is in isolation and cannot receive visitors. But the colonel in charge allows Sasha to see his father and stay overnight. The father realizes that he has no one except Sasha and promises to be there for Sasha when he is released. Sasha, on the other hand, is taken back to the school in Kazakhstan.

Cinematographer:
Iurii Skhirtladze

Art Director:
Valerii Kostrin

Composer:
Aleksandr Raskatov

Editor:
Natal'ia Kutserenko

Duration:
90 minutes

Genre:
Youth Drama

Cast:
Vladimir Kozyrev
Aleksandr Bureev
Svetlana Gaitan
Vitautas Tomkus

Year:
1989

Critique

SER was produced by Mosfilm and based on Bodrov's short story *Cross-Eyed Sasha*. The film enjoyed success outside the Soviet Union, which was rare for a film of this kind. *SER* is not a subversive film that challenges the socialist system: Sasha is brought back to his institution and Sasha's father shows signs of remorse and wants to change at the end of the film. Yet *SER* is also ahead of its time: its cinematic style, simplistic narrative and play on audience emotions are features that would become typical of popular films of the 1990s. Already when the opening credits roll, accompanied by the song 'Goodbye America' of Nautilus Pompilius, Bodrov's immersion in underground and youth culture becomes clear. Nautilus' song about the old jeans becoming too small reflects back on Sasha in *SER* and his desire for escaping the institutions that holds him. The forbidden fruit that Sasha has learnt to love is distrust in the system that has bred him. Sasha is at the bottom, as he once points out, of an allegedly classless society that sees male dominance and militarism ruling people's lives; everyone is encaged, just as the animals Sasha encounters at the zoo. Women are marginalized as paid prostitutes (the woman Sasha robs) or as seeking male patronage in order to get by (Klava). While the men are in command,

Sergei Bodrov, *S.E.R* (1989).

leisurely getting treatment from the children at the school, the women lack maternal instincts (they abandon their kids, as for example Sasha's grandmother). This is a serious simplification of gender roles that has its origin in the stagnation period and in popular films like *Moscow Does Not Believe in Tears* (1980) and continued in post-Soviet films.

Bodrov's film does not pass judgement on its characters (male or female); rather it functions like the snapshots of Japan that one of the orphans shows. Disinterested and formulaic, Japan is reduced to a few learnt phrases accompanied by clichéd pictures. In the same way, Bodrov steps back from deepening and explaining the adult characters of the film; they are one-dimensional, flat stereotypes. However, this leaves Sasha with agency and an internal naturalness. Sasha's environs (human or nature) are reduced – the flat landscape, the road where only military trucks pass, the journeys on bus, train or boat, all of which enhance Sasha's character as he has only one goal: to see his father. Bodrov squeezes the story to the plight of a child, but in turn reveals the absurd world of adults that is the Soviet Union. While Sasha is only one of many boys for whom freedom is paradise, it is the individualized fixation on Sasha that makes the story transgress to a universal level; even Sasha's x-ray offers a chance to 'peek' inside him, to find the 'nail' that causes all the trouble. Yet Bodrov gives no definite answers. Focusing on a child protagonist would become one of Bodrov's trademarks: the child protagonist instils empathy in audiences, which is well illustrated when Sasha hangs from the toilet window of the running train, indicating both how desperate Sasha is and how we, as viewers, have invested our emotion in him. The viewer has become part of his blurry world, and this subjectivity is underlined by the fading colours and slow-motion sequence after the jump. Bodrov excels precisely at placing the spectator inside the main character.

Lars Kristensen

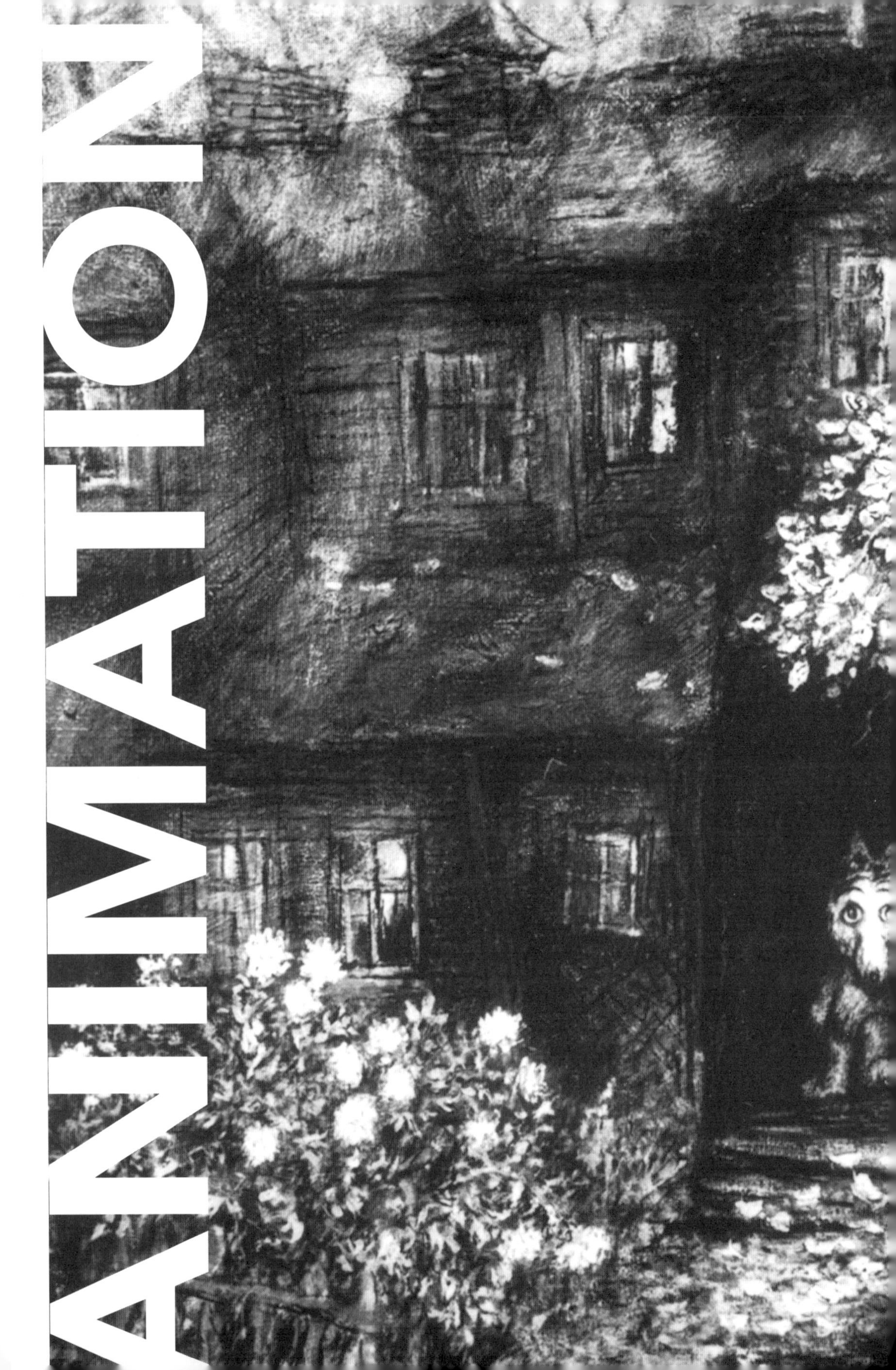
ANIMATION

Władysław Starewicz is traditionally considered the 'father' of Russian animation; he was also the world's first puppet animator (although recently discovered footage of Aleksandr Shiryaev predates and surpasses Starewicz's work – even if these films were not made for the public). *The Cameraman's Revenge* (1912) and *The Dragonfly and the Ant* (1913) were parables of modern life set in the world of insects and flowers. Starewicz's interest in insects led him to use artificially created beetles, turning them into anthropomorphic figures with clear human features.

After the Revolution Starewicz emigrated to France and it was graphic art which came to the fore in the development of drawn animation. Dziga Vertov was inspired by the *Pravda* cartoonist Viktor Deni for his animated film *Soviet Toys* (1924), parodying the New Economic Policy that had introduced some private enterprise to boost the economy. Yet cartoons were still a by-product of a department of Mezhrabpomfilm working on caricatures, ads and film titles. Ivan Ivanov-Vano (1900–1987) agreed with the studio's head that he would make an independent cartoon based on Kornei Chukovskii's story 'Crocodile': the resulting film, *Senka, the African Boy* (1927) opens with real-life footage of a boy visiting the zoo, where he finds a book about African animals. The pictures carry the boy on an imaginary journey to the distant land. This framing device became typical for Soviet cartoons, suggesting that the animated world is a fantasy world. These early cartoons were made by projecting the negative image onto a mirror, as cel became available in the Soviet Union only after 1934. The Leningrad book illustrator Mikhail Tsekhanovskii (1889–1965) created *The Post* (Lenfilm, 1929), based on a story by the Soviet children's writer Samuil Marshak; it consists of sophisticated and detailed black-and-white drawings. A boy is sitting at a table, writing a letter for Boris Prutkov; the cartoon follows the journey of this letter around the world and praises the reliance of the Soviet postal system.

In 1936 the animation studio Soiuzmultfilm was established with a remit to produce cartoons for children. By the mid-1930s Disney

had firmly established the cartoon as a powerful tool for entertainment. Soviet anima-
tors, largely trained as designers and illustrations, were drawn upon to compete with the
Disney output. Later, in 1939, Ivanov-Vano founded the Department of Animation at the
Film Institute in Moscow (VGIK). Moreover, animation had to adapt to sound technology,
setting the movement of characters to melodies. Tsekhanovskii's adaptation of Pushkin's
Tale of the Priest and his Worker Balda, a musical set to a score composed by Dmitrii
Shostakovich, was halted by the censors in 1934 because of the satirical approach to a
classical work. The innovator Aleksandr Ptushko (1900–1973) used combined shots to
achieve tricks in the style of Melies, stunning audiences by life-size humans in the same
frame as little puppets in his *New Gulliver* (1935).

During the war Soiuzmultfilm was evacuated to Samarkand, where the lack of production facilities made it impossible for work to continue. After returning to its production
base in Moscow, Soiuzmultfilm produced a number of drawn cartoons based on fairy
tales, in an attempt to compete with Disney's *Snow White* (1937). The fairy tale suited
propaganda purposes for two reasons: it relied on Russia's national heritage, and it
contained an element of moral instruction. The fairy tale's hero is granted magic help as
a reward for a good deed, while the fairy tale world offers an escape from an unpleasant reality, instructing children while turning both punishment and reward over into the
realms of the magic world. The animated fairy tale also instilled moral values, and thus
occupied a niche left by ideological instruction, namely that of teaching children a sense
of right and wrong.

Animators took full advantage of the possibilities that cel offered for the movement
of animals and humans. Ivanov-Vano elaborated those features that made animals
more comic and flexible than humans. A good example is his animation of the horse in
The Humpbacked Horse (1947, remake 1975), the USSR's first full-length animated film:
the clever, resourceful and witty little horse moves with great expediency across the
country.

The Brumberg Sisters' *Fedia Zaitsev* (1948) revealed the instructive potential of the
cartoon in a contemporary context: the Soviet schoolboy Fedia returns to the newly
decorated school after the summer vacation and draws a smiley face onto the wall. Fedia
does not confess even when his friend is suspected. Plagued by a bad conscience, Fedia
is tormented in his sleep by his toys as they turn on him: he admits his deed the next
day. Fedia lives in a world of toys and tin soldiers and has no contact with the outside
world: the child is essentially secluded and isolated. Indeed, Soviet children of the 1960s
and 1970s no longer have a social role, but withdraw from the collective to the toy world
that teaches human values of love and comfort.

The encouragement of animation to produce cartoons for adults from the 1960s
onwards is indicative of a broader *auteur* tendency in cinema. Fedor Khitruk's *History of
a Crime* (1962) is an example of this, offering a critique of contemporary society (housing
problems, alcoholism, monotony of life), for which the cartoon was criticized in the Soviet
Union but won international acclaim. Cartoons for adults tended to cause more controversy, as they were critical and often satirical of modern life. Indeed, the only cartoon
banned in Soviet history is Andrei Khrzhanovskii's *Glass Harmonica* (1968), a satire on
bureaucracy.

In the late 1960s cartoons for television reach large audiences. *Just You Wait* (1969–1987,
17 series) by Viacheslav Kotenochkin explored the conflict between the wolf and the
hare/rabbit, which has a long-standing tradition in Russian folk tales and fables. It
replicated in a modified way the cat-and-mouse conflict of Disney's *Tom and Jerry*
(1940–1957). The late 1960s also saw adaptations of foreign and contemporary children's
stories, such as Boris Stepantsev's cartoons based on Astrid Lindgren's *Karlsson* stories,
but more importantly the popular cartoon versions of A.A. Milne's *Winnie the Pooh* created by Fedor Khitruk.

During the 1970s cartoons are increasingly concerned with the role of the child in the modern world. Toys appear as cartoon characters and animals acquire toy-like features in their movement, bringing puppets back into animation. Roman Kachanov and the designer Leonid Shvartsman created the most important puppet of Soviet animation: Cheburashka. Kachanov's fine and sensitive understanding of the children's world as superior to the adults' world is evident in his puppet animation *The Mitten* (1967), but it is Eduard Uspenskii's story 'Crocodile Gena and his Friends', which he turned into four cartoons, that brought his success. Cheburashka is a loveable toy: yellow-brown and fluffy, with large ears and rolling eyes; she is a cross-mixture of a teddy bear and an orange. Cheburashka wins our hearts and needs our empathy because she does not belong anywhere. Indeed, Cheburashka became the Mickey Mouse of Soviet animation and the emblem of the studio Soiuzmultfilm.

Uspenskii's stories about Prostokvashino were turned into cel-animated film by Vladimir Popov in the late 1970s. The cartoons trace the loneliness of a boy from the city, which is remedied in the countryside and through the company of a cat and a dog. The theme of isolation also inspired Fedor Khitruk's award-winning cartoon *Island* (1974) about a man stranded on a desert island, and the theme also preoccupied Iurii Norshtein, whose world famous *Tale of Tales* (1979) is a metaphor for isolation composed of memories about a wartime childhood.

With the demise of the Soviet Union in 1991 the main cartoon studio, Soiuzmultfilm, folded its production branch. A variety of animation studios were established, but most cartoons from this decade were screened only at festivals. Many animators moved into advertising to earn a living. Garri Bardin founded his studio Staier, where he created the puppet animated *Choocha* (three parts, 1998–2005), a non-verbal cartoon based on the tunes of Glenn Miller. The studio Pilot was founded in 1988 by Aleksandr Tatarskii, who created the 'Pilot Brothers' series (1990s), featuring two plain drawn characters who comment on modern life, providing a satirical gloss on politics. In 2005 Tatarskii launched *The Mountain of Gems* which produces a series of short cartoons based on folk tales. This project has helped established and young cartoonists to experiment with the short form and to reach an audience through the release of the series on DVD.

A major breakthrough for Russian animation came when the Yaroslavl animator Aleksandr Petrov won Russia the first Academy Award (Oscar) in animation for *The Old Man and the Sea* in 2000, the first cartoon made for 70mm format, in a technique of oil painting on glass. The Petersburg studio Melnitsa, founded in 1992, has played an active part in creating animation that is viable for distribution, co-producing Konstantin Bronzit's feature-length cartoon *Alesha Popovich and Tugarin the Dragon* (2004), a drawn animation about the Russian folk hero Alesha Popovich who features as the Russian superman: he is dumb, but innately good, and although he cannot read or write, his muscles can shift rocks and mountains. His speech caricatures the incorrect language of the New Russians: Alesha's body is muscular, but his brain is underdeveloped. The style was continued in Ilia Maksimov's *Dobrynia Nikitich and Gorynych the Dragon* (2006) and *Ilia Muromets and Robber-Nightingale* (2007), directed by Vladimir Toropchin. The commercial success of these new Russian cartoons – *Alesha Popovich* had a budget of $4 million, grossing $1.7 million; *Dobrynia Nikitich* had a budget of $4.5 million and grossed $ 3.5 million, while *Ilia Muromets* had a budget of $2 million and grossed $9.8 million on the Russia market – gives hope for the future.

Birgit Beumers

The Cameraman's Revenge

Mest' kinematograficheskogo operatora

Country of Origin:
Russia

Language:
Russian (intertitles)

Studio:
Khanzhonkov

Director:
Wladyslaw Starewicz

Producer:
Aleksandr Khanzhonkov

Screenplay:
Wladyslaw Starewicz

Cinematographer:
Wladyslaw Starewicz

Art Director:
Wladyslaw Starewicz

Duration:
13 minutes

Genre:
Puppet Animation

Year:
1912

Synopsis

The Cameraman's Revenge is the story of Mr and Mrs Zhukov, a pair of beetles. Mr Zhukov feels restless at home and frequents a cabaret, the 'Merry Dragonfly' (*Veselaia strekoza*), where a beautiful dragonfly performs as a dancer. On this particular visit, Zhukov fights a grasshopper for the dancer's attention and emerges victorious, taking the dragonfly back to the Hotel d'Amour. Unfortunately for Mr Zhukov, the grasshopper is a cameraman who secretly films the entire affair between Mr Zhukov and the dragonfly, including what the grasshopper sees through the keyhole of the hotel room. Meanwhile, Mr Zhukov's wife sends a note to her own lover, an artist, who comes to visit her. Mr Zhukov returns home and proceeds to find and chase out his wife's lover, despite the artist's attempt to sneak out through the chimney. Mr Zhukov forgives his wife and takes her to the movies. The projectionist is none other than the grasshopper-cameraman, who shows footage of Mr Zhukov's affair, which he titles *The Unfaithful Husband*. The couple begins to fight, accidentally setting fire to the projection room in the process. The final intertitle suggests that their home life will hopefully be less exciting now that they live together in jail.

Critique

The Cameraman's Revenge reflects Starewicz's fascination with technological innovations. The film not only features several of Starewicz's own experiments with technology, such as the use of stop-motion animation of puppet insects and the inclusion of scenes from *The Cameraman's Revenge* itself projected at a cinema within the film, but it also possesses a plot-line that is dependent on filmmaking, a new technology. The resolution of the melodrama in *The Cameraman's Revenge* can only occur after it is filmed and shown on screen. The film also includes several minor, realistic details related to cinema and the filmmaking process. The grasshopper-cameraman is concerned with transporting his large camera and tripod and adjusting the camera to get the perfect shot. His finished product, *The Unfaithful Husband*, even features the Khanzhonkov film studio name and logo.

    The Cameraman's Revenge also serves as a parody of a popular genre of early Russian cinema: the melodrama. The film features the typical characters of an early twentieth-century melodrama and their frivolous lifestyles. Mr Zhukov is a hot-tempered, jealous businessman, with double standards for his behaviour and for that of his wife. His wife stays at home by the fireplace and is waited on by their servant. Both Mr Zhukov's lover, a dancer, and his wife's lover, a painter, are stereotyped by their relationship to art and entertainment, implying that their lives are centred on superficial activities. These characters ride in cars, unlike the grasshopper-cameraman who travels by bicycle, and have the time and means to go to the movies as a leisure-time activity. The fact that these characters are all insects gives the film a parodic tone. The use of insects as main characters facilitates the mocking of the sensationalist melodrama's excessive use of violence and eroticism. Violence turns to comedy as the insects enact scenes that would seem serious if performed by human actors, such as the fight between Mr Zhukov and the grasshopper. Starewicz also uses elements of slapstick comedy, including Mr Zhukov's destruction of a painting by smashing it over his wife's head. Depicting insects in compromising sexual situations ruins the erotic appeal that these scenes would have otherwise had. By applying new experimentation with stop-motion animation and new technology to a familiar genre, Starewicz creates a parodic masterpiece unlike anything that had appeared on the screen before.

Erin Alpert

Soviet Toys

Sovetskie igrushki

Country of Origin:
Soviet Union

Language:
Russian (intertitles)

Studio:
Goskino (Kul'tkino)

Director:
Dziga Vertov

Screenplay:
Dziga Vertov

Cinematographer:
Aleksandr Dorn

Art Directors:
Aleksandr Ivanov
Ivan Beliakov

Duration:
11 minutes

Genre:
Drawn Animation

Year:
1924

Synopsis

This early Soviet animation enacts many of the diverse political and newsworthy events of the early 1920s, which appeared in the newspaper *Pravda*. The animation encourages citizens of the Soviet Union to join the Soviet worker, the Soviet peasant and the Red Army against the evil forces who are working with the NEPman (New Economic Policy) against the Soviet State. The Soviet worker and peasant battle the gluttonous behaviour of the NEPman, work together to control the two priests representing the schism in the Russian Orthodox Church and use a pair of scissors to represent the common man's triumph over the Scissors Crisis, a period in early NEP when there was a widening gap between industrial and agricultural prices. *Soviet Toys* also pays homage to the power of advertisement and the role of film advertising in saving the Soviet economy from NEPmen. Just before the ending of *Soviet Toys* the appearance of the advertising man forces the NEPman to shrink back down to size, so that advertisement of state goods is the ultimate destroyer of the NEPman's power.

Critique

While demonstrating Vertov's early theory and cinematic techniques, *Soviet Toys* offers the viewer a greater understanding of the nexus between 1920s politics and agitational journalism. Like Vertov's *Kinoprada*, his early newsreels, *Soviet Toys* draws directly from the news of the day. The film uses current political events from the newspaper *Pravda* and the work of political cartoonist Viktor Deni as inspiration. Deni's political cartoons and *Soviet Toys* are strikingly similar in their depictions of the position of the so-called NEPmen and NEPwomen (products of the New Economic Policy), the schism in the Russian Orthodox Church, and the union of the peasant and worker.

The image designs and animation in *Soviet Toys* have raised questions about the technical competence of these early Soviet animators. The image design for *Soviet Toys* deliberately alternates crude childish drawings and more elaborate iris shots. Despite the apparently incomplete and primitive quality of the animation for this time, Vertov is intentionally playing on viewers' familiarity of news print media. For

Dziga Vertov, *Soviet Toys* (1924).

example, there is very little depth or detail to the Red Army Soldiers, the Worker and the Peasant who look like caricatures from the newspaper. Early animators rely on an iris shot to economize the drawings and cut-outs and to effectively create more complete personalities for the characters. The iris shot, a transition analogous to the fade-in used in early silent film, forces the viewer to focus on something particular; the rest of the screen is blacked out. One of the most extensive uses of the iris shot is during the section of the film devoted to the Scissor Crisis, the period in early NEP when a widening gap between industrial and agricultural prices appeared. This gap reached a peak in October of 1923 when industrial prices were three times greater than agricultural prices. During this time peasants' incomes fell and it became impossible for peasants to buy manufactured goods. As a result NEPmen were subjected to various taxes and other restrictions on their ability to conduct commerce. In the film the worker and the peasant come together to crush the NEPman's stomach, which the priests are hiding behind. Money rolls out of the NEPman's stomach and straight into the People's Bank. Iris shots magnify the fear in the NEPman's face and in the faces of the Old and the New churchmen.

The last iris shot in the scene is a close-up of the peasant's traditional blunt-pointed hand-woven bast shoe tearing into the NEPman's stomach as if he were made of newspaper like Deni's cartoons.

Vertov's *Soviet Toys* is more than just an animated version of his newsreel featuring newsworthy events; it also pays homage to the power of advertisement and the role of film advertising in saving the Soviet economy from the NEPmen. Just before the ending the audience is once again reminded of the importance of film advertising. A man with a propeller for a mouth and camera lenses for eyes is shown with a sign for film advertisement within Goskino. The appearance of the Soviet advertising man forces the NEPman to shrink back down to size, so that advertisement of state goods is the ultimate destroyer of the NEPman's power. In Vertov's *Soviet Toys* the power of animation and advertisement bolster the Soviet economy through the advertising services of Goskino. In the last scenes of the animation the NEPman, the NEPwoman and the Russian Orthodox priests, who all represent the past, are shown hanging from a tree built from Red Army soldiers.

Lora Wheeler Mjolsness

The Post

Pochta

Country of Origin:
Soviet Union

Language:
Russian (intertitles)

Studio:
Sovkino Leningrad

Director:
Mikhail Tsekhanovskii

Screenplay:
Samuil Marshak

Cinematographer:
Konstantin Kirillov

Art Director:
Mikhail Tsekhanovskii

Composer:
Vladimir Deshevev

Duration:
30 minutes

Synopsis

A boy is sitting at a table, writing a letter for Boris Prutkov. The cartoon follows the journey of this letter from Rostov to Leningrad, where its addressee Prutkov has just left for Berlin; when the letter arrives in Berlin, Prutkov has just departed for London; as the letter arrives in London, Prutkov is already on a steamboat to Brazil; and once the letters is delivered by the postman Don Basilio, Prutkov is already on his way back to Leningrad – where the letter, having followed Prutkov around the world, finally reaches him. The film sings a song of praise to the global postal services and to the reliability of the postmen, but it also tells the story of a journey around the world, returning once more to the new Soviet capital: Leningrad.

Critique

The book illustrator Mikhail Tsekhanovskii (1889–1965) created one of the earliest drawn cartoons with *The Post*, based on a story by the Soviet children's writer Samuil Marshak. The animation consists of sophisticated and detailed black-and-white drawings and uses the new sound technology with music specially composed by Vladimir Deshevov. Tsekhanovskii begins with a white on black paper cut-out showing a boy sitting at a desk. His letter is drawn in subtle grey shades, with an authentic wax seal and stamps in the corner of the envelope, and the squiggly handwriting of a child for the address. The postmen in each country are characterized through elements of local colour that make them typical for a whole nation: the Russian postman is efficient and agile, climbing the stairs with no trouble: he is an example of the new energetic Soviet worker; the German postman is

Genre:
Animation

Year:
1929

fat and plump, proud of his uniform with shiny buttons and plied trousers; the English postman is cold-faced and shows no emotions; the Brazilian postman is dressed leisurely, making his postal round appear like a stroll through the jungle. The means of transport by which the letter is carried from one place to another are carefully chosen and poignantly illustrated. The journey from Leningrad to Berlin is by train and involves going through a tunnel that turns to a vortex, which echoes the motion of the train's wheels. Prutkov, in the meantime, travels by air – with the plane offering a superior, aerial view onto the world. The sea passage to Brazil sees the steamship in turbulent waters, and the vessel seems to be not as safe as train or plane (Soviet symbols of the conquest and appropriation of the vast Soviet lands). Finally, the return from South America to Leningrad happens by plane and zeppelin; both vehicles travel around the globe, which is displayed as a ball with the letters 'USSR' usurping half of the round.

The sound version (1930) with the text spoken by Daniil Kharms appears to be lost. The film was remade by Tsekhanovskii himself in a wide-screen version in 1964. The original 1929 version was restored by the studio Shar in 1996.

Birgit Beumers

The Humpbacked Horse

Konek-Gorbunok

Country of Origin:
Soviet Union

Language:
Russian

Studio:
Soiuzmultfilm

Director:
Ivan Ivanov-Vano

Producer:
Boris Vol'f

Screenplay:
Evgenii Pomeshchikov
Nikolai Rozhkov

Cinematographer:
Nikolai Voinov

Art Director:
Lev Mil'chin

Synopsis

Ivan, the youngest of three sons, catches a magical horse, which has been ruining his family's fields. In return for her freedom the horse gives Ivan two beautiful horses and a funny little humpbacked horse. The humpbacked horse becomes Ivan's faithful companion. After the tsar has purchased the two beautiful horses, Ivan agrees to work as his stable master. Encouraged by the former stable master, the tsar forces Ivan to carry out three impossible tasks, including catching the firebird and capturing the tsar-maiden. With the help of the humpbacked horse, the carefree Ivan is successful, but when he brings back the tsar-maiden she refuses to marry the old tsar. Instead, she suggests that the tsar turn himself young by climbing into three fiery cauldrons filled with cold water, boiling water and milk. The tsar orders Ivan to take his place and the humpbacked horse is locked up to prevent his involvement. At the last moment the humpbacked horse manages to break free and save Ivan one last time. The tsar-maiden's task transforms Ivan into a handsome youth, while the tsar boils himself to death. The story ends as the tsar-maiden and Ivan go into the palace together.

Critique

Ivanov-Vano's animated film *The Humpbacked Horse* is based on a narrative poem of the same title written by Petr Ershov in 1834. Ivanov-Vano selected Ershov's tale for his first full-length animated feature for its folk language, its humorous heroes and its fantastical escapes, which he believed complemented the medium of animation.

Composer:

Viktor Oranskii

Duration:

58 minutes

Genre:

Animation

Voices:

V. Iastrebova
Iu. Chernovolenko
Galina Novozhilova
Anatolii Kubatskii
Alik Kachanov
Georgii Milliar
Valentina Sperantova
Leonid Pirogov

Year:

1947

After World War II many animators turned to folklore as a source of inspiration as it was considered an art form of national importance. Ershov's original has been noted for its folk sense and Ivanov-Vano follows Ershov's path in the creation of his film. *The Humpbacked Horse* features Russian folk paintings, architecture, ceramics, toys and woodcuts to create the mood for the film, but this is only part of what makes *The Humpbacked Horse* stand apart from other animations of this time.

This animation strives to bring the real and fantastic together so that the fairy tale is felt; nevertheless, Ivanov-Vano's focus is on the satirical premise of Ershov's tale, which is rendered chiefly through characterization. Every character in the film has its own personality, distinguishing characteristics and mannerisms. For example, the tsar has a child-like quality about him, which makes him look infantile and capricious. His robes are too big on him and they hang over his hands and over his feet. The tsar and Ivan also have the same baby-round nose and rosy-fat cheeks, which are associated with youth. The tsar also has the tendency to flap his arms and over-gesticulate with his hands, giving him a comical appearance. The power the tsar wields over Ivan contrasts highly with his image creating a satirical version of a ruler. The full-length format of this film allows Ivanov-Vano to successfully create complex characters who reference not only Ershov's original, but also Soviet ideas about past rulers and their relationships to the common people.

The film has both shortcomings as well as strengths in technical competence. The lack of fluidity in movement and lack of rhythm between characters' movements is often noted, but Ivanov-Vano

Ivan Ivanov-Vano, *The Humpbacked Horse* (1947).

worked diligently on the use of colour to strengthen the emotional reception of certain scenes. This colour principle is first used in the scene where the tsar receives the firebird's feather. In his bedchamber the tsar is asleep in half-darkness lit only by the flickering of candle-light and the chamber is depicted in browns, greys and dark reds. The former stable master wakes the tsar and presents the feather. Suddenly a blinding light flares from the feather and engulfs the half-dark bedchamber in light. The chamber is shown in yellows, tans and brighter reds. Ivanov-Vano uses colour in the same manner during the scene when the firebird is caught. This colour principle brings a fairy tale-like and fantastic atmosphere to these scenes and allows Ivanov-Vano to link both the visual and dramatic experiences of the tale, thus creating a stylistic whole. The film pleased audiences and inspired other animators in their artistic endeavours.

The Humpbacked Horse was remade in 1975 by Ivanov-Vano when the negative of the original film was deemed to be of insufficient quality for a re-release. In 2004 new technology allowed the original film to be restored.

Lora Wheeler Mjolsness

Fedia Zaitsev

Fedia Zaitsev

Country of Origin:
Soviet Union

Language:
Russian

Studio:
Soiuzmultfilm

Directors:
Valentina Brumberg
Zinaida Brumberg

Screenplay:
Mikhail Vol'pin
Nikolai Erdman

Cinematographer:
Nikolai Voinov

Art Director:
Anatolii Sazonov

Composer:
Viktor Oranskii

Synopsis

On 1 September, Fedia Zaitsev is the very first child to arrive at school. The school has been freshly painted and cleaned. In his excitement he draws a 'little man' with an umbrella on the wall inside his classroom. In class, the teacher notices the drawing and asks the children to admit to the wrongdoing. Fedia rubs his hands together so that they appear clean, but his friend, with whom he has shaken hands earlier, has dirty hands and is blamed for the drawing. Fedia goes home without saying anything, but he is unable to sleep peacefully because of his guilty conscience. In his dreams his toys begin to taunt him. It is the Little Man himself who decides that the truth must be known. He goes to Fedia's home and on the way he meets other children's drawings including an animal of unknown breed that agrees to give him a ride to Fedia's home. With the Little Man's encouragement Fedia agrees to admit his guilt the next day at school.

Critique

After World War II Soviet animation began to explore new stylistic directions and innovative content. Despite the increased pressure from the Communist Party to clearly illustrate communist ideology in animated films, the Brumberg sisters were able to decisively fill this demand and at the same time to expand their visions as artists with the film Fedia Zaitsev. The Brumberg sisters are best known for their didactic films aimed at getting children to behave better and Fedia Zaitsev is an ideal example of this type of film.

Regardless of the educational message, Fedia Zaitsev holds a valued position in Soviet animation because the film highlights one

Duration:

21 minutes

Genre:

Animation

Voices:

Sergei Martinson
Vera Bendina
Lidiia Koroleva
Vladimir Gotovtsev
Mikhail Ianshin

Year:

1948

of the most important attributes in animated film – the ability to interweave the real world with the fantastic. Fedia Zaitsev's drawing of the Little Man is a funny and primitive drawing by a child, a glorified stick figure with an umbrella and a hat, who represents the fantastic world when he suddenly comes to life. The Little Man is more than a contrast of the real world with the imaginary world. As one of the main characters in the film, the Little Man's iconic appearance contrasts greatly with his personality. The Little Man is the perfect hero: brave, truthful and kind. His sticklike appearance is also at odds with his movement and voice. He moves in an old-fashioned way, displaying a very upright carriage and gesticulating his umbrella with flair. His words, voiced by Mikhail Ianshin, are pronounced in an almost classic theatrical manner. Hence, there is a large difference between the behaviour of the Little Man and his appearance.

The Little Man's upstanding moral character drives the plot of this film and produces a satisfactory ending. The Little Man will not allow another student to take the blame for his existence. He sets out in the middle of the night across an animated Moscow to search out Fedia. Along the way the fantastic and the real come into contact. He talks a chalkboard drawing into taking his place on the wall, he rides a child's street drawing, an animal of unknown breed with eight legs, and he draws with his umbrella his own smaller set of stairs on the wall of Fedia's home in order to climb into the window. This interweaving of

Brumberg Sisters, *Fedia Zaitsev* (1948).

the real word and the fantastic world was inspirational for other Soviet animators who took this idea and adapted it to their own works.

While the Little Man is the most powerful force in the creation of the two animated worlds, this film also brings the child's real world to life. During the night Fedia tries to read Arkadii Gaidar's *Timur and his Gang*, but the drawing of Timur, the perfect Soviet Young Pioneer, comes to life and tells him the book is not for him. Classic nineteenth-century Russian literature is also unfriendly to Fedia. The illustration of Anton Chekhov's *Kashtanka* reaches up from the cover and nips his fingers as he tries to read. Fedia is also left alone by his other toys. His Red Army men march themselves back to the store and his *matreshka* doll reproaches him for not telling the truth. Only the Little Man himself can convince Fedia to go back to school and admit his guilt. The Brumbergs undercut the fantastic world near the end of the film, leaving the animated real world in place. Fedia wakes up to realize that the events of the night were all just a dream. He must face the real world and tell the truth at school that morning.

Lora Wheeler Mjolsness

Story of a Crime

Istoriia odnogo prestupleniia

Country of Origin:
Soviet Union

Language:
Russian

Studio:
Soiuzmultfilm

Director:
Fedor Khitruk

Screenplay:
Michael Vol'pin

Cinematographer:
Boris Kotov

Art Director:
Sergei Alimov

Composer:
Andrei Babaev

Synopsis

Story of a Crime illustrates in a satirical and humorous way the story of how the noise and behaviour of 'uncultured' neighbours brings a simple accountant, Mamin, a good and meek citizen, to commit a murder. The film goes back in time, 24 hours prior to the murder, and depicts a typical day of Mamin's life, from the moment he gets up and goes to work, to the sleepless night, during which he has to cope with his noisy neighbours.

Critique

Story of a Crime can be considered a landmark in a new phase of Soviet animation. After years of cartoons directed exclusively at children, during the Khrushchev's Thaw Soviet animated films branched out to target adult audiences while tackling contemporary topics. With *Story of a Crime*, the director Fedor Khitruk ventured to offer an in-depth reading of that particular time in Soviet history. Posters, slogans and especially hints to the vast building projects of those years concretize the world depicted in the film, suggesting a specific time and space – Khrushchev's era in the Soviet Union. *Story of a Crime* presents an honest picture of the illnesses of Soviet society and attacks the weaknesses of Soviet people through parody and satire rather than heavy criticism.

The style proposed by Khitruk and the art director Sergei Alimov highly differs from the Disney style thoroughly adopted by the studio Soiuzmultfilm since its foundation. The stylized manner adopted for *Story* does not ground on Disney's meticulous attention to details, but on conventionality of the drawings, essential traits in the description of characters and background and lack of words. Principles of

Duration:

20 minutes

Genre:

Animation

Voice:

Zinovii Gerdt

Year:

1962

minimalism and modern design features such as flatness and skewed prospective, together with geometric angularity of the images particularly suit the satirical tone adopted in the film. The environment and the characters are deprived of depth and volume, while pure colours underline the flattening-out effect of the figures. By emphasizing flatness, on the one hand, the animators stress the very specificity of their own artistic medium, the flat surface on which a drawing is traced; on the other, the flat characters in *Story of a Crime* are not perceived as characters with a life of their own, but become conventional signs able to convey with minimum traits a general characteristic; they become 'types' easily recognizable by the audience. The use of 'type' recalls Eisenstein's practice of casting non-professional actors and choosing the characters of his films on the base of their physical characteristics, expressions and postures. Khitruk and Alimov create similar characters, individuals that are not psychologically fully developed, but rather respond to specific behavioural and external characteristics – the idlers at work, the drunk man coming home, the noisy neighbour with an enormous stereo system, the men playing dominoes in the courtyard, the people reading in the subway, the guests singing at a party. These stereotypical personages present a variegated society that displays conflicts within itself; it is not an ideal world, but a collective composed of people violating norms of social order, people who do not belong to the complex field of 'cultured-ness' (*kul'turnost'*, a quite complex term that here can be defined as an unwritten Soviet etiquette which included manners and ways of behaviour). In *Story of a Crime*, each character represents a particular violation of the norms of 'cultured-ness' – self-centredness or not caring for one's neighbours, breaking the rules or idling at work – and the main character's proper attitude repeatedly clashes with this uncultured behaviour. Mamin represents an exception to the general attitude of the people around him; he is depicted as the ideal proper Soviet man, he is nice with children and polite with his fellows, he opens doors, offers his seat in the subway, he observes the rules and is dedicated to his work. The paradoxical result is that 'cultured-ness' in this film is represented by a man who committed a crime.

With this peculiar depiction of the main character and a criticism of Soviet society based on daily life, Khitruk paved the path to a series of cartoons which focused on social criticism and were targeted to adults rather than children. Yet, the innovative style adopted in this film inspired most of the aesthetic of the Soviet animated films made in the 1960s, including also films addressed to young audiences.

Laura Pontieri Hlavacek

The Mitten

Varezhka

Country of Origin:
Soviet Union

Language:
Russian

Studio:
Soiuzmultfilm

Director:
Roman Kachanov

Screenplay:
Zhanna Vitenzon

Cinematographer:
Iosif Golomb

Art Director:
Leonid Shvartsman

Duration:
10 minutes

Genre:
Animation

Year:
1967

Synopsis

The Mitten tells of a little girl, whose mother does not allow her to have a dog, so she creates a loveable puppy from her woollen, red mitten.

Critique

Roman Kachanov caught international attention at the Annecy International Animation Festival, where *The Mitten* won him the main award. The film was based on an original script by Zhanna Vitenzon, which was stripped entirely of the dialogue, using instead music hall tunes to set pace and mood. Leonid Shvartsman, who would later create the famous Cheburashka, designed the puppets.

The girl first appears in a window frame seen from the outside: she lives in a protected world and looks on to the outside world through the window that is, however, frozen over, echoing the emotional coldness of her world. Outside, the courtyard is covered in snow, but here people are walking their dogs. The girl seeks companionship, so she fetches a puppy from the upstairs neighbours. Her mother forbids her this pleasure: adults do not understand children. The girl goes for a walk outside where her dream comes true: her mitten turns into her puppy companion. Back inside the imaginary puppy transforms back into a mitten: the excursion into the outside world has taken place in the child's imagination, which has, however the power of transforming reality.

The girl dreams of another collective than the family: of society at large and of her peers, of lonely dog-owners who can share their emotional life with a pet. The home that fails to provide emotional warmth is set against a world of love and care – for pets. When the mother realizes the child's despair as the girl pours milk for the mitten, she fetches the black puppy from upstairs. As the puppy licks the mother's face, she smiles: at last an emotional response is elicited from this stern face.

The lonely and isolated child creates an emotional rapport with the mother through a pet that she is allowed to keep because of a strong desire as articulated through her imagination. Kachanov shows a sensitive understanding of the children's world as superior to and wiser than the adults' world.

Birgit Beumers

Glass Harmonica

Stekliannaia garmonika

Country of Origin:
Soviet Union

Language:
Russian

Studio:
Soiuzmultfilm

Director:
Andrei Khrzhanovskii

Screenplay:
Gennadi Shpalikov

Cinematographer:
E. Rizo

Art Directors:
Iurii Nolev-Sobolev
Ülo-Ilmar Sooster

Composer:
Alfred Schnittke

Duration:
21 minutes

Genre:
Animation

Year:
1968

Synopsis

The film is a parable on the fate of the artist in a totalitarian society. The music played on the glass harmonica strove towards higher ideals of beauty, and when the authorities destroy the instrument, life turns ugly – until a new glass harmonica appears.

Critique

Based on a tale by Lazar Lagin, *Glass Harmonica* tells about the desire for power that corrupts people, and about the spiritual revival that art can bring. At the centre of the film stands a musician with a glass harmonica, which is broken by a 'man in power' who resembles Magritte's man in a bowler hat. The son of the painter Iurii Khrzhanovskii (who had worked with Pavel Filonov and other masters of the late avantgarde period), Andrei Khrzhanovskii uses multiple references to old masters, such as Hieronymus Bosch, Pintoricchio and Albrecht Dürer to fill his world with beautiful characters.

The love of money turns the people into grotesque and ugly creatures. They destroy their cultural heritage. Only art, represented by the sound of the glass harmonica, and of course by the visual references offered through the art work, allows humanism to surface once again and the people begin to rebuild the clock-tower. The music was specially composed by Alfred Schnittke, while the art work was carried out by Ülo-Sooster, an Estonian non-conformist and surrealist painter, along with Iurii Nolev-Sobolev.

The film was banned for its controversial treatment of the relationship between the authorities and the artist, which had always been a thorn in the flesh of the censors. *Glass Harmonica* remains the only Soviet cartoon of the post-war era that was shelved until after the collapse of the USSR.

Birgit Beumers

Cheburashka

Krokodil Gena, 1969;
Cheburashka, 1971;
Shapokliak, 1974 and
Cheburashka idet v shkolu,
1983

Country of Origin:
Soviet Union

Synopsis

A small furry big-eared creature unknown to science is discovered in a crate of imported oranges by a grocer. The creature is so dazed by his long journey he promptly falls down and the grocer names him 'Cheburashka', from the Russian vernacular term 'topple over'. Cheburashka is lonely but soon finds a friend in Gena, a kind crocodile bachelor who works in the local zoo and who is equally lonely. Together they perform a number of good deeds such as building a social club for lonely animals, constructing a children's playground, halting the pollution of river, and helping repair a school. They become inseparable; always ready to help out those in need and keen to get involved in such worthy social activities such as

Language:
Russian

Studio:
Soiuzmultfilm

Director:
Roman Kachanov

Screenplay:
Roman Kachanov
Eduard Uspenskii

Cinematographer:
Teodor Bunimovich

Art Director:
Leonid Shvartsman

the Young Pioneer movement. The local miscreant, an old woman named Shapokliak with her pet rat, Lariska, at first try to foil these civic-spirited actions, playing all kinds of unpleasant tricks on the pair. However, Shapokliak is soon won over by Gena's gentlemanly conduct and Cheburashka's child-like charm. Finally, Cheburashka is able to go to school and learn to read.

Critique

The four twenty-minute episodes of the Cheburashka series (*Crocodile Gena*, 1969; *Cheburashka*, 1971; *Shapokliak*, 1974 and *Cheburashka Goes to School*, 1983) remain probably the best-loved animations of all the Soviet period. The films manage to excel in every department. The stop-motion animation is of outstanding quality for its time, creating fully rounded personalities out of the

Roman Kachanov, *Cheburashka* (1969).

Composer:

Vladimir Shainskii

Duration:

20 minutes

Genre:

Animation

Year:

1969–1983

sometimes crudely put together puppets and sets. With great economy of movement the animators convey a wide range of emotion and expression in their models. The combinations of a slightly washed-out pastel colour palette for the sets, a strong attention to detail in the modelling of individual realia items and cleverly achieved sense of depth and kineticism (gravity, inertia and momentum are almost tangible to the viewer) create the unmistakable world of Gena and Cheburashka – a world where talking giraffes and well-dressed gentlemanly lions rub shoulders with world-weary school directors, leather-jacketed taxi-drivers, highly strung factory owners and, of course, lonely bachelor crocodiles. Kachanov's adaptation of Uspenskii's stories retains the essentially kind wistfulness and irony of the original but adds a wicked sense of subversive humour to the mix, appreciated by children and adults alike. As well as absurdist moments, Kachanov includes mildly ironic side references to the endemic workplace theft, backsliding and officiousness of Soviet society. Especially memorable is the gentle deflating of the Pioneer movement: its snotty kids aren't interested in the civic aspects of membership – they just want first prize in their contest and the status a uniform brings. Finally there is the unforgettable music – of both the songs and voices. Shainskii's minor-key songs have become as memorable a part of the Cheburashka phenomenon as the animations themselves. The long-serving animation voice-over actor Vasilii Livanov, who went on to play Sherlock Holmes in the Soviet screen version, voices Gena. His, by turns, creaky, grumpily resigned and melodious voice is perfectly complimented by Klara Rumianova's intensely sweet, childlike Cheburashka.

The Cheburashka series is much more than a well-executed quartet of short stop-motion films for children. As a cultural icon of the late Soviet period, the image of Cheburashka has been continually appropriated and reinvented by official and sub-cultures alike. It has served as the official mascot for the Russian Olympic team and its name used as a slang term for a variety of objects, some with ear-like appendages such as an Antonov cargo jet, others that are merely small or cute (a one-third-of-a-litre glass bottle). In sub-culture Cheburashka has long been appropriated for use in narrative jokes some of them bawdy, and more recently in a host of internet parodies, notably of the character of Yoda from Star Wars. Perhaps most interesting is his appearance in the post-Jungian theory of socionics where his character is used to illustrate a personality type that does not fall into any of the sixteen categories of introvert and extrovert types. In addition to Russia, Cheburashka has found success in Japan and Sweden.

Jeremy Morris

Tale of Tales

Skazka skazok

Country of Origin:
Soviet Union

Language:
Russian

Studio:
Soiuzmultfilm

Director:
Iurii Norshtein

Screenplay:
Iurii Norshtein
Liudmila Petrushevskaia

Cinematographer:
Igor' Skidan-Bosin

Art Director:
Francesca Iarbusova

Composer:
Mikhail Meerovich

Editor:
Nadezhda Treshcheva

Duration:
29 minutes

Genre:
Animation

Year:
1979

Synopsis

Tale of Tales operates through a series of returning, metamorphosing motifs. Central among them are an apple, ripe and dappled with raindrops; a baby at its mother's breast; a wolf cub; and people gathered around an outdoors dinner table in the company of a good-natured Minotaur. The little wolf cub, itself taken directly from the words of a lullaby, is comforted by the sight of a human baby, but external events from the adult world spoil this idyll. Initial signs of impending disaster come when the diners are subjected to worsening weather and the peace of the cub's residence is ruined by increasing industry and traffic. Worst of all, however, are a series of references to World War II. Waltzing women on the eve of a frontline draft are slowly robbed of their loved ones, who vanish from the dancefloor with awful speed. Meanwhile the wolf cub tries to steal some paper from a rather lazy poet; the paper becomes a baby, a symbol of the way in which creativity must partake of natural processes of unfettered growth. Yet, for all the cub's efforts to champion creative metamorphoses, the men continue to vanish from the dancefloor. In the competition between life and death, the former is under considerable pressure …

Critique

One of the most straightforward explanations of these motifs, or at least of their provenance, came in an interview with the screenwriter Liudmila Petrushevskaia, where she recalled being approached in March 1976 to work with Norshtein on a new film about his wartime childhood. Petrushevskaia was eight-months pregnant and not keen to shoulder the responsibility of a fresh, probably lengthy project. Norshtein suggested visiting Petrushevskaia's apartment to lessen the workload and thus she consented – with the proviso that after the birth he also walk the baby in a pram. Consequently much of the screenplay was created during long strolls, and the initial childhood of early drafts and motifs became those of a newborn wrapped in the draft papers of a writer. Petrushevskaia said: 'I was full of milk and could think only about children. That's why a baby in the screenplay had to be born swaddled in one of those pages.' Such is the origin of the natural, 'productive' or fertile motifs.

Extra inspiration came when Norshtein both sent Petrushevskaia a book of translated poetry that included lines by Nâzim Hikmet, and then showed her albums with various drawings by Picasso. The Hikmet poem would ultimately sit at the centre of the film, a tiny text also entitled 'Tale of Tales'. A prosaic translation of it might read: 'We stand above the water: The sun, a cat, plane tree, me and our fate. Cool water, a lofty plane tree, the sun is shining and the cat dozes. I compose a poem. Thank Heavens that we are alive! The glare of the water shines in our face; it shines [even] at the sun itself, upon the cat, the plane tree, on me and our fate.' Accordingly Petrushevskaia suggested that perhaps the central human protagonist should be a poet. This explains the literary elements and the 'human' paper.

The wolf comes from a famous Russian lullaby 'Baiu-baiushki-baiu', warning of 'a little grey cub who'll come and grab your sides. He'll drag you off into the forest, under a brittle willow bush'. This character was Norshtein's suggestion; Petrushevskaia, however, countered it with less sentimental memories. She had been seven years old in 1945, too poor to have shoes, and sometimes even ate food from urban gutters. A common and concrete reminiscence they shared, however, was that amateur impassioned music had been used by families and other groups in both times of grief and celebration. A title for the first version of the screenplay was a direct quote from sung lines of the lullaby: 'The Grey Wolf Cub Will Come'. The film studio executives declared it too scary, so the Hikmet title was used instead.

The itinerant little wolf became in Petrushevskaia's drafts 'an eternal soul, who could visit the Golden Age [of Russian poets in the nineteenth century], a quiet seaside abode where a happy fisherman lives with his family. In their pram a chubby child lies quietly. His sister – in a ball gown and hat – skips rope with one of Picasso's Minotaurs … They have guests – a balding poet with a lyre and a young, chance visitor who is a young man, free from material things: a pensive passer-by'. This sketch entered the cartoon, prior to the sequence of young wartime girls bidding farewell to their lovers; thus idylls and tragic transience were slowly juxtaposed, creating a work that has been voted the 'Greatest Animated Film of All Time'.

David MacFadyen

The Old Man and the Sea

Starik i more

Countries of Origin:
Russia
Canada
Japan

Language:
English

Studio:
Ogden Entertainment

Director:
Aleksandr Petrov

Producers:
Pascal Blais
Bernard Lajoie
Jean-Yves Martel

Synopsis

Based on Ernest Hemingway's story written on Cuba in 1951, the film tells of the old fisherman Santiago and his struggle with a marlin. Santiago has not caught any fish for several weeks, and his apprentice Manolin is no longer allowed to fish with him as he is clearly under a spell of bad luck. Once day a marlin takes his bait and Santiago struggles with the fish for three days, when he is finally able to kill the marlin with a harpoon. On the way back to the shore his boat is attacked by sharks that devour the marlin. The old man returns to his home exhausted and falls asleep, dreaming of his youth.

Critique

The story of an old man struggling with nature – the sea, the marlin and the sharks – offers at first sight little action and therefore not much attraction for animation. However, the Yaroslavl animator Aleksandr Petrov, whose technique involves oil painting on glass, turned this story into a poetic sequence of images, capturing the texture of the sea and the sky beautifully on this first animated film made for 70mm IMAX format, produced largely in Canada. *The Old Man and the Sea* went on to win the first Academy Award (Oscar) for a Russian animator in 2000.

Shizuo Ohashi
Tatsuo Shimamura

Screenplay:
Aleksandr Petrov (based on
Ernest Hemingway)

Art Director:
Aleksandr Petrov

Composers:
Denis L. Chartrand
Normand Roger

Duration:
20 minutes

Genre:
Animation

Voices:
Gordon Pinsent
Kevin Duhaney

Year:
1999

Petrov's technique is unique and finds full expression on the 70mm format: his use of oil colour on glass creates an almost three-dimensional texture, not unlike Iurii Norshtein's three-dimensionality achieved through different levels (rather than layers) of cel. The texture of the sea and the sky, uniformly grey-blue in colour, acquires an authentic feel so that the monochrome colour-scheme no longer looks dull. On the contrary, the sparkling drops of water and the shining stars appear almost naturally through a combination of lighting and paint.

The short film explores the relationship of man and nature through subtle and detailed images of sea life, weaving a harmonious entity from the forces of man and nature. Both technically and in terms of the chosen story, Petrov re-established Russia in the world of animation as a country that trains excellent animators and with an industry capable of co-production. It thus opened the path for further development of the art and the commercial exploitation of animation at a time when Russia's animation industry lay in disarray.

Birgit Beumers

Alesha Popovich and Tugarin the Dragon

Alesha Popovich i Tugarin
zmei

Country of Origin:
Russia

Language:
Russian

Studio:
Mel'nitsa

Director:
Konstantin Bronzit

Producers:
Sergei Sel'ianov
Aleksandr Boiarskii

Synopsis

The story takes place in the medieval town of Rostov, focusing in particular upon a boy called Alesha. Although this youngster is blessed with a remarkable strength, he is equally cursed by an inability to control it gracefully. One day, however, he is given the chance to put his prowess to good use.

A terrible danger appears. The feared army of Tugarin the Dragon comes to Rostov and demands that the town hand over all of its gold supplies. A true hero is now needed, for the people cannot defend themselves. The citizens of Rostov therefore turn to Alesha. He agrees to help, but initially the plan goes very wrong indeed: not only does Tugarin escape with all the gold, but Rostov is decimated in the process.

Thus begins the real adventure: Alesha's quest to clear his name, regain the gold and rebuild Rostov. He goes off to lands unknown with some elderly relatives, a talkative donkey, a horse and his fiancée. Over the course of multiple adventures, which at times become so superfluous as to be potentially endless, Tugarin is brought to justice, the gold is returned to its rightful owners, and Alesha settles down with his true love.

Critique

At the time of the film's release, some Moscow newspapers were claiming that children had entirely forgotten folklore and, therefore, Bronzit's witty, self-deprecating use of 'serious' legends was poten-

Screenplay:

Maksim Sveshnikov
Konstantin Bronzit
Il'ia Maksimov
Aleksandr Boiarskii

Composer:

Valentin Vasenkov

Duration:

72 minutes

Genre:

Animation

Voices:

Oleg Kulikovich
Anatolii Petrov
Liia Medvedeva
Natal'ia Danilova
Dmitrii Vysotskii
Ivan Krasko
Sergei Makovetskii
Tat'iana Ivanova
Konstantin Bronzit

Year:

2004

tially detrimental. The serious archetype, said the press, needed to re-establish itself before being subjected to any silliness. Cartoons used to (and still should) address important 'pedagogical' issues, such as correct social behaviour and a respect for authority.

In interviews surrounding the film, Bronzit spoke of this feature as a way to solve and surpass the problems of underfunded, over-commercial animation during the mid-1990s. He also addressed the national issues of a Russian story, made in Russia to aid that same nation's cinema while nonetheless relying on an aesthetic that owes much to American craftsmanship (both verbally and visually). This complicated definition of a nationally specific cartoon recalled some very Soviet insecurities. Bronzit, for example, was keen to point out that his recent employment outside Russia would not lessen the cultural specificity or validity of his art. His time in France working on *At the End of the World* was not of significance to his Russian modus operandi; as additional defence, he referred to Andrei Tarkovskii as a Russian craftsman similarly unaffected by his place of work.

These arguments hoped to deflect some criticism of America's influence in *Alesha Popovich*, in particular the similarity between Alesha's wisecracking horse and Eddie Murphy's garrulous donkey in *Shrek* and *Shrek 2* (2001 and 2004). Although Bronzit said he can only watch *Shrek 2* with a 'gun placed to his head', he admitted that Russian animation has always learned its skills 'like a child, through imitation'. In *Alesha Popovich*, Sergei Makovetskii dubs the voice of a Kievan prince; his performance lacks all reverence for courtly propriety, and presents the prince as 'cowardly, greedy, sly – and homosexual'. All in all, said disapproving voices, this amounted to a loud and irresponsible critique of Putin's role in modern Russian society.

The assumed stability of valued stereotypes is mocked on many occasions in this cartoon. This occurs on both historical and stylistic levels – that is, the degree to which proper storylines are respected (and here again, there is a discernible nod in the direction of *Shrek*). When characters are dispatched into danger, the hero and heroine, we are told, need to survive this tale (of martial conflict) in order to reach its dénouement (of marital cohesion). They therefore should not be sent off to unspeakable danger; minor figures, of little importance to the plot, should do the job. Such is the argument put forward by Alesha's arrogant steed. In a similar spirit, the voice used by Dmitrii Vysotskii to dub that same horse sounds a great deal like comedian Maksim Galkin whenever he ridicules Nikita Mikhalkov's grandstanding in his nationally broadcast skits for a number of TV variety shows.

The dark forces facing these heroes are similarly 'tweaked' in order to make solemn, adequate enemies more modern (and more fun, too). Though the 'Muslim' nature of Tugarin's threat is named explicitly and early on, any geopolitical wrangling of the past is soon displaced by jokes about the mafia, marketplace conmen, suspect lottery tickets and the all-important need for connections in high places to escape any of these threats today. All in all, the film interweaves a large number old ancient stereotypes and modern jokes; whether such techniques vivify or spoil national folklore is an argument that still continues.

David MacFadyen

Russian documentary film begins, as does all documentary film, with actualities, picturesque travel or expedition films and newsreels. While Russia features as an exotic ethnographic topic in Pathé newsreels at least as early as 1908, few significant works were made in the genre until World War I, when Russian, rather than foreign, cameramen were required to film the war effort for domestically produced newsreels. Cameramen such as Petr Ermolov began work here, before building a post-war career first in Soviet newsreel, and subsequently in features.

Russia's first lasting contribution to documentary film came with the work of Dziga Vertov, starting with his *Kino-Pravda* newsreel series, the name of which, in French translation, gives us the term *cinéma-vérité*. Vertov's 1920s films and theorizations of documentary were the most influential and significant of a wider body of work, including that of Esfir' Shub and the ethnographic filmmaker, Vladimir Erofeev. The pivotal importance of documentary film in 1920s cultural politics is evident from the 1927 *New Lef* debates, republished in *Screen* in the 1970s. Throughout, the emphasis is upon the epistemological claims of the form. However, when the state began to invest more resources in documentary towards the end of the 1920s, it was less interested in the niceties of methodology, but rather in the reliable, economically efficient delivery of a message according to a standardized technique. This meant the greater importance of detailed scenarios scrutinized in advance, and a tendency to privilege events that either could be planned ahead, such as with Viktor Turin's *Turksib* (1929), or that could simply be staged, albeit with non-professional actors, as with Mikhail Kalatozov's *Salt for Svanetia* (1930). The short agitational pieces produced by Aleksandr Medvedkin's film train were innovative in their proximity to local problems, but again heavily reliant on staging previously scripted incidents. Such tendencies were strengthened still further with the coming of sound, which again demanded greater investment, and with it came still more political and administrative control. While Vertov's *Enthusiam: Symphony of the Donbass* (1931) was one of a number of early sound films to employ naturalistic sound recorded on location extensively, such experiments were

Mikhail Kaufman, cinematographer of *The Man with the Movie Camera* (1929).

quickly curtailed, in favour of the recording of cliched, highly rehearsed speeches, the dominance of non-diegetic music and the voice-over commentary. Soviet newsreel and documentary of the 1930s was henceforth dominated and stifled by the need to control in advance, and hence by interchangeably predictable films of parades, air shows, military exercises, races and expeditions. Interesting films resulted only on the rare occasion where circumstances conspired against the pre-approved plan, as with the 1934 film *Cheliuskin*, where the ship sank, unexpectedly, and the expedition had to be rescued.

Events, however, were conspiring to jar the Soviet Union, and Soviet documentary, from contemplation of Red Square parades, as the rise of fascist militarism provoked it to use film on the international stage to rally support against this explicitly anti-communist force. The first example of this was *Abyssinia* (1935), directed by former Vertov protégé Il'ia Kopalin, which shows the Italian campaign to subdue the East African state through the feared, new military strategy of bombing the civilian population. More sustained and significant were the efforts of Roman Karmen, rising star of Soviet documentary film in the late 1930s, a former photo-journalist who was sent to Republican Spain to produce regular newsreels conveying the Soviet perspective on the conflict. These reels became the major source for images of the isolated, losing side in the Civil War. This powerful and insightful footage was later edited into *Spain* (1938), a full-length documentary by Esfir' Shub. As with Kopalin's earlier film, Karmen's footage shows the aerial bombardment of civilians, but here it is far more effectively rendered.

The Nazi attack on the Soviet Union of 22 June 1941 forced Soviet newsreel to record a new kind of war: one launched with an ultimately genocidal logic upon 'Judeo-Bolshevism'. The first significant documentary arising from the conflict was Il'ia Kopalin's and Leonid Varlamov's *The Defeat of the Germans near Moscow*, released in February 1942, notable for its dynamic battle-action footage, and harrowing images of Nazi atrocities against Soviet civilians, shown domestically, and then in Britain and the United States, where a re-edited, rewritten version won an Oscar nearly three years before images of the liberation of the camps in Bergen-Belsen and Dachau were screened in spring 1945. Kopalin and Varlamov's film was followed by a number of others showing similar sights. The only example of note for the history of documentary film is Aleksandr Dovzhenko and Iuliia Solntseva's *The Battle for Our Soviet Ukraine* (1943), which, extraordinarily for the time, uses a number of synch-sound sequences, including witness testimony of atrocities, to powerful effect. However, like other Soviet war films, it does not differentiate the fate of the Soviet Jews murdered by the Nazis, and here treats them as Ukrainian losses.

The immediate post-war period until the death of Stalin was as lean for Soviet documentary film as it was for Soviet cinema more generally, although Karmen and Medvedkin continued working in this period, producing films in the established Soviet propagandistic, persuasive mode. The 1960s, however, enabled them to make more interesting films about overseas politics: neo-Nazis, Cuba, Vietnam and Chile. The most noteworthy film of the decade, however, was Mikhail Romm's *Ordinary Fascism* (1965), innovative for its highly personalized voice-over, as well as revelatory use of archive footage. However, alongside films made in this traditional manner, there emerged films and filmmakers whose prime purpose was to develop documentary as an art, rather than a political instrument. For directors such as Gerts (Herz) Frank, the rediscovery of Vertov's *Man with a Movie Camera*, and publication of a selection of his writings in 1966 imparted an important impetus in this direction. Frank was the most notable figure in a Riga-based school of poetic documentary cinema.

Artavazd Peleshian's work also has its roots in the 1960s, when he made his first films, which eschew the voice-over in favour of a more demanding visual style. Likewise, his concept of *Distance Montage* (1974) is the product of the reappraisal and reflection on the form initiated by the filmmakers of the 1960s.

While the artistic and political trends lived in some kind of more or less peaceful co-existence until the 1980s, Soviet documentary was transformed, as it was the world over, by the rise of TV, a decade later here than in Western Europe. The immediacy of TV news reports killed off theatrically distributed 35mm newsreels, but also created a new incubator and outlet for documentary filmmakers. Soviet newsreel studios, where most documentaries were made, were technically backward and slow to adapt to the rise of the technology of video. Nevertheless, the perestroika era meant that Soviet documentary was able to end on a high note, as Frank's *Last Judgment* (1987) and Juris Podnieks's *Is it Easy to Be Young?* (1988) drew huge crowds on their theatrical release. For a brief moment, documentary as an art and as popular social commentary coalesced, before the two went their separate ways once more with the commentary continuing in works such as Stanislav Govorukhin's *This is No Way to Live* (1990), which features the director as a Michael Moore-style presenter-provocateur, but lacks Moore's wit. Probably the most extreme example of documentary as an art without social commentary and almost without an audience is the work of Aleksandr Sokurov, more celebrated for his feature films. With a technique that has its roots in the 'distance montage' method of Peleshian, and Frank's interest in psychology and privileging of the reaction shot, Sokurov has made a number of documentaries aimed primarily at film critics and festivals.

However, Sokurov is one of a number of contemporary Russian documentary filmmakers who have productively explored the potential of digital media to reinvent the genre. His film *Spiritual Voices* (1995) and *Service* (in Russian *Povinnost'*, inexplicably mistranslated for the English DVD release as *Confession*, 1998), which run to a colossal length of 327 and 225 minutes respectively, exploit to the utmost, it would seem, the durational qualities of the long-take to challenge the spectator to find sense. Viktor Kosakovskii's film *Quiet!* (2002) takes almost the opposite approach, by editing an enormous quantity of observational footage into a pithy, allegorical tragi-comedy of repeated failed attempts to fix a hole in the road. Yet another tack is taken by Vitalii Manskii's 2005 'Real Cinema' Manifesto, which explicitly proclaims that digital technology enables documentary filmmakers to witness life as a process, in a way they never previously could, since they can carry a camera with them almost continually. His recent films convey the intensity of the close-up insight into the subject's life.

With the break up of the Soviet Union, and fragmentation of the film industry in the 1990s, many of the prominent contemporary documentary directors are no longer based in Russia, but their films are still, for the most part made in the Russian language and in some sense belong to a Soviet or Russian tradition of documentary filmmaking. Vitalii Manskii's institution of ArtDokFest, a festival for Russian language documentaries which expand the language of cinema, wherever they were made, recognizes and embraces this diasporic dimension of the genre.

Jeremy Hicks

The Fall of the Romanov Dynasty

Padenie dynastii
Romanovykh

Country of Origin:
Soviet Union

Language:
Russian

Studio:
Sovkino

Director:
Esfir' Shub

Editor:
Esfir' Shub

Duration:
66 minutes

Genre:
Documentary

Year:
1927

Synopsis

The Fall of the Romanov Dynasty is essentially a compilation film based on the editing of footage, largely from Western Europe and Russia. It shows events, beginning with tsarist Russia on the eve of World War I and finishing with the Bolshevik seizure of power. Shub's film is edited together to reveal the nature of class exploitation in the country. We are shown, on the one hand, the vast, grand properties of Russian landowners and this is contrasted with the poverty of peasant life. In both the towns and the countryside ordinary people toil in terrible conditions and those who object are punished accordingly. The film then elaborates a story of a conspiring ruling class of elites from Russia and west European states who stand behind the organization of World War I which, at its heart, is seen as an imperialist adventure in the interests of capitalist gain. The film provides a grim portrait of the realities of this war; namely, extreme violence and the consequences of mass death and suffering. The Bolsheviks are presented as the solution with their promises of peace, bread and freedom and the film finishes with the famous image of Lenin shaking hands with a comrade, symbolizing the new era.

Critique

The most important part of the film, from the point of view of the director, is clearly the argument it seeks to convey to the viewer. Shub's edited footage constructs a narrative that suggests that the Russian monarchy of Nicholas II, in a similar way to his royal cohorts in countries such as France and Great Britain, is allied together with government ministers and capitalists to create a transnational conspiracy. The purpose of this is to maintain their collective wealth and power and to accumulate the wealth of other countries through careful collaboration in war that generally involves exploiting the masses as cannon fodder in their wicked game. This type of argument was commonly found in many different forms of art and political literature during the early part of the twentieth century and such conspiracy theories were often related to so-called 'vulgar Marxism', due to their over-simplification of the ideas of Marx himself. Nonetheless, Shub's film was intended for mass audiences as persuasive, punchy propaganda and, therefore, this was clearly her intention.

It is fair to say that this strategy is sometimes very effective. For instance, Shub employs a fairly successful technique to lend her argument historical authenticity. She includes shots of various documents at different stages of the film. So, when Nicholas II abdicates we are shown written proof of this declaration juxtaposed with cheering crowds of workers. The documents and declarations confirm what we see and read in the intertitles: at one demonstration the people demand peace, bread and freedom. The front page of *Pravda* is then shown repeating this demand as a confirmation of popular opinion.

Although the film's argument now looks rather crude, Shub's work is remarkable in other aspects. She uses powerful imagery to contrast the servitude of, for example, sailors scrubbing decks with society's elite dining in highly opulent surroundings. Her film technique also has a distinct rhythmic quality: as the conspiracy becomes more and more obvious to the viewer, her cuts become shorter and shorter creating a sense of momentum towards war. This military rhythm is also emphasized by the cutting of carefully selected shots of columns of soldiers and guards which are always acting in the interests of the wider conspiracy.

The Fall of the Romanov Dynasty is one of Esfir' Shub's major achievements. Regardless of its political tendentiousness, the film preserves images that may otherwise have been lost. The work, alongside Shub's other films is deservedly recognized as an important part of film documentary history. In particular, Shub is remembered as a pioneer of the compilation style of documentary filmmaking which developed in new directions in subsequent years.

Jamie Miller

Man with a Movie Camera

Chelovek s kinoapparatom

Country of Origin:
Soviet Union

Language:
Silent

Studio:
The All-Ukrainian Photo-Cine Directorate (VUFKU)

Director:
Dziga Vertov

Assistant Director and Editor:
Elizaveta Svilova

Cinematographer:
Mikhail Kaufman

Duration:
68 minutes

Genre:
Documentary

Year:
1929

Synopsis

Man with a Movie Camera is a formally innovative silent film documentary, which uses no intertitles, and follows a complex structure. Ostensibly, it shows a cameraman's day, as he records the city around him. Deeper consideration of the film reveals it does not record a city, but create one from elements of several, including Moscow, Kharkov and Odessa. Moreover, while the cameraman is the most recognizable figure, the film shows editing, projection and spectatorship, as well as polemicizing with clichés from feature films. From its opening statement, proclaiming it 'a film on film-language, the first film without words', Man with a Movie Camera celebrates documentary cinema's magical power but also discusses and demystifies filmmaking as a form of healthy leisure and as a form of labour analogous to a dynamic, urban, industrial world.

Critique

Man with a Movie Camera is a landmark in documentary film, a film so formally and conceptually rich it has generated a plethora of competing interpretations, and numerous film scores, including one by Michael Nyman.

Man with a Movie Camera was made by Vertov at the culmination of a decade in which he had pioneered the documentary form, exploring and refining its possibilities as a tool for analysis and persuasion. While often said to be a manifesto, Man with a Movie Camera functions as an essay on the making and meaning of film in the modern world, a defence of Vertov's vision of documentary as a form accessible to all. At the same time, it is important to remember that Vertov's conception of documentary precluded the notion of a rigid scenario prior to the process of shooting, and the film reflects a perceptual process whereby sense is made from the initially dizzying whirr of modern life, itself celebrated and evoked in the film's often frenetic pace.

By contrast, the images of the woman waking up are constructed so as to parody the tropes of feature films, condemned by Vertov as a harmful illusion, preventing people from looking at and analysing the world around them, as his film strives to. Yet, while it is a film about film which articulates a message to filmmakers and critics, the sheer visual merits of this, one of the last great silent films, its dynamic, diagonal compositions, and the associative way the film combines shots, have the widest and most lasting appeal on spectators. Many of the images share the clashing perspectives of constructivist photographers Lazlo Moholy-Nagy or Aleksandr Rodchenko, but Elizaveta Svilova's editing performs the greatest wizardry, as what in other hands might seem an inventory of urban life becomes both a powerful evocation and a clinical dissection of it. Different forms of work, transport or leisure are edited together wittily, and with an eye for corresponding details or contrasting connotations. As the film reaches its crescendo, it is fitting that the editor's art is celebrated as we see her cut splice, play and pause shots at will. The film's last sequence shows Svilova pulling the dominant strands of imagery together, and it is her light blue iris that fittingly ends the film superimposed upon the camera shutter.

Jeremy Hicks

Turksib

Turksib, (Stal'noi put')

Country of Origin:
Soviet Union

Language:
Silent

Studio:
Vostokkino

Director:
Viktor Turin (sometimes spelled Tiurin)

Screenplay:
Iakov Aron
Viktor Shklovsky

Cinematographers:
Evgenii Slavinskii
Boris Frantsisson

Duration:
59 minutes

Synopsis

The film documents the construction of the Turkestan-Siberian Railway, which was conceived by the Soviet government to connect the cotton fields and sheep herds of Central Asia (what is now Kazakhstan) to the grain fields of Siberia. The film begins by stating the problem: Turkestan lacks sufficient water for efficient grain cultivation, but its immediate need forces it to use its potentially rich cotton fields for grain. As animated maps demonstrate and bold intertitles declare, the problem can be resolved by the simple and elegant solution of bringing grain from Siberia. The second half of the film explores the further ramifications of modernization in Central Asia and issues a plea for construction to be completed in 1930.

Critique

Turin's most well-known film illustrates three major facets of Soviet aesthetics in the late 1920s. First, it celebrates the belief in the ability of rational design to conquer natural chaos. This belief was central to the First Five Year Plan which began in 1929 and featured several large-scale construction projects like the Turkestan-Siberian Railway, most of which sought to unite the far-flung production of the Soviet lands into a single transport and electrical grid. The film projects ideals of social and ethnic unity (for instance, in the group of surveyors who include both ethnic Europeans and Central Asians) that will follow from the physical unification of the land into a single grid. The entire Soviet project is summed up in the elegance of an animated

Genre:
Documentary
Year:
1929

map which shows how stubborn, age-old problems can be resolved by a simple bold gesture. The Soviet project is also encapsulated in the totemic image of the locomotive, which is shown to be the literal engine of revolutionary transformation. The image of the camel sniffing the unfamiliar rails became clichés for depicting the clash between old and new in Soviet Central Asia, appearing on the cover of the official history of the Turksib construction project.

The film also demonstrates how documentary genres were deployed as a way for artists to co-ordinate their efforts with those of the overall plan. Since the railway line is itself a bold act of imagination and a thing of beauty, the artist can do no better than to record its projection and implementation. The seeming passivity of the artist before history is actually his participation in its progress. Thus it is in documentary genres that artistic media come to occupy a crucial role in social and industrial praxis. This argument was most famously expressed in the 1929 volume *Literatura fakta*, whose contributors included Viktor Shklovskii, who not only co-wrote the screenplay but also published a 1930 volume on the project utilizing stills from the film. This 'documentary moment' did not last long, as documentary genres increasingly ceded to the new fiction of socialist realism. The role of journalists at the opening of Turksib was specifically satirized in Il'f and Petrov's 1931 novel *The Golden Calf*.

Lastly, *Turksib* demonstrates the linkage between revolutionary activity and rapid montage, the technique pioneered by Sergei Eisenstein. The juxtaposition of images is here the form par excellence of dialectical thinking, and the visual resolution of the manifold contradictions of Central Asia facilitates their elimination in practice.

Robert Bird

Enthusiasm: Symphony of the Donbas

Entuziazm: Simfoniia Donbassa

Country of Origin:
Soviet Union

Language:
Russian

Studio:
Ukrainfilm

Director:
Dziga Vertov

Synopsis

Enthusiasm: Symphony of the Donbas shows images of drunks intercut with hidden camera shots of religion and worshippers accompanied by wailing, accordion music and cacophonous bells. To the beat of a drum, communists and pioneers transform a church, the old world, into a workers' club, symbolic of the new. This is being listened to by a woman sound engineer wearing headphones, who appears only in this section, drawing our attention to the act of listening itself. Marking a transition to the second section of the film, the passage of time is implied through the speeded-up image of clouds passing. In the second part the theme that dominates is work, and the need for the whole Donbas, the whole of society, to work harder than ever to make good the shortfall in coal and build socialism. This they do as work is celebrated in the final part of the work.

Critique

While many of the greatest filmmakers of the silent era, famously including Eisenstein, were sceptical about the benefits of sound film,

Assistant Director and Editor:

Elizaveta Svilova

Cinematographer:

Boris Tseitlin

Composer:

N. Timareev

Duration:

65 minutes

Genre:

Documentary

Year:

1931

Vertov unambiguously welcomed it, and was quick to start work on *Enthusiasm: Symphony of the Donbas*, which he stressed was the first Soviet sound film conceived as such from the outset (rather than having sound added subsequently). Its use of sound is certainly the most interesting element of the film, firstly in the embodied sound spoken by on screen presences which organizes much of its material, rather than relying upon voice-of-God style commentary. Most importantly though, the film uses a great deal of concrete location recorded sound, as we hear a hooter, steam engines, and a pneumatic press intercut with images of industrial production. Initially the noises are linked with their original source, but they are then also used separately to comment upon other scenes. The overall effect here is to redouble the sense of dynamic progress suggested by the images alone. The means of achieving such effects are startlingly original, and only rivalled in avant-garde and experimental post-war western filmmakers.

The film is engaging too in its visuals, with the opening sequence the most arresting in its sharply contrasting low- and high-angle shots: a large number of low-angle shots of churches, high-angle shots of a statue of Jesus on a church, contrasting the immense sculptured form with tiny, barely visible human beings below. Worshippers and drunks are photographed either from a high angle, as they prostrate themselves, or straight on. They are predominantly static, or, like the final drunk's feet, shot with a wobbly hand-held camera, barely able to walk. All this changes when the church becomes a workers' club, after which we see a huge array of low-angle shots of workers framed against a light sky. Frequently they are looking upwards, typically they are hard at work, or in motion, filing past the camera before a red flag. Vertov marshals his considerable resources as a filmmaker to evoke a sense of the energy and enthusiasm of work.

Enthusiasm: Symphony of the Donbas is a film valuable above all for its daring exploration of the possibilities of sound: it is hard to believe Vertov was able to achieve so much in such difficult political and administrative circumstances.

Jeremy Hicks

Ordinary Fascism

Obyknovennyi fashizm

Country of Origin:

Soviet Union

Language:

Russian

Studio:

Mosfilm

Synopsis

In sixteen chapters Mikhail Romm, the film's director and narrator, explores the nature and origins of National Socialism. Chapter I opens with children's drawings and reflections about the universal meaning of childhood and parenting. Suddenly, a photo of a German soldier shooting a mother appears, followed by more images of killed children, demonstrating the inhumane essence of Nazism. Romm discusses the message of Hitler's *Mein Kampf*, its author, his youth and political development. Chapter IV deals with the newsreels of the 1920s and 1930s, Chapters V and IX with the 'culture' and 'art' of the Third Reich. The cult of the 'Führer' (Chapters VII, X, XIII) is linked to the devaluation of the individual, ultimately resulting in the willing participation of millions in unspeakable crimes. The film proves the

Director:

Mikhail Romm

Screenplay:

Iurii Khaniutin

Maia Turovskaia

Cinematographer:

German Lavrov

Composer:

Alemdar Karamanov

Editor:

Valentina Kulagina

Duration:

138 minutes

Genre:

Documentary

Year:

1965

intrinsic link between the ideology of national superiority (Chapter VI) and the racist contempt for other nations materializing in ghettos and concentration camps (XIV). A discussion of neo-Nazi tendencies in West Germany and other countries, as well as the forces that withstand these trends concludes the film.

Critique

Mikhail Romm was not a novice to documentary filmmaking, but for *Ordinary Fascism* he explored new aesthetic paths. A more than two-hour long film essay combining pre-made footage with contemporary shots (often by hidden cameras), narrated by the director himself, was unheard of in Soviet cinema. Moreover, no other Soviet director had dared to focus exclusively on the political, social, cultural and especially psychological roots of National Socialism as did Romm. To be sure, he had already gained the reputation of an eminently political film-maker, from *Human Being # 217* (1944) about a young Russian woman deported to Germany who has to face the ordinary Nazi mentality in the family of a German butcher, to *The Russian Question* (1948), a starkly anti-American Cold War pamphlet. However, in *Ordinary Fascism*, Romm decided for the first time to express his views on Nazism explicitly, without fictional mediation. The preparatory work was enormous: the director and his team previewed hundreds of thousands of metres of German newsreels, propaganda documentaries and personal photographs. The selected material then was arranged in book-like chapters, each opening with a headline and an epigraph, continued by a visual/verbal narration meandering between the objective and the subjective, the analytical and the artistic. The deliberate contrasting of images, juxtaposing peaceful civilization with barbaric destruction, sometimes causes shock effects. Yet Romm's intention obviously went beyond that – he wanted to evoke a viewer's response balancing emotional reaction and rational analysis. The narrator-director exposes the audience to a persuasive arrangement of historical documents, with verbal announcements often preceding the images to follow. Thus, Romm acts as the viewer's personal guide through the realm of images, constantly sharing his own thoughts, expressing dismay, sarcasm or hope, and building a fundamental case against Nazism, racism, anti-Semitism, and militarism. Nazi Germany is depicted as an anti-intellectual society first and foremost, one that reduces individuals to thoughtless minuscule particles arranged geometrically by a ruthless dictator and his minions. Romm's alternative is based on humanism and education, presenting communism as a logical heir to universal cultural achievements. Hitler is portrayed as a dangerous, grotesque psychopath empowered by capitalism, but his opponent is not Stalin – who goes unmentioned – or the anti-Nazi alliance, but decent, rank-and-file people all over the world. This historically reductionist but doubtless humanist concept also implies repeated arguments for a 'better Germany', identified both as the Goethe and Schiller heritage and present-day East Germany. With his open criticism of anti-intellectualism and anti-individualism, Romm implicitly attacked similar trends in the Soviet Union. This and the sober analysis of a totalitarian system's inner functioning, albeit tempered by pro-Soviet and pro-communist statements, alarmed censors on all levels. Only Romm's unrivalled authority as a filmmaker – he had been named People's Artist of the USSR in 1950 and was considered a 'living classic' of Soviet cinema – as well as the relative cultural liberalization in the early 1960s allowed him to embark on this risky project. Indeed, for several months after its completion the film did not get permission for release. Shortly after Khrushchev's demise, though, during a personal meeting of leading filmmakers with the new general secretary Leonid Brezhnev, *Ordinary Fascism* was given the green light. To this day, it remains one of the most astonishing achievements of Soviet cinema and arguably the most brilliant of all of Mikhail Romm's films.

Peter Rollberg

The Seasons (The Seasons of the Year; Four Seasons)

Vremena goda (Tarva yeghanakner)

Country of Origin:
Soviet Union

Language:
Russian

Studio:
Yerevan

Director:
Artavazd Peleshian

Cinematographers:
Mikhail Vartanov
Boris Ovsepyan
G. Chavushyan

Music:
Vivaldi
Dall'Abaco

Duration:
29 minutes

Genre:
Documentary

Year:
1972–1975

Synopsis

'This film is about everything, not only about the seasons of the year or people, it is about everything.' Peleshian's own interpretation of *The Seasons* is quite accurate, taking into account what he generally says about his films: 'It's hard to give a verbal synopsis of these films. Such films exist only on the screen, you have to see them.' Putting aside the director's understandable reluctance to translate this poetic black-and-white firework of montage and rhythm, one could say that *The Seasons* is above all a film about life in the Armenian mountains. Farmers tend to their animals and harvest under incredibly fierce conditions (they transport sheep over boulders and through white-water, or chase huge haystacks down steep slopes); a young couple's marriage excites the whole village. Accompanied by natural sounds or contrasted by Vivaldi's *Four Seasons* and folk music, the images – sometimes manipulated by slow-motion or time-lapse, sometimes interrupted by old-fashioned intertitles – evolve into a dynamic rhythm of faces and hands in close-up, herds of sheep, cloud formations, shadow landscapes and rustic dwellings, rituals of work in the fields and stock breeding. A life of labour and hardship, nature and beauty, handcraft and decoration – the poetry of cultural tradition.

Critique

Two earlier films (*Beginning*, 1967; *We*, 1969) and two later ones (*The End*, 1992; *Life*, 1993) won awards, however, it is *The Seasons* (together with *Our Century*, 1982) which can probably be regarded Artavazd Peleshian's best-known film, marking also a significant shift in his work. For the first time his approach towards a 'contrapuntal' or 'distance montage', as he calls it in his theoretical text 'Distance montage, or the theory of distance', was realized not by using archive footage but original images. For the last time he collaborated with the other Armenian documentary auteur of greatest importance, Mikhail Vartanov, whose cinematography delivered the magic pictures of *The Seasons*.

It took Peleshian three years to create these 29 minutes of cosmic energy and complex structure. The result is so astonishingly strong, both visually and audibly, that once seen, heard and motorically perceived ('relived' in a way), the intensity stays on forever, physically. The beginning and the end especially, where nature, animal and man are bound together in a fierce and yet harmonious struggle, reveal a subtle poetry of rhythm that is developed from an inner quality of the images. The movements constituting the washing of the waves or the floating of the clouds determine the steady flow of the editing, its repetitions or interruptions, its acceleration or retardation. Unlike in the case of Vertov or Eisenstein, the montage is not based on two adjacent shots, but rather on the concept of taking apart ('distancing') that which is related to each other.

Most significantly this also holds true in the relation of image and sound: '[With distance montage] you will not only see the image and hear the sound, but you will also hear the image and see the sound'. In perception, the close-ups of faces and hands, the long and medium shots of the herds, the lashing of the torrents or the high-speed of the haystacks are as 'present' as Vivaldi's 'Four Seasons' or the melodies from the *duduk* at the wedding. It is thus not a synthetic, but rather an emphatically autonomous concept treating film as a hybrid medium with synaesthetic qualities. Even the few intertitles ('he got tired', 'do you think that elsewhere it is better', 'This is your land') do not complement the images or add to up to a plot, rather they figure as an aesthetical index saying – these are the elements of film (like black and white, light and shadow, sounds and images, music and voices).

Formally the intertitles are a reminder of the good old days relating to the archaic traditions celebrated in *The Seasons* (the film is, after all, a hymn to Armenia's cultural heritage). Their 'messages', however, contribute to the creation of the evidential guiding editing principle, namely the mythological time structure, with a focus on 'work' in the first half and on 'leisure' in the second. A spiritual universality lies above all this, an existential drama that is not the product of narration but of the montage of leitmotif (shepherds and sheep intertwined) and other structures of motifs. It's the intrinsic rhythm, the balance of repetition and variation, and the constant competition for mastery between ethnographical detail and cinematographic form that makes *The Seasons* such an outstanding 'poetic documentary' in Soviet film history. Peleshian's cardiogram of the soul and spirit of the Armenian people is a paradoxical 'national monument', being neither nationalist nor monumental. He does not create the story of individuals, but an organic image of the people, his people. A higher form of civilization this is, beyond the limits of progress. Rhythm and beauty, force and love are the ingredients of this alphabet in cinema.

Barbara Wurm

Is It Easy to Be Young?

Vai Viegli Būt Jaunam? (Latvian) / Legko li byt' molodym? (Russian)

Country of Origin:
Soviet Union

Languages:
Latvian
Russian

Studio:
Riga Film Studio

Director:
Juris Podnieks

Producer:
Baiba Urbane

Screenplay:
Abram Kleckin
Evgenii Margolin
Juris Podnieks

Cinematographer:
Kalvis Zalcmanis

Editor:
Antra Cilinska

Duration:
80 minutes

Genre:
Documentary

Year:
1986

Synopsis

The film starts with the court investigation of an incident of vandalism on a train, perpetrated by young rock fans returning from a concert. The film explores different youth sub-cultures, featuring interviews with punks, drug addicts, young artists, students and looks at the burning political and social issues of the perestroika era, namely Chernobyl and the war in Afghanistan through the eyes of the young generation.

Critique

Juris Podnieks's *Is It Easy to Be Young?* is one of the key perestroika films that enjoyed enormous mass popularity and critical attention. Its cultural significance is comparable to the documentary *Ordinary Fascism* (1965) by Mikhail Romm. It is one of the first perestroika films that looked at Soviet society through the eyes of the young genera-tion. What it means to be young in the Soviet Union was one the main themes in perestroika and early post-Soviet filmmaking. The young generation was viewed as the bearer of hope, freedom and change (as in *ASSA*, Sergei Solov'ev 1988) or as the lost generation that struggled amidst hypocrisy and inadequacy of the 'adult' Soviet world (as in *Little Vera*, Vasilii Pichul, 1989). Podnieks's documentary displays a sophistication in weighing both of these options, and personalizing them in the reflections that the interviewed participants share with the camera. The film explores several dimensions of what it meant to be young in the Soviet Union, and Latvia in particular: how youth related to the Soviet system of values and institutions, and the role the young generation played in the dangerous 'hot spots' of the late Soviet history – Chernobyl and Afghanistan. Tracking the participants of a rock concert who vandalize the suburban train and are brought to court, the film seems to be firmly on the side of the young people – misunderstood, constrained and abused by the system of ideologi-cal clichés. The film sides with the youth in a 'j'accuse' moment when it narrates the story of a young woman faced with a criminal trial and psychiatric ward because she stole a ballet dress to pose for pictures. The unruly punks in the film pronounce the judgement that would be reiterated in other perestroika narratives: the young generation despises the Soviet way of life as deeply hypocritical, superficial and stifling self-expression.

However, Podnieks's film goes beyond simple negative identifica-tion of the sore points in the late Soviet history. Another immensely popular film, *This is No Way to Live* (dir. Stanislav Govorukhin, 1990) is a very good example of a documentary in which the sole goal is to dismantle, dispute and debunk the Soviet way of life. Podnieks's film gives a more nuanced picture, making individual fate and moral choice the focus of his story. The variety of subjects interviewed in the film talk about their lives and their experiences. And while these expe-riences are pieced together by history, such as the war in Afghanistan or Chernobyl disaster, they remain in focus as individual existential and moral choices. Thus, Podnieks interviews a young amateur

Juris Podnieks, *Is it easy to be young?* (1986).

filmmaker who shoots a film about young people. His film within Podnieks's film addresses the audience with abstract and allegorical figures – a maze-like hallway, a cloaked figure of death, young people standing in the strikingly blue sea at the end, a symbol of hope. The introduction of abstraction highlights the ways Podnieks's film transcends concrete history and returns to questions of personal choice, of what it means to be young – right now and always. The film is shot in a combination of colour and black-and-white stock, reserved mostly for the to-camera interviews, creating a sense of chronicle, something recorded for history. The variation of film stock serves the purpose of joining historic reference and personal experience, the concrete chronicled time and abstract values that govern people's choices. This combination of acute awareness of individual fate and historic and social experiences that affect us makes Juris Podnieks's film a unique documentary and a landmark in perestroika filmmaking.

Volha Isakava

The Last Judgement: Film Materials (Final Verdict; The Highest Court)

Vysshii sud – kinomaterialy

Country of Origin:
Soviet Union

Language:
Russian

Studio:
Riga Film Studios

Director:
Hertz Frank

Screenplay:
Hertz Frank

Cinematographer:
Andris Seletskis

Duration:
73 minutes

Genre:
Documentary

Year:
1987

Synopsis

The Last Judgement recounts the story of Valerii Dolgov, a man who has committed a murder of a black market trader, at the age of twenty-four. The first part of the film is a piece of investigative journalism, in which the director attempts to establish the facts of the case, the identities of both victim and perpetrator, and then, through interviews, to understand what led Dolgov to commit the murder. The court's verdict of the death sentence changes the nature of the interviews profoundly, and a strong bond develops between Frank, who conducts the interviews himself, and Dolgov. From attempts to justify himself, and explain his actions in terms of his ambition and environment, the condemned man increasingly reflects in more philosophical terms about love, God, conscience, death and the moment of murder. The film seems to grant insight into the course of Dolgov's thinking, the thought processes of someone facing death.

Critique

The Last Judgement is a powerful example of film as a process of analysis and of thought: the filmmaker could not have known when he began shooting, what kind of film he would end up with. Thus the first part of the film seems very much of its time, as the director attempts ever so tentatively to ask why there is crime in a socialist society, and to reveal the then startling insight that even the son of an engineer engaged in the heroic process of the construction of socialism can become involved with organized crime and commit murder. While this portrait is of its time, the time is a historic one, when a generation of Soviet youth rejected the normal steady job with a meagre salary, instead taking advantage of the possibilities for rapid enrichment offered by the expansion of the black market and collapse of the state control over the economy. Dolgov's 'moral collapse' as he terms it, is part of a wider societal shift. The link with broader social themes is made in stylistic terms too by the insertion of footage relating not only to the investigation and legal process, but also to the kinds of honest labour, notably construction, that Dolgov turned his back on.

After the death sentence is passed, the film no longer traces Dolgov's relations with society, but with his own impending death and his parents. He becomes transformed as his rational censor gives way to a free flow of association, and it seems as if Frank's camera has crossed a line, over which, as he says 'the living should perhaps not cross'. There is a eerie sense that this is no longer a normal interview, as the conversations take on a more 'confessional' tone, as Frank later said. The camera records a process whereby Dolgov is stripped down to his palpable fear of death and begins to talk about the importance of love, and of his conscience.

The power of Frank's film lies in its psychological intensity. While the film can be compared to treatments of a similar theme in Richard Leacock's 1965 *The Chair*, and Nick Broomfield's 2003: *Eileen: Life and Death of a Serial Killer*, Frank's command of the documentary form is no less assured: the occasional voice-over is insightful as to his

Hertz Frank, *High Court* (1987).

own feelings and the process of making the film; the music is dramatic at first, but later ceding place to diegetic sound and the subject; and the camera tellingly pinpoints Dolgov's nervous mannerisms, such as his fidgeting with a box of matches. The use of still photographs, however, is particularly effective in the final images of Frank and Dolgov leaving the death row cell, and then of the empty cell. Thus Frank attempts to resist the temptation to show too much after the manner of 1980s and 1990s Soviet 'dark naturalism' or *chernukha*. Nevertheless, when Dolgov's sentence was carried out in the week the film was released, its initial success owed something to its sensational topicality. *The Last Judgement*'s international acclaim, with prizes at Nyon (1987) and Amsterdam (1988) documentary film festivals, however, demonstrated its greater and lasting value. This achievement was subsequently reiterated by Moscow's 'Stalker' Human Rights Film Festival in 1995, which recognized the film's 'artistic honesty.'

Jeremy Hicks

Solovki Power

Vlast' Solovetskaia:
Svidetel'stva i dokumenty

Country of Origin:
Soviet Union

Language:
Russian

Studio:
Mosfilm

Director:
Marina Goldovskaia

Screenplay:
Viktor Listov
Dmitrii Chukovskii

Cinematographer:
Marina Goldovskaia

Art Director:
P. Safonov

Composers:
Nikolai Karetnikov
Marina Krutoiarskaia

Editor:
M. Kareva

Duration:
88 minutes

Genre:
Documentary

Cast:
Dmitrii Likhachev
Efim Lagutin
Oleg Volkov
Zoia Marchenko
Ol'ga Adamova-Sliozberg
Anatolii Gorelov
Samuil Epshtein
Aleksandr Prokhorov
Andrei Roshchin
Savelii Savenko
Fekla Fofanova
Aleksandr Proshkin

Year:
1988

Synopsis

This multiple award-winning documentary describes the prison camp located on the Solovetsk Islands (Solovki) in the White Sea. For centuries a monastery, Solovki was officially converted in June 1923 to a 'Special Purpose Camp', a prototype for what would become the Gulag. Solovki was in operation until August 1939, when some of its prisoners were relocated to Siberian camps such as Norilsk and Dudinka, while others were never seen or heard from again. The film shows numerous excerpts from a propaganda film about Solovki shot in 1927–1928, and interspersed throughout are scenes of a modern-day team unearthing and reading old letters and other documents found at sites on Solovki. The film draws extensively on the personal recollections of those who were at the camp, including Andrei Roshchin (a former member of the Cheka who worked there as a guard), Fekla Fofanova (a cleaning lady at the camp) and Savelii Savenko (a cameraman for the Solovki propaganda film). The most moving testimony comes from those who were imprisoned there: Dmitrii Likhachev (an academic), Efim Lagutin (worker), Oleg Volkov (writer), Zoia Marchenko (stenographer), Ol'ga Adamova-Sliozberg (economist), Anatolii Gorelov (writer), Samuil Epshtein (economist) and Aleksandr Prokhorov (engineer).

Critique

Solovki Power is Marina Goldovskaia's most important and well-known film. Goldovskaia began working on the film near the beginning of the glasnost era, when Mikhail Gorbachev sought greater openness and transparency in discussing and critiquing Soviet history as well as contemporary Soviet policies. Despite the greater freedoms seemingly guaranteed at the time, Goldovskaia was nervous to undertake such a project at a documentary film studio or a television station. To secure herself greater control over the content and design of the film, she made it within an otherwise fiction-film unit at Mosfilm, which at the time was run by a friend of hers from film school. To get the project approved and funded, she downplayed her interest in the prison camps and cleverly assembled a very different proposal for a documentary on the historical and cultural artifacts to be found on Solovki.

The film helped to make public the issue of past government oppression and abuse, something that most people certainly knew of but had only cautiously talked about in private. Sensationally, the film showed that Solovki started taking prisoners on 6 June 1923; thus, the system that would develop into the 'Chief Administration of Corrective Labor Camps and Colonies' (Gulag) began under Lenin – not Stalin, as many had believed. In addition to detailing the capricious cruelties that prisoners suffered, the film exposed camp hierarchies, in which actual criminals usually were treated more favourably and often were assigned to terrorize the intellectuals and religious devotees deemed enemies of the state. The film's title is a bastardization of the oft-championed phrase 'Soviet Power', and the film demonstrates that on those islands of Solovki, there was an altogether distinct, perverse

Marina Goldovskaia, *Solovki Power* (1988).

regime – a different authority and a separate set of rules under which one was forced to endure.

The film's strength lies in its powerful resonances and striking juxta-positions. The accumulation of stoic testimony from the eight featured survivors details the vast range of experiences they underwent at the same time that it confirms the shared depth of their suffering. They recount how they came to be sentenced and brought to Solovki, and their stories reveal the systemic arbitrariness that governed their lives: Oleg Volkov refused to be an informant for the secret police, Zoia Marchenko was found in possession of correspondence from her brother revealing the tortures that he had endured in prison, Efim Lagutin was simply a teenage runaway who stowed away on a ship that had been abroad. Their stories are often most compelling when they overlap on specific events. They reveal how they hid or cow-ered on the night of 28 October 1928 as 300 prisoners were brutally executed as a warning to the others. They object to the footage from the Solovki propaganda film and describe a very different reality from the one shown on screen.

Throughout the film, we are generally left with verbal accounts in place of any visual evidence of abuse. For example, despite hearing of the extensive range of torture administered on Sekirny Hill – con-sidered the most terrible place on Solovki – what we see instead is the desolate, rugged allure of that landscape. The many shots of quiet, scenic beauty optimistically suggest renewal, as this place bears little trace of its past horrors. However, in the very stillness and emptiness of these shots, we are also made to realize the absence and loss of those who did not live to tell their stories. We are cautioned that nature and architecture alone will not preserve this history, and are reminded that, as the narrator declares, 'We do not have the right to forget'.

Vincent Bohlinger

Moscow Elegy

Moscow Elegy

Country of Origin:
Soviet Union

Language:
Russian

Studios:
Leningrad Studio of
Documentary Film (LSDF)
Union of Cinema Workers

Director:
Aleksandr Sokurov

Producers:
Georgii Bagoturiia
Vladimir Mikhailov
Tat'iana Aleshkina

Cinematographers:
Aleksandr Burov
Aleksei Naidenov
Liudmila Krasnova

Editors:
Liudmila Feiginova
T. Belousova
A. Zhikhareva
Leda Semenova
L. Volkova

Duration:
88 minutes

Genre:
Documentary

Year:
1988

Synopsis

Moscow Elegy is Sokurov's homage to his mentor Andrei Tarkovskii on the occasion of his death on 29 December 1986. Sokurov augments extensive excerpts from Tarkovskii's films *Mirror* (1975), *Voyage in Time* (1980) and *Nostalgia* (1983) with video footage from the shoot of *Sacrifice* (1986, supplied by Anna-Lena Wibum) and of Tarkovskii's fatal illness and funeral (supplied by Chris Marker). Photographs document Tarkovskii's childhood. Original footage documents Tarkovskii's homes in Russia. The broader historical context is suggested by footage of the funerals of Brezhnev and Iurii Andropov. Eschewing chronology or analysis of Tarkovskii's cinematic oeuvre, Sokurov's quiet but emotional narration presents Tarkovskii's passing as the end of an epoch in Russian spiritual existence.

Critique

Moscow Elegy culminates with video footage of Tarkovskii's final months, his funeral and his grave. Sokurov features French TV reports on Tarkovskii's death, highlighting the disconcerting way that this epochal event became trivialized as breaking news communicated over modern mass media to an indifferent public, to be forgotten on the morrow. But Tarkovskii's traces are also captured only within technological media, both documentary footage and an audio recording of Tarkovskii reading his father's poem 'I fell ill in childhood'. By posing the problem in this way *Moscow Elegy* links Tarkovskii's death to a central concern in Sokurov's cinematic aesthetic, especially in the genre of the documentary elegy: the tension between the intimate experience of time, loss and death and the modern, mechanical media by which we access it.

In Sokurov's numerous other cinematic homages, from *Sonata for Viola* (1981, about Dmitrii Shostakovich) to *Conversations with Solzhenitsyn* (1999), he has tended to focus his camera on the physical presence of his subject. Though Sokurov begins *Moscow Elegy* as a search for Tarkovskii's presence, it ends up registering his absence: from Russia, from his own homes, from the public record and even from his own films. Sokurov highlights three key moments of Tarkovskii's life: Russian childhood, Italian exile and death in Paris. The only specific places featured are Tarkovskii's now-empty homes: in Zavrazh'e, Shchipok (in Moscow), Miasnoe, Mosfil'movskii pereulok; he takes us on a posthumous tour of the latter three, noting their sparse furnishings and their present state of abandonment. He shows footage of Tarkovskii in Marlen Khutsiev's *Il'ich Gate* (1962) and in a documentary study of cinema protagonists (1969), but only to stress Tarkovskii's seemingly alien guise in these 'roles'. Only sparing traces of his grown presence remains. One stunning sequence imposes Viacheslav Ovchinnikov's soundtrack to *Ivan's Childhood* (1962) over documentary footage of Sheremet'evo airport, Tarkovskii's final port of call in the USSR, culminating in the discovery of the birch woods that surround the airport. Sokurov tries to recover the sense of Tarkovskii's final glance at his loved ones and his home landscape by reproducing the autobiographical elements of Tark-ovskii's fiction films.

Throughout the film Sokurov eschews the words 'USSR' or 'Russia', preferring 'rodina' – homeland, a concept symbolized by this birch forest. Narrating Tarkovskii's final days, he laments that 'We in the homeland knew next to nothing about the state of his health'. One wonders what would have changed had they known; it is, of course, a typically illogical expression of grief, of irredeemable loss. Sokurov's despondence over Tarkovskii's death (to which he also devoted a 1987 memoir *Death: the Banal Equalizer*) reveals a sentimentalism and nostalgia capable of paralyzing those who remain. All we can do, it would seem, is to open museums on the sites of his homes, lovingly preserving the arrangement of objects as he left them.

Made at the peak of perestroika, Sokurov's lament for Tarkovskii was perceived as mourning 'the Russia we have lost' (to quote the title of another perestroika-era documentary by Stanislav Govorukhin). Recent history – most notably the funerals of Brezhnev and Andropov – feels as distant as if it is the history of another planet. In this sense *Moscow Elegy* is less about Tarkovskii per se that about the condition of historical abandonment symbolized by his death.

Robert Bird

The Russia That We Lost

Rossiia, kotoruiu my poteriali

Country of Origin:
Russia

Languages:
Russian, some French

Studio:
Mosfilm

Director:
Stanislav Govorukhin

Producer:
Vladimir Dostal'

Screenplay:
Stanislav Govorukhin

Cinematographer:
Gennadii Engstrem

Synopsis

A political documentary, directed and narrated by Stanislav Govorukhin, which seeks to rehabilitate pre-Revolutionary Russia, while debunk-ing the Soviet mythologies of the Revolution. The film is divided into three parts, the first of which delineates the pre-Revolutionary idyll. Part I paints modern Russian history in broad strokes, using newsreel footage from the period, and crosscutting it with scenes from contem-porary life in Russia. Here, Govorukhin makes his general argument that Russia was already advancing toward modernity before the Revolution, and that real progress was stunted throughout the Soviet period. The director tackles other claims made by the Communist Party, such as the equality of women, only to dispel them. The second part of *The Russia That We Lost* provides detailed portraits of Tsar Nicholas II, Lenin, Prime Minister Petr Stolypin, alongside analyses of the Russian Army during World War I, and the meaning of 1917. The third part details the early crimes of the Bolsheviks, in particular the murder of the royal family and the Cheka's violent campaign against Russian Orthodoxy.

Critique

The Russia That We Lost is a none too subtle piece of political propa-ganda, at times delving into Russian nationalism with its whitewash of the period of Nicholas II's reign. In pre-Revolutionary Russia, according to the film, peasants and industrial workers happily labour. And the elite are harmless purveyors of social ritual and good taste. Imperial Russia in this conception is a space of traditional values and at the same

Art Director:

Al'bert Rudachenko

Music:

Petr Tchaikovsky

Sergei Rachmaninoff

Editor:

Nina Vasil'eva

Duration:

106 minutes

Genre:

Documentary

Year:

1992

time developing into a modern nation on the cusp of joining Western Europe. While there is poverty and inequality in such a space, there is little social conflict. Russian (as opposed to foreign) capitalists were in control of the economy and managed relations with workers in a just and patrimonial fashion. The first part of the film does not yet provide evidence of the director's claims, only a juxtaposition of early *actualités* shot during the first decade of the twentieth century with contemporary footage. The moving images suggest a vibrant and rich society on the eve of revolution, rather than the picture of a declining empire that Soviet historiography had emphasized previously.

The second part of *The Russia That We Lost* introduces the recurrent visual and narrative motif of the archive. The film constantly cuts between an objective examination of old photographs and newsreels and Govorukhin's deliberately subjective tour through the archives and written documents. In one case, the camera pans across the record of a politburo meeting, while Govorukhin reads the text aloud, tapping his pen underneath the words as he goes. The archive becomes the director's key source of credibility in the film, even as it highlights the subjective act of selecting and interpreting historical documents. In this respect, the archive motif in *The Russia That We Lost* is highly unusual in documentary filmmaking, a tradition which usually obscures the process of constructing evidence.

Govorukhin's organization is also unusual in *The Russia That We Lost*, contributing at times to the film's sprawling quality. The second part, for example, is sub-divided into the following categories: Petr Stolypin; Nikolai Romanov; Vladimir Ul'ianov; The Russian Army; and The First Russian Revolution. The first two individuals serve to represent the positive values of the empire: order; love; family; and culture. The film details the everyday lives of the royal family, emphasizing the storybook quality of the Romanovs. Govorukhin then addresses Lenin's upbringing in Simbirsk. While remaining without direct comment, the director emphasizes the Soviet leader's hidden Jewish ancestors, suggesting a contrast between the Romanovs' moral authenticity and the Bolsheviks' amoral duplicity. In the following section, the director details a movement from a united and patriotic army in the imperial period to a military force that revealed the incompetence of Soviet leaders and the deep fractures in Soviet society.

Key to Govorukhin's argument is that the First Russian Revolution in February 1917 had already led the country down the path of violence, chaos and destruction. Even though Russians were initially celebrating their new political freedoms that emerged from revolution, Govorukhin cites political intrigue, an immediate degradation of morals and the loss of legitimate authority as factors that led to the complete breakdown of Russian society during 1917, even before October. The only factor that the Bolsheviks introduced to the context of 1917 was political terror, which he details in the film's third part.

In the conclusion to the film, 'The Epoch of Degeneration', Govorukhin suggests that the amorality of Lenin and the Bolsheviks produced an amoral society. Consequently, the only Russians who maintained not only their culture, but also the morality of the empire, were the émigré communities in Paris and Berlin.

Joshua First

The Belovs

Belovy

Country of Origin:
Russia

Language:
Russian

Studio:
Studio of Documentary Films
St Petersburg

Director:
Viktor Kosakovskii

Cinematographers:
Viktor Kosakovskii
Leonid Konovalov

Duration:
59 minutes

Genre:
Documentary

Year:
1992

Synopsis

'What is so interesting here that you are filming it? This is my brother Misha. We are ordinary people. We live here where the river has its source. There is nothing special about us and this place.' – Anna Fedorovna Belova's words are directed straight into the camera. The ordinary rules in the old Belovs' everyday village life. Mikhail, self-appointed philosopher and part-time drinker sits at the kitchen table, smooches his dog and occasionally leaves the house for a short check-up of his sister's working progress in the kitchen-garden. Anna, two times widow, milks the cows and talks to them (in a far more human way than she does to Misha), she works, laughs, cries and sings *chastushkas*. One day their two brothers from the city come to visit. *The Belovs* exchange opinions on perestroika politics and meta-physical problems as well as a handful of hard-core curses. Left behind in their twosome loneliness Anna and Misha continue to swear their guts out and end their day in the living room: the drunkard crawling on the floor, his sister enchanted by a dance of grief and anger, of lust and exaltation. After all, this is quite an unordinary life.

Critique

Viktor Kosakovskii's *The Belovs* is maybe the perfect example of a deconstructivist documentary. On the threshold between cinema-vérité realism and mythology, this one-hour movie in sepia unfolds its quality by functioning on both levels, the face value of a story set in 1992 Russia, in a run down provincial shack on the one hand, and the symbolic decoding of classical topoi on the other (like the universal brother-and-sister-plot, the 'typical Russian' aspect of it, matching a male drinking theoriser and a female practical family-sustainer, or the mythological setting of a place 'where the river has its source'). Everything seems to happen in an actual, short time span (something like 'one day in the life of …') but is at the same time part of a ritual of much larger dimensions.

This radicalizes the relationship between actuality and potentiality on the level of the representation, between realism and idealism on the level of existence, whereas on a temporal level it brings together a linear and a circular structure, thus creating an interference or rather tension that in turn produces the scaffold for a convincing yet open editing policy. A long sequence of Misha the philosopher sitting at the kitchen table is followed by a sequence shot of the river landscape, the image being confronted with music from a popular old Indian movie; Anna's simultaneous talking to the camera and her cows as well as her restless activities are countered by Misha's coincidental metaphysical monologues on justice, freedom, singularity, the bour-geoisie, Russian imperialism, Yeltsin, Gaidar and his personal peda-gogical doctrine: to forbid the public production of toys, so girls can knit their own puppets and boys construct their own buildings.

It is not the peculiarity of these characters as such, but rather Kosa-kovskii's way of portraying them that makes *The Belovs* such an out-standing documentary and an unofficial role model for the generation to come. Whereas the typical perestroika non-fiction film, fighting the old paradigms of Soviet documentary stylistics, turns to the subaltern in order to enforce 'true', 'authentic' outings of the dirt and decay of the time, Kosakovskii never drives his protagonists into revealing their souls in front of the camera. He doesn't inspire or analyse or generalize anything; above all, he never accuses anyone.

Kosakovskii's camera depicts wonderful, spontaneous moments, like Anna's furious comment on one of Misha's endless tirades ('Karamazov – sit!'), her useless attempts to keep the dog from playing with a hedgehog ('Here you go, take the candy instead!'), her reading of a letter to the son who left ages ago ('Don't forget to take the propolis, and keep your feet warm!') addressed to a birch tree, the brothers' lashing in the bathhouse (accompanied by the tender melody of 'The moon was yellow, and the night was young'), or the chasing of cows, chicken, babushka and ants (this time with some Latin samba as the musical background). But the very subtlety of Kosakovskii's moves and takes, his documentary credo, is displayed at the very end; during a verbal battle of sheer incredible cruelty ('All you possess are two balls between your legs, and those are dirty!' – 'I need to kill you in order to liberate society. You need to be eliminated, you are interfering with our lives.') Kosakovskii decides to turn off the sound, only to have Anna listen to the recorded quarrel through earphones later, while Misha ultimately falls over. Anna seems shocked by what she hears, she is ashamed, and breaks out into hysterical laughter and crying. The film has become part of her life. And we realize that watching *The Belovs* we have been on the edge to voyeurism. On the edge only.

Barbara Wurm

Bread Day

Chlebnyi den'

Country of Origin:
Russia

Language:
Russian

Studio:
VKSR (Higher Courses for Directors and Scriptwriters)

Director:
Sergei Dvortsevoi

Cinematographer:
Alisher Khamidkhodzhaev

Synopsis

A deserted settlement, 80 km from Saint Petersburg. Only a few elderly people are left. It is Tuesday again, 'bread day'. In deep snow they are already waiting for the wagon. Excitement. The locomotive disappears, the wagon stays. Half a dozen of people, female mainly it appears, have to push the wagon themselves, along the rails, 2 km, towards the settlement. An endless shot. They are desperate. Pan across the settlement. Glorious nothingness. A she-dog bites away her own puppies who want to feed. They are desperate. Two goats find each other through the window. They kiss, it seems. Unloading of the bread. The first bags are being stuffed. In another eternal shot, a man buys out nearly all the bread there is, engaging in a fierce verbal battle with the shop assistant ('the ruler of fate'). All other customers remain still. There won't be any bread left. A goat enters the shop, also desperate for food – or bored, who knows? A drunkard, too, wants bread. There is nothing left. Another quarrel. This time it gets physical. Sunset. Sunrise. The empty trays are put back into the wagon. The wagon is pushed back along the rails. Fifty-five minutes – or seventeen shots of classical documentary.

Duration:

55 minutes

Genre:

Documentary

Year:

1998

Critique

Dvortsevoi once said: 'To be ready for a shot means that I can wait for a week, for two weeks, three, a month … I will wait for exactly the shot I want, and I know that I can wait for it and that I will get it'. Beginning in the early 1990s and together with one of Russia's best camera-men, Alisher Khamidkhodzhaev, Sergei Dvortsevoi has developed a convincing method in documentary ethics and stylistics. He observes and waits and tries to be prepared for 'the event' to happen (again). Then he shoots, without the slightest interference. This way, each scene takes the time it needs. In his earlier masterpiece *Happiness* (1995), a clumsy little nomad kid eating his porridge absorbed the attention of an astonished international film community – for an eter-nity, it seemed. In *Bread Day* – the depiction of one day required a three-month presence on site – wagons, goats, dogs and seniors take the scene, as if each was performing its role, a little autistic somehow, busy with themselves, reluctant to communicate with others of their species.

Whereas the Central-Asian setting of his first two films contributed to an outstanding anthropological and ethnographic quality of con-templation, Dvortsevoi's 'thick' observations of this classical (not-yet-post-)communist scenario on Russian soil – peripheral remoteness, constant shortcomings, silent despair, tedious yet useless activity, greed, mismanagement and endless debates over the sales counter – bring in an additional political layer. 'This film is about us, don't you realize!? It's the wagon they uncoupled from world civilization in 1917, and we have spent an entire 70 years pushing it towards communism, wasting our time in queues.' Even if this interpretation might seem somewhat forced, the essential political insight put forth by Dvortse-voi is that these people did and still do not seem to even notice the misery and deadlock they are living in. All they do is continue their daily routines (small-minded talk of shortages with an extra pinch of maliciousness and some great sarcastic humour) and struggle for some loaves of bread. 'Poekhali', is their slogan: let's go! – and this is not an expression of enthusiasm but a quote from Gagarin.

The outstanding ethical quality of *Bread Day* lies in its rigorous aesthetic form. Each shot is so deliberately established that it seems to be staged but isn't: the orchestration takes place on the spatial and temporal level only. The animals and humans do not act, but they do not hide either. Every movement, gesture or verbal utterance (includ-ing some serious swearing) is caught by a stubbornly fixed camera filming from a respectable distance and closing the shot only when the sequence itself has come to a conclusion. Thus *Bread day* deliv-ers images humble in intention but strong in expression. The balance between the director's cinematic intervention and the protagonists' sovereignty of action seems unique in the history of documentary film. As a result one feels compassionate but far from being drawn in by manipulation, reinforced voyeurism or external pathos. The turn of the millennium, says Dvortsevoi, was a 'time for documentary filmmak-ing'. *Bread Day* is the perfect example for that. Its appropriately quiet and patient pace reflects the ambiguity of the 'radical changes' in society. Not much is happening here, in this deserted periphery. And everything seems more or less the same as it used to be. Complaining remains complaining. Swearing remains swearing. Getting upset is useless – but happens. And the name-calling ranges from hyper-offensive to super-cautious. There are snakes in the grass. 'If you want a change, why don't you look for another shop assistant', mumbles the grumpy old woman behind the sales counters. 'We will do that', the nagging pain-in-the-ass customer answers, 'and it won't be hard to find another such *beauty* (*krasavitsu*)'. 'Beauty – why did you just use this word?'

Barbara Wurm

Private Chronicles: A Monologue

Chastnye khroniki. Monolog

Country of Origin:
Russia

Language:
Russian

Studios:
MV Studio
REN-TV (Russia) with YLE-TV2 (Finland)

Director:
Vitalii Manskii

Producers:
Natal'ia and Vitalii Manskii

Sceenplay:
Vitalii Manskii

Composer:
Aleksei Aigi

Duration:
86 minutes

Genre:
Documentary

Year:
1999

Synopsis

Private Chronicles: A Monologue is a compilation of amateur film footage which is used to narrate the life of a fictional individual born on 11 April 1961, a day before Iurii Gagarin's successful flight into space. By adding a voice-over commentary identifying himself and various figures in his life, as well as commenting on various rites of passage (such as the death of elderly relatives or sexual awakening), cultural institutions (such as the *dacha* or the *subbotnik*), social trends (such as migration to Moscow) and wider political events (such as the Moscow Olympics or Brezhnev's death) the film traces the life of a kind of Soviet everyman of the post-war era, a cynical child of the idealistic 1960s generation. The structure of this narrative is further stressed by the titles marking the changing of the year which have images of major national or international events. The narrator drowns in the *Admiral Nakhimov* naval disaster on 31 August 1986, at the beginning of the Perestroika era, before the failed attempt to reform, and subsequent death throes and demise of the system with which he is identified.

Critique

Private Chronicles: A Monologue is a groundbreaking film through its pioneering of a totally new form: it makes a work of art, a biography, out of amateur footage. The purpose is to attempt to illustrate a sense of private life as a positive achievement, as something wrested from and maintained in spite of the symbols and demands of the Soviet political system, but somehow still defined by it. The urgency of the project is all the greater, as the generation it speaks to attempts to mediate their mixed attitudes towards the years of their youthful vitality lived under a moribund political system. Manskii's film stresses a sharp line between the official political culture, which is consistently ridiculed by the voice-over and barely reflected in the home movies, and the physiological processes of growth and death, the sexual, the sub-cultural life of fashion and popular music, of parties and leisure time, which dominate the images. This often means the narrator commenting upon the meaning and importance of various stages of life or institutions: childhood as a brief window of freedom, marriage as the only ritual of personal life where the state helped, holidays on the Black Sea and the flexible nature of the flat.

This device of describing and commenting upon the life around him, like a visiting anthropologist, enables Manskii to get around the fact that the footage does not follow a specific group of people, or indeed, even any one single person consistently enough to identify them. It also means that his film shows someone he calls a 'representative of the last generation of Soviet people', rather than a single individual. This is a paradox, since the nature of the footage and much of the commentary stresses the primacy of the individual and family life over that of the collective. While this contradiction maybe attributed to this generation's ambivalent attitude to the Soviet past, the effect is to transform the material of private memories into a broader, rather monolithic, vision of the Soviet past, centripetally-focused on Moscow, permitting little space for specifically individual, ethnic or other variations. In this regard, the initial image is a telling one, in that it starts as a tiny box in the middle of the screen, and slowly, to the sound of Aleksei Aigi's mesmerising violin, expands until it occupies the whole of the screen. This seems to suggest the way in which Manskii makes the private, note the Russian sense of the term *chastnaia*, the partial, the fragmentary, expand until it occupies the whole of the screen, until it becomes central.

If this is a problem, it is also an incredible achievement to have moulded these fragments, which he has been collecting since 1996, into a whole. While the amateur films have a certain intrinsic warmth, they often frame their subjects poorly, and suffer from other technical faults, which would be forgiven when shown to the filmmaker's family and friends, but not by us outsiders. Manskii's editing of each sequence and the whole structure, create a sense this is a whole. Yet the sound too plays a pivotal role, especially the voice-over, brilliantly paced by Aleksandr Tsekalo, the use of various sounds to accentuate themes such as that of water and Aleksei Aigi's virtuouso, Nyman-esque score, which encapsulates and welds together the moods of menace and merriment, the mixed emotions about this past.

Jeremy Hicks

The Siege

Blokada

Country of Origin:
Russia

Language:
Russian

Studio:
Studio of Documentary Films, St Petersburg

Director:
Sergei Loznitsa

Synopsis

Loznitsa's *The Siege* presents a series of seemingly random episodes from the siege of 1941–1944. The director found these materials dispersed and collecting dust in various Petersburg archives. Many of his findings chosen for inclusion are the censored remains of the *Battle for Leningrad* (1942), the main cinematic text of the official propaganda of the Siege. Six decades after the events, Loznitsa has created a film that radically reverses the rules and expectations of the Soviet ethos of Siege representation. The film concentrates on the most unbearable topoi of life in the besieged city – corpse-filled streets, buses and trucks frozen into ice, Way to Calvary-like expeditions to obtain bread and water; it also empathically follows the changes in the city's image – the disappearance of monuments, the embankments and facades 'wounded' by the constant shelling and bombing.

Producer:
Viacheslav Tel'nov

Screenplay:
Sergei Loznitsa

Duration:
52 minutes

Genre:
Documentary

Year:
2005

Critique

This film challenges the overpowering desire for a teleological master-narrative that would ascribe meaning to the hellish world of the Siege. The final version of *Battle for Leningrad* was permeated by the consoling commentary of its voice-over narration and uplifting soundtrack, and the montage principle of organization took the Smolnyi Party headquarter's point of view on the Siege. Loznitsa's film, on the other hand, works rather as a Siege diary, reflecting on the notions of limited space and the difficult progression of time. As would a citizen caught unawares in the besieged city, this film dashes from one impression, experience and tragedy to the next.

Loznitsa's editing keenly follows one element of urban life that many inhabitants of the city came to see as a crucial leitmotif of their existence in Leningrad both before and during the Siege – the street-car, that for many symbolized the distinction between the 'life' and 'death' of/in their city. If one were to seek unifying strategies in the fragmented body of Loznitsa's film, one might claim that the streetcar becomes this film's protagonist. Its task is to signify the flow of time in the city, where time, according to many diarists, was experienced as having come to a halt. We see the streetcar in October, stubborn and still energetic, we see it in November, as a suffering victim of dystrophy (its slow movement here might be explained by the constant possibility of sudden shelling), and then in January. By now the streetcar is frozen, covered with incrustations of ice, its function changed as well – now turned into an improvised morgue. The streetcar becomes the embodiment of the spectacle of the Siege, signifying both the memories of and hopes for the time without the Siege as well as the new meanings inscribed into the urban text by the reality of the Siege.

Another aspect of the Siege site that interests Loznitsa is how people look at one another. The camera allows us to participate in the dramatic exchange of gazes between passers-by on Nevskii Prospect and German soldiers taken in captivity in the Fall of 1941. The faces of Leningraders express rage, disgust and a certain disbelief – captive

Sergei Loznitsa, *The Siege* (2006)

German soldiers were rare that autumn, when millions of Russian soldiers were taken in captivity. These gazes are active, almost material, weapon-like. They are markedly different from the gazes that Loznitsa studies in the episode depicting perhaps the most painful instance of the Siege existence – citizens walking by corpses in the centre of the city. This condition defines the tension of the episode: we, the audience, are horrified by the spectacle of corpses on Nevsky and along the Griboedov Canal, and equally we are petrified by the expectation – will the urban flow slow down for the dead? According to Loznitsa, sometimes it does and sometimes it doesn't.

One of many sensorial contradictions of the Siege was that though it established a new and poignant version of the urban spectacle, visibility was simultaneously severely compromised and consequently a unique auditory environment was created. In a city robbed of electricity and where windows were blacked out, people had to learn to interpret many layers of acoustic information. Besides the famous 'voice of power' embodied by the Leningrad radio (and almost entirely absent in Loznitsa's film), the system of sounds and noises of the Siege was dense and diverse; it was largely defined by the gripping contrast between the regular sounds of air-raid sirens, shelling and bombing (citizens learnt to define the location of bombing according to the intensity of sound, thus establishing a new kind of interpretive topography) and an unusual silence caused by the lack of cars and public transportation, the relative scarcity of people and fading industrial activity in the city. Since the actual 'raw' footage material that Loznitsa used for his film had no sound, the director's task was to recreate, to evoke, to invent the sounds of the Siege. In Loznitsa's film, sounds are also fragmented, superimposed over each other, disorganized; while creating a disconcertingly ambivalent 'dialogue' between the background 'white' noise of the Siege and ambiguous solo sounds, Loznitsa highlights meanings and sensations by exaggerating volume. In episodes depicting explosions and fires, the sound becomes overwhelming; the rawness of destruction emerges even before its visual counterpart: we hear death before seeing it.

Polina Barskova

RECOMME READING

(Listed here are only English-language books)

Attwood, Lynne (ed). *Red Women on the Silver Screen: Soviet Women and Cinema from the Beginning to the End of the Communist Era*. London: Pandora, 1993.

Barker, Adele Marie (ed). *Consuming Russia: Popular Culture, Sex, and Society since Gorbachev*. Durham: Duke University Press, 1999.

Beardow, Frank. *Little Vera* (KinoFile 8). London: I.B. Tauris, 2003.

Berry, Ellen E. and Anessa Miller-Pogacar (eds). *Re-Entering the Sign: Articulating New Russian Culture*. Ann Arbor: University of Michigan Press, 1995.

Beumers, Birgit (ed). *24 Frames: The Cinema of Russia and the Former Soviet Union*. London: Wallflower Press, 2007.

—— (ed). *Russia on Reels: The Russian Idea in Post-Soviet Cinema*. London: I.B. Tauris, 1999.

—— (ed). 'Special Focus: Soviet and Russian Blockbuster Films', *Slavic Review* 62.3 (2003).

Beumers, Birgit and Mark Lipovetsky, *Performing Violence*, Bristol and Chicago: Intellect Books, 2009

Beumers, Birgit. *A History of Russian Cinema*. Oxford: Berg, 2009.

——. *Burnt by the Sun* (KinoFile 3). London: I.B. Tauris, 2000.

——. *Nikita Mikhalkov* (Kino Companion 1). London: I.B. Tauris, 2005.

——. *Popular Culture Russia!* Santa Barbara, Denver, London: ABC Clio, 2005.

Bird, Robert. *Andrei Rublev*. London: BFI Classics, 2004.

Bordwell, David. *The Cinema of Eisenstein*. Cambridge, MA & London: Harvard University Press, 1993.

Brashinsky, Michael and Andrew Horton (eds). *Russian Critics on the Cinema of Glasnost*. Cambridge: Cambridge University Press, 1994.

Bulgakowa, Oksana. *Sergei Eisenstein: A Biography*. Berlin & San Francisco: PotemkinPress, 2001.

Cavendish, Phil. *Soviet Mainstream Cinematography: The Silent Era*. London: UCL Arts and Humanities Publications, 2007.

Cherchi Usai, Paolo, *et al* (eds). *Silent Witnesses. Russian Films, 1908–1919*. Coordination by Yuri Tsivian. London: BFI, 1989.

Christie, Ian and Richard Taylor (eds). *Eisenstein Rediscovered*. London: Routledge, 1993.

Condee, Nancy (ed). *Soviet Hieroglyphics: Visual Culture in Late Twentieth-Century Russia*. London/Bloomington: BFI/Indiana University Press, 1995.

Condee, Nancy. *The Imperial Trace: Recent Russian Cinema*. Oxford and New York: Oxford University Press, 2009.

Dobrenko, Evgeny. *Stalinist Cinema and the Production of History*. Edinburgh: Edinburgh University Press, 2008.

Faraday, George. *Revolt of the Filmmakers: The Struggle for Artistic Autonomy and the Fall of the Soviet Film Industry*. University Park, PA: Pennsylvania State University Press, 2000.

Galichenko, Nicholas. *Glasnost: Soviet Cinema Responds*. Austin: University of Texas Press, 1991.

Gillespie, David. *Early Soviet Cinema: Innovation, Ideology and Propaganda*. London: Wallflower, 2000.

——. *Russian Cinema*. New York: Longman, 2003.

Golovskoy, Val and John Rimberg. *Behind the Soviet Screen*. Ann Arbor: Ardis, 1986.

Goodwin, James. *Eisenstein, Cinema & History*. Urbana & Chicago, IL: University of Illinois Press, 1993.

Goulding, Daniel J. (ed). *Post New Wave Cinema in the Soviet Union and Eastern Europe*. Bloomington: Indiana University Press, 1989.

Graffy, Julian. *Bed and Sofa* (KinoFile 5). London: I.B. Tauris, 2001.

Graffy, Julian and G. Hosking (eds). *Culture and the Media in the USSR Today*. London: Macmillan, 1989.

Hashamova, Yana. *Pride and Panic: Russian Imagination of the West in Post-Soviet Film*. Bristol and Chicago: Intellect Books, 2007.

Haynes, John. *New Soviet Man: Gender and Masculinity in Stalinist Soviet Cinema*. Manchester and New York: Manchester University Press, 2003.

Hicks, Jeremy. *Dziga Vertov: Defining Documentary Film*. London: I.B. Tauris, 2007.

Horton, Andrew. *Inside Soviet Film Satire*. Cambridge: Cambridge University Press, 1993.

Horton, Andrew and Michael Brashinsky. *The Zero Hour: Glasnost and Soviet Cinema in Transition*. Princeton: Princeton University Press, 1992.

Hutchings, Stephen and Anat Vernitski (eds). *Russian and Soviet Film Adaptations of Literature, 1900–2001. Screening the Word*. London: Routledge, 2005.

Johnson, Vida T. and Graham Petrie. *The Films of Andrei Tarkovsky: A Visual Fugue.* Bloomington: Indiana University Press, 1994.

Kelly, Catriona and David Shepherd. *Russian Cultural Studies.* Oxford: Oxford University Press, 1998.

Kenez, Peter. *Cinema and Soviet Society, 1917–1953.* Cambridge: Cambridge University Press, 1992.

——. *The Birth of the Propaganda State: Soviet Methods of Mass Mobilization, 1917–1929.* New York: Cambridge University Press, 1985.

Kepley, Vance (ed). 'Contemporary Soviet Cinema' [special issue], *WideAngle* 12.4 (1990).

——. *The End of St Petersburg* (KinoFile 10). London: I.B. Tauris, 2003.

Laurent, Natacha. *L'oeil du Kremlin: Cinema et censure en URSS sous Staline.* Toulouse: Privat, 2000.

Lawton, Anna. *Imaging Russia 2000. Film and Facts.* Washington: New Academia Publ., 2004.

——. *Kinoglasnost: Soviet Cinema in Our Time.* Cambridge: Cambridge University Press, 1992.

—— (ed). *The Red Screen: Politics, Society, Art in Soviet Cinema.* London and New York: Routledge, 1992.

Le Fanu, Mark. *The Cinema of Andrei Tarkovsky.* London: BFI, 1987.

Leyda, J. *Kino: A History of the Russian and Soviet Film.* Princeton: Princeton University Press, 1960.

Liber, George. *Alexander Dovzhenko: A Life in Soviet Film.* London: BFI, 2002.

MacFadyen David. *The Sad Comedy of El'dar Riazanov.* Montreal and London: McGill-Queen's University Press, 2003.

Marshall, Herbert. *Masters of the Soviet Cinema: Crippled Creative Biographies.* London: Routledge, 1983.

Mayne, Judith. *Kino and the Woman Question: Feminism and Soviet Silent Cinema.* Columbus: Ohio State University Press, 1989.

Michelson, Annette (ed). *Kino-eye: The Writings of Dziga Vertov.* Berkeley: University of California Press, 1984.

Miller, Jamie. *Soviet Cinema. Politics and Persuasion under Stalin.* London: I.B Tauris, 2010.

Nesbet, Anne. *Savage Junctures. Sergei Eisenstein and the Shape of Thinking.* London: I.B. Tauris, 2003.

Neuberger Joan. *Ivan the Terrible* (KinoFile 9). London: I.B. Tauris, 2003.

O'Mahony, Mike. *Eisenstein.* London: Reaktion, 2009.

Petric, Vlada. *Constructivism in Film: The Man with the Movie Camera.* Cambridge: Cambridge University Press, 1987.

Rimberg, John. *The Motion Picture in the Soviet Union, 1918–1952: A Sociological Analysis.* New York: Arno Press, 1973.

Roberts, Graham. *Forward Soviet. History and Non Fiction film in the USSR.* London: IB Tauris, 1999.

——. *The Man with the Movie Camera* (KinoFile 2). London: I.B. Tauris, 2000.

Salys, Rimgaila. *Laughing Matters. The Musical Comedy Films of Grigorii Aleksandrov.* Bristol and Chicago: Intellect Books, 2009.

Sargeant, Amy. *Vsevolod Pudovkin: Classic Films of the Soviet Avant-Garde.* London: I.B. Tauris, 2001.

Schmulevitch, Éric. *Réalisme socialiste et cinéma: Le cinéma stalinien (1928–1941).* Paris: Editions L'Harmattan, 1996.

Shlapentokh, Dmitry & Vladimir. *Soviet Cinematography, 1918–1991.* New York: Aldine de Gruyter, 1993.

Stites, Richard. *Russian Popular Culture. Entertainment and Society since 1900*. Cambridge: Cambridge University Press, 1992.

Synessiou Natasha. *Mirror* (KinoFile 6). London: I.B. Tauris, 2001.

Tarkovskii, Andrei. *Time within Time: The Diaries, 1970–1986*. London: Faber, 1994.

Tarkovsky, Andrey. *Sculpting in Time*. Austin: University of Texas Press, 1986.

Taubman, Jane. *Kira Muratova* (Kino Companion 4). London: I.B. Tauris, 2005.

Taylor, R and Derek Spring (eds). *Stalinism and Soviet Cinema*. London: Routledge, 1993.

Taylor, Richard. *Film Propaganda: Soviet Russia and Nazi Germany*. London: I.B.Tauris (original edition 1979), 1998.

——. *October*. London: BFI, 2002.

——. *The Battleship Potemkin* (KinoFile 1). London: I.B. Tauris, 2000.

——. *The Politics of the Soviet Cinema, 1917–1929*. Cambridge: Cambridge University Press, 1979.

Taylor, Richard (ed). *The Eisenstein Collection*, London, New York, Calcutta: Seagull Books, 2006.

——. *The Eisenstein Reader*. London: BFI, 1998.

Taylor, Richard and Ian Christie (eds). *Inside the Film Factory. New Approaches to Russian and Soviet Cinema*. London and New York: Routledge, 1991.

——. *The Film Factory. Russian and Soviet Cinema in Documents 1896–1939*. London and New York: Routledge, 1988.

Taylor, Richard, with Nancy Wood, Julian Graffy and Dina Iordanova (eds). *The BFI Companion to Eastern European and Russian Cinema*. London: British Film Institute, 2000.

Tsivian, Yuri (ed). *Early Cinema in Russia and its Cultural Reception*. Chicago and London: U of Chicago Press, 1994.

——. *Ivan the Terrible*. London: BFI Classics, 2001.

——. *Lines of Resistance: Dziga Vertov and the Twenties*. Pordenone, 2005.

Turovskaya, Maya. *Tarkovsky: Cinema as Poetry*. London: Faber, 1989.

van Geldern, James and Richard Stites (eds). *Mass Soviet Culture in Soviet Russia*. Bloomington: Indiana University Press, 1995.

Widdis, Emma. *Alexander Medvedkin* (Kino Companion 2). London: I.B. Tauris, 2005.

——. *Visions of a New Land: Soviet Film from the Revolution to the Second World War*. New Haven: Yale University Press, 2003.

Woll, Josephine. *Real Images. Soviet Cinema of the Thaw*. London: I.B. Tauris, 2000.

——. *The Cranes are Flying* (KinoFile 7). London: I.B. Tauris, 2003.

Woll, Josephine and Denise Youngblood. *Repentance* (KinoFile 4). London: I.B. Tauris, 2001.

Youngblood, Denise. *Movies for the Masses: Popular Cinema and Soviet Society in the 1920s*. Cambridge: Cambridge University Press, 1992.

——. *Russian War Films: On the Cinema Front, 1914–2005*. Lawrence: University Press of Kansas, 2007.

——. *Soviet Cinema in the Silent Era, 1918–1935*, Austin: University of Texas Press, 1985.

——. *The Magic Mirror. Moviemaking in Russia, 1908–1918*. Madison, WI and London, University of Wisconsin Press, 1999.

Zorkaya, Neya. *The Illustrated History of the Soviet Cinema*. New York: Hippocrene Books, 1991.

RUSSIAN CINEMA ONLINE

Animator.ru
http://www.animator.ru
Searchable database of Russian animation, in Russian and English.

Encyclopedia of National Cinema (Entsiklopedia otechestvennogo kino)
http://www.russiancinema.ru
Created under the editorship of Liubov Arkus, this is the most complete
and searchable catalogue of films, filmmakers and other artists, festivals and
organizations. In Russian.

Directory of World Cinema
http://worldcinemadirectory.org
The website for the *Directory of World Cinema* series featuring film reviews and
biographies of directors.

Gosfilmofond
http://www.aha.ru/~filmfond
Catalogue of the archive, in Russian.

Internet Movie Database
http://www.imdb.com
Leading source of information for international cinema and industry news, with
pages devoted to individual films, directors, actors, crew members and regularly
updated links to breaking news and interesting articles.

Iskusstvo kino (Film Art)
http://www.kinoart.ru/main.html
Leading Russian film journal, covering international film studies and published in
Russian (index in English).

KinoKultura
http://www.kinokultura.com
Founded in 2003, the journal is published four times per year with reviews of new Russian films, articles on visual arts and trends in filmmaking and festival reports. Two special issues focus on national cinematographies of former Soviet republics and Central European countries; these are guest-edited.

Kinoglaz.fr
http://www.kinoglaz.fr
A French-based database and information portal on Russian cinema, with a searchable catalogue (partly transliterated and partly translated), offering annotations or synopses in French (not always in English) and information on festivals with Russian films.

Kinovedcheskie zapiski (Film Scholars' Notes)
http://www.kinozapiski.ru
Scholarly journal on Russian cinema, published by the research institute NIIK in Moscow, in Russian.

Russian State Documentary Film and Photo Archive (RGAKFD), Krasnogorsk
http://www.russianarchives.com/archives/rgakfd/index.html
Searchable catalogue for the archive's holdings.

Séance
http://seance.ru
An important journal on film, edited by Liubov Arkus. It appears at irregular intervals.

Senses of Cinema
http://www.sensesofcinema.com
Online journal devoted to a serious discussion of cinema. *Senses of Cinema* is primarily concerned with ideas about particular films or bodies of work, but also with the regimes (ideological, economic and so forth) under which films are produced and viewed, and with the more abstract theoretical and philosophical issues raised by film study.

Questions

1. What is the Russian term for 'auteur cinema'?
2. Which Russian director was the son of an opera singer and a famous zither player?
3. Which film by Evgenii Bauer is often referred to as an 'encyclopedia' of Russian life?
4. Extensive use of radical montage is a recurring feature in which Russian director's works?
5. The life of which tyrannical tsar was depicted in Eisenstein's 1945-48 historical epic?
6. Who developed the 'kino-eye' method of filming?
7. Which American writer wrote the short story on which Andrei Tarkovskii's 1956 film was based?
8. Name the director who, as a youngster, was famously expelled from school for skipping classes in order to film.
9. Mikhalkov's 2007 film *Twelve* is a re-make of which American classic starring Henry Fonda?
10. What is the name of the controversial Sokurov film that follows the home life of Adolf Hitler and Eva Braun?
11. A taxi driver becomes an opera singer in which of Aleksandr Ivanovskii's comedies?
12. Name the director who, as well as being widely recognised as the 'father' of Russian animation, also holds the title of the world's first puppeteer?
13. What was the name of the cartoon character that during the 1970s became the Mickey Mouse of Soviet animation and the emblem of the Soiuzmultfilm studios?
14. Which documentary captured more drama than was anticipated when its subject unexpectedly sank in the Arctic Sea?
15. The true story of the events leading to Iurii Gagarin's historic flight into space in April 1961 inspired which recent film?
16. Which 1993 film follows the life of a Russian music teacher who discovers a magic portal to Paris in his room?

17. Which musician composed the soundtrack to Andrei Khrzhanovskii's *Glass Harmonica*?
18. Which Russian film won the 2000 Academy Award for Best Animated Feature?
19. What was the name of the radical Russian film (and rock) festival that later became known as 'Kinotavr'?
20. Who played the title role in Grigorii Kozintsev's *Hamlet*?
21. Before the first stationary cinema venues emerged in Moscow in 1903 where were early Russian films often shown?
22. Which 1986 documentary scrutinized the political and social issues of the perestroika era?
23. Which literary movement of the 1920s and 1930s inspired revolutionary avant-garde cinema during this period?
24. What country served as a major source of artistic inspiration for Sergei Eisenstein in the early 1930s?
25. Which of Iurii Zheliabuzhskii's comedies can be described as a film about a film?
26. Which festival devoted to Russian Cinema has been held annually in Sochi since 1991?
27. Name the two government-owned studios that were set up in the mid-1930s for the purpose of creating films for young audiences.
28. In 1967 Sergei Bondarchuk's adaptation of a literary classic won him both an Oscar and a Golden Globe Award for Best Foreign Language film. What was the name of this film?
29. Who directed sci-fi classic *Solaris*?
30. Which short animated feature by Roman Kachanov tells the story of a little girl who creates an imaginary puppy from a red woollen mitten?
31. Who starred as Rasputin in Elem Klimov's classic biopic?
32. What is the most common label for Soviet action films of the 1960s and 1970s?
33. Which Russian comedy film depicts a time-travelling Ivan the Terrible?

34. When was the first cinematograph presented in Russia?
35. Which documentary ends with the famous image of Lenin shaking hands with a comrade, symbolizing the beginning of a new era?
36. Artavazd Peleshian's documentary *The Seasons* is accompanied by the music of which famous composer?
37. Who wrote the novel on which Aleksandr Sokurov's *Lonely Voice of a Man* was based?
38. Which director cast his brother in his films *Nest of Gentlefolk* and *Siberiade*?
39. Which of Vasilii Shukshin's films caused waves on its release for being the first film to show and explore prison life?
40. What is the title of the only Soviet film to have won a Golden Palm at Cannes?
41. What is the literal translation of 'Karabalta,' the name of Bolotbek Shamshiev's male lead in his 1972 film *The Red Poppies of Issyk-Kul*?
42. Which melodrama won an Academy Award in 1980?
43. Vasilii Goncharov's *The Defence of Sevastopol* related the events of which War?
44. Who starred as the title character in Vitalii Mel'nikov's *Poor, Poor Paul*?
45. Which 1995 comedy film explores the Russians' notorious love for vodka through a series of anecdotes?
46. Which famous director made cinema a family affair, in the early part of his career employing his brother as cameraman and his wife as editor of his films?
47. Pavel Vasil'evich and Oleg Pavlovich are characters in which Dinara Asanova drama?
48. 'Four friends… In a life without rules… One incredible adventure…' was the English tagline for which recent film?
49. Which famous Russian cartoon was scripted by Liudmila Petrushevskaia?
50. Which 1935 film is often read as a communist adaptation of Jonathan Swift's *Gulliver's Travels*?

Answers

1. avtorskoe kino
2. Evgenii Bauer
3. *Silent Witness*
4. Sergei Eisenstein
5. *Ivan the Terrible*
6. Vertov
7. Ernest Hemingway
8. Nikita Mikhalkov
9. *12 Angry Men*
10. *Moloch*
11. *A Musical Story*
12. Wladyslaw Starewicz
13. Cheburashka
14. *Cheliuskin*
15. *Paper Soldier*
16. *Window to Paris* (by Iurii Mamin)
17. Alfred Schnittke
18. *The Old Man and the Sea*
19. Moscow Outskirts
20. Innokentii Smoktunovskii
21. Fairgrounds
22. *Is it Easy to be Young?*
23. Formalism
24. Mexico
25. *The Cigarette Girl from Mosselprom*
26. Kinotavr
27. Soiuzdetfilm and Soiuzmultfilm
28. *War and Peace*
29. Andrei Tarkovskii
30. *The Mitten*
31. Aleksei Petrenko
32. Red Western
33. *Ivan Vasil'evich Changes Profession*
34. 4 May 1896
35. The Fall of the Romanov Dynasty
36. Vivaldi's *Four Seasons*
37. Andrei Platonov
38. Andrei Konchalovskii
39. *Red Guelderbush*
40. *The Cranes are Flying*
41. Black Axe
42. *Moscow does not Believe in Tears*
43. The Crimean War
44. Viktor Sukhorukov
45. *Peculiarities of the National Hunt*
46. Dziga Vertov
47. *Tough Boys*
48. *Bimmer*
49. *Tale of Tales*
50. *New Gulliver*

NOTES ON CONTRIBUTORS

The Editor

Birgit Beumers is Reader in Russian Studies at the University of Bristol. She specializes in contemporary Russian culture, especially cinema and theatre. Her recent publications include *A History of Russian Cinema* (2009) and, with Mark Lipovetsky, *Performing Violence* (2009). She is the editor of the online journal *KinoKultura* and of Intellect's journal *Studies in Russian and Soviet Cinema*. She is currently working on Russian animation and post-Soviet Russian cinema.

The Contributors

José Alaniz is Associate Professor in the Departments of Slavic Languages and Literatures and Comparative Literature at the University of Washington, Seattle. His research interests include post-Soviet Russian culture, death and dying, disability, cinema, eco-criticism and comics. He is the author of *Komiks: Comic Art in Russia* (2010). His current projects include a history of Czech comics and a study of disability, death and dying in the American superhero comics genre.

Erin Alpert is a graduate student in the Department of Slavic Languages and Literatures at the University of Pittsburgh. She received her BA in Russian Studies from the College of William and Mary and her MA in Slavic Languages and Literatures from the University of Pittsburgh. She serves as co-editor for the journal *Studies in Slavic Cultures*. Her publications have appeared in *KinoKultura* and *The Slavonic and Eastern European Review*.

Joe Andrew is Professor of Literature and Culture at Keele University. He has been researching feminist approaches to literature and film, while his main focus has been nineteenth-century Russian literature. He has published five monographs, as well as many edited volumes in that field. More recently, both his teaching and research interests have expanded into film studies, and he has now published several articles on Russian cinema. Among his research plans are books on Politics and the Cinema, and on key moments in Russia film.

Anthony Anemone is Associate Professor of Russian and Assistant Dean for Faculty Affairs. at The New School in New York City. A specialist in modern Russian literature and cinema, he is the editor of *Just Assassins: The Culture of Terrorism in Russia* (2010).

Polina Barskova is Assistant Professor of Russian literature at Hampshire College. Her scholarly publications include articles on Nabokov, the Bakhtin brothers, early Soviet film and the aestheticization of historical trauma. She has also authored seven books of poetry in Russian. She is currently working on a book project entitled *Petersburg Besieged: Aesthetics of Urban Rereading.*

Robert Bird is Associate Professor in the Department of Slavic Languages and Literatures, Cinema and Media Studies at the University of Chicago. His main area of interest is the aesthetic practice and theory of Russian modernism. He is also the author of two books on Andrei Tarkovsky: *Andrei Rublev* (2004) and *Andrei Tarkovsky: Elements of Cinema* (2008). His works in progress include a biography of Dostoevsky.

Otto Boele teaches Russian literature and film at the University of Leiden, Netherlands. He is the author of *The North in Russian Romantic Literature* (1996) and *Erotic Nihilism in Late Imperial Russia: the Case of Mikhail Artsybashev's 'Sanin'* (2009). Currently he is working on Lev Tolstoy's private correspondence with his admirers in the Netherlands.

Vincent Bohlinger is Assistant Professor of Film Studies in the Department of English at Rhode Island College. He is currently working on a book on Soviet socialist realist film style.

Mariya Boston received an MA from Moscow State University and is a PhD candidate in Comparative Literature at the University of California, Davis, writing on Russian and American modernist literature and silent film. Her research interests include Russian and American twentieth-century literature, silent film, contemporary Russian film and popular culture, and Russian postmodernism.

Nancy Condee is Associate Professor of Slavic Studies and member of the Film Studies Program at the University of Pittsburgh. Her publications include *Imperial Trace: Recent Russian Cinema* (2009) as well as the edited volumes *Soviet Hieroglyphics: Visual Culture in Late 20c. Russia* (1995); *Endquote: Sots-Art Literature and Soviet Grand Style* (with M. Balina and E. Dobrenko, 2000); and *Antinomies of Art and Culture: Modernity, Postmodernity, Contemporaneity* (with T. Smith and O. Enwezor, 2008).

Frederick Corney is Associate Professor in the Department of History at the College of William and Mary in Williamsburg, Virginia. He is the author of *Telling October: Memory and the Making of the Bolshevik Revolution* (2004). He is interested in issues of cultural memory in modern Russia, specifically the refractions of that memory by various collectivities.

Joe Crescente is a PhD student in socio-cultural anthropology and the programme in Culture and Media at New York University. His research concerns the creation of new forms of sociality, belonging and social distinction in urban Siberia.

Sergey Dobrynin is a Russian cultural scholar and teacher. Born in Ulan Ude, Russia, he received his PhD from the Central European University in Budapest. He currently lives in Toronto.

Miriam Dobson completed her PhD at the School of Slavonic and East European Studies, University College London. Since 2004 she has worked as a lecturer at the University of Sheffield. She recently published a monograph entitled *Khrushchev's Cold Summer: Gulag Returnees, Crime, and the Fate of Reform after Stalin* (2009).

Greg Dolgopolov is a Lecturer in Film at the University of New South Wales, Australia. He completed his PhD on the transformations of post-Soviet television culture at Murdoch University. His primary areas of interest are Australian cinema and television, screen theory, video production, mobile devices and documentary. He has published on Australian and Russian cinema, new media and documentary. He has worked as an actor, director and a 'spin doctor'.

Milla Fedorova is Assistant Professor in the Department of Slavic Languages at Georgetown University. Her area of expertise is twentieth-century literature and film. She is especially interested in relations between the visual and the verbal, and the intercultural dialogue between Russia and America.

Joshua First received his doctorate at the University of Michigan in 2008 and is Croft Assistant Professor of History and International Studies at the University of Mississippi. He has published articles on Soviet film sociology, 1970s Soviet melodrama and on Ukrainian poetic cinema. He is currently working on a monograph on the history of Ukrainian cinema during the 1960s.

David Gillespie is Professor of Russian language at the University of Bath. His research concentrates on modern Russian literature and film, and he has published books and articles in both areas. He is the author of *Russian Cinema: Inside Film* (2002) and *Early Soviet Cinema: Innovation, Ideology and Propaganda* (2000). He is currently working on a monograph-length study of the construction of masculinity in post-Soviet literature, film and TV.

Seth Graham is Lecturer in the Russian Department, School of Slavonic and East European Studies, University College London. He taught previously at Stanford University and the University of Washington, Seattle. He has published articles and chapters on Russian humour, Russian and Soviet film, Central Asian film and contemporary Russian literature, and he is the author of *Resonant Dissonance: The Russo-Soviet Joke in Cultural Context* (2009). He is currently working on a book-length analysis of genre in post-Soviet Russian cinema.

Yana Hashamova is Associate Professor of Slavic Studies and Director of the Center for Slavic and East European Studies at the Ohio State University. She is the author of *Pride and Panic: Russian Imagination of the West in Post-Soviet Film* (2007) and editor (with H. Goscilo) of *Cinepaternity: Fathers and Sons in Soviet and Post-Soviet Film* (2010).

Jeremy Hicks is Senior Lecturer in Russian at Queen Mary University of London. His research interests lie especially in documentary and film history. He is the author of *Dziga Vertov: Defining Documentary Film* (2007) and various articles on

Russian and Soviet film, literature and journalism. He is currently writing a book about Soviet wartime film representations of the Nazi genocide.

Emily Hillhouse is a PhD candidate in Modern European History at the University of Texas, Austin. Her Masters thesis explored Russian national identity in 1960s Soviet film. She has recently returned from her Fulbright research trip to Bulgaria, which will provide the foundation for her dissertation on the role played by images of Bulgarian peasants in the formation of the modern Bulgarian nation.

Stephen Hutchings is Professor of Russian Studies at the University of Manchester. He is Director of Research at the School of Languages, Linguistics and Cultures, and is currently President of the British Association for Slavonic and East European Studies. His major publications include *Russian Modernism: The Transfiguration of the Everyday* (1997), *Russian Literary Culture in the Camera Age: The Word as Image* (2004), *Television and Culture under Putin: Remote Control* (with Natalya Rulyova; 2009), and *Russia and its Other(s) on Film: Screening Intercultural Dialogue* (2008).

Volha Isakava is a doctoral student in the Department of Modern Languages and Cultural Studies at the University of Alberta, Edmonton, Canada. Her research interests include perestroika and contemporary Russian cinema, literature and culture, American *film noir* and critical theory.

Andrew Jenks is Associate Professor of History at California State University, Long Beach. His is the author of *Russia in a Box: Art and Identity in an Age of Revolution* (2005) and *Perils of Progress: Environmental Disasters in the 20th Century* (2010). His biography of the first cosmonaut Yuri Gagarin is forthcoming.

Vida Johnson received a PhD in Slavic Languages and Literatures from Harvard University. She is Professor of Russian language, culture and film at Tufts University in Boston. She is the author of articles and reviews on literature and film and co-author, with Graham Petrie, of *The Films of Andrei Tarkovsky: A Visual Fugue* (1994). Her current area of research is contemporary Russian and Central Asian cinema, as well as the cinemas of the former Yugoslavia.

Sergei Kapterev is Senior Researcher at Moscow's Research Institute of Cinema Art (NIIK). He received his PhD in Cinema Studies from New York University (2005). He specializes in the intellectual and political aspects of the interaction between Soviet and American cinemas. Other interests: Soviet film propaganda; cinema of the late Stalin period, the Thaw and the Cold War; Russian and Soviet films about the Far East; practice and theory of film editing and sound.

Vance Kepley, Jr is Professor of Film and Director of the Wisconsin Center for Film and Theater Research at the University of Wisconsin-Madison. He is the author of *In the Service of the State: The Cinema of Alexander Dovzhenko* (1986), *The End of St. Petersburg: The Film Companion* (2003), and several essays on Soviet cinema.

Svetlana Khokhriakova is the cinema section editor of the weekly *Kul'tura* newspaper in Moscow. She consults and acts as press officer to a range of national festivals.

Lars Kristensen completed his PhD in Film Studies at the University of St Andrews in 2009 and is a Research Associate as the University of Central Lancashire. He has published several articles on cross-cultural issues related to Russian cinema and is currently working towards a monograph entitled *Russians Abroad in Postcommunist Cinema*.

Daniel Levitsky is a Teaching Fellow in Modern Russian History at the School of Slavonic and East European Studies, University College London. He is currently completing his PhD thesis, entitled *Soviet History in Thaw Cinema: The Making of New Myths and Truths*.

Mark Lipovetsky is Associate Professor of Russian Studies at the University of Colorado-Boulder. He has written on Russian literature and culture, including *Russian Postmodernist Fiction: Dialogue with Chaos* (1999); *Modern Russian Literature: 1950s–1990s* (co-authored with N. Leiderman, in Russian, 2001); *Paralogies: Transformation of (Post)modernist Discourse in Russian Culture of the 1920s–2000s* (in Russian, 2008) and *Performing Violence* (with B. Beumers, 2009).

David MacFadyen is Professor of Slavic Languages and Literatures at UCLA. He has authored and edited eleven books on various aspects of Russian or Soviet culture, including on filmmaker Eldar Riazanov; on Soviet animation; on popular song; on the poet Joseph Brodsky; on Russian television serials and other fields of cultural expression. Currently he is researching social networking in the Russian internet, and is busy with the biggest online resource dedicated to new music from Russia, Ukraine, and Belarus: www.farfrommoscow.com

Louise McReynolds is Professor of History at the University of North Carolina at Chapel Hill. Specializing in the growth of commercial culture in the nineteenth century, she explores the evolution of civil society and questions of the formations of identities within it. Her publications include *Russia at Play: Leisure Activities at the End of the Tsarist Era* (2003), *The News Under Russia's Old Regime: The Development of the Mass-Circulation Press* (1991), and numerous articles and translations.

Milena Michalski is a Research Associate at King's College London. She is author (with J. Gow) of *War, Image and Legitimacy: Viewing Contemporary Conflict* (2007), and of various articles on film. She has worked on projects with the British Film Institute and Tate Modern. Current research focuses on film and photography of the 1920s–1930s in the USSR, and Joris Ivens' *Komsomol*.

Jamie Miller is Lecturer in Russian at Queen Mary, University of London. He specialises in the relationship between politics and film in the USSR under Lenin and Stalin. He is the author of *Soviet Cinema: Politics and Persuasion under Stalin* (2010) and journal articles on film politics of the 1920s and 1930s. He is currently researching the history of the Mezhrabpomfilm studio from 1923 to 1936.

Lora Mjolsness received her PhD from the University of Southern California in Slavic Languages and Literatures. She is currently a lecturer at the University of California, Irvine and the Director of Program in Russian Studies, teaching interdisciplinary courses on new Russian cinema and on the history of Soviet animation. Her primary research interests include early Russian and Soviet animation.

Jeremy Morris is an Area-Studies specialist with extensive in-country experience and knowledge of contemporary Russia, having lived and worked there in the 1990s. He has written on contemporary Russian literature and visual culture. His current research focuses on ethnographic and interpretive approaches to understanding 'actually lived experience' in the former Soviet Union.

Joan Neuberger is Professor of History at the University of Texas at Austin. She is the author or co-author of an eclectic range of publications, including *Hooliganism: Crime and Culture in St Petersburg, 1900–1914* (1993); *Ivan the Terrible: The Film Companion* (2003); *Europe and the Making of Modernity, 1815–1914* (2005); *Imitations of Life: Melodrama in Russia* (2001) and *Picturing Russia: Explorations in Visual Culture* (2008).

Stephen Norris is Associate Professor of History at Miami University, Ohio. He is the author of *A War of Images: Russian Popular Prints, Wartime Culture, and National Identity, 1812–1945* and the co-editor of *Preserving Petersburg: History, Memory, Nostalgia* (with H. Goscilo) and *Insiders and Outsiders in Russian Cinema* (with Z. Torlone). He is currently finishing a book entitled *Blockbuster History: Movies, Memory, and Patriotism in the Putin Era.*

Karen Petrone is Associate Professor of History at the University of Kentucky. Her research interest is in twentieth-century Russian (and Soviet) cultural and gender history. She is the author of *Life Has Become More Joyous, Comrades: Celebrations in the Time of Stalin* (2000); she is co-editor of *The New Muscovite Cultural History: A Collection in Honor of Daniel B. Rowland* (2009) and of *Gender Politics and Mass Dictatorship: Global Perspectives* (2010). Her latest book, *The Great War in Russian Memory,* will be published in 2011.

Laura Pontieri Hlavacek completed her PhD on 'Russian Animation of the 1960s and the Khrushchev Thaw' at Yale in 2006; she examined the evolving functions and styles of Soviet animation during the Thaw period, providing a case study of the dynamics of interaction between art and power. Her research interests include twentieth-century Russian literature and theatre, Russian and Czech cinema and animation. She is currently writing a book on Russian animation.

Alexander Prokhorov is Associate Professor of Russian and Film Studies at the College of William and Mary. His research interests include Russian visual culture, genre theory, and film history. He is the author of *Inherited Discourse: Paradigms of Stalinist Culture in Literature and Cinema of the Thaw* (in Russian; 2007). His articles and reviews have been published in a number of specialist and scholarly journals.

Elena Prokhorova is Assistant Professor of Russian at the College of William and Mary, where she also teaches in Film and Cultural Studies program. Her research focuses on identity discourses in late Soviet and post-Soviet media.

Sasha Razor is currently a doctorate student at UCLA where she received her MA degree in Slavic Languages and Literatures in 2009. Her research interests include: new media, film and video games; theory of adaptation; artistic mechanisms of social transitions; hybrid literatures and contemporary Russian-American writers.

Peter Rollberg is Professor of Slavic Languages and Film Studies at George Washington University in Washington, DC. He earned his PhD in 1988 at the University of Leipzig and came to GWU in 1991 after teaching at Duke University. His publications include articles on nineteenth- and twentieth-century Russian literature and Soviet cinema. Since 2000, he has directed the GWU Film Studies Program. He is the author of *Historical Dictionary of Russian and Soviet Cinema* (2009).

Rimgaila Salys is Professor of Russian Studies at the University of Colorado at Boulder and a specialist in twentieth-century literature, culture and film. Her most recent books are *Tightrope Walking: The Memoirs of Josephine Pasternak* (2005) and *The Musical Comedy Films of Grigorii Aleksandrov: Laughing Matters* (2009).

Natalia Ryabchikova holds a degree in Film Studies from the Russian State University of Cinematography (VGIK). She has contributed articles on Soviet film history to Russian and English-language scholarly journals.

Amy Sargeant is Reader in Film at the University of Warwick. She has written extensively on British and Russian cinema history and contemporary representations of Russia. Her publications include *Vsevolod Pudovkin: Classic Films of the Soviet Avant-Garde* (2000) and *Storm over Asia* (2007).

Dawn Seckler received her PhD in Russian Cinema from the University of Pittsburgh. She is a Visiting Assistant Professor of Russian at Williams College. Her research interests include Russian genre cinema and representations of a masculine crisis in late Soviet culture.

Vadim Shneyder is a graduate student in the Department of Slavic Languages and Literatures at Yale University. His research interests include Russian and Soviet intellectual history, Stalinist ideology and Soviet Jewish culture.

Vlad Strukov is Assistant Professor at the University of Leeds. He has published on contemporary Russian film, animation, digital media, especially the internet, and popular culture. He is the editor of *Celebrity and Glamour in Contemporary Russia: Shocking Chic* (2010) and of *Digital Icons: Studies of Russian, Eurasian and Central European New Media* (www.digitalicons.org).

Anna Toropova is completing a PhD at the School of Slavonic and East European Studies, University College London. Focusing on the cinema of the Stalin period, her research explores the relationship between affect, ideology and genre. She teaches Russian language and courses on Soviet mass culture at undergraduate level.

Jasmijn Van Gorp received a PhD degree in Communication Studies from the University of Antwerp with a dissertation on post-Soviet Russian film policy. She conducted research at the Russian Film Institute (NIIK) and the Sociological Research Institute (INION) in Moscow. Since 2009 she is a postdoctoral fellow at Utrecht University, where she is investigating the role of Dutch popular television in the identity construction of East European migrants.

Boris Wolfson teaches Russian culture, film and language at Amherst College. He is completing a study of literature, theatre and modes of self-understanding in the Stalinist 1930s.

Barbara Wurm is currently Assistant for Film Studies at the Slavic Seminar of the University of Basel, Switzerland. She works as freelance curator and film critic. Her publications include articles on the bio-politics of seeing in early Soviet non-fiction film and a booklet on Gerbert Rappaport; with Klemens Gruber she co-edited *Digital Formalism. Die kalkulierten Bilder des Dziga Vertov*.

Denise J. Youngblood is Professor of History at the University of Vermont. She has written extensively on Russian and Soviet cinema, most recently *Russian War Films: On the Cinema Front, 1914-2005* (2007) and *Cinematic Cold War: The Soviet and American Struggle for Hearts and Minds* (2010).

Eugénie Zvonkine defended her PhD in 2009 on Kira Muratova's work, entitled 'States of Dissonance in Kira Muratova's œuvre, 1958–2009'. She has published in English a paper on the narrative structure in *The Sentimental Policeman* and is currently teaching film history and aesthetics at the University Paris 8, France.

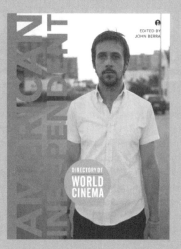

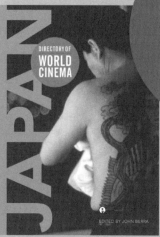